South-East Asia

A POLITICAL PROFILE

South-East Asia

A POLITICAL PROFILE

DAMIEN
KINGSBURY

OXFORD
UNIVERSITY PRESS

OXFORD

UNIVERSITY PRESS

253 Normanby Road, South Melbourne, Australia

Oxford University Press is a department of the University of Oxford. It furthers
the University's objective of excellence in research, scholarship, and education
by publishing worldwide in

Oxford New York

Athens Auckland Bangkok Bogotá Buenos Aires Calcutta Cape Town Chennai
Dar es Salaam Delhi Florence Hong Kong Istanbul Karachi Kuala Lumpur
Madrid Melbourne Mexico City Mumbai Nairobi Paris Port Moresby São Paulo
Shanghai Singapore Taipei Tokyo Toronto Warsaw

with associated companies in Berlin Ibadan

National Library of Australia
Cataloguing-in-Publication data:

Kingsbury, Damien.
South-East Asia: a political profile.

Bibliography.
Includes index.
ISBN 0 19 551003 8.

1. Asia, Southeastern—Politics and government—1945– .
I. Title.

Edited by Lisa Mills
Cover designed by Silvia Witte
Typeset by Desktop Concepts P/L, Melbourne
Printed through Bookpac Production Services, Singapore

For Fiona, Cailan and Alexandra

Contents

List of Abbreviations

ADB	Asian Development Bank
AFPFL	Anti-Fascist People's Freedom League (Burma)
ARF	ASEAN Regional Forum
ARVN	Army of the Republic of Viet Nam (South Vietnamese Army)
ASEAN	Association of South East Asian Nations
BCP	Burmese Communist Party
BIA	Burma Independence Army
BSPP	Burma Socialist Programme Party
CGDK	Coalition Government of Democratic Kampuchea
CP	Communist Party of the Philippines
CPP	Cambodian People's Party
DAP	Democratic Action Party (Malaysia)
DMZ	Demilitarised Zone
DRV	Democratic Republic of Vietnam (North Vietnam)
EU	European Union
FDI	Foreign Direct Investment
FUNCINPEC	National United Front for a Neutral, Peaceful, Cooperative and Independent Cambodia
GATT	General Agreement on Tariffs and Trade
GDP	Gross Domestic Product
HDI	Human Development Index
ICP	Indochinese Communist Party (Vietnam, Laos and Cambodia)
IMF	International Monetary Fund
InterFET	International Force in East Timor
ISA	Internal Security Act (Malaysia)
KIA/O	Kachin Independence Army/Organisation
KMT	Kuomingtang (Chinese Nationalist Army; also Guomindang)
LPNLA	Lao People's National Liberation Army
LPRP	Lao People's Revolutionary Party
MCP	Malayan Communist Party
MILF	Moro Islamic Liberation Front (Philippines)
MPAJA	Malayan People's Anti-Japanese Army
MRLA	Malayan Races Liberation Army

NAM	Non-Aligned Movement
NCP	Nanyang Communist Party (Singapore)
NLD	National League for Democracy
NLF	National Liberation Front (South Vietnam)
NPA	New People's Army (Philippines)
NUFK	National United Front of Kampuchea (Cambodia)
OCAJNSA	Overseas Chinese Anti-Japanese National Salvation Association (Malaysia)
OPM	Organisasi Papua Merdeka (Free Papua Organisation)
OSS	Office of Strategic Services (United States)
PDI-P	Partai Demokrasi Indonesia—Perjuangan
PKI	Indonesian Communist Party
post-WWI	post-World War I
post-WWII	post-World War II
PPP	Purchasing Parity Power
RLG	Royal Lao Government
SEA	South-East Asia
SLORC	State Law and Order Restoration Council (Burma)
SPDC	State Peace and Development Council (Burma)
UMEH	Union of Myanmar Economic Holdings Company
UMNO	United Malay National Organisation
UN	United Nations
UNDP	United Nations Development Programme
USA	United States of America
UWSA	United Wa State Army
VAT	Value Added Tax
VC	Viet Cong
VPA	Vietnam People's Army (also North Vietnamese Army, or NVA)
VRYL	Vietnam Revolutionary Youth League
WWI	World War I
WWII	World War II
ZOPFAN	Zone Of Peace, Freedom And Neutrality

Acknowledgments

There are many metaphors for writing generally and in particular for undertaking a project such as this. All of them involve significant challenge, self-doubt and what Pierre Bourdieu once called 'the small change of madness'. Without the unstinting support of friends and colleagues, I am certain that this project would have come to an ignominious end on a number of occasions. I therefore owe a debt of thanks to numerous people.

To Jill Henry, academic publisher at OUPANZ, I am grateful for continued faith and support. I once used to imagine the ideal publisher; Jill is that ideal. To Maggie Way I am grateful for her constant encouragement and for holding out a lifeline to OUPANZ. I would also like to thank Lisa Mills for her fine work in correcting my sometimes tortured use of language. The research and writing of this book was undertaken while working at the Monash Asia Institute at Monash University, Melbourne. My colleagues there, including Professor John McKay, Emma Hegarty, Emma Barling, and Juliet Yee, have offered nothing but support for this project.

A book covering as wide a field as this relies greatly on the advice and critical comments of a number of readers. To that end, I would like to acknowledge the helpful comments and criticisms of Dr Laine Berman, Professor Arief Budiman, Dr Ian Chalmers, Sue Downie, Dr Herb Feith, Professor Kevin Hewison, Emeritus Professor John Legge, Dr Mark McGillivray, Keryn O'Sullivan, Dr Garry Rodan, Kelvin Rowley, Professor Martin Stuart-Fox, Garry Woodard, and two anonymous readers. Any text covering a field as broad as this is bound to make some errors of interpretation, or of fact, for which I apologise in advance. Such shortcomings are in no way attributable to those who have in different ways assisted with this project and, unfortunately, are my responsibility alone.

Finally, I would like to thank my wife, Fiona Delahunt, and my children, Alexandra and Cailan, for putting up with my time away undertaking research, and for providing such a loving and warm home to come back to.

Introduction

The fine, rich mud slid with familiar sensuality way between his toes as Ni stooped down to continue planting the rice seedlings in the carefully flooded field. It was an oft-repeated ritual, one that he had practised twice every year, since he was a small boy, helping his parents. Ni's older bother and sister were there then, too, but they had now long since left to work in the city, that magnificent, confusing, crowded, noisy, dirty place of impossibly tall buildings and too many motor scooters and cars and trucks and too much to buy; that place where no one knew each other. That was the way of it these days, and Ni had considered leaving also. But his parents were getting old now: his father was well over fifty and by local standards an old man, and his mother could not do enough work to keep them both. His sense of respect and loyalty, shared to different degrees by all the children, held him close.

Then there was Ni's two younger sisters and the youngest child, another brother, who were still at school. There would have been seven, but one had died in infancy of a water-borne disease. The clinic had advised his parents about medicine but by then it was too late. Babies and young children had always died easily, though for a while subsidised medicine had made it seem better. But now treatment was more expensive as the clinic was no longer able to provide the subsidised medicine. The three younger children who had survived the lottery of childhood helped in the paddy or around the house in the half-day they each had off from school, but their help alone was not enough to support both themselves and their parents.

There was also Ni's own family, living in a small and simple house close to his parents. His young wife helped at planting and harvesting time, as well as tending the fruit trees and chickens, selling their small surplus at the local market and looking after their own two small children. They would have no more because, despite the long-standing tradition of large families, the cost of education and the limited amount of land left meant that children were becoming too expensive. Besides, the government encouraged smaller rather than larger families and offered a small amount of help to those families who limited themselves to just two children.

Ni's sister, the oldest of the six children, worked in a clothing factory and returned to the village by bus less and less frequently. The days off

were fewer and the overtime more, she had said, although this overtime was usually not paid. It was just a way of keeping her job, when so many others would willingly work the same hours for no more or possibly less. She had seemed unhappy when she returned, but then she had also seemed unhappy with village life. His older brother returned even less often, just for special celebrations, saying that he had to work from dawn until well after dusk every day just to keep his street-side food stall running. He had married a young woman in the city and he too had his own family now. This older brother was drifting further from the family, and from the life of the village. He spoke disparagingly about the sameness and backwardness of the village, which Ni regarded more as the slow but constant rhythm of life.

There were problems, of course. Ni's own health was not always good, which sometimes made it hard to work. The water from the well was poorer than it once had been, although that was the only water readily available. Water collected from the roof during the wet season fall was good but did not last long. The water from the nearby river had not been drinkable for years due to contamination by more and more people living on the riverbank and because the processing factories upstream used it as an open drain. There were regulations about this, he had been told, but they had never been enforced. The factory owners had money and paid the local officials a small amount to look the other way. It was always the same: if you had enough money you could buy anything. If you had little or none you were at the mercy of those who had plenty.

Even his ownership of the family's land was in doubt. They had long borrowed a small amount each year from a money-lender in the next town to pay for the grain to plant. The rice crops were bigger than in the old days, but the special, high-yielding grain had to be bought, along with fertilisers and pesticides. The increased size of the crops had tapered off, but money was more expensive to borrow and even though the money-lender had to pay more himself he was not well liked in the area. Not being indigenous only further prejudiced feelings against the money-lender.

Perhaps if the land was claimed as forfeit he could challenge the claim in court. But even the courts were open to financial persuasion and often interpreted the law very widely. The police, who often adjudicated such matters in the first place, were not to be trusted. Sleek and well fed in their smart uniforms and sunglasses, they were quick to spot offence and only a little slower in extracting some form of 'fine'. There were many such problems, but the village chief was rarely interested in them, seeming more concerned with keeping the local government member happy. The local government representative lived and worked in the city and only sometimes would he send someone to the villages and towns, usually around the time when Ni and his neighbours were told for whom to vote, every few years. The village chief, the police, the local politician, though all seen sufficiently often to be familiar, had a smug air to them, as though they held the secret which granted them the privilege of demanding the deference and respect he held only for his father and mother. Once he and some other villagers had protested over their high-handedness, but they were beaten and nothing had changed. There was much he wanted to see changed, but Ni recognised there was little hope of achieving this.

Still, it was not a bad life in some ways. The village was safe and familiar, within the confines of clearly ordered, close social relations. And he had his faith, which was comforting, and shared by his fellow villagers. This helped make sense of the world. But for closer events, the small things of everyday life, there were also the local spirits who lived in the fields and the groves. One did not speak too openly about the spirits, but they were there none the less. Sometimes they could only be acknowledged through more officially sanctioned worship, but alongside the official religion they better explained the change of the seasons and the wind and the summer rain.

It was hot in the field. In late morning the sun was high and the sky bright blue, with just puffs of cloud beginning to gather for what would be the late afternoon downpour. Even shaded by the long cloth of his shirt and wrap, and under the wide brim of his woven conical hat, Ni's skin was darkened by the sun. This was the mark of a field worker, not the refined skin and lighter tones of someone who spent their time in the shade. Ni stood upright for a moment and straightened his back after being bent double, looking across the paddy to the cluster of houses and palms of the village. His gaze rested on the rusting iron and thatched roofs of the simple houses scattered around a rough, unsealed road.

Trying to understand his world and his life, the past held him, providing patterns and contexts, reassurance and familiarity, as well as bonds and restrictions. The tension between the way things had always been done and how they could be tugged at him. He was also confused by the distant echo he had heard of the government in the city talking about the way things had been and were still done, linking that with the bigger world in ways which failed to make sense to him. But like his need to finish the planting, the present held Ni with its immediate concerns and prosaic requirements. The future shimmered on the horizon, holding out faint hopes of a better material life, blended with seemingly impossible desires. He noted, with some wryness, that the somnolent cycle of the seasons seemed quick compared to the speed at which his life moved towards these nebulous aspirations.

The fictional character of 'Ni', presented above, could be from any of the countries of South-East Asia. While there are many considerable differences between them, in culture and politics, there are also many similarities. This is especially so at the level of the villages, where most people in South-East Asia still live. The concerns of the people of such places are, if not exactly the same everywhere, then increasingly similar across this region. If the basics of village life are not so different, then neither is the dichotomy between this life and the process of 'development', exemplified by increasingly crowded industrial cities, materialism, and very often self-serving political elites.

Of course, the approximately contemporary situation that each of these societies finds themselves in, as a transitional moment in the trajectory of history, varies from place to place. The circumstances of each manifests in both common and particular ways. To this end, this book attempts to canvass some of the general political issues affecting the countries of South-East Asia, noting differences and, where they exist, broad tendencies. It then considers each of the countries of the region in their own right. In this sense, while each of the countries can be identified in a formal sense, they all have intertwining histories that cannot be neglected. It also mentions, albeit fleetingly, some of the states of the region that no longer exist.

Indeed, the contemporary states of South-East Asia are all constructions, in one form or another, of the period of European colonialism. Had this colonialism not happened the political make-up of the region would undoubtedly be very different. But it did happen, and aspirations for independence by some groups within post-colonial states, along with historical memories of former imperial glories of others, have in part been relegated to the dust-heap of history—at least for the time being. But, like culture, history is far from static and perhaps the political constructions we see now are but a fleeting moment when seen from a future historical perspective.

Like the region itself, the politics of South-East Asia is heterogenous, diffused, and a product of local conditions, histories and influences. There are some parallels between political processes and attendant ideologies within the region, but anything more than a quick glance reveals local distinctions, the intricacy of which is indeed fine. As a result, no one analysis can hope to adequately cover the extent of the diversity, complexity and richness of the various political forces at work in this geographic region. However, it is possible to propose methods that could be useful as a point of departure when looking at particular political situations. It is also valuable to consider political situations not necessarily for how they are portrayed (although possibly why they are thus portrayed), but for what they actually mean in terms of the people they affect.

This book takes a longer term view of political development, tracing the construction of the current states of the region to their pre-colonial and colonial past. It considers them in so far as they correspond to the idea of 'nation', how the states are conceived, and how this conception matches local historical memory. It also considers some of the recent major issues that have affected these states, and how some of the institutions of these states have responded to such issues. Any book trying to deal with South-East Asia at the moment cannot possibly hope to keep pace with the rate of change there, and this book does not attempt to do so. Rather, it attempts to chart the trajectory for political development, to indicate the possible directions of the region's states.

METHODOLOGY

In terms of methodology, most readers and especially those from other 'disciplines' will probably consider this work to belong within the category 'political science', at least based on previous comments on my work. However, I do not believe that politics is or can be a science, or indeed even a discipline that is somehow removed from other disciplinary bases in the humanities. A quick glance will soon show a reasonable appreciation of history, without which I believe nothing can be understood. All events exist within an historical context, and are a product of preceding circumstances. I trust this is implicit in the text. Those who look at politics from a 'political economy' perspective tend to regard my work as being 'culturalist' or 'institutionalist'. From such a culturalist perspective, however, my work is seen more as 'political economy'. To clarify, politics is based in the real, material world and responds to real, material pressures. In this sense, its prime concerns are with economic matters, broadly defined, and particular economic interests will therefore usually end up dominant in the political sphere. I regard this as a given. However, cultural elements also often reflect, or shape, the way interests are defined and decisions are taken. In many respects, as states and their constituent components become more deeply entrenched, decisions are also taken by and reflect the interests of institutions. Such institutions are semi-permanent bodies or organisations themselves reflecting a coherence of values or concerns, and can be seen to be represented by political offices (presidency, cabinet and so on), the judicial structure, the armed forces or civil groups such as the media, trade unions, students, and others. All of these contribute to the actuality of the political process, their respective contributions varying according to the prevailing circumstances. If there is one criticism in all of this it is that it tends to focus on the political activities of the elites. This, sadly, is true. In simple terms, the broad sweep of politics is most easily reflected in the affairs of the elites, and is a consequence of decisions taken by them. Yet this should not be seen to imply a disregard for non-elite people. To quote David Wurfel, an exemplar of a generation of scholars on South-East Asia for whom I have nothing but respect, 'If readers should find passages in this book characterised by cool calculations of power, they may be assured that my work is informed by continuing concern for the fate of the powerless' (1988: xiv). If this text, then, has an agenda, it is one predicated on such a concern.

By definition, any book attempting to consider this region in some sort of totality will necessarily dip only lightly into various issues. Clearly, not just each country but each period of each country's development and, indeed, contemporary issues within each country are each deserving of a book in their own right. Specialist South-East Asian scholars will not learn much that is new to them here, although those who are less familiar with the region might gain some preliminary insights. As an introductory text, then, this book hopes to have raised at least some of the more salient points, and offered some explanations for why things have been as they appeared. Perhaps, more than anything, after opening the door to at least some newcomers, they will invite themselves in to further explore in greater detail the vast richness of events, issues and ideas that contribute to the conception of the region the world knows as South-East Asia.

The structure of this book is intended to introduce readers to some of the key themes and issues in South-East Asia, then to consider each country in the region. It is hoped that this structure makes the subject clear, intelligible and accessible.

Part 1

1

Constructing the
Modern State

What constitutes statehood in South-East Asia (SEA) is open to debate. Challenges come from within the state and, sometimes, outside the state, while questions of legitimacy regarding the institutions of the state are also often open to debate. To this end, it is necessary to consider the styles of government of SEA, which have been, in large part, predicated on methods of achieving power. This chapter will then move on to discuss the role of revolution in state development and national identity, including military-supported or -derived governments whose origins continue to determine political parameters. Further, this chapter will note the style and forms of governments that have been peacefully inherited and how they have been modified to suit the requirements of various interest groups, such as elites and ethnic majorities. The adoption of modern state forms will be considered within the context of the adoption of Western ideas of statehood (the idea of the nation-state), bureaucratic ordering, and the process of 'modernisation'.

SOME POLITICAL DEFINITIONS

In any study of political matters, it is necessary to clarify some definitions, which has been largely undertaken throughout this text. However, particularly in relation to distinctions within the broad political structure, I would like to offer a brief clarification of the conceptions of nation, state, state apparatus, regime, and government. In the first

instance, a 'nation' is intended here to mean a group of people who understand themselves to have common interests and world views and who usually share a common language. This may or may not comply with the 'state', which is the organisational territory under a political authority and which can (or can attempt to) claim or compel the compliance of its citizens for its laws.

The idea of 'state apparatus' implies the functional ability of the state; the means (legislative, institutional) by which it achieves (or attempts to achieve) desired outcomes. Within this text I refer to specific apparatus by their formal names (for example, the armed forces). The idea of a 'regime', which is often used within the context of South-East Asian governments (for example, 'the Hun Sen regime'), literally means the method or system of government (democratic, communist, authoritarian and so on), but is usually regarded as a pejorative term for the institution of government, tending to imply an authoritarian government and, as such, a pre-existing antithesis and is not used here for that reason. The term 'government', which instead is used throughout this text, implies the political institution that makes and implements decisions for the citizens of the state. The term 'sovereignty' or 'sovereign' is used here to denote the political independence of a state or institution within a state to act fully within its defined area of authority. A 'sovereign' power therefore does not share authority within its defined area, or will resist attempts to do so. This might apply to the 'sovereignty' of the courts to decide legal matters, or of the state to determine matters within its territorial boundaries. The population of each state is usually defined as its 'citizens'. A citizen is a member of a state who is entitled to such political and civil rights that exist in the state, and who owes an obligation of duty as defined by the state. Citizenship has been, since modern times, regarded as universal for all legitimate inhabitants of a state. However in the past citizenship was conferred on select members of the state, based on wealth, gender or status. Finally, the term 'ideology' requires some minor clarification, as it has become an often abused term. An ideology is a basic or first principle set of ideas through which an intellectual order is made of social and political experience. For an ideology to function as such, it must have a common core of values that are largely internally consistent. Better known examples of ideologies include Marxism and liberalism, although religious beliefs such as Christianity or Islam, or ideas about the nation ('nationalism') or the state ('unitarianism', 'federalism'), can also function as ideologies.

CONCEPTIONS OF THE STATE

The state, as it is understood in the contemporary sense, refers to a specific and delineated area in which a government exercises (or claims to exercise) political and judicial control and claims a monopoly on the legitimate use of force. Of course, the state is not just its territory, however that may be defined. But the spatial quality of the state 'is integral to its functions and agencies' (Smith 1986: 235). That is, the area of the state defines the functional reach of its agencies. In the modern sense, this implies up to the limits of its borders, although in more 'traditional' societies this historical border area was far more ambiguous. This conception of the 'state' is distinct from that of the 'nation', which, as noted, refers to a group of people who regard themselves in common, usually through language although sometimes through or with other cultural signifiers such as religion.

Within a given territory, the state can be identified by the activities of its agencies. Such agencies include state bureaucracy, the armed forces, educational institutions, state industries, the judiciary and a police and penal system. It should be noted, however, that while these are typical agencies of the state, the size and role of the state at the end of the twentieth century was under challenge, from ideological influences, world bodies such as the International Monetary Fund (IMF), and from globalised economics. In particular, state industries and government bureaucratic services (including penal systems) were being sold to private providers. The state, however, has generally retained legislative responsibility for these agencies.

GLOBAL CHALLENGES TO THE STATE

The question of the sovereignty of the state has become increasingly open to debate in the late twentieth century, as ideas of what constitutes state sovereignty have been challenged (see Weber & Bierstaker 1996: 282; Hinsley 1978: 285–6; Camilleri 1994: 130–1; Camilleri & Falk 1992). For example, the role of the United Nations (UN) and some other international bodies, such as the IMF and the General Agreement on Tariffs and Trade (GATT), can and do use a degree of compulsion in requiring sovereign states to bend to their requirements. This can perhaps be seen as a parallel to the state itself, where the state can use compulsion in relation to its citizens, usually with their consent in principle, while the UN, for example, can use compulsion in relation to its members, also usually with their consent in principle. By consent in principle, I mean that the rules consented to are agreed to apply to all members in principle but may be applied in a way that might have precluded consent in practice to specific members.

Further, a global trend towards the removal of restrictions to trade and the related growth of global capital has removed from many states their capacity to make independent economic decisions. Both the Indonesian and Malaysian governments noted this loss of 'economic sovereignty' during the regional economic crisis of 1997–98. Yet the idea of the state continues to be adhered to, as a viable means of geo-social organisation and, in many cases, as a reflection of national (or nationalist) aspiration.

While no contemporary states seriously challenge the idea of fixed and clearly defined borders, many do disagree about where those borders should be or, indeed, about whether existing states do or do not contain embryonic states. Examples of embryonic states include East Timor, Aceh and Irian Jaya within Indonesia, the Karen and Kachin states of Burma, Bangsa Moro in the southern Philippines and so on (see Fowler & Bunck 1995: 1–62). Further, there have been disputes about the exact location of borders, for example between Thailand and Laos, Indonesia and Malaysia, and a number of states over sea-bed boundaries.

THE MODERN STATE

There is also the question of the relationship between the government and the state. In principle, the state has an existence independent of the government and, with its institutions, continues while governments come and go. However, the distinction between the state and the government was historically less clear, especially in SEA. Prior to the colonial period, the strength or ability of a government or ruler created, maintained or expanded the state. With the loss of that government or ruler, the state was often prey to the interests of other states or dissolved due to a lack of internal cohesion.

A state within the contemporary political context, in SEA or elsewhere, can be determined as having a number of characteristics that define it as a state. As outlined by Morris (1998), these include the following: the state and its institutions must have an enduring quality, in particular being able to survive changes of government or political leadership. In this sense, the state must also transcend both the rulers and the ruled, while the agents (or institutions) of the state must be able to continue regardless of political change. These agents must be differentiated from other, non-state agents and must, if the state is to function, be coordinated with each other. For example, the police and the judiciary must be coordinated in their support and application of the rule of law, while the executive and the military must act together to protect the political sovereignty of the state. The state must therefore also correspond to a clearly defined territory, so that its sovereignty is identifiable and its application enforceable.

Within that territory, the agents of the state must have full and equally distributed authority. The territory of the state must be sovereign, in that the state can legitimately claim a monopoly on the use of force within its territory. Jurisdiction must extend to the full extent of the territory of the state. The legitimacy of the state and its right to claim a monopoly on the use of force (or compulsion) should preferably be consented to and must be adhered to by members of the state, and in that the state is the ultimate authority (Morris 1998: 45–6; see also Laski 1934: 21–4). This adherence should be in the form of allegiance to the state, superseding all other allegiances. To ensure this allegiance, the state should function to protect and promote the interests of its members. However, in some circumstances it can be claimed that the state does not do this, but that it still claims adherence to its right to the monopoly of force.

MODELS OF THE STATE

In the post–World War II (post-WWII) period there has been a general acceptance in principle of the idea of a separation between the government and the state (see Morris 1998: 21–2). However, the practice has been somewhat different. In part this has been a consequence of the role played by certain agents, especially armies but also political parties or individuals, in the creation of the state. There has also been a tendency to draw on or re-invent pre-colonial traditions that characterise the state as being embodied within the army, the party or the person of the political leader. The distinction between the army and the state in Burma, for example, is effectively non-existent, while the separation of the party and the state in Vietnam or Laos is similarly difficult to discern. In Indonesia under Sukarno (Guided Democracy period) and Suharto, and to a lesser extent in Singapore under Lee, the state has been reflected in the person of the president or the prime minister. In the cases of the state being reflected in the person of the leader, each state has shown itself to be greater and more permanent than the leader. However, in each case the independence of state functions, especially the judiciary and the electoral system, has been seriously compromised.

The idea of the state as it is now understood is relatively new; it was only beginning to be formulated in Europe from the time of the Treaty of Westphalia in 1648 and only in the nation-state sense from the early nineteenth century. As an established idea, it is still disputed in areas where the authority of the state is challenged by assertions of the nation. The most obvious examples of this outside SEA are the former USSR, Yugoslavia, and Czechoslovakia and, to a lesser extent, in Belgium, Italy and Canada. Within SEA, Indonesia, Burma, the Philippines, Thailand, and Laos all have had localised 'nationalist' rebellions against the spatial–functionalist claims of the state. In spite of these protests against incorporation into established states, these rebellions are not opposed to the idea of the state as such and, indeed, are aimed at creating their own, new states. As a borrowed, if useful, model then, the modern idea of the state is uniformly accepted by the governments and other political movements of SEA.

All of the current states of SEA were colonies, with the exception of Thailand; and even Thailand had its contemporary borders defined by colonial powers and was in large part economically colonised by Britain. Hence, the physical characteristics of the state were defined not so much by geography[1] or national cohesion, but by the methods and requirements of colonial powers. Further, with the exception of Thailand, all of these states had their traditional or indigenous models of political authority dismantled or emasculated, which required the establishment of new forms of state authority. Even in the case of Thailand an approximation of the British model was adopted there in 1932.

There is no single idea of the state, although there are some general guides to what can constitute a state. In the most simple, anthropological sense, the state could simply be a shared agreement among a group of people about the rules under which they jointly live. It may, indeed, imply a form of government without a state (Krader 1968: ch. 2; see also Gamble 1986; Crone 1986). However, this view of the state does not include more 'explicit, complex and formal' agencies of government, which are the usual markers of state existence (Krader 1968: 13). Indeed, it probably bears closer relationship to the idea of culture, as a shared world view or set of values, or nation, which is a group of people so identifying themselves.

Another marker of the state is its internal integration, although this tends to apply more to modern (fixed boundary, post-colonial) states than to pre-modern (usually pre-colonial) states in which issues of integration were more ambiguous. Claims to state control in, for example, the Javanese Majapahit Empire of the fourteenth century were far more rhetorical than they were actual. A further characteristic of the state is the degree to which it is established and, similarly, the degree to which it can operate independently of external agencies. This idea of the 'embeddedness' of the state refers to the degree to which the state is able to implement its programs and policies within its given territory (Evans 1995).

Most, though not all, states are marked by a type of 'social contract', in which the ruler and the ruled agree to conditions of participation in the state.[2] This implies a type of *modus vivendi* connected with a sense of mutual consent (Plamenatz 1968: ch. 1) or mutual advantage (Rawls 1973: 4), but might in fact be a non-jural consideration. That is, being born into a particular state and with few or no realistic options for change or flight, participation in and effective acceptance of state rules might be a *fait accompli*. There are even some states that have been referred to as 'predatory', in which the state elites prey on their constituent populations (for example, as discussed by Evans 1995: 12, 43–7).

Morris has noted in particular that strong (authoritarian) states have a greater tendency to engage in harmful behaviour, to their own citizens or to others, and that democratic states do not have a record of going to war with each other (Morris 1998: 14–19). The implication of this is that where the power of the state is not in balance with a duty to its citizens it can act contrary to their interests. Such a balance is most recognisably achieved through the agencies of the state being accountable to the government and the government in turn being accountable to the citizens. In SEA there are numerous examples of strong states and of states acting in ways that do not accord with the best interests of their citizens.

THE CULTURAL AS POLITICAL

The main purpose here is to offer some observations about the intersection between culture and politics and to consider the deployment of power as the embodiment of political practice. Politics is, in a practical sense, the practice of the attainment, exercise and maintenance of power. Yet like all things, politics does not exist in a vacuum and reflects a particular set of historically-based circumstances and the variables of social relations. Many of the governments of SEA claim that their political forms reflect their prevailing cultures and cite this as a justification for their behaviour, which is often criticised by observers. This raises the dual questions of the validity of cultural relativism and of the accuracy of these governments' representations of the cultures of their citizens.

If culture is defined as a shared set of codes of behaviour or a world view common in its basic principles, there is necessarily social pressure to conform to such codes or principles. Without a degree of conformity, societies cannot function cohesively. Equally, conformity to social codes is often, generally quite willingly, undertaken by the individual to ensure retention within a social framework. That is to say, social organisation identifies itself as contextually located and is, via its constituent members, conscious of the maintenance of its principle or system of continuation through defining the past to represent a continuum of a particular set of values. This continuum is manifested as 'tradition, combined with the needs of practical adjustment, [which] are the main elements guiding overall system reproduction' (Giddens 1987: 153–4).

Conforming to particular codes of behaviour, or ascribing to a version of events which locates the present, helps to ensure a form of normative social cohesion. In cases where individuals or sub-groups do not conform, which by definition represent a challenge to social cohesion, both formal and informal sanctions may be placed upon them. Much depends on the types of challenges or threats facing the social collective and how much tolerance can be expressed before non-standard forms of behaviour become unacceptable. However, social codes of behaviour are often defined under the auspices of a non-representative power-oriented institution, authoritarian government being the most obvious example but also including the military, capitalists, a non-reflexive bureaucracy, in some cases religious institutions and others. As a consequence, such codes may be interpreted to suit the needs of the powerful, to preserve or enhance their authority.

In assessing such issues, one must consider who it is that acts as the keeper of social codes of behaviour; who has the authority to be the 'cultural police'. In this sense, the term 'culture' is here intended to define that aspect of social relations within a bonded group that refers to obligation, hierarchy and authority. It is not intended to refer to those qualities that reflect taste or preference.

In regard to the resolution of conflict and the control of violence, social codification is usually enacted as law (the legal code) and is policed in a literal sense. Beyond social conflict and violence, codes of behaviour take on more of a moral rather than legal tone. For instance, abusive language may imply the threat of violence and so be restricted, but critical language is merely offensive to certain sets of sensibilities or as a challenge to a position, such as that of a dominant religion. Yet the law can and does often rule on both under the one set of statutes. Conformity to social codes, then, occurs both within a legal framework designed to ensure a society's physical security and to ensure its cultural security, as well as through non-legal, socially based (cultural) mechanisms. Throughout

SEA, adherence to formal social codification is flexible, reflecting in part traditional forms of social sanction but, more importantly in a contemporary context, allowing considerable flexibility for the achievement of politically influenced outcomes. In this way, where traditional cultural values or the law conform to the requirements of government they are maintained or enforced. Where they do not, they are reconfigured or disposed of and replaced by other, often malleable, codes, sometimes dressed up as tradition and sometimes not.[3]

IDEOLOGY

All political systems represent ideological assumptions, even where such an assumption is not explicit. To paraphrase the economist Keynes, those who claim themselves to be without an ideology are usually the followers of some unspoken ideology (see Keynes 1936).[4] That is to say, political leaders might claim to be pragmatic, to assert the good of the state or the nation above ideology or to represent not contemporary ideologies but traditional patterns of political behaviour. But in each case, they are usually representing ideas that derive from classical or neo-classical economic theory, from Leninist interpretations of Marxism, from nationalist ideologies or from resurrected feudal or pre-feudal traditions. Such has often been the case in SEA, where political rhetoric, say on land redistribution (the Philippines), free markets (Singapore), socialism (Vietnam), the role of the armed forces (Burma, Indonesia) or human rights, is not necessarily matched by corresponding political practice.

Hence, the ideological assumptions that underpin each state might not be those that most accurately represent the interests or wishes of most of the people of such states. As a consequence, one must ask of the extent to which the political interests of state constituents—the citizens of the state—are represented or to what extent such constituents are satisfied that their interests are represented.

CITIZENS

The modernist term 'citizen' implies political rights and obligations, which in some political contexts in SEA is not necessarily the case. However, it also implies being a constituent member of a state, being subject to its laws, the rights under which might vary considerably, and being internationally recognised as such. The idea of a 'citizen' did not effectively apply in much of SEA until the post-WWII period, as a large proportion of its inhabitants were colonial subjects and not citizens as such. Prior to the colonial period, the conception upon which the state was based often granted little political status to those other than the ruling elites and their functionaries. It is only with the establishment of the modern state, in particular with delineated borders and (at least theoretically) full and equal legal authority up to those borders, that citizenship became available and applied to the people of SEA.

NATIONALISM

It has been suggested that 'nationalism' is itself an ideology. The detailed form of this ideology varies from place to place, for example from the organicist (proto-fascist) idea of the Indonesian state to the Leninist model of the Vietnamese state. What they feature in common, however, is not just a desire for independent unity and, consequently, self-determination, but the creation of an idea of a common bonded identity (see Anderson 1991; Smith 1986: 231–5). Means of creating such a common identity are various, but usually revolve around a (sometimes manufactured) common history, an (often manufactured) common language, more broadly shared (or imposed) cultural values, and, importantly within the SEA context, the bonding born of fighting against a common colonialist enemy. In this last sense, the common aspiration and struggle for 'liberation' has been a strong component in forging a common identity. This common bonded identity, then, has been regarded as the basis for an assertion of legitimate control over the 'nation's' territory (see SarDesai 1997: chs 18, 24).

As a consequence of the role of the military, in some instances, in both the liberation and hence the state-creation process, military thinking has also come to exhibit characteristics of an ideology. This is especially relevant in terms of the relationship between the state and its institutions and individual citizens, and in terms of more broad conceptions of power, hierarchy and authority. The role of the military can be clearly seen in a number of SEA countries, including Burma, Thailand, Cambodia, Laos, Vietnam, Indonesia, and perhaps the Philippines. In some places the role of the military in political affairs has declined (Thailand, Cambodia, Philippines and, it seems, Indonesia), in some increased (Burma) and in others simply changed (Vietnam, Laos). The lessening of military involvement in political affairs has usually been regarded as a sign of the political maturity of the state, a sign that the state is capable of assuming responsibility for its affairs (Dodd 1972: 50–4).

The modernist adoption (or imposition) of fixed borders clashed with the ebb and flow of traditional SEA polities, not to mention the drift of migrants from one region to another. In the contemporary political world, the free flow of people is regarded as challenging state control of its borders, upsetting patterns of established land use and ownership, and threatening loyalty to the state. Historically, however, such migration was encouraged, as a means of strengthening the state in both economic and military terms. This had implications for pre-colonial state formation and how that has influenced contemporary states. But the ideas that derive from the pre-colonial period also inform, sometimes consciously and sometimes subconsciously, the way political leaders look at their own country and those around them.

With the establishment of European colonies in the region, colonisers sought to extend their authority either to or beyond the limits of the state as they found it, as a part of their empire creation. To that end, the Dutch included not just Java in their colony of the Dutch East Indies, but also islands which had only peripheral relations with Java (despite what has been claimed, albeit briefly, for the Majapahit Empire). Similarly, Britain incorporated not just the core state of Burma within the Irrawaddy Valley, which it acknowledged as 'Burma Proper', but also states that had a separate or conflicting history in relation to Burma, which they also acknowledged, as the 'Frontier States'. The French correctly assumed the connectedness of the three states of Vietnam, as they found them, as Cochin-China, Annam and Tonkin. However, it was only through the shallow establishment of a Vietnamese claim to suzerainty that they then annexed the Lao state of Luang Prabang, extended to incorporate the other Lao states of Vieng Chan (Vientiane) and Champassak. That Thailand also claimed suzerainty over these states little worried the French. Further, to compound this lack of acknowledgment for what political arrangements did and did not exist, the French then chose to delineate their newly acquired Lao territory along the Mekong River, with the exception of small northern and southern sections. The Mekong had traditionally been the main artery *within* the Lao nation, and earlier within the Lao state of Lan Xang. This had little meaning for the French, but left a majority of ethnic Lao Loum in what was thereafter defined as Thailand rather than in Laos.

MANDALAS

Prior to colonialism, nowhere in SEA was there a state that had clearly delineated borders or which ruled with any permanent authority in all its outer regions. Almost by definition, the states which existed in pre-colonial SEA were in a constant state of expansion or retraction, with all authority located at what was often seen as an 'exemplary centre'. In an idealised state, it is from this centre that a monarch ruled, his authority radiating outwards. Acknowledged in practice but less so in rhetoric, that power receded the further it travelled. At or near the centre, authority was greatest; at the periphery it was dispersed, often through local rulers of increasing independence (Tambiah 1976: 114; see also McCloud 1995: 93–7) and increasingly doubtful loyalty, until it ceased to exist in practice. At this point the authority from another centre would begin to resonate. Where two centres of authority came into contact, other than through truces, suzerainty or rare marriages of convenience, conflict was almost inevitable. A state that could not maintain or continue to expand its authority was by definition in decline and, given the quasi-magical or metaphysical qualities associated with power, once a loss of power was manifest, decline, usually total, was inevitable. Without wishing to overstate the point, aspects of this model continue to be reflected in contemporary states, in particular in Suharto's rule of Indonesia, Hun Sen's rule of Cambodia and Ne Win's dominance of Burma.

A further elaboration of this idea is that, with the power of the state strengthening towards the centre, the highest source of authority within the state is the individual who resides at its centre: the monarch (or absolute ruler). Through patronage, as opposed to bureaucracy or feudal obligation, the monarch dispenses favour or otherwise, balancing competing forces within their sphere. In a practical sense, the monarch might also need to enter into arrangements with other powerful individuals, or substates, diminishing the purity of this centralising model. However, there remains not just a parallel but also a direct relationship between the central patrimonial system of monarchy and the notion of a deeply centralised state. The centralisation of power and the distribution of patronage continue to be hallmarks of SEA political models, to varying degrees applying in each of the region's states.

This idea of state organisation has, generally, been referred to as a *mandala*, the Buddhist model of the universe in which all matter radiates from and revolves around an exemplary centre (Wolters 1999; Stuart-Fox 1997: 2–4; Moertono 1981: 71, nb207; Wilson 1969: 7).[5] The idea of the *mandala* as a political model derives from India and has been used to describe the construction of early Buddhist states of SEA. However, a similar model for political authority applied to China and the states it directly influenced, including Korea, Vietnam, and Japan as well as its own western provinces.[6]

MANDALAS OR IMPERIA?

Wolters (1999) and Stuart-Fox (1999, pers. comm.) have suggested a distinction between the state as *mandala* and the state as an imperium. Vietnam, both suggest, was an imperium, based on two criteria. The first is that Vietnam, as a state originating in the Red River Delta region, only ever expanded and hence did not exhibit the expansion and contraction of a classic *mandala* (Wolters 1999: 144). Further, they both claim that Vietnam had more clearly defined boundaries and that its authority was complete up to that clearly defined boundary. Wolters also claims that Vietnam enjoyed a hereditary form of government that reflected dynastic succession that was not in keeping with a *mandalic* rise and fall of individual rulers and that it retained a constant political focus on Hanoi (see 1999: 143–54).

In part both Stuart-Fox and Wolter's definitions are based on a distinction between the 'Indianised' states of SEA and the 'Sinicised' state of Vietnam. Vietnam certainly had a different historical experience as a consequence of China's cultural and political influence, and the form of Buddhism it enjoyed (and continues to enjoy) was the more inclusive and syncretic Mahayana version, also derived from China. The rest of the mainland, in particular, converted to the Theravada version of Buddhism, founded in Sri Lanka. However, this sets up a dichotomy in Buddhism that is perhaps overstated.

More importantly, though, its logic also suggests that the notion of a *mandala* was reflected in the way society organised itself, rather than the *mandala* being conceived to describe that pre-existing social construction. To this end, one need only look at the feudal states of Europe or the pre-colonial states of Africa and Latin America to find numerous other political forms that parallel the construction of a *mandala*, even though Buddhism of either main variety was completely unknown to them. By way of illustration, it has been suggested that the political forms which, until the period of colonisation, dominated much of Asia were in fact similar to those which dominated Europe until the end of the Middle Ages or later (Steadman 1969: 26–7). In this respect, these states reflected a particular stage of economic and related political development.[7]

A parallel idea of the *mandala*, that the universe revolved around the earth (and that the state was centred on the court), was dominant in Europe until at least the mid seventeenth century. Weber discussed a similar idea in his model of 'patrimonial-prebendal' states, in which the ruler dispensed with patronage and ensured loyalty from a central point (Weber 1958, 1968; see also Bakker & Ferrazzi 1997). In that sense, as is often the case, the idea (in this case the *mandala*) reflected and ratio-nalised a pre-existing state of affairs or corresponding world view, rather than helped to shape them.

By contrast, the idea of an imperium suggests immutability. Vietnam has enjoyed a series of capitals at or near the site of modern Hanoi, but has also had capitals at a number of other sites across the length of the state. Similarly, Vietnam experienced dynastic succession but also saw dynasties fall and individual rulers last for short periods. Even the boundaries of the state, most clearly defined by the Annamite Cordillera, are physical rather than political. Where geography has allowed it there has been a lack of clarity over what did and did not constitute the terri-tory of the Viets, especially in the highland areas of the north-west and in the expanding south. There were at various times different methods of delineating the boundary of the Vietnamese state, but these were often similar to those used elsewhere, such as language, architectural style and regional loyalty. Further, while the Vietnamese maintained a fairly clearly defined sense of national identity and expanded south at the expense of the Chams and later the Khmers, their efforts to do so were not without reversal. The state of Champa attacked and occupied much of Vietnam in 979 CE, while the Khmer empire of Angkor occupied territory claimed by Vietnam during the period 1112–50 CE (Smith 1964a: 598; Nguyen 1993; 29; Osborne 1997: 20, 26, 32). All of this, of course, does not include the tendency of the Vietnamese state to fragment and reform, which it has done several times since the end of China's main period of occupation in 938 CE. The ideas of the *mandala* and the imperium are therefore like Weber's types of power, being idealised, with the reality being a variation on or a diluted or combined form of the models.

EMPIRES

In so far as the above discussion can be applied as a model for pre-colonial SEA states, it can also be used for pre-colonial SEA empires (superstates). The empire is but an extension of central authority: in the traditional format the greater the power of the central authority the greater its reach. Within a single linguistic or cultural group the reach of authority can be regarded as encompassing the state as a nation. How-ever, once the state uses force to encompass other linguistic or cultural groups—other nations of peoples—it becomes an empire. In pre-colonial times, empires encompassing diverse nations of peoples were not only common throughout Asia but were a logical, perhaps necessary, extension of the successful state. But in the post-colonial period, empires in the classical sense are almost universally disapproved of in the strongest possible terms. Colonialism does not have to be exercised by Europeans to be regarded as normatively undesirable.

Each of the contemporary regional states reflects attributes of empire (imperium), especially with the imposition of clearly defined borders and nominal judicial and administrative authority up to those borders, usually in spite of 'national' difference. But each also reflects attributes of a *mandala*, with practical political authority often not being fully implemented. Examples of such are found in the ethnic states of Burma, the minorities of Laos, the separatist aspirations within Indonesia, and the warlordism of Cambodia (especially around Pailin), and parts of Thailand, Laos, Burma, Indonesia and the Philippines. The idea of the *mandala*, then, lives on in a practical sense both in the form of modern states, in how they sometimes arrange their internal structures of authority and, not surprisingly, in particular cases of interstate relations.

COLONIAL INFLUENCES

Having noted the above, most SEA states more closely represent the area of their former colonial boundaries than they do states based on single cultural or historical groups. In this sense, a number of dominant nations have come to exercise authority over often reluctant smaller nations, thus comprising some modern states effectively as empires. Javanese domination of Indonesia, Thai domination of T'ai[8] and non-T'ai minorities, and Bhamese domination of Burma's minorities are but a few examples of states which, in historical terms, would have been considered empires.

While the idea of the nation-state inspired much post-colonial political thinking, there are few states that are also single nations of peoples. Vietnam is in its core areas a relatively homogeneous nation-state as is Cambodia. But even these have exceptions of numerous indigenous minorities—Cambodia has 100 000 or more Chams in its population of ten million—while Vietnam counts some fifty-three minority groups among its people, and other states are much more heterogeneous. This has led to a number of post-colonial states striving to manufacture a sense of national identity, for example through a common language or what are claimed to be shared historical events. Indonesia is the outstanding example of attempted nation building, bringing together numerous diverse cultural groups with usually very separate histories into a unitarian state. The means of achieving this have been the use of a common, if synthetic, language (Bahasa Indonesia) and a glorified common history, in this case under the Majapahit Empire and through the claimed unity of the anti-colonial struggle. Thailand also conducted an exercise in the construction of national identity in the latter part of the nineteenth and the early part of the twentieth century, as have most other states with varying degrees of effort and success.

Further enhancing the composite form of a number of contemporary SEA states, a number of European colonies that later became states were either based on pre-existing regional empires or regions of political dominance, or were in effect empires in their own right. The borders of Burma were determined by the British, with marginal regard for the significant ethnic minorities of the region. Malaysia comprises a number of earlier sultanates and modern Indonesia is a state based on the composite empire of the Dutch East Indies, reflecting Dutch colonial control in the archipelago.

Yet again, other ethnic and linguistic groups were divided by colonial boundaries, which have translated into modern states. Examples of this include the Lao of Thailand,[9] the ethnic T'ai (Shan, Wa, and so on) of Burma, the Papuans of Indonesia and the somewhat arbitrary division between Sumatra and the Malay Peninsula. In the case of Thailand, its modern boundaries include the old Thai principality of Lanna, based on Chiangmai, which was not formally incorporated into the state until 1907. Even until 1930, Chiangmai remained outside Thailand's taxation system and retained its own currency. Similarly, the eastern border of Thailand was not defined until 1907, incorporating as it did a majority of the Lao people in the north-eastern Korat Plateau, although there were to be short-lived readjustments during WWII under the auspices of imperial Japan. Similarly, although Vietnam's invasion of Cambodia in 1978 was in response to attacks by Khmer Rouge units across the border, its occupation until 1989 was perceived by many, including in Cambodia and Thailand, as a renewal of age-old Vietnamese imperial or expansionist ambitions.

Beyond this tendency towards expansion or retraction, SEA was and largely remains politically divided by its geography which, allowing for colonial reorganisation, is reflected in the borders of the region's contemporary states. By way of illustration, the rise of the Han, the preceding Ch'in, and the unification of the Chinese empire drove numerous ethnic minorities from China's southern provinces into SEA, forcing them to follow the natural contours of the geography. The spread southwards of Annamites (Vietnamese) was channelled by the Annamite Chain of mountains, which divides Vietnam from Laos, and in part from Cambodia. The various T'ai groups settled in geographically distinct regions; the various Lao in the region of the upper Mekong River, the

Thai in the Menam Valley; and the Shan in the Salwein Valley, while Tibeto-Burmans settled in the Irrawaddy Valley. The Mon-Khmer settled in the lower Mekong region of Cambodia (originally including the Mekong Delta) and across what is now southern Thailand and around the Irrawaddy Delta of Burma. Later cultural and political influences also followed the local geography, with Hinduism and the more formal Theravada Buddhism spreading from India and Sri Lanka along coastal routes into SEA, while the more syncretic Mahayana Buddhism flowed into China and south into Vietnam.

EXPANSIONIST AMBITIONS

This process of settlement and influence was not without conflict, however. Earlier settlers were often displaced or absorbed, such as the Chams of central Vietnam by the Annamite community (a Cham community continues to exist in Vietnam, with a larger community living near Phnom Penh in Cambodia); the Mon by the Burmans; and numerous ethnic minorities (not least of whom were SEA's original Austronesian aborigines) by numerically and militarily superior regional majorities. As late as 1828, Thailand resolved the problem of its rebellious Lao subjects by physically shifting tens of thousands of them from the eastern mountains and valleys of what was to become Laos into the northern part of the administratively more convenient Korat Plateau on the west side of the Mekong River. Although already a Lao region and once a part of the ancient Lao empire of Lan Xang, this relocation effectively divided the Lao between those under direct administration and those who owed suzerainty to Bangkok. The subsequent French occupation of the non-Thai region of old Lan Xang formalised this division.

In considerable part, the placement and displacement of peoples in turn reflected the rise and fall of regional powers and empires, which in turn reflected the aforementioned idea of expansion or contraction of political authority. This state of affairs was still dynamic when, in the sixteenth century, Europeans first began to encroach on the region, originally as traders and sometimes missionaries and then simply as other powers in a wide ranging field of political competition. But as European technology and political manipulation took effect in the form of colonies and 'protectorates', the border regions of Asia began to solidify, although not reaching their final colonial form until the early years of the twentieth century.

Yet there are still competing interests between the states of SEA, and much of the political manoeuvring, both within and between states, can be attributed to the solidification of a formerly fluid political environment. Border disputes have been prevalent between Thailand and Laos, Vietnam and Cambodia, Burma and China, the Philippines and Malaysia, Indonesia and Malaysia, Indonesia and the Netherlands (in West Papua) and, over the Spratly Islands, between China, Taiwan, Vietnam, the Philippines and Malaysia. The colonial anomaly of Portuguese Timor was absorbed into the post-colonial construction of the state that is Indonesia and while this made sense geographically it did not reflect the wishes of the great majority of East Timorese and again recalled the *mandalic* idea of imperial expansion.[10]

There also continues to be a tendency for some states to play an active role in the affairs of their neighbours, acting out in what were perceived to be 'areas of influence', or what was once, in more practical terms, called suzerainty. China has been active in Cambodia and briefly in Vietnam and has been forging close links with Burma, Laos and Thailand. Vietnam has also engaged in neighbourly intrigues, influencing and, at times, contributing to events in Laos and Cambodia, as has Thailand. Indonesia has sought to influence affairs in Malaysia to the extent of opposing the state in its entirety. Perhaps states have always and will always seek to influence their neighbours, despite the non-interference principles of the Association of South East Asian Nations (ASEAN), which now comprises all the SEA states. Such influence can be interpreted as an effect of 'manifest destiny' and continues to give strength to the idea of the *mandala* as a political model.

Within the states, often quite distinct ethnic groups can be amalgamated or brought together under a single political structure, usually under the tutelage of a dominant ethnic group that controls the administrative and military mechanisms. In Burma, for instance, there are significant minorities of Shan, Chin, Kachin, Kyah, Karen and others in their own regions as well as other absorbed minorities. In Indonesia, there is a continuing history of rebellion in the northern province, but once separate sultanate, of Aceh, and in West Papua, as well as serious levels of disaffection elsewhere. East Timor, incorporated by force in 1976 (invaded in 1975), was separated from Indonesia in October 1999. There are separatist claims by Muslims in the southern Philippines. And there are disputes between majority lowland and upland Lao (such as the Hmong, Yao, Kha), including conflict with the government in Vieng Chan, in part over political control and in part over the production of opium. There also remains disaffection between mainstream Thai and Lao of north-east Thailand, and with the minorities of the north and Muslims of the south, which in the late 1960s and early to mid 1970s spilled over into revolutionary rebellion.

Faced with competing historical interests, conceptions of national or tribal identity and a requirement to forge a unified state which more or less complies with contemporary requirements to be self-administering, viable and independent, the post-colonial states of post-war SEA have drawn strongly on their respective local histories and political styles as well as many of the organising principles of government derived from the West. In this sense, as the states of SEA have sought to model themselves on the relatively recent European idea of a legally delineated territory, they have often also sought to implement political institutions that could correspond to administering that territory. This has become especially important to those states that have engaged in increasingly complex interstate relations, including trade and diplomacy, which, within the modern context, traditional political forms were unable to adequately provide for.

This political process does not then imply a particular ideology of government, but it does imply a government which (theoretically at least) exercises full sovereignty to the limits of its borders (Morris 1998: 21) and which acknowledges citizenship of the permanent residents within those borders, as well as having independence from external powers (Morris 1998: 174). In a formal sense, sovereignty is, or should be, absolute, inalienable and indivisible (Morris 1998: 178). Sovereignty can be limited, however, where governments may be constitutionally deprived of certain juridical powers (for example, making state religion) (Morris 1998: 205).

The idea of the state, then, is not immutable and especially not so in SEA. Localisms challenge existing states from within, while global tendencies challenge them from without. Even the simple management of states can present a challenge to their cohesion, while many states only partially fulfill the requirement regarded by Morris as standard for their legitimate claim to existence. Yet each state continues to assert itself, assuming in some senses an existence beyond that of the group or area it claims to represent. Here we see the morphing of the institutions of state with the state itself, and the role and ideology of government as defining the style and scope of the state. In this, the states of SEA perhaps reflect older conceptions of statehood, or more universalist ones. There was little guarantee that the states that existed at the end of the twentieth century, or even what was understood to be meant by the term 'state', would continue in some precise form indefinitely. The idea of the 'state' has been fulsomely adopted throughout the region but, like other political forms, how it has been interpreted has been shaped by local desires, values, requirements, and impositions.

NOTES

1 Contemporary river boundaries are a European convention. Rivers were a means of travel within states in pre-colonial times.

2 The idea of a 'social contract' has been extensively discussed by Hobbes, Locke and Rousseau, among others, although rejected by Mill (1961: 552).

3 See Pemberton (1994) for a useful illustration of this point in relation to Indonesia.

4 To clarify my own position, I favour democratic or representative government, with enough checks and balances to ensure qualification of political decisions and processes.

5 In its original cosmic sense, the *mandala* was intended to be a metaphorical rather than literal interpretation of the universe. It reflected a desire for order and balance as much as it did a method of explanation. Further, particular models of *mandalas*, like other forms of cultural expression, also varied from one cultural environment to another, and, while retaining the same basic characteristics, said as much about their makers as about the thing they were supposed to represent.

6 Stuart-Fox (1996: 5–6) suggests that within the SEA context, Vietnam was not a mandalic state, in that it had clearly defined borders. It was, he says, an *imperium* in the same manner as China. Vietnam did have more formally defined borders than other pre-colonial SEA states. However, its expansion southwards into what was Champa and into Cambodia and the poorly defined nature of its boundaries and suzerainty to its north-west suggest a similar pattern of authority to other SEA states. (Similarly, the extent of the authority of the Chinese *imperium* has waxed and waned according to internal circumstances and external forces.)

7 A related idea is that power is radiated in concentric circles, but with those circles alternating in favour and disfavour towards the centre. That is, my neighbour is by definition my enemy, hence his neighbour must be his enemy and is perforce my ally, although his neighbour in turn will again be my enemy (see Moertono 1981: 71 nb207; Steinberg 1971: 400).

8 The term 'T'ai' refers here to the linguistic family of T'ai speakers, including the Shan, Thai and Lao, as well as T'ai who are spread from Assam in India to north-west Vietnam and southern China.

9 About 6 000 000 ethnic Lao live in Thailand, while only about 4 000 000 Lao live in Laos.

10 Further, the Indonesian government argued that to allow East Timor independence would encourage separatism on the part of Indonesia's other provinces, reflecting the *mandalic* idea that a state, or empire, which is not expanding (or at least maintaining) is threatened with shrinkage.

2

Authority and Legitimacy

This chapter will consider models of political legitimacy and their application in SEA, with particular reference to the nature of authority and its relationship to notions of legitimacy within the SEA context. Central to discussions of legitimacy are issues of how governments organise themselves and how they behave towards their constituent members, which is usually referred to under the rubric of civil and political rights.

REPRESENTATION AND PARTICIPATION

One way of understanding political processes is to ask whether or not people are satisfied with their lot, and to then look at the conditions which offer that degree of satisfaction or otherwise. This could be seen as an indicator of whether or not a political system is working and indeed what type of political system it is and whose interests it primarily represents. In most cases, representation of interests is determined by participation, which can be either active or passive, or exclusion from the political process.

The positive version of political participation means having some constructive input into the political process to which a citizen of a state is subject. In the negative, this could mean being opposed to such political processes. Somewhere in between lies passive participation. Passive participation implies that citizens are not prepared to engage in the political process but not to reject it; that they are sufficiently satisfied to disregard it and get on with other matters or that they see no practical value in actively opposing it. That is, the political process is, for all practical intentions, accepted. This does, however, raise the issue of what could be termed 'political psychology'. It has been suggested that in some circumstances membership in a political process is not a question of will, but a fact of life. Members born into a political community are sometimes not asked if they are happy with the order of things but rather are expected to accept this order and comply with it (and it is at this point that 'culture' blends with politics). In instances where there is dissonance between the desires of the individuals and the circumstances in which they find themselves, and where they have little or no control over those circumstances, there is a tendency for individuals to try to reduce that dissonance by complying with their circumstances. That is, passive acceptance of a particular political situation does not necessarily reflect acceptance, but a recognition of the futility of rejection.

Within such a discussion, the question of lawful behaviour becomes implicit. It is a normative requirement that states act within the laws they themselves have framed, through their institutions. And it is a normative requirement that those institutions that have framed the law have done so in an equitable and just manner; that they are broadly socially acceptable and reflect the values of the society to which they are intended to apply. If the state behaves in a way that corresponds to law, it can be said in one sense to be legitimate (Morris 1998: 103). However, if the state does not behave in a way that corresponds to its own laws, or if its laws are not broadly socially acceptable, or they do not reflect the values of the society to which they are intended to apply, then the state could be said to be illegitimate. It may be claimed that accordance with law is not a sole criterion for the legitimacy of the state, and clearly there are complicating factors when agents of the state act outside the law. But if the state does not generally act lawfully, or if the laws it acknowledges are arbitrary or predatory, the legitimacy of the state could come under fundamental challenge, both from within and without.

Beyond lawful behaviour lies coercion. Coercion is a product of force, or power, and is perhaps the primary ingredient in any political process and especially in many of those found within SEA. Coercion is closely related to the above mentioned resolution of dissonance in that it implies a lack of choice on the part of the individual. In the case of accepting an unchangeable situation, an individual does not necessarily run into conflict. However, coercion implies that the individual is behaving a particular way and that some greater power enjoins them to change that behaviour against their will, usually with the explicit or implicit threat of violence. In that the individual will usually seek to avoid such violence, or through the use of violence against them or others understand that future violence is best avoided, they are in effect complying with circumstances over which they have little or no control.

The scale between passive acceptance and coercion is often ambiguous and is frequently misrepresented. It is often difficult to determine at what point coercion is no longer being used, and what the lingering effects of coercion can be on individual behaviour. In that sense, it is unclear at what stage a threat, especially an implied threat, ceases to have force. It is even more difficult, given the process of resolving individual dissonance, to determine whether even relatively happy or satisfied passive acceptance can constitute endorsement of a regime of threat. This creates problems when political leaders claim that there is no objection to their rule based on its passive acceptance by others. We cannot know, for example, whether in other circumstances there might not be a more active rejection of that rule. Nor can we know the extent to which such passive acceptance has been the product of earlier intimidation or coercion. In this sense, an apparent lack of discontent with particular political rule does not necessarily imply support for it, as has so often been claimed by SEA political leaders. Rather it is, or should be, beholden upon political leaders who make such claims to provide evidence to support their assertions. Invariably, however, they cannot be compelled to provide such evidence and, as a consequence, they do not.

APPROACHES TO THE PRACTICE OF POWER

The single most crucial issue in regard to the exercise of power is that of legitimacy or the right to exercise power that, within an organisational context, is translated as authority (the other manifestation of power being force). Of the various formulations of legitimacy, the great social theorist Max Weber proposed that its foundations are based on three, usually interactive, sets of criteria. However, qualifying his definitions of types of legitimacy, he noted that it was not necessarily correct to assume that every case of submissiveness to persons in positions of power was primarily (or even at all) oriented to the belief that 'appropriate attitudes' and 'corresponding practical conduct [from the power holder] will ensue'. 'Loyalty', he said, 'may be hypocritically simulated by individuals or by whole groups on purely economic grounds, or carried out in practice for reasons of material self-interest. Or people may submit from individual weakness and helplessness because there is no acceptable alternative' (Weber 1964: 326).

This qualification of legitimacy is important, as while authority might be exercised and might be held to be legitimate as a consequence of the acquiescence of its subjects, the motivation for acquiescence may be a product of inflexible circumstances. Therefore, what passes as political legitimacy might only be through lack of free subject choice. Otherwise, legitimacy can be understood to mean the rightful or appropriate rule or exercise of power based on a principle, such as consent, which is accepted by both the ruler and the ruled. Such a relationship may imply force within particular, usually prescribed, circumstances, such as the enforcement of laws.

Of Weber's three types of 'ideal' legitimate authority, 'rational–legal' authority is based on the acceptance of 'the "legality" of patterns of normative rules and the right of those in authority under such rules to issue commands (legal authority)'. Traditional authority is based on 'an established belief in the sanctity of tradition and the legitimacy of the status of those exercising authority'. Charismatic authority is based on 'devotion to the specific and exceptional sanctity, heroism or exemplary character of an individual person, and the normative patterns or order revealed or ordained by him' (Weber 1964: 328). The distinctions noted by Weber were proposed as 'ideal' types and were, in part, intended to highlight the differences between types of authority. In this, they tended to exaggerate or 'purify' most circumstances, which were and remain in reality considerably more blended and affected by other considerations.

Rational–legal authority presupposes the rational and consistent nature of the legal apparatus or the subject's compliance with it. However, the legal apparatus might not be 'rational'—it might not necessarily act consistently or may be unduly influenced by a diminution of 'the separation of powers' (of the judicial and political systems[1]). Similarly, the subject's compliance might be rational only in so far as to not comply would invite an unwelcome response.

However, legal authority can be regarded as rational if, and to the extent that, the rules on which it is based are in 'pursuit of the interests which are specified in the order governing the corporate group within the limits laid down by legal precepts and following principles which are capable of generalised formulation and are approved in the order governing the group, or at least not disapproved in it'. Further, the application of such laws or rules must be applied impersonally and consistently, and they must be equally obeyed impersonally rather than as an obligation of obedience to an individual (Weber 1964: 330).

POWER AND GOVERNMENT IN SOUTH-EAST ASIA

A number of governments in SEA do not, in practice, recognise a separation of powers between the state and the judiciary, and encourage the law
to be applied in ways that reflect political rather than legal concerns. This
might be through customary law, which incorporates cultural values not
formally codified into the legal process. Where the law is codified, it may
still be repressive, or operate within a flexible and highly interpretable
framework and be quite open to political influence. In this latter case it is
where courts return verdicts or sentences that reflect the wishes of politicians rather than reflecting the balance of evidence or the seriousness of
the crime. Further, an obligation of duty is owed to the state as a manifestation of legal authority, but in practice—and in some aspects in law—an
obligation of duty is also owed to political leaders or wielders of authority. Hence the 'legality' of patterns of rules and the right of those elevated
to authority under such rules to issue commands might apply only in a
qualified sense. This situation could have been said to apply to Indonesia
under Suharto, Singapore under Lee, Thailand under Sarit, Burma under
Ne Win, and perhaps Cambodia under Pol Pot.

In this sense, it follows Weber's view that 'traditional' authority is
open to a 'sanitisation' that renders what passes as traditional not so
but rather a politically convenient cultural reconstruction. In traditional
authority, loyalty is based on allegiance to a 'personal chief' (a political
patron), where 'his administrative staff does not consist primarily of officials [public servants] but of personal retainers [clients]'. Further, loyalty
is not to the office of the 'chief' [the presidency and so on], but to the
'person of the chief' [the individual concerned] (Weber 1964: 341).

Where tradition has been reconstructed and sanitised, what constitutes traditional limitations on chiefly behaviour is equally reconstituted,
while 'the obligations of obedience on the basis of personal loyalty
[which] are essentially unlimited' is enhanced. In the case of administrative staff, senior officials may be appointed on the basis of their closeness
or loyalty to the 'chief', as a consequence of patron–client relations, or
'personal retainers' may be appointed to official positions. Wright–
Neville might have been specifically thinking about much of SEA when
he said that such sanitised tradition tends to emerge in non–reflexive
societies, usually after its rigorous reinterpretation by state-affiliated
bodies. These 'traditions' are then disseminated in a non–critical manner
through the state apparatus, including schools and universities, and via a
media industry that is dominated by, usually beholden to and often dominated by the government. As a consequence, there is no way of knowing
whether what passed as legitimacy actually reflected the views or aspira-

tions of ordinary people, or whether it just served elite interests (Wright-Neville 1993: 21–2).

Absolute traditional authority has always been a rare occurrence and in a period of competing interests spurred on by rapid technological and economic change, such as the late twentieth century world, it was effectively non-existent. However, traditional authority where a personal administrative staff (or where a staff of officials) owe their positions to their 'chief', 'especially a military force under control of the chief, traditional authority tends to develop into "patrimonialism" '. Such patrimonialism is where the 'patron' personally looks after the interests of his clients, and they are personally loyal to him.

Under such patrimonialism, citizens of the state are treated as subjects. Authority of the chief which was previously regarded as exercised on behalf of such citizens becomes personal authority, which the chief appropriates in the same way as any ordinary possession. The chief might choose to sell it, to pledge it, or to divide it. The primary means of support for such patrimonial authority is an army or paramilitary police. Through these instruments of force the chief may broaden the range of arbitrary power which can then become free of traditional restrictions, and put the chief in a position to dispense patronage at the expense of the traditional limitations typical of patriarchal and gerontocratic structures (Weber 1964: 347).

Suharto, Lee, Ne Win, Marcos and Sarit, among others, come to mind when considering this broadening of arbitrary power. Further, the tendency for authoritarian leaders to engage in corrupt practices, in particular Suharto and Marcos but also others such as Sarit, paralleled Weber's view of authoritarian rule that was organised partly by profit-making businesses, partly by fees (or corruption) and partly by taxes. This could be conducted under a monopoly situation. With the economy dominated or influenced by such a ruling group, its growth is usually hampered by their personal ambitions and ability to influence its direction (Weber 1964: 355).

The orientation of charismatic authority towards the individual rather than the office or pre-existing forms of authority has on one hand allowed the expectation of a duty of obedience to the individual regardless of legal or traditional proscription. To fail in this personal commitment is to be regarded as delinquent in duty (Weber 1964: 360). However, charismatic authority is vulnerable to misfortunes which may be beyond the leader's actual control, but which are assumed to reflect on the control vested in him through his charismatic status—that his 'gift of grace' has deserted him (Weber 1964: 360). In cases of a challenge, the victor is implicitly in 'the right' (Weber 1964: 361).

Within the traditions of a number of SEA states, power had (and still often has) a quasi-metaphysical (magical or religious) quality for many people, particularly those whose education remains limited. In this sense, power is still sometimes understood not as a system of social, economic and political relations, but as an independent quality which reflects the purity (or holiness, in a normative ethical sense) of the individual. One of the better contemporary examples of this phenomenon was the leader of the Indonesian Democratic Party struggle, Megawati Sukarnoputri. Megawati was a classic case of representing little in a concrete sense, but standing for the only vaguely articulated aspirations of millions of Indonesian people. Megawati was perceived to stand not for particular policies but for 'change' (even though she was a political conservative), for an end to authoritarianism (even though she was close to the top ranks of the army) and for 'democracy' (even though her party did not encourage or reflect local level participation). But, as a symbol, she could do no wrong. In this she embodied 'purity'. To a far lesser but still valid extent, Suharto was similarly seen as pure by at least some of Indonesia's population, as perhaps too were some of the political leaders of the Philippines (especially Corazon Aquino). Having such qualities, diluted, modified or cynically reconstructed though they may be in the contemporary context, the leader is perceived as representing not just his office, but also himself (or herself), as leader. Many SEA political systems thus reflect a mix of forms of authority, as defined by Weber, with a notable continuation of 'charismatic' and 'traditional' models.

THE SUBTLETY OF POWER

While Weber's analysis of power can be seen to apply, in broad terms, to issues of power and authority in South-East Asia, it does not take into account the range of subtleties through which power can be manifested, and how these can shape peoples' lives, values and actions. Lukes discussed the range of influences of power by proposing that power be defined as 'dimensional' (Lukes 1974). The first dimension of power, as discussed by Dahl (1971), focuses on behaviour in making decisions on issues over which there is an observable conflict of interests. This may be expressed as policy preferences and demonstrated through political participation (Lukes 1974: 15).

What Lukes called a 'two-dimensional' view of power, as elaborated on by Bachrach and Baratz (1962: 947–52), incorporated not just active or overt uses of power, but passive or covert uses of power. This could be said to parallel Weber's 'capacity' for the exercise of power. This is when a person or group creates or reinforces barriers to the public discussion of conflict, such as through media control, limits to free speech or other more subtle forms of control of communication (see Berman 1998, for discussion of this last point in relation to Java). This places much greater emphasis on exclusion or what Lukes calls 'non-decision making' (Lukes 1974: 18). That is, power is not just about acknowledging certain subjects being legitimate for discussion, but about the delegitimisation of certain subjects for discussion (for example, the political role of the armed forces) or the removal of certain subjects from the public agenda (for example, the legitimacy of the king). This developed 'behaviouralist' perspective is sometimes referred to as 'culturalism' (for example, Pye 1985[2]) or 'institutionalism' (for example, Liddle 1996), or 'political order' (Robison, in Higgott & Robison 1985: 295–6).

Lukes saw this type of analysis of power as still relying too heavily on observable conflict. This follows Weber, who stressed that power was the realisation of one's will despite the resistance of others. Yet power may be exercised by shaping the thoughts and desires of another, to have them act in a required manner that may not be in their interests. Such 'thought control' may take 'more mundane forms' than Huxley's *Brave New World*, such as 'through the control of information, through the mass media and through the processes of socialisation'.

Lukes suggested that because grievances about a power structure may not be aired or be able to be uncovered does not necessarily imply that the grievances do not exist. If a person or group does not have access to sets of ideas that inform them they may have a grievance, they continue to experience 'an undirected complaint arising out of everyday experience, a vague feeling of unease or sense of deprivation'. Further, power may be exercised by shaping understanding in such a way as to legitimise respective roles in the existing order of things. This legitimisation comes about because individuals cannot see or imagine an alternative, because it is seen as natural and unchangeable or because it is valued as 'divinely ordained and beneficial'. The absence of grievance does not necessarily equal genuine consensus, as it deletes the possibility of false or manipulated consensus by definitional fiat'[3] (Lukes 1974: 24). Lukes' definition of power, then, closely accords with the conception of 'hegemony' as articulated by Gramsci. Hegemony in this sense implies the establishment and maintenance not only of political and economic control, but also of agreement by a subordinate social group or class with a dominant group or class that a prevailing state of affairs is desirable (Gramsci 1971: xii–xiv). Applied to SEA governments, it could be seen that what are regarded as social and political norms, and the processes by which they are maintained, operate at both conscious and unconscious levels. Further, they are reinforced both overtly and covertly by existing power structures and this tends to act primarily in the interests of the power brokers who exercise them. Some governments can therefore be seen to act primarily in their own interests, that of their close associates and of the elite in general.

MARXIST AND RELATED APPROACHES

Lukes was also critical of the focus on a methodology in which power is about individuals realising their wills (Lukes 1974: 21). He argued that the power to control the political agenda and exclude potential issues could not be adequately analysed unless it is seen as a function of collective forces and social arrangements. This then leads to a more broadly Marxist or 'political–economy' approach, such as that taken by Robison. Robison summarised it as an 'analysis of the development of capitalist relations of production and the development of a class of capital accumulators'. He said that the state (in this case Indonesia) is crucial because of its strategic role in the process of capital accumulation and, consequently, class formation and conflict (Robison 1985: 298). This role of the state in capital accumulation has indeed been critical in many SEA states, and classes, in the conventional industrial sense, have begun to emerge. However, their emergence has been fitful and weak and class conflict in a traditional Marxist sense has been less important than other forms of communal rivalry, in which challenges for ownership of farming land and religious affiliation were critical. In the case of capital accumulation, in some instances this has occurred not through conventional capitalist practices, but through economic systems that rely on patronage and corruption and cronyism.

In his 1985 analysis, Robison posited the other main analytical grouping as the 'dependency approach', which agrees with the idea that classes in the conventional sense 'were too weakly developed to constitute the basis of politics'. Instead, it was proposed that networks of patrons and clients provided a more substantial basis for political organisation (Robison, paraphrasing Mortimer, 1985: 298). While this was intended to apply to Indonesia under Suharto, the relationship between SEA governments and foreign capital is more complex than just an 'outflow of surplus'. A considerable surplus also accumulated to indigenous (*comprador* and 'nationalist') elites and there has been a considerable economic strengthening of the state and its infrastructure. Further, broad living standards have in most cases improved rather than declined, even if in some cases this has been marginal, and even if longer term trends have been reversed (seemingly temporarily).

ASIAN VALUES

Any discussion of political legitimacy in SEA must at least acknowledge the claim made by some of the region's political leaders to what has been called 'Asian values'. These 'Asian values' are intended to cover a broad range of social relations but have a particular application to politics as a consequence of their emphasis on hierarchy, order and obedience. Notable proponents of 'Asian values', or the cultural specificity of an Asian approach to politics, have included Singapore Prime Minister Lee Kuan Yew, Malaysia's Mahatir Mohamad, Indonesia's Suharto (and, as Research and Technology Minister, later President Habibie), Brunei's Sultan Hassanal Bolkiah and Burma's various political leaders. Interestingly, the leaders of the states of Laos, Cambodia and Vietnam have usually appealed to either ideological dogma or the exigencies of running a state, while the political leadership of Thailand and the Philippines has rarely in recent times made such appeals the basis for their legitimacy. This then begs the question of what are 'Asian values'?

In one sense, the whole notion of 'Asian values' is nonsensical, if for no other reason than it implies a commonly held set of principles that apply across the region known as 'Asia'. Yet the idea of 'Asia' is itself problematic, being a European construction developed at a time when the unity of 'otherness' was defined by its geographical location; that of east of Europe. If Afghanistan is taken as the 'beginning' of Asia, one would be hard pressed to find some cultural affinity between it and, say, Japan. Meanwhile, many Indians identify themselves as quite Asian but at the same time as quite distinct from their Chinese counterparts, for example.

If the definition is further narrowed to East Asia there are distinct differences between societies as diverse as Japan and the Philippines, China and Indonesia, Korea and Laos, and Taiwan and Brunei. Narrowing further to South East Asia there are increasing areas of overlap between each of the states of the region, but there remain distinct areas of difference. The Thai and Lao, for example, can claim some broad cultural affinity although, beyond religion, the Bhamese of Burma and Cambodians would have difficulty in making a similar claim. Vietnam, by comparison, is set aside, at once very much reflecting long-standing

Chinese influence as well as the Vietnamese' own well developed sense of cultural identity. In the archipelagic region, there is some commonality and mixing between the Proto and Deutero Malays,[4] as well as literally hundreds of linguistic and cultural groups. But with the exception of some parts of Sumatra and the Malay Peninsula it would be difficult to establish any significant claim to cultural commonality. This, of course, defines culture as belonging to states, which are administrative regions, rather than nations, which are social collectives. Yet among the states of the region are numerous 'national' or ethnic distinctions: more than 300 in Indonesia, more than a dozen in Malaysia, almost 70 in Laos and more than 50 in Vietnam, with many more in Thailand, dozens in the Philippines and Burma, in Cambodia and even in Brunei. Within these groups, perhaps only a small minority are numerically significant, but claims to cultural homogeneity in SEA exist only on very poorly supported evidence (see Vervoorn 1998: ch. 4). Beyond ethnic distinction are others, such as status and class, which create further levels of identity and the value systems that inform such identity. In these myriad 'localisms', some overarching Asian value system starts to look very poorly grounded.

The claim to 'Asian values', then, reflects less a common cultural framework of the people it is suggested to represent and more the values of a particular group of people who make such claims.[5] This is not to suggest that there is not some authentic cultural commonality, however, between these political elites. Rather it is to suggest that the claim to cultural commonality is misidentified, probably quite intentionally, for overt political reasons. More accurately, if the political leaders of SEA and their supporters require a particular value system, they might be better and more accurately served by considering one of the political universal theorists, such as Machiavelli.[6]

Considering who has been making such claims, the one characteristic they have in common is their political leadership, usually acquired or maintained through means that are neither openly participatory nor genuinely representative. Singapore opposition leader Chee Soon Juan made both this point and stated that many people in Asia do not subscribe to the 'Asian values' idea (Chee 1998). Beyond this core group, there are its supporters, beneficiaries, hangers-on and a grab-bag of pro-authority sycophants. The intellectual coherence of an idea does not have to be particularly strong in order for it to exercise a powerful grip over the imaginations of some. Rather, it can achieve allegiance through its promise of stability and, supposedly as a consequence, security. However, as has been demonstrated in Burma, Cambodia and Indonesia (and elsewhere if one cares to look closely enough), authoritarian stability has been brittle and usually comes at a high, repressive price. If, then, we are to look for some cultural commonality in the claim to 'Asian values' it is connected to the attainment, maintenance and exercise of political power.

The models of government of modern Asia, or at least East Asia, have been identified by some commentators as having a common thread running through them, in part reflecting the economic development of many East Asian countries but more reflecting a tendency towards authoritarian forms. This common thread has been identified by Segal (1990: 117–24), among others, as deriving from the Confucian principle of respect for authority and a strong central government. Thus, the authoritarian tendencies of many East Asian governments have been claimed by some observers to be able to be explained by appealing to the ethical precepts of the dominant country of the region, China.

What is referred to as Confucianism is indeed an important cultural factor in a number of East Asian states, including Vietnam, North and South Korea and, of course, China. As a predominantly ethnic Chinese city-state, it could also be said to apply to Singapore. However, any claim to Confucian political values having a more widespread application confronts the reality that a number of states in the region find their ethical inspiration elsewhere. Indeed, Confucius' *Analects* have been argued to not support the claims made for it by apologists for contemporary authoritarian governments (Leys 1997). Moreover, Confucius himself[7] formulated the *Analects* in response to the political turmoil of the Chou Dynasty in the period in which he lived (circa 551–479 BCE). Within the *Analects* can be found a prevailing humanist theme (Ping-chia 1965: 19–23; Schurmann & Schell 1977: 10–11, 48), which was noted by scholars of Enlightenment Europe such as Voltaire (1979: 78–95). Confucius has been regarded as a social reformer (as illustrated in his Analects 1995: iii) and in favour of dissent (Leys 1997), rather than as a supporter of an authoritarian status quo.

If Confucianism has been seen as endorsing authoritarianism, it is because as a highly interpretable text it was bent to the requirements of China's absolutist monarchies (which, in a benevolent, enlightened form, it endorsed), in particular from the period of the Sung Dynasty (960–1279). It was from this time that Confucianism was reconstructed in neo-Confucian form in which 'conservative and nationalistic, it imposed narrow shackles on men's minds down to the nineteenth century' (Ping-chia 1965: 45). But even here there is confusion. The early Vietnamese nationalists wished to dispose of Confucianism, as identified by the traditional scholar class (Steinberg 1971: 305), while one of their leaders, Phan

Boi Chau, was 'himself a Confucian revolutionary, more at home with Mencius than with Montesquieu', admiring the 'unhurried mythological "democracy" of Chinese sage-emperors, who acknowledged that their throne belonged to the people, not to themselves'. Chau's objection was to an 'ossified' Confucianism (Steinberg 1971: 306).

More appropriately, what should be considered in Asia's contemporary political philosophy is not some overarching Confucian contribution to its practice, but the degree to which political systems derive their style from traditional forms of authoritarianism, the basis of that authoritarianism, the degree to which traditional authoritarian models have been reinvented, and the extent to which current authoritarian models reflect recent or contemporary circumstances and sectional interests. Examples of all of these factors can be discerned in Brunei and Burma, in the late Sukarno and late Suharto periods of government in Indonesia, and to a lesser extent in a number of other governments, including Cambodia under Prince Norodom Sihanouk, in post-unification Vietnam, in Singapore, and in Thailand. If traditional political models, or a re-invention and re-configuration of such models, informs at least some of contemporary Asian political behaviour, so too has Western political thinking. Western ideologies have come to the states of SEA either through the free will of an influential national (or nationalist) group, sometimes a majority and sometimes not, or have been left behind as a legacy of colonial intervention.

THE COLONIAL LEGACY ON FORMS OF GOVERNMENT

In the latter case it has been suggested that of the colonial powers, Britain tended to impart its political traditions but not its culture, while France and, to a lesser extent, the Netherlands imparted their culture but not their political traditions (Scalapino 1989: 29–32). In the first instance, probably the most important institution that reflected British culture was and is its parliament. The history of British parliamentarianism dates to the thirteenth century[8] (Pirenne 1939: 421) while the ideas that inspired it are considerably older. Perhaps the major distinction between the colonial powers was that Britain occupied its colonies and protectorates in a way that preserved significant aspects of traditional political society, while France tended to impose its own administrative structures (in conjunction with compliant 'traditional' rulers) on its colonial population. Technically, only Cochin-China was directly administered, although all of Indochina was, in practical terms, directly ruled by France (Jumper & Normand 1969: 384).

Following the turmoil of the period of WWII, France returned to Indochina to reassert its colonial authority, to restore its economic interests and, when conflict arose, to suppress linked nationalist and communist aspirations. The policy it adopted in the immediate postwar years differed little from that it had pursued as an imperial power. The Netherlands was also loath to release what was to become Indonesia as, 'Economically, the Netherlands was more dependent on its colony than any other Western colonial power in Asia' (Feith 1969: 193).

Britain gave up its colonial possessions in SEA in the postwar period in a somewhat more equitable manner. Weakened by WWI and then by WWII, Britain regarded the cutting of such colonial ties as inevitable and, in most cases, desirable. In Burma it chose to acknowledge rather than fight the Burma Independence Army, while in Malaya it supported political moderates but launched a 'police action' against communist guerrillas. By generally acceding to more moderate demands for independence, Britain was able to leave behind a number of institutional structures, including both a political system and a more or less workable bureaucracy. Yet the political model which Britain bequeathed did not survive unscathed.

It has been suggested that, as a non-indigenous political model, parliamentary democracy has been modified in line with local circumstances where it has been adopted in SEA, in particular reflecting the considerable authority and legitimacy that the first post-colonial governments derived from helping found the new state. Parliamentary politics has been more stable in Malaysia and Singapore, although this has been at the expense of its democratic component. Both states have had one governing party since independence. The Malaysian United Malay National Organisation has retained power through a coalition arrangement based on the country's three main (broad) ethnic groups: Malays, Chinese and Indians. This domination of Malaysian politics by one party has resulted in an autocratic style of government with distinctly authoritarian overtones, including hobbling the judiciary and restrictions on freedom of expression. In Singapore, the dominant People's Action Party has subverted the political system by making it very difficult to stand against the government or, more importantly, to criticise it. An authoritarian state, Singapore retains the shell of parliamentarianism without the substance.

The parliamentary system can also be seen at work in Thailand, which has proven increasingly resilient despite numerous coups, attempted coups and threatened coups. The pivotal aspect of Thai politics is, again, the legitimacy or otherwise lent to governments by the Thai king, who retains the position of head of state. Brunei retains an absolute sultanate (the king is not elected and appoints his own, non-elected cabinet), perhaps being able to do so because of the oil-based prosperity of the tiny nation's people, and at least in part because of successful counter measures against democratic reformers in the 1960s.

As a republic, the Philippines has a system essentially similar to that of parliamentary democracy, though with the president being elected separately from ordinary representatives, and the executive being separate to the legislature. This model was derived from the United States but was underscored by the establishment of a landed economic elite derived from the nation's Spanish colonial past. This has led to disaffection culminating in rebellion and, from 1972 until 1986, the suspension of democratic participation under martial law. In the late 1980s there was a series of attempted coups against the government, but the government and the country's political processes survived intact.

As a consequence, at least in part, of the role of the military in independence movements, the armed forces have continued to play a dominant role in the affairs of both Burma and Indonesia, and for different reasons in Thailand, the Philippines, Laos and Vietnam. In the case of Burma, its early attempts at parliamentary rule were destabilised by both the significant role of the army in political affairs and the separatist ambitions of its ethnic minorities. Conflict between ethnic minorities and the state in the late 1950s and again from the early 1960s onwards provided an opportunity for the army to be granted and soon after to assume power, which it retained into the twenty-first century.

Although increasingly wearing a more civilian face, from 1958 Indonesia was run with the backing of the army, its electoral process only superficially satisfying the form and certainly not the function of democracy. Indonesia initially adopted a parliamentary democratic system in which political, religious, geographic and ethnic distinctions were balanced. However, largely because of the pressing of claims by the central, Jakarta-based, government, this mixture proved to be unstable and was eventually abandoned for 'Guided Democracy', introduced in the period from 1957–59. Under this strongly presidential system, Indonesian politics polarised into a split between the Indonesian Communist Party and the armed forces, resulting in a showdown in late 1965 and, as anti-communist purges, into 1966 and beyond.

The New Order government that developed in Indonesia between 1966 and 1999 was underpinned by the armed forces and, until 1999, allowed extremely limited political activity. Reflecting the rise of wealthy and/or militarily powerful individuals within a context dominated by Suharto, a political system in which patron–client relations are fundamental has been allowed or encouraged to develop.

Both France and the Netherlands, while perhaps even more weakened by the two world wars than was Britain, were reluctant to let go of
their colonial possessions, in part for economic reasons and in part for
reasons of national prestige. As a consequence, with the exception of
Cambodia, the peoples of these colonies were obliged to fight for their
independence and consequently neither inherited, nor generally desired,
the political institutions of their former colonial masters.

In the case of Vietnam, Marxism–Leninism—generically referred to
as communism—was not just a guiding ideology but was also explicitly
anti-colonialist and in favour of economic redistribution. Initially allied
with other nationalist forces under the name of Viet Minh, the Leninist
element of the ideology was a particularly useful organisational tool for a
nationalist struggle (Salisbury 1971: xi; Steinberg 1971: 308). Indeed, the
early nationalist movement, from 1927 the Viet Nam Quoc Dan Dang
(VNQDD), which was closely modelled on the Chinese nationalist
Guomindang, adopted a version of Leninist organisational structure (as
did the non-communist, later anti-communist, Guomindang itself),
while the socialist principles of economic redistribution and collective
action were also popular with early Vietnamese nationalists (although the
VNQDD neglected the issue of land redistribution). In large part, the
VNQDD failed as a consequence of French repression in 1929 and an
abortive uprising in 1930, in which it was effectively broken as a viable
organisation. This left Vietnam's political stage to the communists,
although they too were repressed in 1931. Drawing on a small 'proletarian' base, in the late 1930s the Vietnamese communists expanded their
appeal by claiming that 'poor people are proletarians' (Steinberg 1971:
312), thereby adopting the tactics of China's communists in bringing
rural peasants to the revolutionary movement.

The Marxian element of the politically successful Vietnamese ideology also appealed to notions of revolutionary liberation. The war against
France up to 1954 brutalised and hence radicalised many Vietnamese and,
in the later 1950s and until 1975, the war against the French and later the
US-supported Republic of Vietnam in the south, further radicalised
much of the population. Issues which pushed much of the population
into supporting the communists included the corrupt and inefficient
government in Saigon, the brutality of the Army of the Republic of Vietnam and its military allies, indiscriminate bombing campaigns, forced
relocation and the widespread understanding that the war was not just, or
even primarily, pro or anti-communist but a continuation of the war of
liberation against foreign powers (after France, the United States). Marxism–Leninism might not have been universally endorsed, but various of

its elements were popular and it was in so dominant a political position that even from the early 1950s there was little doubt that Vietnam, once independent, would become a communist state.

Similarly in Cambodia, granted independence in 1953, the quietly pro-Chinese and pro-North Vietnamese 'neutralist' policies of Prince Norodom Sihanouk eventually brought American wrath in the form of intensive, socially dislocating bombing. These bombings were directed against North Vietnamese military bases inside Cambodian territory, and against the supply routes from north to south which entered Cambodian territory. Unwilling to tolerate his unsupportive position on the conflict in Vietnam, the USA endorsed the overthrow of Sihanouk in March 1970, seeing him replaced by the pro-US Lon Nol. Already on the offensive, the Cambodian communists, the peasant-based Khmer Rouge, toppled Lon Nol in 1975 (Sagar 1991: 93–6).

The Khmer Rouge adopted a version of the then Chinese (peasant-based) interpretation of communism, and, supported by a largely illiterate peasant army, it was unable to administer an urban-centred state. The Khmer Rouge policy of emptying the cities and establishing a rural society, complete with murderous prejudices against perceived urban elites, initiated a period of terror, famine and increasing paranoia. That paranoia spilled over into wrath against erstwhile military allies but historical enemies, the Vietnamese. In response to Khmer Rouge border attacks and a policy of violent discrimination against ethnic Vietnamese in Cambodia, in late 1978 Vietnam invaded Cambodia, installing a puppet government under the leadership of Heng Samrin (Sagar 1991: 132–41). This event, and the subsequent Chinese attack on Vietnam, indicated that historical animosities and competition for regional hegemony could be, and in this case were, more powerful political factors than strategic or ideological considerations.

The intrigues of US-influenced Laotian politics, in which a right, 'neutral' and left faction had juggled for power since 1954, was also tipped in favour of the peasant-based communist Pathet Lao in 1975, with the communist victories in Vietnam and Cambodia. The pro-Vietnamese Pathet Lao added another aspect to the regional political matrix, which had permutations for Laotian support of a pro-Chinese communist insurgency in north-east Thailand, although support was withdrawn and the insurgency collapsed.

In each case, the states of SEA have drawn on a colonial legacy, the examples provided by the colonial powers (such as industrialisation) or other Western conceptions (such as parliamentary or republican democracy, or Marxism) for their models of legitimacy. In some cases these legacies have been retained in form but not in content, such as Malaysia and

Singapore, and in some cases they have been entirely abandoned, such as in Burma and, until 1999, in Indonesia. But even Indonesia subscribes to the republican model, although modifying it in ways that suit Javanese conceptions. The Burmese state, though, only matches contemporary conceptions of legitimacy in that it retains some of the institutions of state that ordinarily imply a functioning government, such as a bureaucracy and a nominal legal system. The Burmese government itself could not be said to be legitimate in any meaningful sense of the term, nor does it generally correspond to ideas of government in a modern sense (although it would no doubt claim it does).

THE RULE OF LAW

Issues of legitimacy revolve mainly around maintaining codes of behaviour, usually understood as the application of the rule of law. In so far as a degree of certainty about rules and responses is a requirement for legitimacy, consistency in the application of the rule of law is a key criterion for legitimacy (Morris 1998: 24, 105–11; Rawls 1991: 7). In each case, the political systems and processes adopted by the states of SEA reflected not just a range of styles and types, but indicated that even within the respective categories there was considerable scope for interpretation and reformulation to suit the needs and interests of prevailing political groups or organisations. In this respect, the issue of the separation of powers between the executive and the judiciary did not just allow laws to be interpreted inconsistently, but allowed for the development of tyranny (see Morris 1998: 287). That is, the application of the rule of law was not applied consistently in practice and, in some cases, was not intended to be applied consistently even in principle. This has then begged the legitimacy of some governments or, indeed, some states.

In this sense, what is perhaps important is less the particular political model used by a contemporary state but rather whether or not it accurately reflects the needs and desires of its citizens. To that end, theoretically, pluralist liberal democracy might not be regarded as an appropriate political model while paternalist authoritarianism or Marxist– Leninist centralism might. Alternatively, paternalistic authoritarianism or Marxist–Leninist centralism might not be regarded as necessary or desirable by the citizens of a given state but, because these political systems do not allow open expressions of meaningful dissent, it is difficult to know. Further, with the shift towards market economies in all previously Marxist–Leninist states, such as Vietnam, Laos and Cambodia, and the central control exercised over the economies of many effectively single-party, supposedly free capitalist states, such as Singapore, Malaysia and, until 1999, Indonesia, such definitions are becoming increasingly redundant. Where major problems with legitimacy of the state have arisen, it has often reflected the state taking on a life of its own, as separate from or above those citizens it represents.

Yet the state as the state cannot claim to have a legitimate interest in the preservation of particular laws. Laws that do exist owe their legitimacy to popular support, so it would be analogous that those laws are not or should not be immune from popular rejection or change (Schauer 1982: 190).

The problem is that this only applies if the government derives its legitimacy from free support. Implicit in the notion that law is not beyond popular change is the idea that government legitimately represents the interests of its people and that among those interests is free expression in favour of such representation. Notions of justice, on the other hand, are not predicated on the legitimacy (or otherwise) of governments, but find their home in conceptions of natural rights.

To that end, the question of contemporary politics in Asia resides less with what label a political system has or is given and more with whether it is a representative and hence participatory state or whether it is an authoritarian and hence coercive state.

OPPOSITIONS

Political oppositions exist in SEA across the full spectrum of dissent from government. At one end, for example in the Philippines and Thailand, the opposition is formalised within the political process and is considered 'loyal'. In some countries, however, at some times, the opposition has been fundamentally opposed to the existence of the government and indeed sometimes even the principles by which the state is constructed. These fall into two categories: those that wish to overthrow the state and rebuild its structure, for example the New People's Army of the Philippines, the pre-1975 Lao People's Revolutionary Party, and Cambodia's Khmer Rouge. Then there are those that wish to secede from the state, for example some ethnic minority states of Burma and some provinces of Indonesia. In between, oppositions can and have existed within government factions, in extra-governmental state apparatus (such as the armed forces), through trade unions, non-government organisations, religious groups and others.

Western assessments of political development in SEA usually derive from the normative premise of liberal democracy. However, very few states in the region could be said to be moving towards a liberal democratic model. Indeed, the tendency has been to contest such a model. For example, Malaysia and Singapore have become less rather than more democratic, although Indonesia was, at the onset of 2000, establishing more democratic credentials. Thailand and the Philippines were largely democratic at the time of writing, although Brunei, Burma, Laos and Vietnam were not, while Cambodia was only marginally so. Also important is the fact that very few of the oppositions that existed in the region also embraced liberal democracy. Most were interested in re-ordering power structures or in creating political space within which they could exercise a greater degree of self-determination, but these aspirations were not synonymous with participatory representative government.

In this sense, the Western notion of democracy, perhaps only a fleeting historical moment in the West itself, has rarely been translated to SEA with much success. Indeed, there has been considerable debate not from the political elites but from ordinary people about what 'democracy' actually means within local contexts. Many ordinary people have been enthusiastic about the voting process, for example, and desired answerable politicians, in countries as diverse as Thailand, Burma, the Philippines and Indonesia. But in Malaysia and Singapore, for example, it has been much harder to find widespread enthusiasm for a genuine application of this idea.

CONSENSUS

One idea that did have some currency throughout SEA, especially among elites mostly for its ability to avoid open conflict, was that of consensus. Consensus politics is essentially about reducing the greatest objections to arrive at a workable formula. The source of the consensus model in SEA is generally held to be the village or small social grouping, in which face-to-face contact is a regular occurrence and in which the maintenance of harmonious social relations is important. To this end, when a matter affecting the broader community was to be decided, it was not so much done by a majority which had the potential to seriously disadvantage the minority, but by reducing the objections of the minority to make the outcome more broadly acceptable. This, then, helped ensure social cohesion and mutual cooperation.

As a political system, however, consensus is taken out of its original context and is often decided by elites, who might not be representative of larger groups of people. While consensus in this circumstance retains its quality of removing major objections and making outcomes more broadly acceptable, it also has the distinct problem of not being directly answerable to individual voters and rather relying on the good will or good judgement of elites. It also tends to be favoured by such elites for its ability to ensure continuing elite control of political processes. A consensus candidate for the presidency, for example, would ultimately not be beholden to any group, but rather amorphously to 'the nation'. This then opens the possibility of the abuse of power, and of corruption, both of which are common enough. Established in power, a consensus politician could then build a coterie of sycophants to ensure that consensus remained with them. This was most clearly seen during Suharto's tenure in office in Indonesia, but could also be applicable to Lee in Singapore and Mahatir in Malaysia.

RIGHTS AS CULTURALLY RELATIVE

Before proceeding with this discussion, the question of what constitutes a human right needs to be established. A human right, according to Pettman, 'is a general moral claim. It is the assertion of a just entitlement pertaining anywhere, any time, ... to the enjoyment of certain goods or the satisfaction of particular interests deemed fundamental in some way' (Pettman 1979: 76). As a general moral claim, the rights pertaining to being human are not contingent upon their cultural or political location. However, human rights constituting a moral claim does represent a value judgment and, as such, necessarily reflects culturally located values. The question is: at what point can morality claim to have stepped beyond the particular into the universal? Pettman argues that there is a universal foundation to human rights, not only based on common humanity but, in UNESCO, 'globally shared norms' agreed to by 'transcultural consensus', including social solidarity; the sense of self; the value of life, and the duty to protect the lost, sick or weak; the idea of the legitimacy of power and a duty to rebel when power's legitimacy is lost; the limitations to be placed upon the arbitrary exercise of power; the idea of juridical impartiality; the civil freedom to travel and to work elsewhere; the freedom to think and publicly criticise; tolerance of social rights (to strike, work and so on); securing freedom by securing material wellbeing; the right to knowledge and learning; the right of a people to their identity; and the universality of human enterprise or endeavour (Pettman 1979: 80).

It has been widely claimed throughout SEA, at various times and by various people, that the whole idea of 'human rights' is ethnocentric, being based on European values (and specific ones at that) and not reflecting South East Asia's own values and rich traditions. In one respect this generalised assertion is correct. Notions of human rights, particularly civil and political rights, do derive from European tradition generally and the Enlightenment in particular. However, as has been equally widely pointed out, although notions of human rights can be traced back to ancient Greek and early Christian tradition, there are parallels in other traditions. Basic human needs such as freedom and dignity are implicit in some of the earliest written and oral codes. Hindu and Buddhist texts focus on the human condition, while notions of human virtue and compassion characterise early Confucianism. Many local traditions throughout SEA include sanctions on the exercise of power, the reciprocal nature of political relations, and often high degrees of local autonomy.

To illustrate how these less universal traditions reflect similar sentiments towards issues of human rights, Burmese political leader Aung San Suu Kyi has drawn on the Theravada Buddhist tradition as a basis for a tolerant and lawful society, in opposition to the military government (which itself draws on an equally strong martial tradition). Vietnamese monks have drawn on a similar, Mahayana Buddhist, tradition, opposing both the authoritarianism of the former government of the Republic of (South) Vietnam as well as the later Socialist Republic of (united) Vietnam. Indonesian Islamic scholar Nurcholish Majid has argued for tolerance and mutual support based on Islamic principles, as did Indonesia's President Abdurrahman Wahid, as leader of the Nahdlatul Ulama before his rise to political power. Throughout the region, among ordinary people and many of their leaders, there is a recognition that some principles will always hold and that some common standards of behaviour are universally valid and applicable on the basis of common humanity and international law, not their ethnic specificity and local law. Further, governments which have argued against a universal conception of human rights, including those that have signed the relevant UN covenants, have invariably done so because it suits their immediate political interests.

Apart from culturally relativised reasons for rejecting the universality of notions of human rights, the Marxist–Leninist approach to the role of the individual in the state, based on that of Hegel, and its co-option by quasi-Marxist states such as Vietnam and Laos, is that notions of human rights are a liberal subterfuge. The general Marxist critique is that human rights are ineffective because a capitalist world order requires human rights abuses as a method of enforcing hegemony within a potentially dissenting framework. Such rights are held, in this type of argument, to be only genuinely possible within complete economic, political, social and cultural emancipation (Campbell 1983: 7). Perhaps there is some ground for this argument, but it did represent a utopian condition for the enjoyment of more prosaic human rights and, as such, tended to disqualify them from serious consideration.

A somewhat different critique of human rights derives from the 'organicist' or 'proto-fascist' model of the state, in which the citizen is regarded as an integral part of the state and without an independent political existence. This was the model first conceived of in the foundation of Indonesia, and in a practical sense informs states such as Burma and, to some extent, Vietnam. To illustrate this position, the chief framer of Indonesia's 1945 constitution, Supomo, argued against a formal acknowledgment of human rights, saying, 'There is no need to guarantee the fundamental rights and liberties of the individual against the state, because the individual is an organic part of the state, with his own position and an obligation to help realize the state's greatness ...' (Supomo, in Feith & Castles 1970: 191) In drafting the 1945 constitution, Supomo had himself 'envisaged a compromise between basic human rights and the right of the government to suppress them when necessary' (Vatikiotis 1993: 114).

This view on human rights was not, of course, monolithic. Nasution asserted that the relativisation of human rights via cultural difference 'confuses what is, or what happens, with what is right. This kind of argument ignores the fact that in the struggle for Indonesian independence (since the beginning of the twentieth century and during the national revolution from 1945–49) as well as in the post independence period to the present, democratic tendencies have always existed alongside authoritarian ways of thinking' (Nasution 1993).

It should be noted that within the assertion of 'Asian values' it has been said that there is a greater focus on the collective than the individual, that there is no tradition of explicit rights, and that there is a social requirement for group members not to express dissenting opinions. This issue of 'cultural authenticity' then raises concerns not so much about a broad notion of 'rights' but about what 'rights' retain validity and how they might work *vis-à-vis* social obligations. All societies impose some sort of requirement upon their members to conform to social codes and the question of 'rights', in all cases, exists within this context.

This raises a number of subsequent issues, the first of which begs the question of whether cultures and hence the values they express are static or dynamic. The various cultures of SEA have been remarkably dynamic over the nineteenth and twentieth centuries, no more so than in the last decades of the twentieth. There is, then, a political tension between change and tradition, or between varying interpretations of tradition. However, change is not always easily or comfortably accepted, especially when it upsets established norms of behaviour, or contravenes established political practices. In this there is legitimacy in asking whether or not particular rights retain applicability and, if so, in what ways they could be accommodated to local conditions. Alternatively, if such rights are claimed to be not applicable there needs to be a fairly closely scrutinised case for such rejection.

Related to this issue is the source of such values that may impose them as a consequence of an unequal power structure. They may or may not be accepted or internalised, but it cannot be claimed that they are 'natural' or immutable. A further issue, noted elsewhere, is that by taking the structure of the nation-state, the states of SEA have adopted a form of political organisation derived from the West in which there are certain organisational and structural arrangements. One of these is the identification of citizenship, which implies certain basic rights thereof.

The question of human rights, including social and political rights, economic rights (see UNHCHR 1999) and so on, is therefore a site of significant political contest. There may be no absolute answer to this debate—although its protagonists usually argue strongly that there is— but it is very much at the core of social content or, more often, discontent, and how that manifests itself in power relations within states.

AUTHORITY AND LEGITIMACY REVISITED

In some traditional political forms, to hold power, such as military power, was synonymous with holding political power, and to hold political power was synonymous with legitimacy. To draw on the traditional Javanese model (which found parallels elsewhere), power included conventional notions of political power, legitimacy and charisma; it either existed or it did not, and questions of legitimacy were not a part of the equation. At various times in the post-WWII period throughout SEA, political leaders have exercised a very similar style of political power, neither relying on public consent nor allowing their right to rule to be called into question. Political power has been concentrated largely, if not exclusively, in the hands of assertive individuals who have sometimes ruled almost as autocratically as their pre-colonial and colonial forebears.

This is not to suggest that the governments or political leaders of SEA are re-inventions of the past, even though in many instances they have clothed their rule in 'tradition', or 'tradition' modified to suit modern conditions. And it is further not to suggest that issues of legitimacy and the use of authority are not more open to question, in most cases, than they have ever been. In part, this has been a consequence of the globalisation of ideas, in particular normative ideas about political behaviour.

But in the symbols of state power, in the rationalisations for political styles and methods, in the patrimonial forms many political leaders employ, and in the often repressive apparatus they employ, authority is actively wielded. The question of legitimacy, on the other hand, often finds itself floating on a sea of hegemony and formal opposition to the articulation of alternative aspirations.

NOTES

1   That is, a separation of the two institutions so that the judiciary, which is supposed to be neutral in its adjudication on the law, is not influenced by political considerations.

2   It has been suggested by some that my views on the connection between culture and politics puts me in a similar position to Pye (1985). Our positions are, in fact, quite different. Pye tends to use culture as the explanation for political forms, while I see those aspects of culture reflecting authority and status as essentially political in the first place, and often reinvented for the purposes of the maintenance of power.

3   Lukes' analysis was challenged by Clegg, who argued that it was surpassed, particularly by approaches under the general rubric 'post-structuralism' (Clegg 1989: 147, 150). Lukes' broadening of the power framework to incorporate the subtleties as well as the bluntness of power indicates a tolerance for ambiguity (a central post-structural theme) in the diffusion of power.

4   Proto-Malays are those 'first' wave Malays, who may be distinguished from later, or 'second wave', Deutero-Malays by language, social organisation (including shifting rather than wet rice agriculture) and other aspects of culture. The former tend to live in highland regions or in the more remote parts of the east, the latter in low-land or valley areas and predominantly in the west (see Fisher 1968: ch. 8).

5   To illustrate this point, while I believe that Pye (1985) overstates specific cultural inputs into political processes, he does identify the respective cultures of the region and their impact on politics as quite distinct.

6   Niccolo Machiavelli (1998), a sixteenth century writer and political theorist, proposed that the attainment, exercise and maintenance of political power was universal in scope and application.

7   His actual name was Master K'ung, or K'ung-fu-tzu, being Latinised in a Jesuit translation.

8   In 1297 Edward I formally acknowledged the right of parliament to vote on questions of taxation.

3

Economic and Political Development

More than any other issue, that of 'development' has been the overriding rhetorical concern of the governments of SEA. Development has been the point by which governments have attempted to legitimise their rule and policies[1] and it has been the goal of development that has acted as a major rationalisation for the employment of authoritarian methods of political control.

Any discussion of development begs the question of what exactly has been meant by the term. For much of the two or three decades after WWII, the term 'development' was almost exclusively defined as meaning growth in per capita gross domestic product (GDP). It was this ratio of how much money a country earned in a year from local production divided by its population that was viewed as the primary indicator of development. This formula, as the sole or primary indicator, is still adhered to by some more conservative development economists and some governments. It is worth noting that once countries move away from low levels of per capita GDP, there is often a correlation between this formula and median standards of living. Indeed, some economists have noted that the higher the per capita GDP ratio, the smaller the relative discrepancies in income distribution, meaning that not only is there more wealth but also that it is more evenly shared (McGillivray 1991). However, the factors that come in to play in income-sharing of overall wealth themselves require closer attention, as they are sometimes the result of long processes of political struggle as well as economic development, such as in developed Western countries. Further, some other countries with growing per capita GDP reflect increasing disparities in income distribution.

COMPARATIVE DEVELOPMENT

In SEA, aspects of both situations have arisen. Singapore, for example, had at the beginning of the twenty-first century a high level of per capita GDP by world standards, at $US30 000 per annum, but a 'purchasing parity power' at a level slightly lower than that. This had also resulted in a relatively high median rate of income, although critics have noted that the purchasing parity power of lower paid workers only allowed them to attain the most meagre of existences. Purchasing parity power (PPP) is the purchasing power of a country's currency relative to a 'basket' of goods and services that can be bought in another, denominated currency, usually US dollars. The purpose of the PPP system is that it shows not just how much people might have in a given currency (usually US dollars) at a particular exchange rate but, more importantly, what can be purchased in each country with that particular income. For example, a kilo of rice might cost two dollars in the United States, but significantly less in exchange rate terms in the currency of another country. To this end, the PPP is intended to illustrate the capacity for material standard of living, rather than simple exchange rates presuming a commonality of prices of goods.

In contrast to Singapore, Indonesia, until the economic collapse starting in mid 1997, had relatively strong economic growth, a claimed per capita GDP of $US1100 per annum and a significantly better PPP for basic commodities, at a claimed $US3350, but an extremely poor rate of income distribution. That is, although the average purchasing power of an Indonesian person was more than three thousand dollars a year,[2] the vast majority of people earned much less than this. In part the rate of income distribution in both these countries reflected not so much the absolute level of income but, to a considerable extent, the income distribution policies of their respective governments. While Singapore could be fairly accused of having an authoritarian government, at least initially it was one which saw benefit in raising the standard of living of most of its citizens by helping to ensure some degree of income distribution. Indonesia, on the other hand, throughout the period of the New Order government, retained a policy which kept ordinary incomes at artificially low levels, to help ensure Indonesia's 'competitive advantage' (low wage rates) and hence its attraction to foreign investment compared to other developing economies, such as that of the Philippines.

Perhaps more important, though, is the fact that the per capita GDP definition of development is inadequate in a broader sense. If development is intended to refer only to material issues, then nutrition, literacy, health care, sanitation, education, housing, environmental degradation, fertility, infant mortality rates, average life expectancy, and causes of death also need to be taken into consideration. This is generally referred to as the Human Development Index (HDI), although the formal HDI as used by the United Nations Development Programme (UNDP) is significantly more limited in its scope than this model.[3] More than this, though, ideas of development have increasingly begun to take into consideration non-material qualities, such as notions of human dignity, personal fulfilment, self-determination, and access to political participation and representation. These somewhat more nebulous areas are not yet fully accepted in debate about development, but increasingly there is disquiet about a purely material focus on what constitutes 'development'.

POLITICAL DEVELOPMENT

In development circles, which are dominated by economists and to a lesser extent geographers of one type or another, the notion of political development is rarely discussed. However, at one level it is the most fundamental aspect of 'development', if that term is understood in its wider sense. Hutchcroft notes that, in the Philippines, political under-development is the prime cause of continuing economic under-development (Hutchcroft 1998). Political development can be thought of as reflecting a process of change from archaic political forms, such as single-source (prebendal) patrimonialism or feudalism, through to authoritarian or oppressive political systems, at the most extreme end of the scale a parasitic or predatory type of government. A more developed or mature political system could be typified by being benign, inclusive and participatory, accurately reflecting the aspirations of most citizens. There is debate about such definitions and many more authoritarian governments try to argue that they represent a maturation of local politics more suited to local conditions. This does, of course, imply an approximately normative model of government.

Often discussion about normative models of government defaults to notions of 'democracy'. The problem with this default is, however, that it very rarely spells out what is intended by the term 'democracy' and whether other types of political systems cannot also fulfil the needs of political citizens. It also assumes that a model of democracy as practised in the West is an ideal aspiration, not taking into account that there is no single Western democratic standard. Nor is such an approximate Western standard necessarily applicable to countries in which illiteracy is high, communication is poor, patronage is dominant and consensus is preferred. However, it must be conceded that some governments' attempts to appropriate the word 'democracy' for what are clearly non-democratic systems of government tends to imply the need for some particular definitions for a meaningful use of the term.

For the purpose of this exercise, the term democracy is taken to mean a form of rule in which citizens either act as the policy-making authority (direct democracy) or are represented by others to make policy on their behalf (representative democracy). The former tends only to exist in small or closed societies, while the latter is the more applicable model. The issue of participation might also be included in such a definition, allowing citizens opportunities to both stand for election as representatives and express their views outside the formal policy-making or representative-election process.

Finally, a strong argument has been put claiming that economic development precedes political development and that a 'strong' government is a necessary precondition for the economic development of the state. There is some (though far from overwhelming) evidence to suggest that this proposition could be at least partially correct. Political 'stability' is a preferential environment for investors to instability, and policy consistency is preferred to a political environment in which policy can change from year to year, depending on the whims of the electorate or the influence of pressure groups.

Somewhat ironically, this argument is usually put forward by political conservatives, yet the idea of economic development providing the foundation of political development comes directly from the revolutionary Karl Marx. There have, however, been exceptions both for and against democratisation reflecting economic development. For example, Singapore has become less democratic even though it has become more economically successful. On the other hand, the Philippines and Indonesia have both embraced democracy despite both being very poor and having continuing economic troubles. So, while the argument of political development being built on economic development might have some validity as a general tendency, it is far from a rule of politics and other factors can also influence political outcomes.

'FULL BELLIES'

This idea of economic development first before political development has been referred to as the 'Full Bellies Thesis': the idea that people need and want to have full bellies before considering other, more esoteric, issues such as political participation (Howard 1983). This was nowhere more clearly stated than at a major regional statement on human rights, the Bangkok Declaration of the World Conference on Human Rights (1993), which said that civil and political rights, which are the preconditions for political development, were conditional on economic development. The declaration agreed to 'Underline the essential need to create *favourable conditions* for effective enjoyment of human rights at both the national and international levels' [my emphasis] (*World Conference on Human Rights* 1993: 3.2). Such 'favourable conditions' usually include limitations on political activity and censorship of the media. Such an approach has been suggested to be in keeping with the 'Asian' experience. Yet not all 'Asians' accepted such conditions:

> Two justifications for authoritarianism in Asian developing countries are … that Asian societies are authoritarian and paternalistic and so need governments that are also authoritarian and paternalistic; that Asia's hungry masses are too concerned with providing their families with food, clothing and shelter, to concern themselves with civil liberties and political freedom; that the Asian conception of freedom differs from that of the West; that, in short, Asians are not fit for democracy. Another is that developing countries must sacrifice freedom temporarily to achieve rapid economic development that their exploding populations and rising expectations demand; that, in short, government must be authoritarian to promote development. The first justification is racist nonsense. The second is a lie; authoritarianism is not needed for developing; it is needed to perpetuate the status quo. Development is not just providing people with adequate food, clothing and shelter; many prisons do as much. (Diokno 1981)

The president of Third World Lawyers, Clarence Diaz, concurred, when he said at the Bangkok meeting: 'The notion that in order to get bread you have to sacrifice freedom doesn't hold true in the region. We've had a number of governments giving that as a rationale and in fact they've ended up providing their people—significant sections of their people—with neither bread nor freedom' (Diaz 1993).

Also against the argument in favour of authoritarian government is the fact that a representative government is less prone to corruption and is less likely to spend vast sums on an unproductive 'security' force. Such a government is also more likely to offer 'soft' political changes rather than the more abrupt, often violent changes that occur when an authoritarian leader is finally dumped and their usually tainted bureaucracy requires a fundamental overhaul. Further, the free flow of ideas in such a system is more likely to invigorate market development as opposed to a culture of silence in which original ideas are not encouraged, indeed sometimes regarded as dangerous (see Howard 1983: 478; Donnelly 1984: 258; Goodin 1979).

But in SEA, as elsewhere, the biggest political issue has been and remains the material wellbeing of citizens of the state. This then returns to 'development' in the more constrained, economic sense of the term, and the approaches that have been taken to development in the post-war period.

THE ORIGINS OF 'DEVELOPMENT'

Notions of development have been far from static since they first began to be discussed by governments, world bodies, and academics in the post-WWII period. In part these ideas corresponded to conceptions of what development meant in a more broad sense. But in part they also reflected, and continue to reflect, the ideological paradigms of their respective periods. In this the debates and discussions have been led by academics and social critics, referred to and sometimes acted upon by world bodies, and, via policy, enacted (or ignored) by governments.

The growth of development as a major issue in world affairs began after 1945 in direct response to the process of decolonisation. That is, the creation of new states, and the attendant rhetoric of liberation, implied an improvement in standards of living. This was supposed to arrive as a consequence of the end of exploitative colonial relations. However, neither the process of decolonisation nor the improvements in standards of living was as easy to achieve as the rhetoric had implied.

While some colonising states agreed to the process of decolonisation relatively peacefully, others were quite reluctant to give up their lucrative possessions. In SEA, the Dutch fought a bitter campaign in what was to become Indonesia while the French became involved in an even bloodier conflict in Indochina. The United States had already agreed to independence for the Philippines prior to the Japanese invasion and occupation, so the process was interrupted but not unnecessarily delayed by the colonial power. Burma, meanwhile, had in effect secured its own independence in cooperation with the Japanese, although it too had been moving in this direction prior to WWII. The actual agreement to grant independence was based more on resolving issues of internal representation, which ultimately failed in practice, than on whether or not such independence should be granted. In Malaysia, Singapore and

Brunei, independence was more a matter of ensuring adequacy of domestic systems of representation and administration, and defeating an indigenous communist insurgency, than any quibble over the ultimate desirability of independence. After choosing not to join Malaysia, Brunei was somewhat slower in achieving independence, although not because of Britain's reluctance to break its colonial bonds. Indeed, as a state that relied on Britain for military support, Brunei was reluctant to be granted independence at even its own late stage, in 1984.

The process of decolonisation was a two-sided affair, however, and it was not simply a case of emergent or proto-states claiming the right to self-determination. The reality of Japanese occupation had shown that the European powers were not invincible in SEA (and elsewhere), and that there was nothing inherently superior about European rule. Further, the European powers were deeply damaged by the conflict at home, and their economic resources, such as they remained, were more in demand for postwar reconstruction than they were for maintaining increasingly troublesome colonies. The United States, on the other hand, was determinedly in favour of decolonisation and, outside its own concerns with the Philippines, used its economic power (under the Marshall Plan for reconstruction) to pressure the European states. The break, in political relations at least, was inevitable. The two questions that were only partly answered were what would be the shape and style of the new, post-colonial states, and to what extent would those states be economically viable.

MODELS OF DEVELOPMENT

The first, most clearly identifiable model of development, which arose in the immediate postwar period and lasted more or less unchallenged in the non-communist world until the mid 1960s, was that of 'modernisation'.[4] 'Modernisation', in this context, was intended to be the glue that held together the fragile new states that were emerging in the post-war period. With development such states would be strong and cohesive and better able to build a 'national' self-image around mutual prosperity. More importantly for new and often insecure governments, development through modernisation also acted as a method of legitimation (see Hettne 1990: 29–31). Such 'modernisation' was based on a particular view of the world, including the ideas that development and economic growth were identical, that economic growth was separate to other political considerations (Hettne 1990: 28), and that growth could be achieved by applying technological answers to development problems

(McKay 1990: 55). Further, according to this model, all societies should pass through a series of stages of technological advance, usually prompted by investment. At a certain point, this technologisation would become self-fulfilling, leading to 'take-off'. The consequent economic growth then led to the 'modernisation' of social, institutional and political forms, including the establishment of the primacy of the individual over the collective and the establishment of democratisation (Rostow 1991). This 'modernisation' process would have the benefit not only of assisting the societies concerned but, according to this theory, lessening ideological tension between states (the logic being that capitalism and democracy would become the dominant forms).

Needless to say, at the time this theory was being promoted there did exist sharp ideological divisions in the world order. The Cold War, between capitalist countries spearheaded by the United States and communist or centrally planned economy countries led by the Soviet Union, offered starkly contrasting models of modernisation and development (Cohen 1995; Leffler & Foner 1994). According to the Soviet model, largely adopted by China and later other allied countries, the economy could be planned and run from the centre, and modernised and supplied according to central command. This view was a part of a wider understanding of the value of communism to newly emerging states, a significant part of which was also based on political liberation (Brewer 1980; Rhodes 1970). While some elements of a Marxist critique were useful for explaining the iniquities of feudalism, capitalism and colonial capitalism (Brown 1974), the organising principles of the Leninist interpretation of revolutionary Marxism were equally as useful as tools for organising nationalist, anti-colonial movements (see, for example, Lacouture 1969).

To this end, every state of SEA has had at some stage a revolutionary communist organisation that has had the explicit goal of overthrowing the prevailing political order.[5] In those states that had the most oppressive colonial governments and which were least willing to depart quietly, Marxism–Leninism took strongest root. This was especially the case in Indochina, led by Vietnam, where the less left-leaning anti-colonial forces were routed before they could adequately organise themselves, and where the communist forces had battled the occupying Japanese during their own interregnum. Conversely, communist and leftist forces in Indonesia were targeted for special attention by the colonial Dutch forces, which left them in a state of relative disorganisation when Japan encouraged Indonesia's declaration of independence in 1945 (Hindley 1964: 18). Communist and leftist forces in the Philippines were poised to assert some degree of authority in the postwar period. However, US assistance in excluding them from the legitimate political process and then in crushing their consequent rebellion reduced that challenge to the level of regional threat rather than a direct threat to the state (Wurfel 1964: 698–701).

MODERNISATION STUMBLES

By the mid 1960s, it was clear that for many countries the 'modernisation' project of post-colonial growth was failing to deliver its promised development. Further, when and where development did occur there was sometimes disquiet about what were perceived to be assumptions about cultural identity implicit and often explicit in the idea of 'modernisation', in particular the appeal of individualism and consumerism (Frank 1981). If the aspiration and achievement of the capitalist version of modernisation was proving to be problematic, the centrally planned economy version fared no better. In particular 'The market incentives that imposed discipline on firm managers and encouraged producers to increase output were not always provided by the state' (Rapley 1997: 47). Similarly, the values that derived from centrally planned systems did not always fit easily with existing methods of production, while the application of the Leninist model of top-down political organisation and control, while suiting many political leaders, was often not favourably received by ordinary people.

Many countries, especially in Asia, Africa and Latin America, were also not willing or able to embark on a radical course of economic and political revolution. Simply, the task being proposed was in many cases too radical a leap from prevailing circumstances and, even where it was seen as desirable, it was not always practical. Moving directly from a peasant-based agricultural society directly to industrialisation is a rare achievement and, in two cases where it has been at least partially achieved (the former Soviet Union and China) it came with an enormously high cost in human life. In other cases, even where the goals were more modest, many newly emerging countries found that while they had achieved political independence, their economies continued to be subject to the often one-sided demands of former colonial trading partners, or new countries which took the place of former colonial masters. All colonial powers in SEA continued to maintain significant investments in their former colonies long after independence had been achieved.[6] In this they were often later assisted or buttressed with investment by other industrialised (or post-colonial) states.

If the modernisation project, as a general program, was not as successful as had been hoped for, at least the elites of each country tended to benefit, or were able to preserve their privilege. This alone ensured a resistance to change. In particular in SEA, by the early 1960s Burma had opted out of the international process and Indochina was moving towards the Second Indochina War. Malaysia and Brunei were attempting to ward off threats from Indonesia, and Indonesia itself continued a downward economic spiral, in part abetted by and in part producing polarised political positions. This resulted in the political and civil convulsion of 1965–66, which left the state firmly in the US-led camp. Thailand and the Philippines were economic beneficiaries of American strategic policy in the region. However, while Thailand developed economically (though with political convulsions of its own), the Philippines slid into a Latin American-style leadership of corrupt power, characterised by a weak state and a strong, predatory oligarchy.

Absorbed by its own, critical events, during the 1960s the attention of the SEA states was inwardly focused. As a battleground by proxy for a larger ideological conflict, pro-capitalist governments were too directly supported by the US to be critical of the capitalist model of modernisation. Indeed, for many of the region's elites the idea of emulating the US, at least superficially, was extremely attractive. With the deepening of ideological division, the anti-capitalist or revolutionary leftist groups were in no mood, or position, to offer a more moderate critique of capitalism. However, outside the region a number of developing countries which were not caught up in the throes of revolutionary processes or outright warfare were more ambiguous about fully accepting the supposed benefits of the international capitalist system. The experience in many developing states had been one of greater acceptance of international capitalism leading to the greater impoverishment of their people. The economies of many developing states were still linked to those of their former colonial masters, or new 'neocolonial' economic masters. Rather than wealth coming into these countries the experience was more that it flowed out.

DEPENDENCY

This situation led to a new critique of development that came to be termed the 'dependency' theory. While the dependency critique came primarily from academics and intellectuals, it was also accepted in varying degrees by some governments. Dependency theory relied for its analytical foundation on a Marxian critique of relations between rich and poor countries, in which the latter were exploited by the former (Hettne 1990: 82–7).

Broadly, aspects of this 'dependency' theory of development focused on the idea that development could not take place while developing countries were in the process of having their economies systematically exploited by developed countries. Indeed, based on this analysis, the 'third world' state of these countries was a direct result of earlier economic exploitation. However, 'dependency theorists' were not classical Marxists and their critique of relations between developed and developing countries took on a number of guises. These included universal as opposed to particular analyses, external versus internal causal factors, socio-political versus economic causes, sectoral and regional analysis versus class analysis, absolute under-development versus cyclical under-development, and voluntarist (actor-driven) versus determinist (material-driven) analyses (Hettne 1990: 89–90).

In practical (if simple) terms, especially from the mid 1970s many countries, mostly those without a manufacturing base, were encouraged to export, usually primary commodities such as crops and minerals. However, the international economy was shifting orientation and these countries found the value of their exports falling on the world market. To counter this loss of revenue they produced and exported more, flooding the market and further lowering prices. This overall situation led to the identification of an international economic centre, linked to but not reliant on an economic periphery. The centre was dominant, while the periphery was subservient. Further, some groups and individuals within these countries, including government officials, assumed the often lucrative role of 'middle-men' in exploiting their own countries' wealth. These were known as the 'comprador elites'. Accordingly, the only hope for these countries to develop was to cut their links with developed countries.

These ideas manifested themselves in a number of forms, from total isolation, as practised by Burma throughout the 1960s and 1970s, to revolutionary activity[7] to the more common focus on creating industries that met local needs rather than importing (expensive) foreign goods. The Philippines was a strong example of this policy during the 1950s to the 1970s, although there was in this case also the significant influence of President Marcos offering lucrative and protected industries to his associates. In the later 1990s, Malaysia and to a lesser extent Indonesia re-adopted variations on the Dependency critique in their relations with international finance. In particular, after the economic down-turn from mid 1997, Indonesia and Malaysia only partially accepted the economic remedies proposed by the IMF. Malaysia in particular tightened financial regulations to slow the outflow of capital and to rebalance the exchange rate in mid 1998, while Indonesia moved to limit some of the conditions which impacted directly on ordinary people, including the provision of subsidies on essential commodities.

As a critique of the failure of the modernisation project, dependency theory itself had two main failings. The first was that, given the right circumstances and incentives, developing countries could constructively engage in the process of modernisation through industrialisation and export-driven policies. Both McKay and Missen noted that economic (though not necessarily political) development could come from a close alliance between large-scale capital and a participatory state (McKay 1991; Missen 1991). The second was that, where there continued to be failings of the modernising capitalist state, dependency theory's 'conception of the domestic bourgeoisie as parasitic and dependent on foreign capital was simplistic ... time would show that many Third World capitalists were anything but parasitic, sluggish, or dependent' (Rapley 1997: 48).

'NEO-CLASSICAL' ECONOMICS AND EXPORT ORIENTATION

The dominant model for economic development throughout SEA at the beginning of the twenty-first century was the 'export orientation' model. In short, this model was based on a number of related premises, all of which linked into the international market and to the dominant economic paradigm of 'neo-classical' economic theory and practice developed in the early 1980s. The first premise was that growth in exports based on 'competitive advantage' would produce an inflow of foreign currency and would enhance economic growth more than could be achieved by domestic consumption. This so-called competitive advantage could, in theory, be anything from exploitation of particular natural resources to an uncanny ability in one particular economic area. In most cases, however, such competitive advantage has started and sometimes remained with low cost production via low wages.

The second premise was founded on general neo-classical economic theory, that government was an only marginally necessary evil that should be limited in its functions and that markets would find their own 'natural' equilibrium in a 'free' or unregulated environment. Following on, if individuals or individual enterprises prospered then the whole of society would prosper through a flow-on effect. Under this system enterprises prospered or failed in their ability to meet market demand

and that, as such, the market was the greatest incentive for and determinant of efficient production. Under such a system, that which was not 'efficient' lost its right to exist.

Further advantages of this were that industries that replied on state support to exist, often engendering cronyism or corruption, were required to survive or otherwise on their own merits. De-linking business and government had the effect of limiting cronyism and corruption, although it would be a gross overstatement to suggest that such practices were ended by introducing free market principles.

DISADVANTAGES OF THE FREE MARKET

The disadvantages of this system included the fact that many industries that were only marginally competitive but which offered other benefits, such as high levels of employment and related social welfare, were challenged and often closed. While this begged the question of the purpose of industrial development, the logic of 'neo-classical' economics was such that those who pondered too long the value of the system were left behind in the mad rush for competitiveness and profitability.

A related disadvantage of the 'neo-classical' economic model was that it tended to reduce the whole of society to its ability to fit into or become a part of a globally efficient production machine. In particular, there was (and at the beginning of 2000 remains) a focus on short-term profits often at the expense of long-term investment—in education, social welfare and the environment. In a related sense, so-called 'free markets' do not usually fully account for their production costs, especially in terms of disposal of waste, which was frequently inadequate, or use of infrastructure. Finally, even where this model worked, it tended to enlarge gaps between the rich, through capital accumulation, and the poor, through having to compete for a position in the workforce, in which their only bargaining position relied on the cost of their labour. In those societies that did create more wealth, as McGillivray noted, the disparities between the rich and the poor tended to shrink rather than increase and overall standards of living rose (McGillivray 1991).

However, some sectors of society and indeed some whole societies were left out of this process, creating political tensions over the distribution of income and, in more humanitarian terms, simply causing high levels of seemingly unnecessary misery. One need only consider the specific examples of each SEA country to see where such 'neo-classical' policies have been introduced and where some sections of society have been left behind. Illustrations of this included the rural populations of Thailand, the Philippines, Indonesia, Laos, Cambodia and Vietnam (see Cowen and Shenton 1996: 433–7). Industrial workers (especially women) were also left behind in Indonesia (see Berman 1998: 160–213) and the Philippines. The 'labour pool'[8] of unemployed and underemployed in all of these countries, but especially in those which have developed urban industrial-isation, such as Indonesia and the Philippines, was to become their 'competitive advantage' *vis-à-vis* higher cost economies. Further, where the 'free market' could potentially work in favour of employees, especially through unionisation and collective bargaining, governments have tended to limit the rights of union organisation and collective bargaining. This is one of the clearer illustrations of how 'neo-classical' economic theory was less a commitment to an absolute principle than it was an ideological position that could vary in practice according to the ability of prevailing circumstances to meet business needs.

A COMPETITIVE ADVANTAGE?

The premise that each country had a 'competitive advantage' that it could exploit to secure a niche in the world market could be in the production of a particular good, or type of goods, or service. Such a competitive advantage would be achieved by using the available resources to produce those goods or services at a lower cost than their competitors, hence securing a position in the world market. Available resources to assist such competitive advantage could be the educational level of the constituent population, prior experience with particular types of production, access to cheap raw materials or, quite commonly, access to cheap labour.

In this last case, a country which did not have access to an educated work force, prior experience or raw materials was obliged to reduce the cost of its labour to make its products more competitive on the world market. The problem with this was that, with so many countries only having potentially cheap labour as a competitive advantage, they tended to undercut each other to strengthen that advantage. This in turn meant that the real incomes relative to hours worked for many people did not rise but rather shrank. The sweatshop culture which pervaded Indonesia's textile and footwear manufacturing industry, for example, got worse rather than better as a consequence of the dramatic fall in the interna-tional value of the rupiah. Working hours went up and, already disin-clined to pay the minimum wage, textile manufacturers trimmed wages further and increased hours.[9]

While low wages and other forms of 'competitive advantage' assisted some countries in exporting into the world market, other countries frequently undercut them through cross-subsidisation programs. This was especially prevalent during the 1980s, when the EU and the US subsidised agricultural exports which were then dumped on the world market, often below cost price. Without similar subsidies, even otherwise efficient agricultural producers could not compete without similarly slashing prices, which in turn cut income to farmers. The process of subsidisation has decreased since the late 1980s, in particular since the finalisation of the 'Uruguay Round' of the GATT which cut subsidies to agricultural products. But the world has still not managed to get to the stage of presenting a 'level playing field' on which all competitors start without any advantage other than that based on their ability to produce efficiently.

More positively, however, a number of SEA states have managed to lift their export income quite significantly through the adoption of export-oriented economic planning. Singapore, Thailand and Malaysia are the strongest examples, while Indonesia has also moved ahead, with Vietnam coming more slowly behind. Laos has too little infrastructure to actively participate in export-oriented industry except at the level of selling unprocessed logs, while Cambodia has been in a similar position (although with the added export of gems). Similarly, Burma has relied on logging, oil and gem exports for its legal income, while all three latter countries derive considerable income from the export of illicit drugs. As an oil producer and exporter, Brunei is in the fortunate position of having virtually a single product but one for which there is great and seemingly inexhaustible demand and hence a generally high price.

FOREIGN INVESTMENT

It is taken as given by virtually all states throughout the world, with the exception of those very few that run a consistent budget surplus, that foreign investment is a necessary ingredient for economic growth. This is not to suggest that foreign investment alone can produce economic growth (it can, but that growth is shallow and vulnerable to collapse), but that the inflow of capital from external sources is a primary means of replacing domestic capital formation for investment in economic development.

In SEA, foreign investment has been eagerly sought by all governments (with perhaps the exception of Brunei), though by some more keenly than by others. Such foreign investment has taken two broad forms, the first of which has been what is termed Foreign Direct Investment (FDI).

This refers to foreign investment by private companies in wholly owned or joint ventures. This is the primary means of foreign investment by business and is that which is most eagerly sought by regional governments. Foreign investment can also come from private loans to in-country financial institutions, which in turn disburse those funds on a commercial basis to private companies. A third major source of foreign income for the countries of SEA is by way of loans from development banks, such as the Asian Development Bank (see ADB 1999: Policies).

The major development banks are the World Bank, or its local arm the Asian Development Bank (ADB), and the IMF. The primary difference between the two is that the World Bank or ADB are intended to provide long-term loans for infrastructure projects, with the aim of assisting local governments in building the foundations of their economies. The IMF, on the other hand, operates more as a direct source of funds for government consolidated revenue, or to assist in financing economic restructuring programs (IMF 1999: ch. 1).

In order to meet eligibility for such loans, recipient countries usually have to agree to conditions of repayment (see IMF 2000). Such conditions do not only include a timetable for repayment, but often also the adoption of economic policy prescriptions intended to ensure such repayment. From the early 1980s, such policy prescriptions imposed a small government-free market ideology, the assumption being that this would not only better guarantee the repayment of loans but would also ensure the financial viability of the recipient government into the future. There has been considerable debate about the appropriateness of such policy prescriptions, particularly in regard to their impact on the poorest people of recipient countries (IMF 2000: 27), often in Latin America and, more obviously, in Africa. However, broadly speaking, these policies (IMF sponsored or otherwise) have appeared to work in SEA.[10]

INDOCHINA

The process of attracting foreign investment has not been easy, however. The communist or former communist states of Vietnam, Laos and Cambodia have all sought foreign investment, but have either intentionally or unintentionally erected hurdles to that investment, not least through inefficient bureaucratic administration, and, like some other places, through high levels of corruption. A further issue for foreign investment has been governments' willingness to offer a floating currency, the rationale being that a floating currency will rest at a level designed to balance the flow of capital into and out of the country. A high-value currency will increase imports and send money out, a low-value currency will decrease imports, which become proportionately more expensive, and proportionately increase cheaper exports. In most cases, the desire is to increase exports in order to strengthen the local economy. A fixed exchange rate, conversely, may make exports more expensive, as fixed exchange rates generally (though not universally) tend to overvalue the currency they are designed to protect.

Vietnam has generally been the most successful of these states in attracting foreign investment as a result of its stable government, relatively large and seemingly industrious population, natural resources (such as oil), and relatively low labour costs. However, Vietnam's slowness in adopting reform, especially of its exchange rate, saw a downturn in its FDI towards the end of the 1990s. Cambodia has also had success in attracting foreign investment (it has a floating exchange rate), although much of that investment introduced to the country has, in fact, been a blind for importing goods made elsewhere (such as China) and exporting them under Cambodia's preferential (low tax) trading arrangements. Laos, on the other hand, has had Vietnam's stability and a floating exchange rate, but a serious lack of skills and infrastructure. Added to a small and economically not very dynamic population base and the fact that it is far removed from most trans-shipment points, Laos has not been sought out by the international investment community as a desirable destination for funds.

INDONESIA

Indonesia has had one of the more interesting foreign investment policies of any SEA state, if only because it has varied from period to period depending on the economic circumstances of the domestic economy, divided by the level of official corruption operating at that particular time. The underlying tendency within Indonesia has been for its governments to accept foreign investment only grudgingly, this position being predicated on a perceived sense or desirability of economic 'nationalism'. That is, the preference of most Indonesian economic decision makers has been to assert the country's economic independence where and when possible, which has positioned it against the free flow of foreign investment. In particular, although the New Order government under Suharto openly encouraged foreign investment in the late 1960s, government policy and practice became increasingly restrictive as the price of oil rapidly increased during the 1970s, encouraging what many Indonesians then believed to be the establishment of the country's effective economic independence (Winters 1996: ch. 3).

However, with the collapse of oil prices in the early to mid 1980s, government policy returned to a more open encouragement of foreign investment, especially in regard to dropping requirements for foreign investors to enter into 'joint investment' arrangements. Such arrangements usually meant that the foreign investor was required to put up the funds, which would then be administered by domestic management. Needless to say, a number of foreign investors had their financial fingers burnt through such exercises. From the late 1980s onwards, though, foreign investment was allowed without joint partnership, which raised the problem of foreign companies reaping considerable profits at the expense of Indonesia's low-paid workers.

In this varying and, at times, unpredictable scenario has been Indonesia's now internationally appreciated penchant for official and unofficial corruption. It is now common knowledge that the Suharto period of government saw official corruption scale previously undreamed of heights, both through simple skimming from other ventures to the allocation of lucrative contracts (with payments or shared ownership) in often monopoly situations (Kingsbury 1998b: ch. 11). For example, almost any investment in Indonesia required the services of a 'consultant', often a Suharto family member or someone who had close links to Suharto. This 'consultant' would, for a percentage of the total proposed investment, ensure that the investment was approved and went ahead unhindered. In reality, what this amounted to was a type of protection racket, whereby the potential investor could not be guaranteed an investment licence or other permits without first paying a bribe to a Suharto crony. Indeed, there often was a guarantee: that the proposed investment would meet insurmountable hurdles if such payments were not made! Beyond this debilitating official corruption, large numbers of senior and middle management employed to oversee foreign (and often domestic) owned operations in Indonesia lined their own pockets through various means. These included claiming wage bills for staff not actually employed (making up the difference with enforced, unpaid overtime) and through entering into preferential purchasing and selling deals which ensured a financial kickback.

Needless to say, foreign investors only looked closely at Indonesia because, up until mid 1997, it offered what appeared to be a stable political and economic environment with low wage rates and low levels of labour unrest (due to tight government restrictions on labour organisation). However, once it became apparent that Suharto's tenure was coming to a close, domestic investors rapidly took their money off-shore, precipitating a meltdown of the economy and ensuring Suharto's political demise. This then turned Indonesia from a relatively secure if corruption-ridden investment climate into one that was dominated by economic collapse and political unrest. Most foreign investors simply wrote off their losses in Indonesia, refusing to tip more funds into the political and economic quagmire, while potential investors stayed well away from the wreckage of the Indonesian state.

MALAYSIA

Malaysia had a more consistent foreign investment policy and, indeed, much of its economic growth from the mid 1980s was predicated on high levels of off-shore investment, often in platform assembly of knocked-down products manufactured in Japan, South Korea or Taiwan. While Malaysia had a significantly cleaner government than that of Indonesia, it was still prone to the letting of contracts to sources close to the ruling clique within the government. It also enforced the paying of lip service to the requirement that companies have a positive discrimination policy up to the highest levels of corporate administration. That is, ethnic Malays (*bumiputeras*) were often employed to satisfy government requirements rather than to actually do a job (Crouch 1996: 181–9, 200–3; Milne & Mauzy 1999: 23). This meant that when the so-called 'Asian economic meltdown' began in mid 1997, Malaysia was also vulnerable, although not so much so as Indonesia.

When Malaysia's notoriously irascible prime minister, Dr Mahatir Mohamad, castigated foreign investors generally, the West most of all and Jews in particular, he further alienated already wary foreign investment opinion (Skehan 1998b; Singh & Oorjitham 1998). Mahatir's emotional outbursts were taken as a sign of political unpredictability and a very clear unwillingness to play the foreign investment game according to internationally established rules.

In the end, in August 1998, Mahatir broke with the international investment community by limiting the convertibility of the Malaysian ringgit and the repatriation of investments or profits from Malaysia. In this, Mahatir was opposed by his deputy prime minister, finance minister and heir-apparent, Anwar Ibrahim, who was promptly sacked and made the object of unrelated and seemingly unsubstantiated charges. Needless to say, the international financial community looked askance at Mahatir's manoeuvring and promptly ceased further investment. However, Mahatir's bid to run contrary to global finance was successful. Malaysia's economy did not slide further and, after stabilising, began to improve into late 1999. If nothing else, this showed that there was more than one policy prescription for economic management.

SINGAPORE

Singapore was hit by the economic crisis of the late 1990s primarily as a consequence of its exposure through investment in Indonesia. However, while this affected sections of the Singaporean economy it did not go to its heart.

Singapore had built a robust economy from the mid 1960s by linking government and business within a free-investment framework. At a time when, in economic terms, 'government' is almost synonymous with 'undesirable', Singapore has continued to retain a high level of government involvement in its economy, in particular in industries linked to the government through official or quasi-official investment. Like most countries that have one political party or leader in power for too long, Singapore had begun to exhibit some of the characteristics of a corrupt state, if nepotism and favouritism can be taken to imply corrupt practices (see, for example, (Singapore) *Business Times* 1996). However, such 'corruption' tended to occur primarily at the upper reaches of government, being quarantined from the larger sectors of the bureaucracy and work-force below, and was small in scale relative to the size of the Singaporean economy as compared with, for example, Vietnam or Indonesia. In very large part, Singaporeans either did not know or did not want to know about such official abuse when, on the whole, the economic system worked well for them compared not only to their neighbours but also to most other countries globally.

THAILAND

Thailand was perhaps the star of the 'miracle' economies of SEA, managing to post growth rates in excess of ten per cent a year for the decade to 1997. The Thai government had wholeheartedly adopted export-oriented industrial policies and provided several incentives for both local and foreign investment in the Greater Bangkok region. The scale of development in this region was staggering, with the face of Bangkok being transformed from that of a large but pleasant urban centre to that of a mega-metropolis almost bursting at its seams.

The fate that befell Thailand in mid 1997, as discussed in the chapter on Thailand, was in part in response to the overenthusiasm for lending into what had become a stagnant economic environment, corruption and, in part, the boom and bust nature of capitalism. In simple terms, when world demand for Thai products slowed in the early to mid 1990s, investment and easy credit continued to flow into the country, with much of it being siphoned off into artificially high property prices, bad businesses and corrupt schemes. When the time came for these debts to begin to be repaid the defaults began, with businesses and then financial institutions going to the wall (*Asiaweek* 1998b; Chalongphob 1998). In turn, the value of the Thai currency, the bhat, collapsed by around half, ensuring that remaining debts denominated in foreign currencies effectively doubled. A similar problem also hit Indonesia, although there it was much worse due to the vastly greater scale of corruption and the capital flight that had preceded the resignation of Suharto as president. In part a flow-on effect, in part a response to similar issues in other regional countries, the Thai economic crisis quickly spread throughout the region, affecting virtually all countries.

In Thailand's case, due in part to new economic measures aimed at cleaning up marginal financial practices and some corruption, the economy began to rebound by 1999 (see Gearing 2000). Capitalism's cycle appeared to be on the upswing again. However, this effect was slower to take place in other SEA countries, although it did appear as though it would occur. But more importantly, the human cost of this economic collapse, in terms of the shattered lives of ordinary people who lost their livelihoods through no fault of their own, indicated that, as a system, SEA's 'boom capitalism' was probably an immature approach to economic development.

PHILIPPINES

The Philippines had the highest level of per capita GDP of any country in SEA in the 1950s, and considerable capacity for building on that, including relatively high literacy levels and widespread use of English. Yet within two decades, the Philippines was mired in corruption, poverty, economic turmoil and a dictatorial government.

If one was to seek out the primary ingredient in this descent into chaos—a chaos from which the Philippines has yet to fully recover—it would be the weakness of the state. In simple terms, the government has been too close to or too easily manipulated by the country's oligarchy, which in turn has raided the economy on a regular basis (see Hutchcroft 1998). Even in the post–Marcos period, social change was very slow in being achieved; economic change through land redistribution or the strengthening of regulations and institutional support was effectively non-existent, and political change reflected a return to the cosy relationships between government and vested interests of the pre-Marcos period.

Regardless of policy prescriptions implemented at a public level, little had changed in the Philippines from the 1950s other than the decrease in its support from the United States. With an elite steeped in the art of self-enrichment and the government essentially being hostage to that elite, notions of policy outside short-term elite interest were alien concepts.

THE 'BALANCE SHEET'

Economic development in SEA has therefore been mixed, with some countries making impressive strides towards 'modernisation' while others have languished. The respective abilities of the countries of the region to link into the world economy have been determined in part by their state ideologies, but more so by aspects such as adequate regulatory and other state systems, and issues such as political stability and corruption. In many cases, so-called 'development' has been little more than elites further entrenching and enriching themselves at the expense of the people who have historically been excluded from both political and economic participation. In this sense, economic development has not exclusively but most often reflected political development:

> The distribution of development's fruits typically reflects the pattern of political power, not the pattern of human need.
>
> All too often this happens because development efforts are simply hijacked, to their own material advantage, by proximate power-holders. In particular, intended beneficiaries at lower levels of power and income will suffer from the political process which Porter has labelled—simply if inelegantly—'the rip-off upward' (Porter 1986: 243).
>
> *(Goldsworthy 1988)*

At the beginning of the twenty-first century, it could be suggested that the broad trajectory for both economic and political development in SEA was looking up. Indeed, Fukuyama's thesis (1993) on the seeming inevitability of the success of both free market capitalism and democracy incorporated the normative assumption that both were not only desirable but inevitably had some support. Yet the sometimes supposed structural linkages between free market capitalism and democratisation, as inferred by Fukuyama, was disproved by the economic success of Singapore and Malaysia, while Indonesia and the Philippines embraced versions of democracy while retaining weak capitalist economies. Other states have both economic growth and democratisation, or have little of either. It may be that democracy, however it is defined, is but a passing historical phase and that there is nothing inevitable about its application. Similarly, free market capitalism, as Marx suggested, has shown itself to have in-built contradictions which could limit its existence. If both can be taken to be a product of a particular historical and perhaps cultural environment, like civilisations before them, they too could collapse, wither away or, due to their broad environmental unsustainability, die from lack of clean air and water.

In the interim, governments and their critics, states and individuals, all compete with varying degrees of success for influence over or ownership of ideas that define social organisation. To date there has been no proven correct answer to the questions this raises, nor perhaps can there be. In many senses, the competition between ideas on these and other questions—perhaps the only true subject for a free market—is the foundation stone of real development. It may also be that such reflection is difficult without first securing immediate material needs. But the assertion that one without the other can comprise anything deserving of the name 'development' is to sell short not just the idea but the people to whom it applies.

NOTES

1   To illustrate, former President Suharto referred to himself as 'the Father of Development'.
2   This is an official claim of income for 1993 and, like many other economic statistics from Indonesia under the New Order government, its accuracy is at best dubious.
3   The UNDP version of the HDI includes average life expectancy, adult literacy rates, per capita GDP, and PPP. Discussion about what should be included in an HDI has also raised the question of weighting (for example, whether infant mortality should be given the same weighting in such an index as literacy).

4   There is some debate about whether the term 'modernisation' should apply to the post-war development process in its entirety. I have used 'modernisation' in its more limited context to differentiate it from other theories and practices of development.

5   It is worth noting that the largest communist organisation in SEA, the Communist Party of Indonesia (PKI), attempted to work within the government to achieve political change.

6   The major exception is North Vietnam.

7   Revolutionary models picked up by dependency theorists were usually Latin American based, although the various communist insurgencies of SEA could probably (though not explicitly) illustrate the same critiques of existing political and economic orders.

8   It is a common critique of free market capitalism that it requires a pool of labour, based on unemployment or underemployment, to draw on in order to keep down wages and hence production costs.

9   This observation is based on a discussion with NGOs working in that area.

10   Malaysia in particular and Indonesia to some extent have bucked the IMF's policy prescriptions, in the former case by rejecting them and the IMF entirely in 1998. Indonesia successfully bargained with the IMF for 'softer' conditions for its own bail-out package in 1999.

4

Security Issues

The region of SEA sits at a geographic, cultural, and political juncture between the two great regions of the earth known as South Asia and North East Asia. These land masses between them account for two thirds of the world's population. Situated half in the Indo-Chinese peninsula and half in the archipelago north of the Australasian continent, dominating the sea lanes between the Indian and Pacific Oceans, SEA has since time immemorial been regarded by other states as one of the most strategically vital regions in the world. Historically, whoever controlled the Straits of Malacca between Sumatra and the Malay Peninsula was, by definition, a world power. In the nuclear age, whoever controls the Ombai–Wetar Straits, which marks a tectonic divide immediately to the north of East Timor, controls the passage of nuclear capable deep water submarines between the Indian and Pacific Oceans, with all the implications this has for threats to five of the world's seven acknowledged nuclear armed states. This is not to mention the oil producing capacity of the archipelagic states, the fact that the regional population exceeds 600 million or that, in the middle, Indonesia is the world's most populous Muslim country and the 'lynchpin of regional security' (Feinstein 1998). For these, and many other reasons, the security and stability of SEA is of global strategic importance.

This chapter is intended to consider issues which have influenced strategic policy considerations in the SEA region. In particular, it will focus on the role of nationalist movements, communist insurgency and revolution, and the influences exerted by the USA/USSR/China.

Despite the apparent stasis of the states of SEA, the competing historical claims that produced these states continue to be worried about by his-
torians and, by extension, by contemporary political actors. It seems that
anyone who writes about a SEA state is in some way trying to legitimise
current state formation or, more subtly, rationalise irredentist claims.

Each state seeks to base the legitimacy of its existing borders on a
claim to territory within that greatest area occupied during some real or
imagined period of imperial glory. At different stages of the region's history, different states rose to regional prominence, and many occupied or
claimed suzerainty over areas vastly greater than currently exist. In this
historical memory, the concept of the *mandala* comes into play, in which
states, based on an 'exemplary centre', expand when strong and contract
(or disappear) when weak. The general structure of such a political (as
opposed to metaphysical) *mandala* was that outlying regions were not so
much directly ruled by the centre but were semi-autonomous and owed
allegiance or were suzerain. The greater the distance from the centre, the
greater the autonomy of the peripheral localities.

Texts abound on the validity of each of the states, how the others have
behaved in a perfidious or grasping fashion and, often, how the territorial
and cultural claim of each state should, in a better world, extend beyond
its present horizons. As survivors, or imaginative recreations of former
states, these states are able to make such claims, or at least justify their continued existence. But almost identical types of texts could have been written about, for example, the state of Lan Na, except that due to the
vagaries of history it failed to survive as a state and is now a part of Thailand. The difference between it and, for example, what became Laos was
more luck based on geographic proximity to a particular colonial power
at a particular time than any intrinsic quality. Still, to write of Lan Na as
one might now write of Laos would be to invite allegations of treason to
the state of Thailand. There but for the grace of history went Laos.

Similarly, the once important state of Brunei is now but a shadow of
its former territorial self. Champa, in what is now Vietnam, has long
since ceased to exist, although Islamic Chams are still found in Vietnam
and Cambodia, while the southern Lao province of Champassak continues to reflect its former influence. Cambodia still lays an historical
claim to Kampuchea Krom, in what is now southern Vietnam, while the
early T'ai states of Sipsong Chu Tai and Sipsong Panna, among others,
have completely disappeared, even though their people have not. Not
surprisingly, as people continue where states disappear, an historical
memory also exists, to a greater or lesser degree. The sack of Vieng
Chan by a Thai army in 1828 is a date that is still bitterly remembered

in Laos, in particular in that city. When French explorers came to the site that was once the city of Vieng Chan some forty years after the event, all that was left was a handful of Buddhist ruins. The Thais had been successful in obliterating this rebellious vassal state, while managing to transport tens of thousands of its surviving citizens to populate an otherwise barren region under its authority. Prior to the colonial era, people were more of a commodity to a regional state than was produce, and captives of war were a conventional benefit of military success.

The predecessor state to Laos, Lan Xang, was for a time the greatest state of the Mekong region. However, its decline and disintegration into three competing states allowed it to be vulnerable to incorporation into the growing Thai state. Yet that state was itself vulnerable, especially to the resurgent Burmese. Resentment and suspicion lingers between the Lao and the Thai, and the Thai and the Burmese. Formal relations might be cordial, or might not, but historical memory cannot be completely erased. With the complete destruction of Ayudhya by the Burmese in the eighteenth century, the Thai state centred on this city dissolved, freeing the periphery. However, under the remarkable leadership of Taksin, the Thai state was quickly restored, with the capital being removed to Thonburi (now part of Bangkok). In reassembling the state, Taksin reasserted authority over the Lao states. The states of Vieng Chan and Luang Prabang had an established history of conflict, often one siding with an invading power against the other, for example Vieng Chan with the Burmese against Luang Prabang in 1765, and then Luang Prabang with the Thai against Vieng Chan in 1779. This aided their disunity and made them more vulnerable to control by the resurgent Thai state. Internal state divisions therefore also exist.

Similarly, later conflict between the Thais and Vietnam reflected competing imperial agendas. When one looked at Thailand's close support for the Khmer Rouge of Cambodia, for example, what one saw was not some ideological agreement, but a continuation of an historical battle against the expansionist Vietnamese. Looking at it like this, there is no moral right or wrong, but only survival, and alliances that helped secure survival. In this sense, Cambodia has been allowed to exist as a buffer state, in much the same way that the states of Laos secured their pre-French existence. As imperial Britain and France did not wish to come into conflict over a border dispute in SEA, hence maintaining Thailand between their territories, so too have Thailand and Vietnam come to an understanding that good buffer states make good neighbours.

In the archipelago, the Javanese retain, or have reinvented, the glories of the Majapahit empire of the fourteenth century as a means of providing a link between Indonesia's present and its somewhat mythologised past. The unity of the state is, according to most observers, desirable, at least for the purposes of regional stability. But desire does not always match outcomes, and for each territorial desire there is usually a competing desire. Only one can claim success. In a contemporary sense, there is still considerable support for the idea of being 'Indonesian'. But there is far less support for the idea of being a Javanese colony. With the meaning of 'Indonesia' increasingly contested, it is not surprising that its various groups have asserted their distinct visions against one they feel is imposed from outside.

Similarly, in the Philippines, the construction of the state is not accepted by a relatively small but none the less militant Islamic minority in the south, nor has it ever been. Why should anyone be surprised that Muslim separatism continues to afflict Mindanao, and Aceh in northern Sumatra, when it has done so since the first attempts to incorporate these regions into greater states. Similarly the only glue holding Malaysia's western state together with the peninsula is economic prosperity. The vast majority of the population of these states, both indigenous and Chinese, is otherwise disinclined to be dominated by the peninsular Malays. In Burma, where no such economic prosperity exists, there is no tangible reason for the non-Bhamese population to remain as a part of what continues, in effect, to be an extension of an older Bhamese empire.

The shape of the political world we now look at is vastly different to that which existed in the past. It is, therefore, not necessarily the same as that we will always look at. Historical memory runs deep and, as continues to be demonstrated, some grievances, both ancient and contemporary, remain to be settled.

IDEOLOGICAL CONFLICT

In more recent history, ideology has come to play a significant role in SEA, especially as a means of nation-building. The first Indochina War, from 1946 until 1954, was clearly a war of national liberation on the part of the Vietnamese. It was participated in by both Cambodia and Laos in so far as both had indigenous nationalist movements and, perhaps as importantly, in so far as their communist groups were influenced by or agreed with the central claim to independence by Vietnamese communists. Perhaps another nationalist model might also have worked in Indochina, but communism had a number of points in its favour. It had a clear organisational structure, offered a rational analysis of colonial exploitation, supported the poor, and, perhaps most importantly, could neither be bought off by nor would compromise with colonial capitalism. It was this implacability and consequent success that led to a further attempt to quash it.

The division of Vietnam at the 17th parallel in 1954, which marked the end of the First Indochina War, was intended purely as a device to allow the separation of combatants before the holding of elections. However, with the Cold War well underway by this stage and with a communist victory likely, if not inevitable, France and the US were unwilling to allow the strategically important state of Vietnam to fall into the communist camp. Having secured a stalemate on the Korean peninsula in 1952, and with Germany and the rest of Europe having been partitioned along communist and non-communist lines from 1945, the US in particular believed that it was possible to stall the communist advance in SEA. Indeed, if it did not, the states of the region could, as the later theory outlined it, fall one by one like a series of dominoes (McNamara 1995: 31, 32).

The US was in some small measure reassured by the minor cultural distinction between the north and the south of Vietnam, that it had spent a part of its history divided and that it comprised three separate states when occupied by France in the late nineteenth century. The fact that the US easily found willing accomplices for its anti-communist crusade among the local elite further bolstered its contention that an independent South Vietnam was not only viable but legitimate.

The Second Indochina War is now formally recognised by the US, for its own purposes, as having begun in October 1956, with the declaration of the state of the Republic of Vietnam. For others, especially in the south, there was no break between the conflicts. The US was initially reluctant to involve itself in a major military commitment, believing that high levels of economic and military aid coupled with the provision of 'advisers' to train South Vietnamese troops could be enough to hold the line. It was not, and the escalation of the conflict into the 1960s was for many, perhaps most, Vietnamese a continuation of their already long struggle for self-determination.

The success of communism in both Laos and Cambodia can be seen as a spill-over effect of the conflict in Vietnam. While both these countries had their own domestic causes for conflict, they were undoubtedly pushed along by forces competing in Vietnam. A further spill-over also affected Thailand, albeit in a more limited manner. And a general strategy of communist insurgency promoted by China was also active in British Malaya, North Borneo and, later, in the Philippines. Interestingly, the biggest communist party in the region until 1965, the Indonesian Communist Party (Parti Komunis Indonesia – PKI), had not, since the creation of the state of

Indonesia in 1949, ever attempted to overthrow its government. The Suharto-ist 'New Order' rhetoric about the PKI's 'attempted coup' of 1965 is, logically, absurd. Certainly communism was gaining ground in the most populous country in the region and that might have been cause for concern for opponents of communism. But the events of 1965 and 1966 reflected more a desire by pro-US generals to seize control of Indonesian politics than they did the likelihood of a communist takeover.

NATIONALISM

More problematic for Indonesia was the Permesta–PRRI rebellion of 1958, which threatened to dismantle the state, raising issues of both ideology and conceptions of nationalism. Interestingly, many of the tensions that led to the Permesta–PRRI rebellion, such as poor economic distribution, excessive centralisation of government and corruption, were those that fed into events tearing at the fabric of the state at the end of the twentieth century.

Indonesia's claim to securing West Papua resulted from that territory being a part of the Dutch East Indies and the fact that the basis of the Indonesian state was defined by the totality of the Dutch territories. That a number of early nationalist leaders had been imprisoned at Bovun Digul, near the Papua New Guinea border, further added to a sense that the territory had a legitimate, some claimed special, reason to be included in the new republican state. The Dutch, however, did not view West Papua in the same light as Indonesian nationalist irredentists. Indeed, the Dutch administrative conception of the East Indies was that it comprised a collection of separately administered colonies that were coordinated from Jakarta. West Papua in particular did not fall into any greater conception of an overarching or single colonial territory, nor were its indigenous people, being Melanesian, in any way related to the Malays who comprised the vast majority of the rest of the population. As a consequence, the agreement of 1949 that secured Indonesian independence specifically excluded West Papua, to be negotiated at a later date.

The Dutch were strongly supported in their position by Australia, which directly administered Papua, the south-east quarter of the island and, under a League of Nations and then United Nations mandate, the north-east quarter of the island, New Guinea. During WWII, Imperial Japanese forces had advanced as far as the southern coast of Papua New Guinea before being halted by Australian troops on the ground and US ships and aircraft in the Coral Sea. It was clear to Australia's strategic planners that any future threat to Australia's security would probably come through the island of Papua New Guinea. Australia was therefore concerned to either maintain a 'friendly' Dutch presence in the western half of the island, or even bring that part of the island also under Australian administration (Osborne 1985: 18–28). The Dutch had been allies during the war, after all, while the Indonesian government was at least in part a creation of retreating Japanese who, moreover, were increasingly seen to be influenced by communism. However, the United States, concerned to shore up relations with the government of the strategically important archipelago and with a tendency towards supporting the movement towards decolonisation, pressured the Dutch into surrendering the territory in 1962, to take effect in 1963. A vote of specially selected village chiefs in 1968 'confirmed' the incorporation of West Papua into the republic of Indonesia (Osborne 1985: 30–9), to be known thereafter as Irian Barat (West Irian), then Irian Jaya and finally, in 2000, West Papua. The obviously rigged and unrepresentative vote pushed many West Papuans into rebellion against the government in Jakarta.

The Organisasi Papua Merdeka (Free Papua Organisation, or OPM) was born as a result of this forced incorporation. Although militarily never a threat to the Indonesian government or its forces, the OPM has continued with a low-level guerrilla campaign aimed at harassing Indonesian troops and settlers and continuing representation of anti-Indonesian sentiment. The displacement of indigenous people as a consequence of government-sponsored resettlement of other Indonesians in West Papua, and the often disruptive and exploitative practices of mining companies in the province, further exacerbated tensions between colonisers and colonised.

The two main strategic issues which have arisen as a result of this rebellion include the potential for the break-up of the state, and the conflict spilling over into neighbouring states. In the first instance, the conflict in Irian Jaya stands with that which existed in East Timor and Aceh as those which had the greatest potential to bring undone the idea of Indonesia as a unitary state comprising more than 300 separate ethnic groups. Beyond this, there are some fears, strongest in Jakarta and among the Indonesian military, that if one region was successful in pulling away from the state this would then give impetus to others, destroying the state of Indonesia as a cohesive entity. This concern also exercises the minds of more distantly placed strategic analysts, who regard the idea of the archipelago comprised of several independent, potentially non-viable and possibly confrontational states as a problem of major proportions. In this respect, though, West Papua was situated a long way behind East Timor in the possibility for success of its bid for meaningful independence.

The second major issue concerning West Papua was that, in their enthusiasm to pursue OPM guerrillas, Indonesian soldiers have crossed in 'hot pursuit' over the Papua–New Guinea border, raising the spectre of a confrontation between Indonesian troops and PNG troops. Further, with Australian soldiers still patrolling the border region as a part of Australia's assistance to PNG, there was thought to be the possibility of clashes between Indonesian and Australian troops. Given the historical unease felt by Australian defence planners towards Indonesia, this then raised the issue of such a confrontation becoming the trigger for a full-scale conflict between the two neighbouring states. Although such a fear was strongest in the early 1960s, when Indonesia's left-leaning government under Sukarno was regarded in Australia with considerable hostility, the 'hot pursuits' which aroused the most controversy occurred in the mid 1980s, when diplomatic relations between Australia and Indonesia were again at a low ebb.

The point at which Indonesia and Australia, along with Malaysia, Great Britain and New Zealand, did come into more direct conflict was the creation of the new state of Malaysia, in 1963. Indonesia's President Sukarno viewed the creation of the state of Malaysia, comprising the former British Straits territories and a number of local sultanates, as both artificially dividing the Malay world and creating what he saw as a neo-colonial state which could be used to destabilise Indonesia.

Sukarno's vision was for all Malay peoples, including those in the Philippines, to be united in a 'Greater Indonesia'. This accorded with the 'Indonesia Raya' plan developed by some Indonesian nationalists in 1945. However, the move was not well supported by Indonesia's army, which conducted secret negotiations to end the conflict throughout its duration. While Indonesian 'volunteers' were active in Sarawak and Sabah,[1] and there were forays into the Malaysian peninsula, it never presented a major military threat to Malaysia. The confrontation was primarily a diplomatic battle, although Australian, New Zealand and British troops did engage Indonesian irregulars on a number of occasions. The Australian government felt so concerned about the potential for a full-scale conflict with Indonesia that it ordered, off the drawing board, the F111 aircraft. The F111 had the capacity to both bomb as far distant as Jakarta and to carry nuclear weapons (which Australia has never had). The F111 was not built or delivered to Australia until after this perceived threat had disappeared, although it was still in service in Australia in upgraded form in the first years of the twenty-first century.

In a military sense, the confrontation was declining when Sukarno was deposed as president, ending the conflict. A military coup against Sukarno appeared increasingly likely, especially as his health was beginning to fail and the Indonesian Armed Forces (then Angkatan Bersenjata Republik Indonesia – ABRI) desperately wanted to forestall the accession to power of the PKI. Some junior officers intent on protecting Suharto moved against the senior ABRI officers on the night of 30 September 1966, killing six of the most senior generals. In the counter-attack the following day, Brigadier-General Suharto began the first part of his campaign to defeat the '30 September Movement' and moved on to eliminate the PKI as a force within Indonesia. The confrontation, which was already dwindling to a war more of words than bullets, was quietly cancelled.

EAST TIMOR

Where a greater danger emerged, at the end of the twentieth century, was between Australia and Indonesia over East Timor. Following the referendum in East Timor on autonomy or independence, which overwhelmingly supported independence, and the subsequent anti-independence violence, Australia led an international peace-enforcement team to East Timor under the mandate of the United Nations. However, the very direct response of many Indonesians was that Australia was interfering in Indonesia's domestic affairs. The Australian embassy in Jakarta was attacked as was an Australian school, and many Australian businesses in Indonesia found their customer base disappearing due to quasi-official sanctions. At one stage, when Australian lawyers from the International Commission of Jurists said they would travel to East Timor to investigate war crimes, Indonesia's Justice Minister, Mauladi, said such a move could lead to a break in diplomatic relations.

Similarly, comments by the Australian Defence Minister, John Moore, that Australian troops could cross into West Timor in 'hot pursuit' of militia members if they attacked the international force, InterFET (International Force in East Timor) raised a great deal of concern in Indonesia and led the regional military commander to say that such an 'invasion' of Indonesia's sovereign territory would be met with force. Moore quickly backed down on his statement. However, the pro-integration militias were given safe haven near the East Timor border in West Timor and from that position continued to harass East Timorese civilians and the international force. Further, Indonesia's regional commander at that time, Brigadier-General Adam Damiri, said that while he would not order East Timorese troops in the Indonesian army to attack the InterFET forces he could not stop those who wished to 'volunteer' to do so. As with the 'volunteers' who were active in Malaysia in the Confrontation (Konfrontasi) and in West Papua, no one believed that these troops were in fact 'volunteers', or that the Indonesian army was unable to exercise authority over them. After the election of Abdurrahman Wahid as Indonesia's president, while the border skirmishes continued they were of reduced diplomatic consequence. This reflected a lack of formal Indonesian government support for the armed forces (reconstituted as the Indonesian National Military, Tentara Nasional Indonesia – TNI) or militia groups operating in the area.

Perhaps what East Timor represented most to Indonesians was its potential to lead the way for the break up of the state. At the time that East Timor achieved effective separation from Indonesia, in September 1999, Aceh was at its most violent and dangerous since perhaps the late 1950s, while thousands had died in ethnic conflict in Ambon and in other parts of Maluku, and West Kalimantan was beset by ethnic conflict. Throughout Indonesia there seemed to be considerable tension over the idea of what 'Indonesia' actually meant. Pro-Indonesianists formed into a strongly 'nationalist' camp, while those with other ideas split along factional and regional lines. It increasingly seemed, however, that Indonesia as a unitary state had a limited life expectancy and that its future was, at best, uncertain. Many analysts suggested that the break-up of the state could present a strategic nightmare for other countries in the region. But others pointed to the erratic and problematic nature of the state as it had already existed, suggesting that separate smaller states might be more accommodating to their neighbours. Within Indonesia itself, such discussion was effectively forbidden, even though a plan for political and economic decentralisation was put in place by the government.

BURMA

Burma has long been considered a major strategic crossroad in Asia, sitting as it does across the only readily passable route between the world's two largest and often antagonistic nations, India and China. In recent history, the only external threat to Burma has come from Japan, which occupied it in 1941 as a part of its push towards India. While the target of that attack was never achieved, Burma was until 1945 a battleground across which raged some of the Asian conflict's bloodiest and most destructive fighting.

Burma has always been influenced by its two giant neighbours but, perhaps more importantly, it has been more dominated by its internal geography and ethnic make-up. Historically dominated by its two-thirds majority Bhamese, Burma has a history of aggression both towards its neighbours and towards its internal minorities. While internal conflicts and the demands of coming to terms with a rapidly changing external world have focused the attention of Burma's military dictatorship, there have also been signs that conflict could spill over into neighbouring Thailand, Burma's traditional enemy.

Since the late 1980s, Burma's army (*Tatmadaw*) has more than doubled in size, from fewer than 200 000 troops to more than 400 000. Given that Burma faces no credible external threat, this rise in troop numbers can only be attributable to the role of the army in domestic oppression, both towards the country's ethnic insurgents as well as towards its pro-democracy activists. In building up the strength of its army, Burma has established increasingly strong ties to China, which at the beginning of the twenty-first century was the country's biggest arms supplier. Reliable figures are unavailable, but a number of estimates put Burma's acquisition of Chinese arms, ranging from automatic rifles to jet fighters, at around US$1 billion a year.

The second biggest arms supplier to Burma was Singapore. In conjunction with Israeli consultants, in February 1988 Singapore had shipped to Burma's Directorate of Defence Industries a prefabricated factory designed and built by Chartered Industries of Singapore[2] to produce small arms and weapons up to 37 mm calibre. The first item thought to be produced in the new factory is the EMERK-1, a locally designed assault rifle/light machine gun. Singapore previously supplied the Burmese government with weapons at critical times and has also built a cyber-war centre in Rangoon capable of telephone, fax and satellite communications. Chartered Industries of Singapore had previously supplied the Burmese government with tonnes of ammunition, mortars and other war materials at the time of the pro-democracy protests in 1988 (*The Irrawaddy* 1998a: 13).

Further concerns have been raised over Burma, in a contra deal, allowing China access to the Indian Ocean. Although still little more than a gesture, and a base from which to gather intelligence, Chinese access to the Indian Ocean has the potential to alter the strategic balance of power within the region and provided further fuel for tension between India and China (see Malik, in Pedersen, Rudland & May 2000: 249, 251, 253–4).

In large part, ASEAN's invitation for Burma to join the organisation was aimed at this increasing Chinese influence. The partial aim of ASEAN was to reduce Burma's reliance on China, which was widely perceived throughout ASEAN as the region's most significant long-term threat. In this respect, the addition of Burma to ASEAN and hence the strategically oriented ASEAN Regional Forum completed the 'cup' which encapsulates the southern flanks of China. This then establishes a strategic bloc that is the only realistic way in which the smaller and more diffuse countries of SEA could contain a potentially expansionist or belligerent China. The lesson here is an old one: when China has been weak at the centre it has withdrawn its focus to matters close to home. When China has been strong it has tended to exert or extend its influence well into the SEA region.

As China's economy moves to become the world's largest within the next few decades, with the world's largest population, China is again being perceived as growing in strength. Regional leaders look not so much towards what the present Chinese government has done or is doing, but to the actions of Chinese leaders dating back to the rise of the Han Dynasty, some two thousand years before. Finally, it is widely hoped within SEA that, while China could well become a threat, it might also become an economic friend. To this end, Burma's increasingly close links with China offered the ASEAN states an opportunity to engage more closely with China in business, especially in the much vaunted (but underdeveloped) Yunnan–Burma–Laos–Thailand region.

Stuart-Fox has identified the relationship between the SEA states and China as one of big brother–small brothers, where the regional states act in such a way as to recognise China's interests and concerns. In this, China is seen to prefer not to act but to have its wishes anticipated. This relationship is seen to reflect a traditional sense of Confucian hierarchy (acknowledging one's 'proper place' in the world) which allows for 'non-intervention' (*wu wei*: inaction) (Stuart-Fox 1998b). Stuart-Fox also noted that China's regional significance has considerably developed as the United States has diminished its presence in the region, first by withdrawing from mainland SEA by 1975, and later from the Philippines, and by the withdrawal of the Soviet Union from its base at Vietnam's Cam Ranh Bay.

While the *Tatmadaw* has been preoccupied with quelling internal dissent, as ethnic refugees have spilled across the border to Thailand, Burmese troops have followed in 'hot pursuit'. This has raised tensions between Thailand and Burma, especially as many of the Burmese refugees are Shan, who are linguistically related to the Thai and who have, on various occasions, suggested their geographic incorporation into the Thai state.

Tension between Thailand and Burma was illustrated by the 'Thai–Burmese Friendship Bridge', which crosses the mutual border at Myawaddy–Mae Sot, north-west of Bangkok. The bridge was opened on 15 August 1997, but closed by Burmese authorities on 14 April 1998 after a bomb was planted in the town of Myawaddy. The bomb was suspected as having been planted by members of the Karen National Union, which had launched sporadic attacks against Burmese troops in the area. Thailand enjoyed a significant surplus in trade across the bridge, which it built, and the Burmese government was thought to be using its closure as a means of pressuring the Thai government into helping destroy the Karen forces on the Thai side of the border (Saritdet & Nussara 1998). Later activities by Burmese separatists in Thailand were met by considerable Thai force, indicating that Thailand did not want to become a party to Burma's internal problems.

LAOS

Territorial control over Laos has always been contested to some degree. Its border areas expanded and shrank according to the fortunes of the state. But within the state there have always been groups of people who only distantly, if at all, recognise the sovereign authority of the state. This has particularly applied to the highland regions, which have traditionally had a relatively independent existence from the rest of the state. Most recently, that assertion of independence has focused on the Hmong, or Meo, people, who migrated from southern China into highland Laos from early in the nineteenth century.

The Hmong have relied, for their own use and for trade with the outside world, on the growing of opium poppies, which are well suited to the region's rugged terrain. When the production of opium was legal, this was the source of revenue for the state, notably under the French. However, as opium production has become an industry of international pariah status, there has been increasing conflict between opium producing Hmong and the Lao government. Since the 1960s, this conflict has been exacerbated by an ideological conflict, fed by the US, which recruited Hmong to form an anti-communist private army under General Vang Pao. The interest of the US was twofold: it wanted a private army that could harass the Pathet Lao, but it also wanted an unofficial military force located in Hmong territory, in particular in the middle of the strategically important Plain of Jars, which sits astride the major routes from northern Vietnam into northern Laos, including to Luang Prabang and Vieng Chan. The US Central Intelligence Agency has been claimed to have assisted with the export of opium in exchange for (and to help finance) Hmong military support.

When the US abandoned its attempts to control events in Indochina from the early 1970s, it abandoned its Hmong allies. However, the Hmong, more deeply entrenched in opium production, continued with the lucrative trade. To a lesser extent they also continued to battle with rival Hmong groups and, for more obscure ideological and cultural reasons, with Lao government forces. Over the last decade of the twentieth century, the Hmong were increasingly brought under the control of the Lao government, especially with the completion of a sealed road through the western section of the Plain of Jars, from Luang Prabang to Vieng Chan. A large number of Hmong have been resettled near this road, allegedly to curtail their traditional slash and burn agricultural practices, but more accurately to make them susceptible to military control. However, sporadic attacks against both the Lao military and civilians continued along the road in the area of Kasi, and the area further to the east remains disputed, while there have also been bombings in Vieng Chan and a guerrilla attack from Thailand at Pakse in the south.

THAILAND AND MALAYSIA

As the 'Malayan Emergency' subsided from the 1950s, Malaysia's remaining communist insurgents increasingly withdrew to the mountainous and relatively isolated region along and across the Thai border. While low level campaigns against them by the Malaysian government remained in place, their major saving grace was an effective refusal by the Thai government to act against them. Had the Thai government done so, the guerrillas of the Malayan Communist Party (MCP) would have been caught between the two forces. But it did not. It was not as if the Thai government was sympathetic to the MCP's cause, however, especially as during the 1970s it had its own communist insurgency to counter. Rather, it was unsympathetic towards appeals by the Malaysian government, because of the latter's effective harbouring of Thai Islamic separatists just south of the Thai border.

The effective stand-off over the issue of both Thai and Malaysian insurgents on either side of the border was a result of the mixed history of the region and the imprecise nature of pre-colonial political control. The sultanates of the Malay Peninsula had at various times been vassal states to precursor Thai states, as well as at various times to other powers such as Sri Vijaya in Sumatra, possibly Majapahit in Java, and even occasionally achieving relative independence. However, the northernmost sultanates were the most susceptible to Thai influence and control, and there was a long history of *mandalic* expansion and contraction of Thai influence. In particular, the northern Malay states were most firmly brought under Thai suzerainty after 1782, under the resurgence of what was to become the Chakri dynasty.

It was only as a consequence of British pressure, in 1909, that Siam ceded suzerainty of the four states of Perlis, Kedah, Kelantan and Trengganu, bringing them under British 'protection'. However, this left a number of ethnic Malays in Thailand's southern states. Of Thailand's approximately two million Muslims, about seventy-five per cent live in the southern Thai provinces of Yala, Narathiwat, Satun and Pattani.

Since the early twentieth century, there has been strong Muslim opposition to incorporation within the Thai state, which has been manifested in separatist sentiment. Constituting only three per cent of the Thai population, the southern Muslim minority has never been a threat to the Thai Buddhist state. However, the ethnic, linguistic[3] and religious differences, compounded by occasional official repression, have pushed some into rebellion (Hewison 1994). The Malaysian government, responding to populist appeals from its Muslim community as well as reflecting elements of a Malay irredentist sentiment, had not persecuted Thai Muslims operating out of Malay territory. However, by the end of the twentieth century, it seemed that the exigencies of the modern state had started to supersede ethnic identity, and the prime ministers of both Thailand and Malaysia had agreed to work more closely to 'suppress terrorist groups operating along the Thai–Malaysian border' (*The Nation* 1998: A2).

PHILIPPINES

The issues of ideology and nationalism both affect the Philippines, although neither did so in ways that had wider strategic implications. In particular the southern island of Mindanao was deeply beset by insurgencies led by both communist and Islamic groups, reflecting the tenuous nature of the consolidation of the state, as well as issues of economic distribution. As communism has waned internationally, so too has communism shrunk as a threat in the Philippines, even though the issues that engendered it were still largely in place several years later.

Militant Islam, on the other hand, had in the past a lesser grip on the island, but had more consistency in terms of its appeal. Islam has been a driving force in the southern Philippines since the Spanish first colonised the region more than 400 years ago. This Islamic separatism was supported by Islamic groups throughout the world and represented a long-term if localised challenge to state integrity. If there was a wider strategic issue to be considered in the Philippines, it was that the string of islands between Mindanao and the Malaysian state of Sabah were regarded as having considerable strategic value, being an historic trans-shipment route through the archipelago. As a consequence, whoever controlled Mindanao, and consequently these islands, controlled one of the region's main links. In historic terms, the Sultanate of Sulu was a significant regional power because of its control not just over these islands but over much of modern Sabah. But with Sabah fairly firmly within the Malaysian state, there seemed about as much prospect of this region reconsolidating under an Islamic banner as there did the state of the Malay Peninsula forming a federation with the *malayu* states of Sumatra.

Related to Sulu's former ownership of Sabah, the Philippines has claimed the territory as the inheritor state of the Sulu Sultanate. A state of dispute between the Philippines and Britain over Sabah was first lodged in 1962, transferring to Malaysia after Sabah was incorporated into that state in 1963. The claim led to a serious rupture of relations between Malaysia and the Philippines when, in 1968, endorsed by the Philippines Congress, President Marcos formally announced the Philippines' right to the territory. The claim was exacerbated by a report that the Philippines military had been training young Muslims as a force to invade Sabah, which appeared to be confirmed by the arrest of twenty-six armed Filipinos on an island off the coast of Sabah in March 1968. The Philippines continued with its claim to Sabah, although with less conviction after a visit by Malaysian Prime Minister Mahatir Mohamad in 1994.

SPRATLY ISLANDS

The Spratly Islands are a major test case in terms of state control and nationalist assertion in SEA, being a small group of islands claimed at once by China, Taiwan (as a claimant to Chinese legitimacy), Vietnam, Malaysia, Brunei, and the Philippines. The Spratlys are an outcrop of some 400 rocks, reefs, shoals and sandbanks spread over roughly 800 kilometres north to south in the middle of one of the world's major trading routes. The main islands of the group are located a little more than 450 kilometres almost directly north of Brunei (and Sabah and Sarawak) and about 600 kilometres west-south-west of Palawan Island of the Philippines. The next nearest landfall is near Ho Chi Minh City in southern Vietnam, some 750 kilometres away, although Vietnam claims islands that are about 150 kilometres from the nearest of the Spratly group, while the main Spratly islands are some 1300 kilometres south of China.

China's claim to the Spratlys derives from its Nationalist government's claim following Japan's use of the islands as a submarine base and its defeat in 1945, reaffirmed by the People's Republic of China in 1951. Chinese fishermen had previously used the islands, although no previous Chinese claim had ever been made to them. The Philippines lays its claims to the islands as a consequence of an expedition there in the 1950s and a presidential decree concerning sovereignty in 1978. Malaysia's claim dates from 1979, with the publication of a map of Malaysia including those islands closest to the north Borneo coast. Vietnam (South) claimed the islands in 1955 as a consequence of a French claim in the late nineteenth century.

Since the 1980s, both China and Vietnam have placed armed forces on various of the islands, while the Philippines has also sent armed forces to the Spratlys. Conflict over the islands has included the displacement of one military force by another, including a brief naval battle between China and Vietnam in January 1988. In 1999, Vietnamese gunners fired on Philippines reconnaissance planes, while planes from the Philippines and Malaysia also engaged in a stand-off (Tiglao 1999). Mostly the claimants are concerned to secure fishing rights to the region as well as the rights to explore for oil and natural gas. In 1992 China signed a lease with an American oil company to drill for oil on some of the islands that are within waters claimed by Vietnam as part of its continental shelf, while in the following year Vietnam built a lighthouse on one of the islands. There is also concern that China in particular wants to claim the islands as a part of an extension of its authority further into the SEA region.

The Spratlys have been controversial because of the strength, sometimes vehemence, with which China, Vietnam and the Philippines have respectively laid their claims to sovereignty. Indeed, the Spratlys are probably the biggest point of contention between the member countries of ASEAN (Tiglao 1999). However, the Spratlys are uninhabitable, other than by constant externally supplied relief, and were historically uninhabited as a consequence. Fishermen may have visited the rocks in the past, but the legitimacy of each of the claimants is fragile. As a consequence of disputation over the islands, the ASEAN states agreed to try to seek a peaceful resolution to the problem, although at the beginning of 2000 this was yet to secure a concrete outcome (ASEAN 1976, 1992).

ASEAN

The Association of South-East Asian Nations (ASEAN) was founded in 1967 as a gesture of reconciliation between what had been somewhat antagonistic neighbours in the SEA region. Indonesia had, from 1963 to 1966, been engaged in its *Konfrontasi* with Malaysia (including Singapore), the Philippines disputed Malaysia's territorial claims to the latter's eastern reaches, and tensions had arisen between Malaysia and Singapore over the latter's expulsion from the Federation. Thailand and Malaysia also faced difficulties over the presence of Malaysian communists operating out of southern Thailand and Thai Muslim separatists finding haven in northern Malaysia. Each of these states had also experienced, or was still experiencing, a communist challenge,[4] which encouraged their respective strategic association with the United States.

It was also believed that mutual economic development by these states would contribute to political stability and help reduce or resolve domestic political unrest. By shoring up their economic and political position, these states also believed they would reduce the potential for outside involvement or interference in their domestic affairs.

A continuing focus for concern by the SEA states is China. By 1967, China had established itself as a significant actor in regional dissent. It had promoted predominantly ethnic Chinese communist parties in Malaysia and Singapore, supported the Communist Party of the Philippines (CPP), had close links with the PKI and had supported communist forces in the conflict in Indochina,[5] with which the ASEAN states were deeply concerned. ASEAN was also increasingly concerned over the role of the former USSR in the region, in particular in Vietnam and, by extension, Laos, although it did not formally regard the regional influence of the USA as problematic.

ASEAN has made a number of agreements on security, including the Bangkok Declaration of 1967, the Zone of Peace, Freedom and Neutrality (ZOPFAN) in 1971 and a further Declaration of ASEAN Concord and the Treaty of Amity in 1976. While these agreements reflect a particularly regional view of security matters, they did not imply consensus on how to deal with intra-regional security issues. There has been a longstanding view within ASEAN that internal matters are sovereign and should not invite the 'interference' of others, including other member states (preamble to ASEAN Declaration 1967).

The establishment of the ASEAN Regional Forum (ARF) in 1994 was a significant step towards the creation of an informal security alliance in the region, although on the surface it was intended only as a 'dialogue' group, and also included such 'dialogue partners' as the US, China, Japan, Russia and Australia (Lau 1997: 36). However, the agenda for ARF discussions, as well as chairing of the ARF, were dominated by the ASEAN partners. The key areas of interest for the ARF include confidence and security building, nuclear non-proliferation, peace-keeping cooperation, exchanges of non-classified military information, maritime security, preventative diplomacy and norms and principles regarding political and security cooperation (ARF 1994). The primary purpose of the ARF was to act as a 'preventative' forum, rather than as a forum that could respond after the event (Ball & Acharya 1999: ch. 6).

However, this view was increasingly challenged towards the end of the twentieth century, manifesting itself in a number of intra-regional disputes. There has been disagreement between Indonesia and the Philippines over views expressed in the Philippines about Indonesia's former occupation of East Timor and Thai criticism of more recent ASEAN member, Burma, over 'hot pursuits' into Thai territory. The Philippines has been critical of the treatment of Filipina workers in Singapore, and criticisms have been traded between Singapore and Malaysia over various minor matters, many of which seem to stem from the bitterness that came from Singapore's separation from Malaysia in 1965. Beyond this, there has also been widespread criticism from various sources in ASEAN states over the jailing of sacked Malaysian deputy prime minister, Anwar Ibrahim.

Further, there is no consensus within ASEAN about the role of external powers, in particular the US and its declining military role, under the Guam Doctrine of 1969, in both the Philippines and Thailand. To a lesser extent there was also lingering concern about the roles of Britain (which after 1968 was in practice reduced to zero), Australia and New Zealand (under the Five Power Defence Agreement of 1971). This latter association reflected a lingering unease with the strategic dominance of by far the largest ASEAN state, Indonesia, and a reluctance of the ASEAN states to enter into a formal military alliance with it.

A Malaysian proposal to secure the region's neutrality, presented to the Non-Aligned Summit in 1970, received a generally negative response from the US, the Soviet Union and China. Each state wished to play a more active role in the region at that time, although both the United States and the Soviet Union subsequently reduced their active participation in the region. Indonesia also opposed the proposal, on the grounds that it could imply a less negative corporate relationship with China which, at that time, the New Order government viewed with some hostility. However, with the US moving to redress its own hostility towards China, especially with the announcement in 1971 of President Nixon's visit to Beijing and China's resumption of its seat at the United Nations soon after, relations began to normalise. The Zone of Peace, Freedom and Neutrality (ZOPFAN) agreement the following year was a compromise response to the Malaysian proposal.

Given the commitment of ASEAN's founder states to an implicitly anti-communist position, it is not surprising that the member states found themselves ill at ease with Vietnam after the reunification of the state in 1975. While the ASEAN states were also ill at ease with Laos and Cambodia, after their successful communist revolutions in that same year, Laos was not perceived as presenting a threat, while Cambodia had closed itself off from all but the most limited external contact. At this time, ASEAN was tending to flounder, with no clear purpose and no unifying theme. This was to come at the end of 1978.

In December 1978, when Vietnam responded to Khmer Rouge provocation by invading Cambodia, installing the Heng Samrin 'puppet' government, the ASEAN states leapt to the forefront of international condemnation. Thereafter, the ASEAN states were not only the most vociferous critics of Vietnam but also they actively engaged in supporting the anti–Heng Samrin coalition, which referred to itself as the Coalition Government of Democratic Kampuchea (CGDK). The CGDK comprised a royalist party headed by ousted Prince Norodom Sihanouk and the Son Sann group comprising Lon Nol's republican government. But most importantly, it also comprised the Kampuchean Communist Party (the 'Khmer Rouge'), which had just been shown to have murdered or otherwise been responsible for the deaths of up to two million Cambodian people.

Regardless of the morality of ASEAN's support for the CGDK, this issue served to give the member states a diplomatic rallying point for the next decade.[6] Thailand in particular played an historical game of trying to offset Vietnamese influence in Cambodia, in this case by allowing CGDK units to operate from refugee camps along its border. During this time, Thai officials and businesspeople actively traded with CGDK officers who maintained bases in western and north-western Cambodia. The CGDK, in particular the Khmer Rouge, sold teak logs and gems in exchange for cash that was used to help finance their war with the Phnom Penh government and its Vietnamese allies.

While during the period of Vietnamese occupation of Cambodia ASEAN appeared united, there was actually considerable discord, primarily between Thailand and Indonesia. Thailand, sharing a border with Cambodia, had the most to lose from any potential spillover of the conflict. Similarly, Thailand had an historical interest in influencing events in Cambodia. However, Indonesia did not view the Vietnamese invasion with quite the same concern and, having finally thrown off the effects of its colonial heritage, instilled some respect for Vietnam in Indonesia. Further, at this time Indonesia was still highly wary of China's role in SEA and was not happy with China's active support for the Khmer Rouge, or the implications of its assault on Vietnam after the latter's Cambodian invasion. Tensions were generally kept below the surface, but when talks began to consider resolving the Cambodian situation, Indonesia played a far more active role than did Thailand, especially by hosting the Jakarta Informal Meetings.

By the time Vietnam's involvement in Cambodia had begun to de-escalate, from around 1988, the ASEAN states were mostly riding a wave of economic development. Increasingly the ASEAN states assisted in brokering a settlement, which contributed to the 1993 United Nations mission to hold general elections in Cambodia. Their intention, particularly Thailand's, was to bring peace to the region and, hopefully, engage in business. That this coincided with the collapse of the Soviet Union meant that the logic of the 'Cold War' no longer shaped regional thinking. This movement towards political settlement in Cambodia, the increasing marginalisation of the recalcitrant Khmer Rouge and alienation from its erstwhile allies and the liberalisation of the Vietnamese and Lao economies led ASEAN to the once unthinkable step of inviting Vietnam to join the organisation, which it did in 1995. Laos and Burma followed suit in 1997, although a bloody split between its coalition partners, just days before Laos and Burma joined, precluded Cambodia's inclusion. The initial failure of elections in July 1998 to satisfy the United Nations' concerns over the legitimacy of Cambodia's government further delayed its inclusion into ASEAN, although this was granted the following year.

CAMBODIA

Since its decline as a regional power, Cambodia has long been a battlefield for competing regional forces, in particular Vietnam and Thailand. It would be far too simple to suggest this was the state of play between 1978 and the end of the 1980s, when both countries were actively involved in Cambodia. But there were some historical memories at play when Vietnamese forces pushed the Khmer Rouge up to the Thai border region, which in turn prompted Thailand to unofficially support the Khmer Rouge. Beyond these two neighbouring powers, Cambodia has in recent times also attracted the interest of China, the former Soviet Union and the United States, each backing different factions within the country. In part this international involvement in Cambodia, and the disaster that was the Khmer Rouge era and its aftermath, induced these countries and others to broker an agreement to settle the conflict there.

While the relative success of the UN-arranged elections is now history, what has subsequently happened has been that, as in past times, Cambodia has in part become a collection of semi-independent warlord states (as it was under the Khmer Rouge, and perhaps before that). Military chiefs hold considerable power and a great deal of independence from the central government, although the structure of the Cambodian People's Party, which is deeply centralised, has limited some of their centrifugal tendencies. But like the former *mandalas* of the region, Cambodia seems only to be able to hold together under a relatively strong and centralised authority.

In one sense, however, Cambodia was more important for what it symbolised to the international community, in particular the depredations that could be caused by total civil war, and for the guilt inspired in so many external states for their contribution to that conflict. As a strategic site, however, Cambodia was a relatively safe place in which a number of states could battle each other by proxy, rarely risking their own well being. In that respect, Cambodia was strategically important only in that it provided a site for the release of aggression that could have been expressed elsewhere. By 1998, the international community appeared to have felt that its debt to Cambodia had been paid, beyond normal aid flows, and that the country now had to work out its own problems.

THE INFORMAL COALITION AGAINST CHINA

China looms large in the strategic thinking of SEA. It has always done so and, conceivably, always will. China has perhaps been less at the forefront of regional strategic thinking this century because of its own economic and military weakness, especially earlier in the century and because most of the regional states have been dominated by other external powers. However, as the states of the region have asserted their independence and consequently lost external protection they have become increasingly vulnerable to China's influence. It has even been suggested that China has used the overseas Chinese as an arm of its foreign policy, fomenting dissent and discord, if not revolution, in states it wished to influence.

China has also used its support for regional dissident movements to much the same effect (see, for example, Miller 1967; Roy 1998: 25–8). This can be most clearly seen in early revolutionary Vietnam, Indonesia pre-1966, Malaysia and perhaps Brunei, Thailand in the mid to late 1970s, Cambodia (especially under the governments of Democratic Kampuchea and the Coalition Government of Democratic Kampuchea), in Burma through the Communist Party of Burma, and in the Philippines through the Communist Party of the Philippines/New People's Army. It was not until 1978 that China's leader Deng Xiao Ping said that China would not interfere in the affairs of SEA states and even then, in some cases, this was more rhetoric than reality. But as the 1980s progressed, Chinese support for SEA communist parties disappeared, in part leading to the acceptance of amnesty by the Communist Party of Thailand in 1985, and the truce arrived at with the Communist Party of Malaya in 1989.

But the peoples and states of the region have a long historical memory. As already mentioned, there is a continued recognition that when China is weak its influence is limited, but when China is economically strong it asserts its authority more comprehensively throughout the region. China has been subject to a number of stumbling blocks in its development, from regional economic woes to untenable environmental problems, the inflexibility of the centralised state and, not least, its burgeoning and increasingly less sustainable population. But China has also posted growth rates of around nine per cent or more a year for the last decade of the twentieth century and was predicted to have the world's largest economy, in absolute terms, by the year 2050, along with its existing and growing population of more than 1.3 billion. This has not only positioned China as having the potential to threaten SEA, it has almost ensured that China will want to play a more active, indeed more dominant, role in regional strategic affairs.

To counter this, the states of SEA, informally defined through the ASEAN grouping, have begun to see themselves as constituting a cohesive and substantial bloc as a foil to Chinese strategic ambitions. The extremely poor relations between the Indonesian and Chinese governments in the wake of the anti-communist massacres in Indonesia from 1965 marked a turning point in the establishment of a regional anti-communist bloc. Similarly, China regarded ASEAN as a manifestation of US 'imperialism' (Roy 1998: 14–16; see also Schurmann & Schell 1968: 293, 358, 574–5, on China and the earlier, more strategic South East Asian Treaty Organisation). However, relations between individual SEA states and China have been normalising since 1974, with Indonesia finally re-establishing relations in 1990. The Indonesian government first recognised the communist government of China in 1950, but broke off diplomatic relations in 1967. Similarly, Singapore did not recognise the government in Beijing until 1990. In part, the slowness in formalising relations resulted from the Chinese government's insistence that the Communist Party of China should be able to maintain links with local communist parties even after establishing diplomatic relations. The logic of this was that the party and the government were separate entities. Since diplomatic relations have been restored, the ASEAN states have come to the view that contentious international issues such as China's relationship with Taiwan and its occupation of Tibet are China's domestic concerns (Roy 1998: 175–6, 179–80).

Vietnam showed that it was capable of mounting a strong defence against Chinese aggression[7] when the latter launched a 'punitive' invasion with more than 200 000 troops from 17 February 1979. The maritime states have the advantage of defence in depth, both being beyond the land-based states as well as raising issues of supply lines. The other states, Laos, Thailand, Burma and, to some extent, Cambodia, were far more vulnerable to possible Chinese manoeuvres. To that end, while the countries of the region have formed a sort of informal 'defence club', they have also embarked on a policy of incorporation.

China's incorporation into SEA was primarily commercial and economic, although a diplomatic element was also present. Acting both independently and with the encouragement of their ASEAN partners, both Laos and Burma have embarked on a course of developing cordial relations with China. In the case of Laos, this policy follows a period of relative isolation from China after the falling out between China and Vietnam. However, since the late 1980s and into the 1990s, Laos attempted to restore relations with its northern neighbour, both through diplomacy and trade. The trading element of the relationship was especially important for Laos, being a country with no sea borders and consequently being more reliant than most on having as much access by land as possible. A land route from Laos to China exists but, like many roads in Laos, it was a dry-weather road only. At the beginning of 2000, that road was in the slow process of being upgraded. Road links between Laos and China date back to the period of WWII and the anti-French conflict. However, the quality of the roads did not make them suitable for commercial traffic.

China and the ASEAN states have also presented something of a united front to the rest of the world over issues of government style. There is considerable consistency between the Chinese government's form of progressively more free-market one-party authoritarianism and opposition to liberalism and a number of regional governments. There is also considerable consistency between these states over issues of human rights, especially as identified by the UN and Western countries. China is also a member of the ASEAN Regional Forum (ARF), which includes it in SEA security discussions.

BURMA AND CHINA

Burma's relationship with China is particularly interesting. As noted, Burma has traditionally existed as a 'buffer state' between the two rival powers, China and India. Burma has had poor relations with both countries and, while it has not been invaded by either in recent times, it remains an ideal staging ground should open conflict between the two break out. In contemporary terms, India regards Burma as an international pariah, while China has actively defended Burma's interests in the United Nations (Roy 1998: 173).

After decades of regarding China as an ideological enemy and a significant threat, not least through its support of the Burmese Communist Party, since the late 1980s Burma has more actively pursued a policy of close diplomatic and economic cooperation with China. Indeed, sharing an extensive border, China is one of Burma's major trading partners and arms suppliers and each supports the other in diplomatic affairs, especially in relation to international criticism over human rights issues. In recent times, China has been supporting an economic corridor through Burma by constructing a road from Kunming in Yunnan to the Irrawaddy River port of Bhamo, which then provides access to the Bay of Bengal. China has also been upgrading its naval facilities on the Burmese coast, giving it access to both the Bay of Bengal and the strategically important Straits of Malacca[8] (Roy 1998: 174; Ball 1998: 219–26, 260; Olsen & Winterford 1996: 120).

There are still tensions between Burma and China, however, with Chinese investment in Burma displacing local Burmese, and some Chinese businessmen taking a less than gentle approach to cross-cultural relations. The Chinese government is also less than totally happy, especially with the flow of heroin and its associated problems into Yunnan as a point of dispersal (Roy 1998: 174).

Considering the strategic implications of the region, it is clear that there are numerous local issues that continue to tear at the fabric of peace and unity. Further, tensions both historic and contemporary continue to generate friction between the states of the region, none of which appears to be easily resolved. And given that SEA sits astride one of the major land and water crossroads of the world, there has long been and continues to be considerable international interest in local affairs. The states of SEA were perhaps at the beginning of the twenty-first century more able to determine their own futures than at any time since the eighteenth century. But in doing so, they needed to be cognisant of the fact that, unlike their world view of the pre-colonial era, in which petty kings thought themselves omnipotent and local emperors thought themselves gods, the states and their leaders are small players on the world stage. They were important in their own region, but their continued internal focus was being challenged by the reality that the world was becoming an increasingly integrated place. The twin pressures of local identity and globalisation presented new challenges to many of the states of the world. The states of SEA were at least as vulnerable as any to such challenges.

NOTES

1 While some Indonesian troops did land on the Malay Peninsula, most of the actual fighting (limited though it was) took place in northern Borneo. The southern parts of the island, known as Kalimantan, had passed from the Dutch to the Republic of Indonesia in 1949. But the states of Sabah, Sarawak and Brunei remained under British protection. That Brunei's sultan decided not to join the new federation of Malaysia did not alter Britain's commitment to defending the state against what it then regarded as external aggression (though which was probably more an expression of local political frustration).

2 Chartered Industries is linked to the Singapore Government and is run by a member of the family of former Prime Minister Lee Kuan Yew.

3 The ethnic Malays of southern Thailand mostly speak *Jawi*, a Malay dialect.

4 In each case this had comprised insurgencies, except for Indonesia where the PKI was an open and legitimate party until its destruction by the incipient New Order government.

5 It should be noted that China's contribution to the Second Indochina War was much less than analysts at that time had believed, and that during the 1960s China and Vietnam were increasingly retreating to their historical positions of mutual suspicion of and hostility towards each other.

6 My experience of this derived from being present at a number of media conferences held by ASEAN at the United Nations in 1983, as well as regularly reporting on Vietnam and its position *vis-à-vis* ASEAN in the latter 1980s for Radio Australia.

7   As a consequence, China's People's Liberation Army overhauled its 'human wave' methods of attack and moved to update its weaponry.

8   Ball notes that China's primary involvement in the Bay of Bengal is assisting Burma with intelligence gathering, and in undertaking some intelligence gathering, particularly of shipping, of its own.

Part II

5

Burma:[1] The Garrison State

The Burmese economy was in such disarray at the turn of the twenty-first century that even the Burmese government could no longer afford to change currency at its own official exchange rate of six kyats to the US dollar. Instead, it did what everybody else did who had hard currency, exchanging its currency on the black market, at about 320 kyats to the dollar.[2] However, the truly parlous state of the Burmese economy, along with the government's lack of faith in its own control over monetary mechanisms, meant that the kyat had a tendency to continue to slide in value, which boosted inflation, further damaging the economy. Given that conventional monetary control mechanisms didn't work in this out-of-control economic environment, when the government wanted to protect the kyat from further devaluation it sent troops into the black money markets to arrest the 'illegal' money dealers. Taking these money dealers out of the black market had the effect of restricting money supply, increasing the exchange rate and lowering inflationary pressure. It was a novel way of determining monetary policy and summed up the major elements of official Burmese political society: an almost non-existent formal economy, a rampant black market, government collusion, and the use of force for civil purposes.

This chapter looks at a range of political issues in Burma, including state unity versus national aspiration and identity, and the consequent historical and contemporary role of the military in this ethnically divided state. There will be an account of the collapse of the civilian state and its effective demise, and the eventual rise of the pro-democracy movement, including the role played by Aung San Suu Kyi as a symbol of that

movement. As Burma is the world's largest opium and heroin supplier, this chapter will also look at the opium trade as a source of income, both for separatist organisations and the government, the black market and other forms of economic development (or non-development). With the rise of the pro-democracy movement and continuing separatist movements, the chapter will also focus on the Rangoon government's crackdown on dissent, its international ostracism and its more recent move to join the Association of South East Asian Nations (ASEAN).

The government of Burma has, since 1962, been a classic military dictatorship. The country has been ruled by the military and, despite its claims to do so on behalf of the Burmese people, for the military. As with many other countries in which the military has a prominent role in politics, Burma's military played a leading role in gaining the country independence from its colonial master (in this case Britain), thereby moving some way towards institutionalising itself in the process of government. However, the diverse ethnic nature of Burma, or more accurately the incorporation of separate nations of peoples within a unitary Burmese state, has led to a constant conflict between these ethnic groups and the army, which has established for itself a role as 'guardian of the state'. While the military government rules without the support of the great majority of Burmese people, it is able to maintain its internal cohesion as a consequence of four characteristics. The first is the army's caste-like sense of identity, especially among the officer corps, while the second is a system of patronage by senior officers, which ensures loyalty and obedience even when ordered to fire on unarmed demonstrators. Thirdly, the military is almost the only means of gaining upward social mobility (Pedersen, Rudland & May 2000: 5), and fourthly, with such a large military, almost every family has a member who is in the armed forces. While Burma continues to be constructed of several separate nations under a constitution, as it is interpreted, which ensures ethnic Bhamese domination, the state will continue to be internally riven. This, in turn, means that the military will (or will want to) continue to play a prominent role in Burmese politics.

FOUNDATIONS OF THE STATE

The region now known as Burma has been continuously inhabited since at least 2500 BC, with settlements taking advantage of the rich alluvial plains fed by the Irrawaddy River system. The first group to consolidate control over the central part of the valley, from around the middle of the ninth century, was the Pyu, based in and around Pagan (see Htin 1967: 5–21). The Pyu practised Hinduism blended with Mahayana and, later, Theravada Buddhism (Cady 1958: 4–9). The Pyu were overthrown by invaders from what is now Yunnan in China in the tenth century AD, leaving the northern and central region without any coherent political control. Pagan's decline as a political capital was completed by 1289, with its sacking by the Mongols of Kublai Khan ushering in 250 years of chaos.

In the southern region, the Mon[3] settled in the region between the Irrawaddy and what is now western Cambodia from about the sixth century. After a series of skirmishes with the ascendant neighbouring T'ai,[4] the Mon established their capital at Pegu (about 70 kilometres north of Rangoon) (Htin 1967: 21–8). Around the late eighth or early ninth century, the Bhamese (a group related to the Tibetans) descended into the upper valley from the eastern slopes of the Himalayas. There they quickly supplanted the vanquished Pyu and battled with neighbouring Shans and other groups for dominance within the upper valley. These events set up the framework for competing ethnic divisions that have dominated Burmese politics to this day. By the end of the fifteenth century, the Bhamese had dominance over the northern Irrawaddy Valley and, in the following decades, entered into conflict with the Mon for control of the whole valley. It was not until 1555 that this conflict was settled in favour of the Bhamese, including the defeat of the neighbouring Thais in 1549. A high level of Mon–Bhamese antagonism from that time continues to exist between the two groups. To ensure the protection of the capital from recalcitrant Mons, the Bhamese retained the capital at Ava, moving to nearby Pegu and back again, depending on which king was in power (and which site was regarded as most secure and auspicious). This general location of the capital had the effect of removing the political elite of the state from significant coastal contact and encouraged a sense of cultural and economic isolation, and was a major contributing factor in leading to conflict with the British.

The Burmese state went into decline after the death of the king, Baynnaung, in 1581 and by the mid 1600s the authority of the state had retreated to its core. The hill tribes, including the Shan, began to raid the lowlands and the Mon broke away in the south, establishing a new kingdom at Pegu. In 1752 the Mon even succeeded in taking Ava, but that year a new Bhamese king, Alaungpaya, came to power in Shwebo, 80 kilometres north of Ava. Alaungpaya embarked on a reign of reconquest, destroying all who stood before the rebirth of the new state. Such was the seeming invincibility of Alaungpaya that the Konbuang Dynasty he founded believed that it could not be successfully challenged. When a

Bhamese general who had been installed on the throne of Chiang Mai in 1763 was overthrown soon after in a local rebellion, Alaungpaya's son Hsinbyushin commanded 30 000 (mostly Shan) soldiers to invade the principality. The Bhamese-commanded army then moved on to Luang Prabang (in modern Laos), assisted by troops from Vieng Chan. Having reduced Luang Prabang, they then prepared for an assault on Ayudhya (near what is now Bangkok). The Thai capital was laid to waste, its inhabitants killed, dispersed or led into slavery (Wyatt 1982: 134–7). It was to be the high imperial point of pre-British Burma, to which contemporary Burmese leaders look for cues for the post-colonial Burmese state.

COLONIAL HISTORY

By the early 1800s, the British had consolidated their rule over Assam and the eastern Islamic states of the Indian subcontinent, and established the Straits Settlements along the Malay Peninsula. However, there was British concern about growing French interest in the region (in Thailand[5] and later Indochina) and they wished to extend their authority to the eastern part of the Bay of Bengal. The British and their new South Asian subjects came into contact with the Burmese in Chin and Arakan states, especially over Burmese raids into British territory chasing 'disloyal' Burmese subjects. This gave the British the excuse they needed to extend their control. The British declared war in 1824 and, over the next two years, secured Arakan and the Tenasserim coast along the Thai border on the upper peninsula in the region of the Isthmus of Kra (Htin 1967: 210–32; Cady 1960: 68–74).

Still unaware of British power or intentions, the Burmese king at Mandalay neither improved defences nor engaged in constructive dialogue with the British. In 1852 two British sea captains were held at Rangoon, in lieu of paying a small fine for transgressing port rules, providing Britain with what it believed was sufficient pretext to launch its second offensive, this time occupying the whole of southern Burma. By this stage the Burmese king realised the thrust of British intentions and attempted to establish good relations. However, the firm establishment of the French in Indochina by the 1870s and the growth of French interest in northern Burma in the early 1880s decided the British course of action. In 1885 two events sealed Burma's independent fate. The first was commercial difficulties between the Bombay Burmah Trading Company and the Burmese administration at Mandalay. The second was the bad international publicity accorded a traditional though exceptionally bloody 'massacre of kinsmen' upon the succession to the throne of the new king, Thibaw. This latter event, in which a new king would have dozens, sometimes hundreds, of his relatives and acquaintances murdered to ensure no rivalry for the throne, horrified the newspaper-reading European public, leaving British public opinion in particular with little sympathy for the legitimising claims of the new king.[6] The British launched the third Burma War by sending gunboats up the Irrawaddy River to Mandalay, formally annexing the remainder of the state the following year and administering it from India. Over the next two years, the British crushed any sign of resistance to their rule. The indignity inflicted upon the state of Burma was such that the British established the capital of the colony at Rangoon, in the south, for better sea access, relegating the former capital of Mandalay to second city status, from which it has never recovered (Fisher 1968: 149–56; Htin 1967: 233–65; Cady 1958: 125–54).

THE COLONIAL PERIOD

Under the British, ethnic Indians moved in to southern Burma to take up junior administrative positions and to work the newly cleared swamplands, which were turned into rice paddies, while the Bhamese were relegated to second citizen status. By 1930 half the population of Rangoon was Indian. Commercial cropping turned the country into the world's rice basket, which paid for increasing imports, while new systems of land tenure and moneylending disrupted traditional social patterns. While the British administered 'Burma proper' directly, they formally acknowledged the separation of the 'frontier states', allowing a relatively high degree of autonomy based on ethnicity in the Chin, Kachin, Karen, Shan, and Kayah regions. It was from this recognition and consequent formalisation of 'national' difference that the 'frontier states' later sought to assert their independence from ethnic Bhamese domination.

While a Burmese sense of nationalism grew in the shadow of its Indian counterpart, in a practical sense it exceeded the nationalism of India. From as early as 1897 the British began to allow a degree of local autonomy, granting increasing degrees of self-rule and, in 1937, Burma's own cabinet, based on a parliamentary system. It was noted soon after that, with the exception of the Philippines, no imperial colony had more political autonomy than did Burma and that achieving independence was close (Fisher 1968: 446).

Burma enjoyed four popularly elected governments until it was invaded by Japan in 1941, as a part of the latter's strategic plan for WWII.

Prior to the Japanese invasion, though, there was considerable anti-British sentiment. For example, the student activist Aung San had opposed British colonialism and been arrested for his pro-independence activities. He and twenty-nine others, known thereafter as the 'Thirty Comrades', had fled to Japan in 1939 to receive military training, returning with the Japanese to lead the Japanese-backed Burma Independence (later National) Army (BIA). In a technical sense, by 1942 the BIA and the Japanese Imperial Army shared occupation of the state. However, as it became increasingly clear that Japan was losing the war, Aung San and the BIA switched sides, joining the British against Japan and thereby winning some legitimacy in the eyes of the British at the conclusion of the conflict (see Cady 1958: 427–84).

INDEPENDENCE

Aung San has been celebrated not only as the founding father of Burma, but also as a democrat (Silverstein 1993: 153–6), a mantle that his daughter wears to considerable political advantage. Aung San favoured elections through 'universal adult suffrage by secret ballot' (Aung San, Point 9: 'Fourteen Points', in Silverstein 1993: 69) and representation for ethnic minorities. But he was also a Burmese nationalist and was determined that the state remain united in what its ethnic minorities regarded, with considerable justification, as a unitarian rather than federal state under its ethnic Bhamese majority.

The Communist Party of Burma (CPB) also enjoyed considerable popular support at this time, but Aung San and his colleague U Nu systematically moved to have both its factions (White Flag and Red Flag) expelled from the umbrella party, the Anti-Fascist People's Freedom League (AFPFL)[7]. This was in order to avoid the likely prospect of a coalition government. The more fanatical Red Flag group was outlawed in July 1946 and went underground in 1947, with the White Flag following suit and declaring war on the state in the following year (Shwe 1989: 26–7). It was these two fields of division, over ethnic identity and ideology, which led to the conflicts that beset the state from the end of 1948 and which came, in large part, to shape the state to the present time. In any case, whatever moderating influence might have been claimed for Aung San which, in retrospect, accords him a more politically inclusive approach than his writings suggest, the rest of the Bhamese-dominated AFPFL was far less open to full political representation by Burma's communists and ethnic minorities[8] (Shwe 1989: 27–9).

In January 1947, Aung San reached agreement with Britain for independence to be granted a year later. In February 1947, representatives of all of the states of the proposed federation met at the town of Pin-Lon in Shan State to formulate the process of union. This 'Pinlon Treaty' was incorporated into the Constitution and allowed, under Chapter X, 'The Right of Secession' (with the exception of Kachin State) after ten years if the respective states so wished. With this agreement, Aung San formed a provisional government ahead of full independence the following year.

Before independence was granted, however, in July 1947, Aung San and six cabinet colleagues were assassinated by two men with automatic weapons. The political leader U Saw, who led an opposition movement to the AFPFL, was convicted of organising the murders and was duly hanged. Although the arms and vehicles used in the assassination were traced to the home of U Saw, where further stolen weapons were found, there remains a lingering doubt about his complicity or whether he acted alone. There have been suggestions that the assassination was in fact organised by a rival of Aung San within the military wing of the AFPFL, although some claims that this person was Ne Win plays rather too neatly into contemporary political divisions.

SEPARATISM AND ELECTIONS

Independence went ahead, being granted on 4 January 1948, with U Nu becoming prime minister. No sooner had independence been proclaimed, however, than Burma's ethnic minorities demanded independence and, upon refusal, rebelled against the Rangoon government, claiming (with considerable justification) that it had abandoned the inclusive form of government agreed to with the British and had reasserted chauvinistic Bhamese authority. The main insurgent groups were primarily based on the Arakanese, Chin, Kachin, Mon, Shan, and Karen ethnic groups, as well as the two communist parties, although subfactions coalesced and divided from the late 1940s onwards.[9] By the end of 1949, the insurgent groups were so successful and the Rangoon government so disorganised that almost the whole of the country was in the hands of one rebel group or another. This situation was further complicated by the defeat of the Chinese nationalist Kuomingtang (KMT) army by the Chinese communists in 1949. The remnants of the KMT 8th army and other KMT forces crossed from Yunnan province into southern Shan State between 1949 and 1952, from where they set up new bases. Not only were the KMT units well armed and located in remote regions, they were also supported by the US government, which hoped these military units would continue to keep the new Chinese communist government off balance. Instead, the KMT troops aided Karen rebels, and later turned to the lucrative opium growing business, establishing themselves as an effectively independent state within the state.

Over the following two years, the Burmese army (*Tatmadaw*), under the command of General Ne Win, wrested control of much of the state back from the insurgents. It was helped by their general disorganisation, poor tactics, the lack of unity among rebel groups and the two communist parties attacking the Karen National Union, the troops of which had at their most threatening advanced to within 16 kilometres of Rangoon. The communist groups attacked the Karen forces on the grounds that the Karens were splitting the state along ethnic lines, as claimed by U Nu and Ne Win, rather than along class lines as the communists advocated. This triangulation of the conflict weakened the anti-government groups, especially the Karen forces that were exposed and spread out along the Irrawaddy plain among its ethnic Bhamese inhabitants. The Karen forces subsequently retreated to the Burmese–Thai border, allowing the Rangoon government time to regroup. Meanwhile, the Arakanese rebels split between their nationalist and communist wings, further enhancing the position of the Rangoon government's forces (Shwe 1989: 30–1; see also Trager 1966: ch. 6). A government amnesty also weakened the anti-government forces, to the extent that by 1951 the government was able to hold elections in some parts of the country. The AFPFL was returned to government with a comfortable majority.

Elections were again held in 1956, returning the AFPFL in Bhamese-dominated areas, but nationalist or ethnic representatives in non-Bhamese regions. The period from 1956 until 1962 has been termed one of 'parliamentary democracy' (Shwe 1989: 31), at least in the Bhamese heartland. In this period the insurgencies were at a low ebb. However, non-Bhamese representatives in the parliament claimed that Burma was not a union of the eight states, as outlined in the Constitution, but rather a unitary state. The regional states received, but did not determine, local policy and the appointment of the head of each state required the approval of the prime minister.

The government of the 'Union of Burma' used the term 'Burma Pyima' to distinguish what the British had called the 'Burma Proper' region from what it had called the 'Frontier States'. However, the word 'pyima' means 'a centre of ruling, administration, civilisation and benefactors'. Similarly, the non-Bhamese states were referred to as 'pyinay', which denotes inferiority and subordination (Shwe 1989: 35). This

placed the non–Bhamese states in a peripheral and subordinate relationship to the Bhamese, which they deeply resented. As a consequence of
Bhamese rejection of a proposed 'Federation of Burma', in 1958, the
Shan representatives chose to secede from the 'union', as was their constitutional right as a result of the incorporation into the Constitution of
the Pinlon Treaty of Chapter X.

THE ARMY MOVES INTO POLITICS

While this further attempted secession of the 'Frontier States' could have
been a cause for Bhamese concern it was, in fact, brought quickly under
military control. At this time the AFPFL was more preoccupied by internal divisions. These divisions were based on personality clashes over the
distribution of power within the government, in particular between the
prime minister, U Nu, and the deputy prime minister, U Kyaw Nyein
(Shwe 1989: 37). As a result of the split, U Nu formed the Union Party,
while U Kyaw Nyein's group retained the name AFPFL.

Unable to command a majority in parliament, U Nu handed political power to a caretaker government headed by General Ne Win, to hold
fresh elections in 1960. In the meantime, however, Ne Win had presided
over the removal of the last vestiges of feudal rights of the Shan and Kaya
lords, which included a guaranteed seat in the National Assembly. He
also presided over the cession of territory to China, based on a Chinese
claim that dated back to Kublai Khan's occupation of Pagan in 1279.
This loss of territory especially affected the Wa National Area and Shan
State, which in response again attempted to secede as per Chapter X of
the Constitution.

Despite acquiring a taste for political power (Cady 1960: 32), the
army allowed Burma's third elections to be duly held in May 1960. U
Nu's Union Party won 159 of 250 seats, the AFPFL won forty-two seats
and forty-nine seats were distributed among state-based political parties.
The army waited in the wings, 'prejudicing' the survival of constitutional
government (Cady 1960: 34). While U Nu's government acceded to
some regional demands by creating the new states of Arakan, Mon and
Chin, to add to the existing Kachin, Shan, Kaya, and Karen states, their
demands for a federated state continued unabated. They also continued
to be rejected by the Bhamese majority. Added to the government
making Buddhism the state religion, protests and riots broke out, especially in Kachin State where Christianity was the majority religion, and
among Muslims. The Rangoon University Students Union and the All

Burma Federation of Student Unions demonstrated against the bill, while opposition parties and the military also expressed their displeasure.

To compound this political unrest, Burma's economy was stagnant while the population was increasing. From February 1962, leaders from the Kachin, Shan, Kaya, Mon, Arakan and Chin groups gathered in Rangoon to finalise their version of a proposed constitution for a Federation of Burma. On 2 March, Ne Win took advantage of the situation by arresting these leaders and launching a coup against the government, replacing the government with a Revolutionary Council of seventeen officers who ruled by decree. This set the stage for the subsequent institutionalised military domination of Burmese politics, with consequent domestic dissent, and the entrenchment of ethnic military opposition to the Rangoon government (Smith, M. 1999: 195–7; see also Trager 1966: ch. 9).

ISOLATIONISM

In his first major act in government, accusing the previous government of putting the nation's integrity at risk and abandoning socialism, Ne Win formulated what was called the Burmese Road to Socialism, which claimed to mix socialist and Buddhist ideas with a policy of isolationist self-sufficiency. At this stage, it could be argued that the army was acting at least in part on principle, even if that principle was misguided. This move towards 'socialism' reflected a high level of popular support for leftist ideas and disenchantment with parliamentary democracy, both for its corruption and for it being a legacy of imperialism. The Soviet Union at this stage looked like a suitable alternative model for economic development, although there was considerable concern about Stalin's influence on the Soviet model and its general rejection of religion (Shwe 1989: 86–7).

To implement its program of Burmese-style socialism, the army formed the Burma Socialist Programme Party (BSPP), which in 1964 became the only legal political party. Through the BSPP, a network of military-dominated councils administered the country, while the BSPP-controlled Peasants' and Workers' Council provided another avenue of political and social authority. Under the BSPP's program, some 15 000 private companies were nationalised, including foreign-owned companies, and international trade was severely limited. In response the economy, which was already in poor shape, atrophied. Meanwhile, some twenty-eight separate organisations formed to oppose the Rangoon government, most through military means (Smith, M. 1999: 219–27; Shwe 1989: 42–4). In July 1962, students at Rangoon University, protesting against strict new regulations, were met by around 2000 soldiers who, after a brief lull, fired on them, killing hundreds and arresting a further 3000 (Shwe, 1989: 47; Sesser 1993: 202–3). This event set the tone for BSPP rule for the next three-and-a-half decades.

As a result of instituting the 'Burmese Road to Socialism', between 1962 and 1987 Burma's economy had become a shambles. Rice production from the one-time rice-bowl of Asia dropped from 2 000 000 tonnes to 200 000 tonnes, with consequent food shortages for the first time in memory. In 1987 the BSPP admitted its poor economic management, and asked the United Nations for 'least developed country' status, making it eligible for additional foreign aid. As the per capita income was then about US$210 a year, this was granted. The formal acknowledgment that Burma had slid so far as to join the world's ten poorest countries came as a shock to the country's educated class, and did much to undermine confidence in the military government. Burma's black market economy was by this stage already well developed.

In September 1987, the Rangoon government took a further economic initiative that was both inexplicable and deeply damaging. In a claimed bid to curb inflation and wipe out the black market, the government demonetised the three highest bank notes, of 75, 35 and 25 kyats. This made worthless around fifty-six per cent of the money in circulation in Burma at that time. Given that most people kept their savings in cash, including most of the military and public service, and in particular the farmer parents of most of the army's soldiers (due to the difficulty in accessing bank accounts), this wiped out much of the savings of most Burmese. The now-worthless banknotes were replaced with the equally oddly denominated notes of 45 and 90 kyats, reflecting Ne Win's obsession with variations on the number nine. In so far as the move was intended to curb inflation, the effect was the opposite. With no public faith in the future of cash, people spent it as quickly as possible, pushing up the price of goods and increasing inflation.

DISSENT

The central Irrawaddy Valley was, for the most part, relatively peaceful from 1962 until the late 1980s, indicating more the BSPP's firm grip on power and the effectiveness of its intelligence (Ball 1998: 61) and security apparatus than satisfaction with its rule. However, among a number of relatively minor disturbances, there were two serious incidents in Rangoon that indicated that all was not well within the Burmese heartland. The first incident, in 1967, was anti-Chinese riots in response to a perception that China was attempting to export its Cultural Revolution to Burma. In this incident, hundreds of ethnic Chinese Burmese citizens were killed by other Burmese, although the riots were almost certainly instigated by the Rangoon government, which, at that time, had poor relations with China. The next major incident, seven years later, revolved around the death and funeral arrangements for the Burmese former secretary-general of the United Nations (1962–71), U Thant.

U Thant died in New York in 1974 and his family brought his body back to Rangoon for burial. Tens of thousands of people lined the road to pay their respects, the gathering of which worried the government. Ne Win also harboured some animosity towards U Thant, because of the latter's close association with Ne Win's predecessor, U Nu. The government wanted a quick funeral at the Kyandaw Cemetery, but students and monks removed the coffin from the hearse at Kyaikasan Stadium, where it had been in state, and took it to Rangoon University, where it was draped with the banned Student Union's 'fighting peacock' flag. Four days later, on 7 December, the army attacked the university, killing 135 students and arresting thousands more. The student union building, a symbol of Burmese nationalism since the 1930s, was dynamited at midnight that night. U Thant's body was exhumed from the university grounds and buried by the government in a rough mausoleum near the Shwedagon Pagoda in central Rangoon (Shwe 1989: 50–3; Sesser 1993: 203–4).

In 1976, there was a falling out between the then defence minister, General Tin Oo and Ne Win, with the former being sacked from his position and jailed for four years. Tin Oo was allegedly aware of a plan to assassinate Ne Win, but did not report it. Tin Oo later joined the National League for Democracy (NLD), becoming one of its leaders, along with another former Ne Win associate, Aung Gyi. Aung Gyi resigned from his powerful position in the army when Ne Win seized power and moved towards socialism. He was jailed for three years in 1965 and again, briefly, in 1988. Aung Gyi broke with the NLD in 1989, saying that he had always been close to Ne Win, despite having twice been jailed, and accused NLD leaders Tin Oo and the daughter of Aung San, Suu Kyi, of being associated with 'communists'. It is possible that Aung Gyi reached an accommodation with Ne Win, probably in the mid to late 1980s, and was planted by him to discredit the opposition. Within the NLD, a distinction in political style began to emerge, which has subsequently evolved into a type of factionalism. Tin Oo led a more conservative and somewhat more accommodating group within the NLD to that of Suu Kyi, and was seen as pressing this group's claims to a less confrontational style with the Rangoon government. The basic difference has been over tactics, with Tin Oo's group supporting accommodation with the government and Suu Kyi's group in favour of confrontation. The ethnic separatist groups, meanwhile, have tended to regard both accommodation and unarmed confrontation as non-viable options, preferring instead to remain outside the formal Burmese political system.

THE ARMY AGAINST THE PEOPLE

After years of repression, the demonetisation of the three bank notes pushed many people into public protest. A general mood of dissatisfaction was clearly building. Then, in March 1988, a seemingly innocuous fight in a tea shop over music selection sparked a major upheaval. The police came and arrested the participants in the fight, clubbing one to death in the process. Dozens more were left locked in police vans for hours in the midday heat, as a result of which forty-one people suffocated to death. A protagonist in the original brawl was released without charge; as it turned out he was the son of a senior BSPP member. This sparked more protests, which quickly turned into riots. The death toll rose into the hundreds. Then, on 21 June, a student protest at Rangoon University was attacked by police. Hundreds more were killed. In a public response to these events, General Ne Win resigned as chairman of the BSPP and as a member of the party. However, as with his retirement as president in 1981, he continued to hold power from behind the scenes.

Ne Win's replacement was General Sein Lwin, who had directed the dynamiting of the student union building at Rangoon University, the bloody assault on students after U Thant's death, and the attacks on students in March 1988. For this he was known as 'The Butcher' and, not surprisingly, was an unpopular choice as public leader (Lintner 1990: ch. 1). Within weeks of Sein Lwin taking office, tens of thousands of Burmese were protesting in the streets in Rangoon and Mandalay and, between 8 and 13 August, soldiers firing in formation on peaceful, unarmed protesters killed at least 2000 people (Lintner 1990: 94–105). On 19 August, Ne Win replaced Sein Lwin with the civilian Maung Maung, who had been attorney-general in Ne Win's cabinet and who was regarded as more conciliatory. Although still a Ne Win loyalist, Maung Maung announced there would be elections, held under the auspices of the military government. Opposition leaders rejected the proposal, saying that Maung Maung should resign and that a non-military interim government should oversee the election process.

With no movement from the government, protesters again spilled into the streets, now demanding immediate democratisation. The daughter of assassinated Burmese leader Aung San, Suu Kyi, had recently returned from England to care for her ailing mother. Although she had no political background, as a symbol of Burma's initial aspirations for democracy she was immediately pushed into the forefront of the protest movement, being appointed general secretary of the NLD, a position that she took up with great enthusiasm. The protest movement had grown beyond students and monks and now included professionals, workers and even government officials. A general strike was called, which received popular support. The protest movement was now a strong expression of widespread, popular opposition to the government. Government administration ground to a standstill and, after initially taking no action, soldiers began to uncoil barbed wire barricades in the streets of Rangoon. Burma's newspapers, long subject to strict censorship, began to publish articles critical of the government. By 19 August the protesters controlled Burma's second city of Mandalay. It was two years after the Philippines so-called 'People's Power' revolution which ousted dictator Ferdinand Marcos. However, as so widely misunderstood elsewhere, those who took courage from the Philippines movement failed to acknowledge or understand that it was the military, in alliance with a disaffected elite, which eventually toppled Marcos, not the people. Without the army on side, in similar circumstances such an event could not be repeated.

THE ESTABLISHMENT OF THE SLORC

To destabilise this difficult situation, from 21 August Ne Win had Rangoon's prisons emptied. The resulting upsurge in crime included widespread looting, which was joined by ordinary but desperate Burmese. Vigilante committees were established, which themselves acted with violence against suspected criminals and government agents. On 18 September, the BSPP government was dissolved, being replaced by the State Law and Order Restoration Council (SLORC), with the 1974 Constitution being suspended and martial law being declared. The SLORC differed from the BSPP primarily in that it brought all government institutions under the direct control of the *Tatmadaw*, rather than through the military's influence but not control over the party, and allowed for substantial increases in military spending. The *Tatmadaw* effectively doubled in size between 1990 and 2000, and its budget was estimated to consume up to half of total government spending (Callahan, in Pedersen, Rudland & May 2000: 23, note 1).

All state bodies were abolished and their place was taken by representatives of the SLORC (see Smith, M. 1999: 365–73). The SLORC was headed by close Ne Win associate, General Saw Maung, who had previously been defence minister and, since 1985, army chief of staff. The SLORC ordered striking workers back to their jobs, outlawed demonstrations and banned gatherings of more than four people. The following day the bloodbath began. That morning, as protesters moved into the streets, soldiers positioned on bridges and the tops of buildings opened fire on the crowds. In what has been described as an 'ambush' (Sesser 1993: 220), thousands upon thousands of Burmese citizens were killed by their own army.

Perhaps believing their own propaganda, the military-dominated Rangoon government believed that it was sufficiently popular, or had sufficiently rigged the prospective electoral system, that it could now go ahead and actually hold general elections, which it believed would legitimise its rule. Even if the elections had produced a more even division of support for the contesting parties, the SLORC was of the view that it could at least broker a deal that would see the army as the only 'unifying' factor in Burmese politics and hence ensure its continuation in power.

The elections were held in May 1990, but were hampered by restrictions placed on political activities and the arrest of NLD leaders Suu Kyi and Tin Oo, along with the head of the Liberal Democratic Party, U Nu. Contrary to the SLORC's (clearly misguided) expectations, though, the elections were overwhelmingly won by the National League for Democracy. Despite massive vote rigging and electoral fraud by the government, the NLD took 392 of the 485 seats. The BSPP, renamed the National Union Party, won only ten seats. Initially saying they would hand over power, the military refused to acknowledge the results of the elections. When protests ensued, soldiers shot dead hundreds of protestors, including killing some parliamentarians held in custody, and in the following year placed Suu Kyi and other NLD leaders under house arrest (Smith, M. 1999: 412–19).

In 1991 the NLD was barred from political activity. In April 1991, the SLORC formally announced that it would not transfer power to the civilian opposition. In October that year, Suu Kyi was awarded the Nobel Peace Prize, inspiring further protests, the closure of universities and the banning of more political parties. To illustrate the SLORC's alienation from the Burmese people, in Mandalay, in 1992, a protest by Buddhist monks over the government's failure to honour the election results was met by rifle fire, with more than 600 protestors shot dead. Buddhism is highly revered across all strata of Bhamese society, as are its monks. Attacking Buddhist monks was an extreme sign in Burmese society, even for the SLORC, that there was no longer even the faintest resemblance between its rule and notions of political legitimacy.

SUU KYI AND THE NLD

By this stage there was a high level of international concern over events in Burma. The increasingly brave and highly quotable Suu Kyi was lauded by the international media as symbolising honourable opposition to an evil government. In 1991 Suu Kyi won both the Nobel Peace Prize, for what the committee described as 'one of the most extraordinary examples of civil courage in Asia in recent years', as well as the European parliament's Sakharov Prize for freedom of thought. In 1992 Suu Kyi was awarded the Simon Bolivar prize for freedom.

Suu Kyi was released from house arrest in 1995, but kept under the very close eye of the government. The NLD was allowed to hold its ninth anniversary meeting in September 1997, which was seen by some as a concession by the government to the NLD. However, later talks between government representatives and some NLD leaders were regarded as a government attempt to split the NLD. The talks were aimed at having some NLD members cooperate with the government, in exchange for some possible political freedom. Suu Kyi did not agree to such cooperation, leading to division between herself and Tin Oo.[10]

Like other members of the NLD, after being released from house arrest, Suu Kyi's movements were, in theory, free but in practice very limited. Apart from being watched at all times, her freedom of movement was restricted by the government's insistence that she be 'protected' by armed guards and that she not be allowed to move around Burma without first notifying the government. What this did was inhibit her movement on a number of occasions, perhaps the most celebrated of which was a stand-off on a bridge in southern Burma in July 1998. Suu Kyi and her driver had attempted to visit some NLD members, but were stopped on a road about 64 kilometres south of Rangoon. Suu Kyi refused to leave her car and a stalemate ensued. Six days later, after much negative international publicity, government officers forced her driver from the car and drove her back to Rangoon. The government had broken the deadlock, but the incident had only served to focus further international attention on the repressive nature of the Rangoon government (Skehan 1998a). A similar event took place in September 2000.

While the general approach of the Rangoon government appeared consistent, there were also changes at the top levels of government. In April 1992 General Saw Maung had 'stepped down'[11] as head of SLORC, to be succeeded by General Than Shwe, who also assumed the position of prime minister. However, the head of intelligence, General Khin Nyunt, was widely seen as a more powerful proxy figure, being a protégé of Ne Win. A major achievement of Khin Nyunt was to purge the National Convention of dissident voices to allow the armed forces to push through acceptance of the idea of a draft constitution, in January 1994, which enshrined the leading political role of the armed forces (with twenty-five per cent of all seats in the legislature). It would have also removed the armed forces' financial allocation from the budgetary process. That Constitution was not yet ratified at the end of 2000. The proposed constitutional incorporation of the armed forces in the political process also corresponded to the political and security 'dual function' of Indonesia's armed forces. The accession of Generals Than Shwe and Khin Nyunt also led to a change in political and military tactics on the part of the Rangoon government. In 1992, confident of its political control, the SLORC began to release political prisoners, and lifted martial law restrictions (Smith, M. 1999: 425).

THE SLORC AND ETHNIC SEPARATISTS

With the NLD seemingly limited in its ability to oppose it, the SLORC turned its attention to the root of the political problems in Burma: the ethnic insurgencies. The SLORC's first action was to launch an all-out offensive against the Karen National Liberation Army, which was supported by the All Burma Students' Democratic Front. The government then focused its attention on other insurgencies, in particular that which gripped Shan state, large sections of which had fallen under warlord control. The most powerful of these was the Mong Tai army, formerly led by the opium baron Khun Sa. The Burmese Communist Party (BCP) also constituted a major insurgency problem, although its split in 1989 and subsequent abandonment by its Chinese sponsors as they improved relations with the Burmese government led it to become ineffectual. Remnants of the BCP have subsequently regrouped under four other ethnic organisations (Smith, M. 1999: 421).

The following year the SLORC made its first major breakthrough in its battle against separatists, by signing a cease-fire agreement with Kachin Independence Army/Organisation (KIA/O), which was at that time regarded as the most significant anti-government group. This had followed an earlier, but far less important, cease-fire agreement with the Shan State Progressive Party in 1989, and the Pa-O National Union and Palaung State Liberation Party in 1991. The Kayan New Land Party (KNLP) followed the KIA/O ceasefire in 1994, with the New Mon State Party also signing a cease-fire, in 1995. These agreements freed up government troops to focus on Karen and Shan rebels, who were increasingly driven from their bases to the border regions. The situation was further complicated by a split within the Karen ranks over religious differences, with the nominally pro-government Democratic Karen Buddhist Army attacking the predominantly Christian Karen National Union and the Karenni National Progressive Party. The combined strength of these two latter organisations had fallen to less than 10 000 by the late 1990s (Nussara 1997).

In 1996, the Rangoon government had another breakthrough, signing a peace agreement with Mong Tai Army leader Khun Sa. Apart from leading the Shan-based Mong Tai Army, Khun Sa was also the most notorious, and probably the second largest, opium and heroin producer in the world. After the peace agreement, Khun Sa quickly settled in Rangoon, on the shore of Inya Lake near Lieutenant-General Khin Nyunt and on the same street as Ne Win. In Rangoon, Khun Sa established a large business network including mining, transport and agriculture and was believed to be perhaps the largest single holder of wealth in the country. Khun Sa also maintained close relations with the chairman of the State Peace and Development Council (the successor to the SLORC) and commander-in-chief of the armed forces, Senior General Than Shwe, as well as Khin Nyunt (Ball 1999).

Other deals were believed to have been struck with erstwhile separatist groups that allowed them to continue their production and trade of opium and heroin, with a proportion of profits being channelled back to government and military officials. The Rangoon government has since refused to extradite Khun Sa to the US (*The Irrawaddy* 1998b), where he is wanted on drug smuggling charges.

But despite the agreement reached between Khun Sa and the Rangoon government, most of the MTA decided that it had not reached any agreement that assisted the Shan people. To that end and after a brief lull, the bulk of the Mong Tai Army reformed as the Shan United Revolutionary Army and later as the Shan State Army, resuming its battle against the Rangoon government. Smaller breakaway groups, the Shan States National Army and the United Nationalities Shan States Army, were also said to have rejoined attacks on the Rangoon government's troops. From early 1999, there were reports in Bangkok that the Burmese army had launched a major offensive against Karen rebels, who were said to be attempting to sabotage the Yadana oil and gas pipeline from southern Burma to Thailand. According to the *Bangkok Post* (6.1.1999: 1), the Burmese army assault was financed by the main oil companies involved in the construction of the pipeline, the French company Total and the US company Unocal. The two companies denied their support for the military operations.

A total of seventeen ethnic armed groups had signed cease-fire agreements with the Rangoon government by the end of the 1990s, with four holding out. However, the cease-fires were military and did not offer political solutions to continuing problems (Pedersen, Rudland & May 2000: 10). A number of the ethnic military groups, including the United Wa State Party (Army), the New Mon State Party, KNLP and the KIA/O, subsequently broke with the Rangoon government and pursued an independent or oppositionist line. The main complaint by them, which led to the renewed hostilities, was that their cease-fire agreements had been abrogated by *Tatmadaw* troops, who continued to abuse the ethnic minorities. Common complaints against the army included the use of these people as slave labour, rape, looting and arbitrary executions (*The Irrawaddy* 1998b). In the middle of 1999, five ethnic groups had formed an alliance to fight the central government. They were the Karen National Union, the Shan State Army, the Arakan Liberation Party, the Kerenni National Progressive Party and the Chin National Front (*The Irrawaddy* 2000a: 14).

OPIUM AND HEROIN

Apart from Burma's extremely poor human rights record—it is widely regarded as the worst of any existing government in the world—the other main issue that marked it as an international pariah was its involvement in the illegal production of opium and heroin. Burma is the world's biggest supplier of opium, accounting for more than sixty per cent of the world's production of the drug. The views on who produces what vary widely, but it was known that most if not all of the independence groups or former independence groups engaged in the production and sale of opium to finance their battle against the Rangoon government. Further, many ethnic peasants in the hill areas also grew opium as a cash crop, as it is both simple to grow and, unlike many other crops, well suited to the hill terrain.

But there was also significant international concern about the informal and probably formal involvement of the Rangoon government in the opium and heroin trade. At one level, it was widely believed that non-commissioned officers were actively involved in the growing and distribution of opium. At another level, there was belief that the government itself was involved in the opium business, despite the fact that the government had, at least on the surface, begun a crackdown on opium production. For example, in 1996 the Rangoon government publicly burned seized opium to show that it was serious about eradicating it. However, the amount—504 kilograms—was regarded as very small. Almost twenty-three tonnes of opium had been claimed as seized by the Rangoon government between 1988 and 1997, along with almost four tonnes of heroin (Embassy of the Union of Myanmar 1998b).

It was probable that the destruction of the opium crops or stores was primarily if not solely aimed at non-government or anti-government groups, including opium production by ethnic rebels. Many of the people officiating at the 1996 opium burning were 'up to their necks in unofficially promoting production and trade' (*Thailand Times* 1997). Burma's army commander, Major General Maung Aye, for example, had a business arrangement with drug baron Kyaw Win and Thai timber tycoon Choon Tangkakarn, who ran logging operations out of Khun Sa's territory. Kyaw Win later established the May Flower Trading Company and May Flower Bank, which was the only bank to have a foreign exchange licence. From being near bankruptcy in 1995, business was booming by 1998. Kyaw Win also purchased the loss-making Yangon Airways and introduced new air routes, including to the drug towns of Lashio and Mergui and the conduit town at the crossroads of the 'Golden Triangle',[12] Tachilec. The timing of these events was associated with Khun Sa's move to Rangoon (Davis & Hawke 1998). Lin Mingxian, another major opium lord, also enjoyed the protection of the Burmese government, being based in Rangoon. Heroin purchasers had open access to northern Burma, with military assistance with transshipment, in exchange for ten per cent of the purchase price of the drugs.[13]

The secretary-general ('Number One') of the government party, the State Peace and Development Council (SPDC) (number three in the party), Lieutenant-General Khin Nyunt, arranged most of the cease-fire agreements with the ethnic armies, through which they were allowed to continue or expand their opium and heroin production. It was Khin Nyunt who brokered agreements with the Kokang Chinese, allowing Lo Hsing-han to ship their heroin to Tachilec on the Thai border. He also brokered agreements with the Shan State Revolutionary Party, the Wa armies and the Kachin Independence Army. It was believed that Khin Nyunt had personally benefited from these arrangements. Further evidence to support the claim of the government's involvement in the international drug trade appeared strong. The (renamed) Kachin Defence Army, for example, delivered opium from the north-east of Burma to Manipur in India, securing their passage with government issued 'special permits' (Davis & Hawke 1998). Another main route for opium was through the Chinese town of Kunming, in Yunnan province, which had increasingly replaced smuggling routes through Thailand (*The Irrawaddy* 1998b).

Khun Sa's second son, Sam Heung, took over running Khun Sa's old operation near the Thai border (Davis & Hawke 1998), where he conducted his drug trade with the assistance of the army commander of Ho Mong (north-west of Chiang Mai), Brigadier-General Chit Maung.

Probably until his 'retirement', the world's biggest opium baron and warlord was Lo Hsing-han. Lo left the Kokang hills of Lashio, north of Mandalay, in 1973 for seven years in prison and then a pardon. He now has a 'gracious home' in Rangoon, from where he ran 'one of Myanmar's largest business conglomerates—Asia World—with interests in real estate, manufacturing, export–import and construction that includes key infrastructure projects' (Davis & Hawke 1998). Lo had a ten per cent share of Rangoon's five-star Trader's Hotel, along with Singaporean investors, while his son, Steven Law, made regular business trips to Singapore (although he was banned from the US due to his drug connections).

Since the diversification of Khun Sa and Lo Hsing-han into superficially legal businesses, Burma's biggest drug lord has been Lin Min-Shing, who operated out of Mong La opposite the Chinese border of Yunnan. In this, he and others were helped by and shared in the drug business with senior army officers. 'In addition to his heroin interests, Khin Nyunt has recently acquired shares in five amphetamine laboratories in areas controlled by Lin Min-shing near Mong La' (Ball 1999). The SPDC's second secretary (and number four in the Rangoon government), Lieutenant-General Tin Tun, was part-owner of two heroin refineries at Murng Kerng and Kesi in central Shan State. Commander of the South-East Command (Moulmein) and previously tactical operations commander in the Mong Ton area of the 'Golden Triangle', Brigadier-General Myint Aung, was paid large bribes for his protection of heroin refineries. Numerous other regional military commanders and their battalions either conducted, protected or taxed heroin production of some of the largest refineries which are located along both the Indian and Thai borders (Ball 1999).

United States Assistant Secretary of State Robert Gelbard stated that Burma was a minor opium producer when the army came to power in 1962, but that it agreed to allow opium growing in exchange for peace in the frontier areas. Further, he said, since SLORC was formed in 1988, Burma's production of opium had doubled. The US State Department estimated that heroin production in Burma had risen from a little more than fifty tonnes a year in the late 1980s to an average of more than 150 tonnes a year since 1989 (US Department of State 1996). Gelbard said that the government had become involved in the opium trade both through turning a blind eye to it as well as by allowing or encouraging money laundering from opium sales. Gelbard cited the example of the United Wa State Army (UWSA) as a major heroin producer. The UWSA and the Myanmar National Democratic Alliance Army of Kokang, also a major heroin producer, comprised troops who had formerly served with the Communist Party of Burma, but had been allowed to trade freely in heroin since leaving the CPB (Lintner, in Pedersen, Rudland & May 2000: 168, 170). The UWSA in particular had wrested control of a significant part of the opium and heroin trade from remnants of the KMT troops based in Burma and other rebel ethnic groups, and then signed a cease-fire agreement with the Rangoon government. Gelbard called the UWSA 'East Asia's largest heroin trafficking organisation', saying it was allowed to buy property in Rangoon as a means of investing its illegally gained money (AFP 1996; also Davis & Hawke 1998). As well as the production of opium and heroin, these drug producing organisations were increasingly moving into the manufacture of amphetamines and hallucinogens (notably Ecstasy).

Beyond allowing former insurgent groups to produce and traffic in heroin and other drugs, the Rangoon government allowed profits from heroin sales to be laundered through the country's poorly regulated banking system. This turning of a blind eye to heroin profits stemmed at least in part from the government's desperate need to bring into the country hard currency to prop up its ailing economy (see Lintner, in Petersen, Rudland & May 2000). Under this 'blind-eye' system, funds could be deposited in Burmese banks on payment of a thirty per cent tax, a figure that declines during periods of amnesty if certified by the government as 'investment for national development'.

In response to international pressure, the Burmese government announced in 1999 that it had cleared 1386 hectares of opium poppy between September 1998 and February 1999, amounting to 15.25 tonnes of opium. Burma's senior anti-drugs officer, Colonel Kyaw Thein, also announced that 371 tonnes of opium had been destroyed over the preceding decade (probably from non-government linked areas). At the same time, the government announced a new fifteen-year program to end opium production in Burma, to begin in the year 2000. A number of other countries, however, did not take the promise seriously, and a European Union delegation refused to attend the meeting at which these claims were made (AFP 1999b). The director of Interpol's criminal intelligence unit, Paul Higdon, attended the meeting and later said that the Burmese government had to allow the drug trade to flourish in order to first bring under control its insurgency problem. 'Before the government could do anything with heroin, they had to do something with insurgencies,' he said. 'Sometimes you have to make a pact with the devil.' (AFP 1999a). Higdon also endorsed the Burmese government's existing anti-drugs campaign. Some observers wondered aloud about the reasoning behind Higdon's comments and, presumably, Interpol's position.

ECONOMY

It would seem rational for Burma's military to be primarily concerned about the continuing insurgencies in various parts of the country and the general sense of opprobrium felt towards it by both its own population and the international community. But the issue most preoccupying the minds of its leaders was the state of the economy. Even this would seem to make sense, especially given that much of the disaster that was the Burmese economy was a direct result of both Burma's relative international isolation and the structural inability of its citizens to engage in meaningful international trade. This was exacerbated by the downturn in East Asian economies in 1997–98, especially in South Korea, which was claimed by sources in Burma to have been a major supplier of bartered fuel oil.

However, the military's concern was not so much with the poor shape of the economy, for state reasons, but with the fact that the economy had finally become so parlous that it had the potential to affect the operations of the military itself. The state is subservient to the needs of the army, and if the army could not organise the state to meet the army's needs then it has failed in its primary objective. This led to divisions within the armed forces over economic policy and management and offered the greatest scope for some sort of rapprochement. The divisions, such as they existed, were between older, hard-line 'isolationists' and those eager to integrate into ASEAN and the international economy.

The 'isolationists' had the upper hand at the end of the twentieth century, being able to cite the downturn in the East Asian economies as proof of the unreliability of international economic engagement. However, a younger, more outwardly focused generation of officers saw the downturn as a temporary phenomenon in an otherwise broad tendency towards economic growth. Although losing the first round of the battle over policy, the younger officers had on their side the likelihood that the East Asian economies would repair themselves and continue to grow, as well as the impetus from the initial move towards greater economic openness. They also had time on their side, with the 'independence' generation of officers reaching the end of their life expectancy.

There was also concern both in Burma and abroad that there was considerable corruption at the higher levels of the military, with five per cent skimmed off from most major international deals. The change of government from the SLORC to the SPDC in 1997 cleaned up some of the more corrupt officers, but had little real impact on corruption overall or, more importantly, on investor confidence. 'On the contrary, many investors are pulling out of Burma, partly as a result of the regional crisis but also because they have found it impossible to conduct business in the country' (Lintner 1998).

As indicated at the outset, Burma's economy was, apart from heroin production, deeply disorganised and functioning extremely poorly. While it retained significant economic potential, nearly all of that has either been squandered or left unrealised by its military government. There was some economic liberalisation in the 1990s, but this was relatively superficial and had little impact on the lives of ordinary people. Perhaps the most obvious sign of this freeing up of the economy has been the importation of new cars and trucks, supplementing the ancient road transport that had served the country since the 1950s. One of the main reasons why the 'liberalisation' of Burma's economy has not had much impact on ordinary people is because almost all foreign investments are in joint ventures with the Union of Myanmar Economic Holdings Company. The UMEHC was run by the Defence Department's Directorate of Procurement. Other estimates suggest that close to half of Burma's gross domestic product, with the most obvious investments in real estate and with links to the government, was taken up by cash flows generated by the illegal heroin trade.

Perhaps the most important aspect of Burma's economy, apart from its mismanagement, was the fact that the government spent around forty per cent of its budget on the armed forces. The government deficit towards the end of the 1990s was, by comparison, at around twenty per cent of the budget. This is a figure that in most countries would be regarded as unsustainable. Because of its appalling economic management and its even worse human rights record, Burma has been banned from access to funding through the International Monetary Fund and the World Bank, and from export credits and investment protection insurance. Needless to say, there is no open debate allowed about Burma's economic management or direction.

To complicate Burma's parlous economic state, the country had and looked set to retain a grossly inadequate infrastructure, with particular reference to electricity. There were regular power failures throughout Burma, including Rangoon, with power out in some areas all the time and in a number of areas, such as Mandalay, about half the time. This appeared to be increasing as the government was unable to afford diesel fuel to operate its power generators, while hydroelectricity was down due to low water volumes as a consequence of the El Niño effect/drought. The exploitation of natural gas in the Gulf of Martaban could go some way towards redressing the energy problem from the early years of the twenty-first century. However, most of the gas was to be shipped to Thailand and the profits were to go to the controlling companies, Unocal of the United States and Total of France, with Burma's share intended to help service debt repayments. Like Burma's other attempts to exploit existing resources, such as timber and fisheries, there was no environmental impact assessment made. The impact on these geographic areas has been, in most cases, devastating.

Further, government export figures were grossly inaccurate. Government bureaucracy was severely bloated, inefficient, labyrinthine and held no real power in terms of decision making. Government responses to requests were usually to say 'no', as it was too difficult to actually do anything. Further, there was always the risk that any active policy could step on the toes of another government service, or military person, which could have serious repercussions for the individual concerned.

Government employees were unable to live from their meagre salary, so engaged in other businesses, usually to the detriment of government work. The economy was, in effect, the black market. In Rangoon the black market competed openly with the legal market, though it probably has an advantage in terms of consumer goods and access to other more modern requirements, such as medicine. Mandalay was, in effect, a black market town, being a hub for trade throughout northern, western and eastern Burma. An especially large amount of goods came in through Yunnan province in China, which had considerable ethnic crossover with the Kachin and Shan states. Many goods were significantly cheaper than they are even in those countries in which they were manufactured, especially drugs/medicine and electrical goods. This seemed to imply that much of the goods for sale in Mandalay were not just smuggled into the country, but they were the end result of highly organised theft, piracy or, more probably, the cross-border drug trade. In Shan state, the black market was even more rampant, with the border town of Tachilek selling everything that it was possible to pay money for. The cured skins of leopards and elephant tusks vied for business with a huge range of consumer goods and, only just off the shop counters, all sorts of guns and vast quantities of opium and heroin. It was across the bridge from Tachilek into the boom-town of Mae Sai in Thailand that most of the world's opium used to travel and over which drug battles had been fought. Though large quantities were still shipped across the river further upstream it was still an extraordinary clearing site for a significant array of the world's contraband. That the economies of Mae Sai and Tachilek were booming[14] was less a result of industry or the small trickle of tourists through there, who predominantly came to see this infamous place, than because of the vast trade in contraband that washed through, leaving a residue of loose cash.

ELITE DIVISIONS

As well as divisions over economic policy, the military was also in disagreement over tactics to deal with the separatist movements; one view was that they should be crushed, the other that they should be accommodated or effectively left to their own devices. The 'crush' option was made difficult by the economic problems the armed forces were facing, especially in relation to its operational capacity as well as by the fact that, despite having some separatist groups make peace with the government, others continued to present a seemingly intractable challenge. Similarly, there was division within the military over an appropriate response to the NLD. One group suggested accommodating the NLD. The intention of this was primarily to appease international criticism and relative isolation and to open up Burma to more opportunities for both aid and trade. The other faction was more hard-line and oppositionist, asserting the capacity of the military to continue to function in a more constrained economic environment. It should be noted, however, that while there were disagreements about direction, the army remained essentially united, and such differences of opinion did not debilitate the army's political activity.[15]

If these divisions within the military seemed to hold out some small hope for democratisation and greater political participation (or separation), the NLD itself was at least as divided as the military. The major division within the NLD appeared to be between Suu Kyi, who seemed to be under the influence of a younger NLD parliamentarian, and the older 'uncles'—former Ne Win associates—who advocated a less confrontational, more engaged approach to political settlement. As noted by Selth, it was unlikely that the NLD could ever achieve office without at least the passive support of the *Tatmadaw* (Selth 1999: 20). In this sense, the political contest in Burma was not so much about the army versus the NLD, or even factions within either, but, following tradition, about intra-elite rivalry. Aung-Thwin notes that the post-war communist leader Than Tun was Aung San's brother-in-law; that the president of the government-in-exile is Suu Kyi's cousin; that Aung Gyi (former Ne Win confidant and briefly allied with Suu Kyi) was a student leader with Aung San and Ne Win; that seventeen of the twenty-one leaders of SLORC in 1988 had close or overlapping military training; and that more than half of the nine individuals of Suu Kyi's inner circle were former military officers who were friends and followers of Aung San. Patron–client relations remained paramount in Burma's political arena, dominating military–civilian tensions and urban/rural dichotomies, as well as issues over support for market and command economies. 'In short, the contest is a personal, elitist struggle for power that has been shaped both by the continuity of traditional structures and the introduction of modern ideologies' (Aung-Thwin 1998: 94; see also 158–9).

In this respect, the intention of the Bhamese majority appeared to be to maintain Burma as a united, probably unitary, state. The NLD was not very far, in terms of policy, from the SPDC in how it saw the construction of a future Burma, although its fundamentally different approach to resolving differences of opinion and its willingness to talk with ethnic groups did stand as a radically different approach. However, if the NLD could achieve government there remained some possibility that it would continue to confront and perhaps even battle separatist movements in the outlying regions. Suu Kyi's 'vision' for the future of Burma under an NLD government was one in which ethnic minorities would be allowed to 'express their feelings' and through this reach an understanding with Burma's legitimate government (Clements and Suu Kyi 1997: 150–1; Suu Kyi 1991: 226–31). But, like her father (Cady 1960: 558), Suu Kyi did not countenance that 'expression of feeling' to include formal separation.

While factionalism seemed rife within both the government and the NLD, it also hampered the efforts of the ethnic rebels and their supporters. The All Burma Students' Democratic Front was riven by 'rampant factionalism', which was pushing some members of the group to give up their guerrilla struggle to seek refugee status in Bangkok (*The Irrawaddy*

2000a: 2). Meanwhile, the leader of the Karen National Union, General Bo Mya, was replaced by Saw Ba Thin Sein, following military set-backs, factional disputes and armed attacks against the Karen National Union by the breakaway Democratic Karen Buddhist Army (*The Irrawaddy* 2000b: 7–9).

THE SPDC

More in order to satisfy its external critics than appease internal dissent, the SLORC's successor, the State Peace and Development Council (SPDC), made some small rhetorical moves towards political legitimacy. The SPDC was established in November 1997, primarily as a means of rearranging some cabinet positions, especially those noted for excessive corruption (Callahan, in Pedersen, Rudland & May 2000: 39), and bringing some field officers more closely into line with the central government. One move by the SPDC was its claim to have held a constitutional convention, allegedly representing all groups, to draw up a new constitution for implementation, along with elections in 2000. This tended to ring hollow, especially in light of the outcome of the 1990 elections.

After more than fifty years of independence and the same number of years battling separatists, the government was still only in control of about half the country and most areas had an uncertain status or were strictly off-limits to outsiders. While there was good reason for political change in Burma, it was unlikely that such change would take place while Ne Win was still alive. Indeed, in a re-ordering of Burma's senior political landscape in 1998, the 'old guard' had reasserted themselves. Under the newly proclaimed SPDC, the six most senior positions in the government were taken by top-level military officers, while twenty-three of the remaining thirty-five cabinet positions were also held by senior officers (Embassy of the Union of Myanmar 1998a). Ne Win himself was not much directly consulted by the SPDC ministers. Instead, they believed they understood his views so well that they could offer decisions that, if he were ever obliged to do so, he would endorse.

For there to be significant political change, it would probably only follow total economic collapse. The crunch would only really come if the economy deteriorated to the point that the army was unable to function relatively efficiently. It therefore seemed that after Ne Win's eventual demise there would be a power struggle within the government over whether or not it would loosen its grip on the body politic. However, such a decision seemed far away, if at all possible, while the rationale for the military government in the first place—that of ethnic insurgency—remained an intractable problem.

ENDING ISOLATIONISM

Since the attacks on unarmed protesters in the late 1980s, Burma has been an international outcast and is cut off from bilateral aid from a number of significant potential sources, including the United States. Finally deciding to abandon its policy of self-imposed isolation, Burma was in 1999 attempting to reintegrate into the international economy, albeit slowly and very cautiously. However, its path was made difficult by its poor human rights record. By way of example, an offer by the World Bank for a loan of a billion dollars was refused by the SPDC because it had attached to it the condition of political concessions. 'The generals did not budge and claimed to be offended at the notion that they could be bought' (Mitton 2000b).

As an assertion of its independence, Burma had been one of the early members of the Non-Aligned Movement[16] (NAM). But it withdrew from this forum at the NAM Havana summit in September 1979, allegedly over a lack of neutrality in Cuba's chairmanship. This perhaps marked the depths of Burma's international isolation. After criticism from Muslim states over its persecution of its Muslim Arakan minority, Burma sought and was granted readmission to the NAM in 1992. Burma then formally turned its attention towards China. After a long history of strident opposition to Chinese communism, by the late 1980s the Rangoon government began to reach an accommodation with China. To some extent, this was in part China's response to the international opprobrium and isolation it had earned as a result of the Tiananmen Square Massacre of student protestors in 1989. In this respect, Burma and China could view each other as mutual pariahs in the international community. From Burma's perspective, though, more important was gaining China's friendship as a means of having it withdraw support from the BCP, which it had previously backed. The BCP had been a major source of difficulty for the Rangoon government, being perhaps the most organised and potentially the most powerful of the guerrilla groups arrayed against it. China also became a source of trade, especially in weapons,[17] which, by the end of the 1990s, was valued at somewhere towards US$1 billion a year. Smuggling, in such things as electrical goods, clothing and pharmaceutical drugs, was estimated to be worth around a similar amount, while legal trade also flourished. China also assisted in the development of Burma's communications network, although this proceeded far less quickly than did the arms trade. Part of the exchange was to allow China access to the Indian Ocean, as well as a growing Chinese business presence in Burma's northern states.

BURMA AND ASEAN

By the early 1990s, Burma was also making overtures to the Association of South-East Asian Nations (ASEAN). Membership in ASEAN was intended to enhance Burma's international trade and foreign investment. For the ASEAN states, Burma represented a source of cheap labour, and oil, gas and timber, within the structure of a 'stable' political environment. Few of the ASEAN states have ever been concerned with the niceties of genuine political representation and their existing though challenged policy of non-interference in the affairs of member states suited Burma very well. With China's economic development starting to focus the attention of the SEA states, Burma's links there were also seen as very useful. On one hand Burma acted as a bridge to China, as well as a bridge from China, while on the other hand it helped strengthen what could, in an emergency, be quite a powerful anti-Chinese alliance.

Singapore's Prime Minister, Goh Chock Tong, helped move along Burma's regional acceptance when he visited Rangoon in March 1994. Singapore thereafter became a major investor in Burma until the downturn in the SEA economies in 1997. Indonesia's President Suharto also visited Burma, in February 1997, signalling its increasing acceptance (even if by a regional politician who was soon to fall from grace). Among other things, the Rangoon government wanted to talk with Suharto about the 'dual [security and political] function' of Indonesia's armed forces, which they viewed as a potential model. Perhaps indicating his increasing distance from the realities of political events in his own country, Suharto did not point out that his relationship with Indonesia's armed forces was even then under strain. Burma was, in any case, formally admitted into ASEAN in 1997, along with Laos.

However, by early 1998, relations between Burma and Thailand had begun to deteriorate. While an oil and gas pipeline between the two states was about to open up and a number of business deals for logging had been developed, Burmese attacks against Karen National Union refugees along the Thai border soured relations. At the ASEAN meeting in Manila in August 1998, Thailand went so far as to call for the scrapping of ASEAN's cardinal rule of not commenting on the internal affairs of member states. This criticism of Burma's human rights record was in response to Burma's violation of sovereign Thai territory, when troops crossed into Thailand to attack Burmese refugee camps, as well as to conduct armed intelligence gathering missions. The Philippines has also joined Thailand in criticising Burma's poor human rights record. The SPDC responded by taking an increasingly isolationist, indeed paranoid, position regarding external comments on the country's political development. The government newspaper, the *New Light of Myanmar* and other state controlled media, have run regular, quite vitriolic attacks on 'foreign conspirators' and 'neocolonialists who are colluding with traitors' (Lintner 1998).

In contrast to this deterioration of the Thailand–Burma relationship, in early 2000 Thai military forces killed ten members of the Burmese 'God's Army', a Karen rebel faction, who had taken over the Ratchaburi hospital near the Burmese border. The Karen rebels had occupied the hospital in response to Thai military bombardment of Karen rebel positions just inside Thai territory. It was claimed that Thai and Burmese forces had been coordinating their attacks on the rebels, following the peaceful settlement of the occupation of the Burmese embassy in Bangkok by members of the Burma Students' Democratic Front the previous October. It was believed that the coordinated action against the Karen rebels, and others, was part of a 'normalisation' of relations between the governments of the two countries (*The Irrawaddy* January 2000a: 6). Such 'normalisation' continued to be troubled however, by border tensions. In early February 2000, six Burmese soldiers were arrested by Thai troops near Mai Hong Son in western Thailand. Burma responded to their arrest by sending more troops to the border area (*The Irrawaddy* 2000b: 2).

As if Burma was not beset with enough difficulties, its history of military domination and inter-ethnic conflict mixed with its geography has led to the development of a type of regional 'warlordism', especially since 1990. A very high degree of regional autonomy was given over to local commanders to determine activities, necessities and relative freedoms (see Callahan, in Pedersen, Rudland & May 2000: 36–9). This was one of the main sources of human rights abuse and support for the drug trade, given that such warlords were held little accountable to the central government (should it care to hold them so accountable). There was also, according to reliable sources, a high degree of desertion from the army, with patrols going out but not returning. In those cases where they did meet ambush by ethnic separatists, the bodies were usually found.

Burma was a place of fear for ordinary people. Long jail sentences for marginal 'crimes' were common, people were afraid to speak openly for fear of being identified as anti-government, phones and faxes were tapped and security and surveillance were constants of everyday life. Even slavery, in the service of the state, was common, especially for convicts and ethnic minorities. It would be easy and not inaccurate to identify Burma as a totalitarian state. But more accurately, it was a garrison state, where the state exists to serve the requirements of the military and the military, in turn, had little compunction in exploiting in any way it desired. This type of state has also been termed 'predatory' (Evans 1995: 45–7), a term which can only fill with horror those who understand the depredations of existence in such a political environment.

NOTES

1   The name 'Burma' is used here as it better reflects the name of the dominant ethnic group, the Bhamese, after whom the country was named. The alternative name, Myanmar, is also regarded as excluding the interests of the country's ethnic minorities. Nor is it far from a settled question as to whether this name is acceptable to any but a government that, by its own admission, was voted out of power a decade ago and hence is illegitimate.

2   At the beginning of 2000—this exchange rate does fluctuate.

3   The Mon are related by language to the Khmer of Cambodia.

4   The T'ai of this period were the predecessors of the Thai of Thailand. However, at this stage they were not so clearly delineated from the T'ai of what is now Shan State, Chaing Mai (then the state of Lan Na, including parts of Yunnan) or Laos.

5   It was from this time that the Thais developed the term 'farang' to denote 'European'. It is a variation on the word 'France'.

6   The common method of killing royal Burmese was to tie the individual in a velvet sack and beat him or her to death, the intention being that no royal blood was thus spilled.

7   The AFPFL was formed from the BIA to oppose the Japanese.

8   Interestingly, Aung San was close to or a member of the Burmese Communist Party in the 1930s, which was linked to his anti-colonialist stance.

9   The official breakdown of Burma's ethnic composition is: Bhamese 68 per cent, Shan 9 per cent, Karen 7 per cent, Rohingya 4 per cent, Mon 4 per cent, Chin 3 per cent and Indian 2 per cent, while the Akha, Danu, Kayan, Kokang, Lahu, Naga, Palaung, Pao, Rakhine, Tavoyan, and Wa peoples comprise about 3 per cent between them. These figures, however, could be exaggerated to justify Bahmese domination.

10 According to two sources close to the NLD.

11 This change was seen by some observers as more of a 'palace coup'.

12 The term 'Golden Triangle' denotes the region covered by northern Thailand, north-west Laos and north-east Burma, which was said to be the world's primary opium and heroin producing region. After a crackdown in Thailand, most opium and heroin was produced in north-east and northern Burma, with much smaller amounts produced in northern Laos. The 'Golden Triangle' was primarily a conduit for the flow of opium and heroin to the outside world, although even this had shifted to include Assam in eastern India and Yunnan in southern China.

13 This was according to a person who claimed to have been earlier involved in the trade from northern Thailand.

14 The border crossing between Mae Sai and Tachilek was closed in late 1999 by the Burmese government in response to the Thais' handling of the Burmese rebel takeover of the Burmese embassy. The border was also closed for a year in 1995–96, following a gun battle over heroin shipments across the border.

15 It has been noted that, within the *Tatmadaw*, 'Splits along the lines of racial background, organisational origins and political affiliation have been resolved' (Maung Aung Myoe 1998). However, there appears to still be some competition over which officer will succeed Lt-General Khin Nyunt, indicating a return to 1950s-style personality politics.

16 The NAM had 25 member countries in 1961, rising to 113 (with three suspended) by 1995.

17 China came to dominate Burma's weapons procurement program in the late 1990s, although Burma sought to diversify its sources of weapons and to manufacture its own weapons (Maung Aung Myoe 1999: 20).

6

Thailand: The Survivor
Mandala

In mid 1998, Thailand was supposed to still be in the depths of a major economic downturn, what most observers had termed a 'crisis'. Certainly Thailand was undergoing some sort of economic convulsion, which saw the value of its currency, the baht, fall by around half, numerous bankruptcies, and the collapse of a number of banks and other financial institutions. But perhaps most importantly, the 'crisis' also saw an increase in unemployment of huge numbers of workers who had no economic 'safety net'. Yet Bangkok at that time—the epicentre of the crisis from which shockwaves emanated—appeared to be a hive of industrious activity.

Some major infrastructure projects had been put on hold, for example, with work on some of the 'fly-over' freeways being stopped until new funding was made available for their continued construction. But the streets were still jam-packed with near-new cars, the horizon littered with skyscrapers, buildings still seeming to have a high occupancy rate, and advertising and other public displays of commercial activity were at least as pronounced as ever. The air veritably hummed with economic activity. If this was a country in economic crisis, what was it like in boom times? And, more to the point, what did Thailand's inwardly focused and confidence-sapping economic crisis have to say about its underlying economic prosperity, not just compared with its impoverished neighbours but with a number of industrially developed economies? The overwhelming sense was that the Thai people's sense of industriousness and economic opportunism was irrepressible.[1]

Similarly, after eight decades of military intervention in political affairs, Thailand appeared to be adding depth to its somewhat fitful

BURMA

LAOS

VIETNAM

Chiangmai

Vieng Chan

Yom R.

Menam R.

Ubon

Nakhon
Ratchasima

Ayudhaya

Bangkok -
Thonburi

CAMBODIA

*Gulf of
Thailand*

*Andaman
Sea*

Nakhon
Si Thammarat

Pattani

THAILAND

250 kilometres

application of democratic principles to the political process. The role and scope of the military was being reduced, despite some objection from that quarter, and the Thai people seemed to have firmly embraced the idea of participatory politics. Indeed, noting that democracy in the Philippines continued to be marred by two insurgencies, the resurgence of crony-capitalism, negligible land reform and pork-barrel politics, Thailand possessed the most democratic and politically free society in SEA. Like all places, it was less than perfect and some of its problems were greater than others, but on balance Thailand looked like the model of participatory and representative politics when compared with its politically tarnished regional neighbours.

This chapter will look at the rise of the Thai as the core national group and their relations with the state's outlying regions. It will then look at the traditional role of the king in the state, the establishment of the army as a political force, and the regular failure of democracy, although noting that form's resilience. It will then discuss Thailand's economy taking off along with the reassertion of democracy and the 1997–98 currency collapse.

HISTORY

The Thais began to descend into the Menam Valley along with other T'ai-Kadai linguistic groups from around the sixth to seventh century CE. Earlier inhabitants of the region date back as far as 8000 BCE, with rice being cultivated in the north-east of what is now Thailand from around 2000 BCE. Within Thailand there is a belief, supported by some archaeological evidence, that the Ban Chiang culture, upon which this cultivation was based, was using bronze from before 3000 BCE, predating the bronze age of the Middle East by at least 200 years and China by 1000 years.

The most reliable accounts indicate that the T'ai originated in the region of southern China, in the Yunnan and Guangxi provinces, and in the region known as Sipsong Panna ('12 000 Paddies') in northern Laos and north-west Vietnam, which had long been a home to a northern T'ai group (see Cheah 1996). As with the Lao and the Shan, what is known about their migration into the Menam Valley region is that they left southern China and followed the geographic contours of the land. While T'ai peoples had been drifting south for some centuries, the main wave of migration was in response to the aggressive expansionary policies of the Sung Dynasty in China under the Mongols of Kublai Khan. As a result of this migration, the T'ai spread from north-west Vietnam to

Assam in eastern India, dispersed across seven contemporary states.[2] Laos can claim to be a predominantly T'ai state as could Shan State if it was independent of Burma. But dominant among the T'ai states is Thailand, a country that is largely and most successfully T'ai.

The T'ai of what was to become Thailand in particular followed the Chao Phraya River towards the south. Others of the T'ai–Kadai linguistic group followed similar courses, the Shan following the Salween River Valley, the T'ai of Assam following the Bramaputra, the Lao following the Mekong and the T'ai of north-east Vietnam following the Red River. The river and its flood plains assured the migrating T'ai of suitable alluvial soil and a plentiful supply of water upon which to base their wet rice agriculture. In pursuing this southward course, the T'ai came into contact with and mostly assimilated other peoples. These were largely other Austronesian groups and, most notably, the Mon-Khmer who spread across what is now southern Thailand between modern Cambodia and southern Burma. They also came into contact with the Tibeto-Burmans who were themselves moving south. In large part, the incorporation of the different ethnic groups the T'ai encountered was probably assisted by the fact that there were already significant numbers of T'ai living in the region. It was this cultural assimilation that led to the 'Siamese' T'ai becoming distinct from their Shan and Lao counterparts. It is worth noting that the earlier inhabitants of the region north-west of the Gulf of Thailand were referred to by their neighbours as 'Syama' and their country as 'Syam' or Siam. This was in reference to the original people of the region rather than the T'ai who had come to increasingly dominate the local populations (Manich 1979: 1–5). It was, however, a name that continued to be given by outsiders to the T'ai of the 'Siam' region.

The T'ai tended to establish local polities that could be described as districts or small principalities. Like those at the time in north-eastern Laos and north-west Vietnam, they were called *meaung*, a name that continues to be used by the Thai in reference to Meaung Thai (that is, Thailand). In its original usage, a *meaung* was located by a river in a valley and usually demarcated by a mountain range. It could include several nearby villages, under the authority of a main central village or town (Gehan 1991: 163–70). As elsewhere, these *meaung* were usually ruled by an hereditary chief called a *jao* (or *chao*) *meaung* (*meaung* lord). Each *meaung* was based on a section of the river valley and usually extended to the peaks of nearby mountain ranges, with some *meaung* coming together under one powerful *meaung* or through alliances. Such arrangements were, however, short-lived. As noted in the chapter on Laos, one such powerful *meaung* was located at what is modern Dien Bien Phu in north-western Vietnam, while another was located in southern China and later developed as the state of Nan Chao.

While the T'ai were increasingly establishing themselves in the Menam River valley, by the first couple of centuries of the second millennium they were not yet politically organised. In so far as there was any real political organisation in the region increasingly inhabited by the T'ai, it was in the Mon state of Dvaravati. While Dvaravati was a Buddhist state and perhaps a precursor to the T'ai state that followed, little is known about it and, in terms of ethnic dominance, it did not present a consistent genealogy with contemporary Thailand. Further, forestalling any such attempted political organisation by the T'ai, and eclipsing the state of Dvaravati, were two great regional empires. To the east was the Khmer empire with its glorious capital at Angkor. To the west were the Bahmese, with their almost equally glorious capital at Pagan. These regarded the central region of the Mon and later the T'ai, situated along the mountain range of what is now Burma's Shan State and further south towards the Isthmus of Kra, as little more than a buffer state between them. During the eleventh and twelfth centuries, this buffer region and the fringes of the Khmer empire became more substantially T'ai. As the Angkorian Empire underwent internal rifts, an outlying province centred on Lopburi attempted to assert its independence, even appealing to China for recognition, in 1001 and 1155 (Wyatt 1984: 20–8). It was from around this time that the first inscriptions mention 'Syam' and the 'Syama' people.

A PATCHWORK OF PROTO-THAI STATES

By the end of the twelfth century, the T'ai were beginning to organise new states, in the Shan region of Burma, in Nan-Chao in Yunnan province of China, and in Sipsong Panna. Following the fall of the T'ai state of Nan Chao to the armies of Kublai Khan in 1253, the T'ai of that area also began their migration south. Within decades, with the decline of the Angkorian empire, Lopburi had established itself as an independent state, including the nearby centre of Ayudhya, founded in 1450 (Manich 1979: 8–10, 18–26; see also SarDesai 1997: 52–6). Further to the north, the young state of Sukhothai had come to encompass the Menam River valley, a parcel west across to Martaban just south of Pegu, and a further larger parcel east to encompass Vieng Chan and its surrounding territory. To the north, Lan Na, centred on Chiang Mai, extended into southern Yunnan and west into Shan State. Between Lan Na and Sukhothai lay the smaller state of Pha Yao in what is now the eastern portion of northern Thailand (Wyatt 1984: 38–60). In some respects, this rearrangement of the political landscape, splitting up larger regional empires and allowing the growth of new states, was an intentional product of China asserting regional military and political control (Coedes 1968: 250–1). In the face of a Mongol invasion, at the beginning of the fourteenth century under the leadership of Mangrai, the king of Lan Na, his state, Sukhothai and Pha Yao combined forces to defeat the invaders and to conduct raids far into Chinese territory (Coedes 1968: 194–5). Although political stability was not yet a given, it was here that the seeds of the later Thai state were sown.

The T'ai state of Lan Na was one of a number of states that existed from the eighth to sixteenth centuries in the region. However, its central position meant that it was almost constantly buffeted by invading armies from Burma, from Lan Xang or from the southern T'ais of Ayudhya. Lan Na lost the last vestiges of its independence to the Burmese in 1564, and from that time on became a vassal state to one or other of the regional powers, eventually being subsumed into the expanding Thai state (Wyatt 1984: 93).

BURMESE INTERVENTION

Being in close proximity to the states of Burma, the early T'ai states were regularly attacked and often occupied by Burmese forces. Although the historic memory of these events is not strong, there remains a lingering sense of Burmese aggression, although they have attempted to maintain cordial formal relations. In a contemporary sense, Thailand has no formal aspiration to incorporate the T'ai Shan State into its territory. But there is a very clear feeling that the Shan and the Thai are at least ethnic cousins, whereas the Burmese are not. The Burmese state was perhaps the most clearly mandalic of all those in SEA. When it was strong it tended to be aggressively expansionist, at the expense of its local and regional neighbours. When it was weak it tended to recede quite rapidly towards the core polity. The core region of what was to become Thailand evolved as a consequence of this protracted period of conflict with the Burmese state.

By the late fifteenth century, Toungoo had established itself as a prominent state and, in the early 1530s, took control of the Mon state of Pegu. In doing this, it also marched on Chiang Krai, in Moulmein district, then a tributary to Siam. The Siamese responded by driving the Burmese out in 1538. While internal squabbles over royal succession tore at the state in 1547, the Burmese crossed through the Three Pagodas Pass and attacked

Siam. To further complicate Siam's position, the Khmers attacked the state's eastern region (Wyatt 1984: 90–1). After a break of some years and having settled renewed internal conflicts, Burma's new king, Bayinnaung, took advantage of succession turmoil in Lan Na to march from a fresh conquest in Shan state to take Chiang Mai in 1558. The Burmese used Chiang Mai as a forward base for further attacks on Lan Xang and Ayudhya, as well as attacking from Tak. The Siamese king, Chakkraphat, capitulated to the Burmese in 1564, with a Burmese vassal king being installed in Ayudhya five years later (Wyatt 1984: 90–6). Relations between the two states settled, remaining relatively quiet for almost 200 years, as Ayudhya drifted from Burmese control.

During a period of internal conflict, a new Bhamese leader, Alaunghpaya, arose. Settling the conflict in Burma, Alaunghpaya then turned his attention to Siam. Having established such a successful military campaign, Alaunghpaya simply followed the logic of expansion (Wyatt 1984: 133). It was left to Alaunghpaya's successor, Naungdawgyi, to capture Chiang Mai in 1763. In July 1765, a new Burmese army, boosted by troops from Lan Na and the Lao states, marched through central Siam, taking all the major cities including Sukhothai and Phitsanulok. Meanwhile, another Burmese army landed at Mergui and marched down the Isthmus of Kra, taking Tenasserim and Chumpon on the Gulf of Thailand, before marching north to take Phetburi. At Ratburi it met a third Burmese army that had crossed at Three Pagodas Pass and together they took Ratburi and Suphanburi, meeting the northern army just outside Ayudhya in 1766. Siamese resistance was 'both belated and uncoordinated' (Wyatt 1984: 134).

The siege of Ayudhya ensued but, by early 1767, its fate was sealed. A fire broke out in the city, adding to the desolation and starvation already rampant as a consequence of the siege. The Siamese king, Suriyamarin, tried to negotiate a surrender based on his suzerainty to Ava, but the Burmese, from a position of absolute strength, refused anything but unconditional surrender. The ensuing slaughter and destruction was complete. Tens of thousands were led away as slaves. Those survivors left were reduced to an animal-like existence, scavenging for food, often leaves or grass (Wyatt 1984: 136–7).

SIAMESE RESURGENCE

The Siamese eventually pushed the Burmese from their country, under the leadership of General Taksin, who upon victory proclaimed himself king. However, the sacking of Ayudhya was so complete that Taksin removed the Siamese capital downriver to Thonburi on the right bank of the Chao Phraya River. Taksin was successful in pulling together the fractured and fragmented state, but quickly developed delusions of grandeur, in particular of being the next Buddha. Taksin was dethroned and executed in front of his successor, in the traditional manner of being tied in a velvet sack and beaten to death.[3] The current lineage of Thai kings and the founding of the modern state date from 1782, when the powerful general Chao Praya Chakri succeeded the executed Taksin. Because Thonburi was exposed to Burmese attacks, Chakri moved the capital to the other side of the river, to Krung Thep (Bangkok), where it currently resides.

Conflict with the Burmese continued, however, until the middle of the nineteenth century. The ruler of the Lu state of Chiang Hung, in what is now the north-west corner of Laos, had sent tribute to the court at Bangkok. However, the Burmese claimed suzerainty over the region through Kentung, in Shan State. At the request of the Chiang Hung ruler, King Mungkut sent expeditions against the Burmese in 1852–53 and in 1854. The timing of these expeditions followed close on the heels of the second Anglo-Burmese War of 1852 and reflected both Burma's recent military weakness and an age-old desire for long-standing enemies to strike at times of greatest advantage. These Siamese forces were led by Mongkut's younger brother, Prince Wongsathirat, and manned largely by troops from Lan Na (Wyatt 1984: 182). The Burmese capitulated, with Kentung being occupied by the Siamese troops. However, the attack on Kentung upset the regional court at Chiang Mai, which felt closer to Kentung as a 'brother' T'ai state than it did to its master of Bangkok. From the Siamese perspective, however, the attack of Kentung was a pre-emptive strike aimed at securing the border regions of the state *mandala* (Ratanaporn 1988: 311–20).

A EUROPEAN PRESENCE

Thailand prides itself on being the only SEA state not to have been brought under European control during the colonial period. This reflects well on the diplomacy and far-sightedness of successive Thai rulers. However, Thailand has a long history of European intervention and its boundaries were defined by colonial Europeans. The first European to visit the coast of what was then a part of Thailand, the trading ports at Tenasserim, Mergui and Tavoy, was Nicolo di Conti, in 1430. The Portuguese also supplied arms to both the Thais and the Burmese in their various conflicts from as early as 1511 (Manich 1979: 9–10). Spaniards in support of Cambodia engaged Thai armies in 1594. Portuguese, Dutch, English, French, and Japanese mercenaries also assisted the Thais in various conflicts. The English were especially interested in trade with Thailand, which came to more closely shape relations and Siam's responses to colonial intervention in the nineteenth century.

It was John Cruwford's mission to Bangkok in 1822 that first proposed the dismantling of the Siamese king's monopoly of trade. This was initially not well accepted. The Siamese king was primarily interested in purchasing firearms from Britain, which it had already been buying from American and Portuguese traders. Britain initially refused the request, as its firearms were then needed for its campaigns in Burma (Ngaosyvathn & Ngaosyvathn 1998: 109–11). However, seeing an economic opportunity wasted, Britain finally acceded to the Siamese request. In the early 1820s, Thailand bought firearms from Britain, some of which had been used in the final Napoleonic conflict, the Battle of Waterloo. While Thai use of these weapons was not yet up to European standards they did give the Siamese army unparalleled military superiority over its near neighbours[4] (Ngaosyvathn & Ngaosyvathn 1998: 117–20).

THE MANDALA EXPANDS

By 1828, Thailand reached what was probably the greatest extent of its territorial expansion and regional power, claiming or exercising control as far west as Shan State in Burma, all of the old empire of Lan Xang, and most of the kingdom of Cambodia. To the east it exercised control of regions now occupied by north-west and south-west Vietnam and as far south as Kedah, Perlis, Kelantan and Trengganu states in what is contemporary Malaysia (Corfield n. d.). In traditional mandalic fashion, the empire of the first Chakri, Rama I, exercised authority over these regions through the maintenance of minor kings or princes seated on suzerain thrones: 'In looking at Rama I's empire as a whole, one of its remarkable features is the large number of power centers that existed' (Wyatt 1984: 158). Wyatt noted that at the furthest reaches of the empire, local rulers were semi-independent and did little more than pay tribute. Among these were the later Malaysian states, Cambodia and Luang Prabang. States, usually principalities, closer to the centre included Chiang Mai, Vieng Chan, Champassak, and Pattani. Closer still were quasi-independent provinces including Songkhla, Nakhon Si Thammarat, Battambang-Siem Reap (which had been claimed by the proto-Thai state since the collapse of the Angkorian empire), and possibly Nakhon Ratchasima (Wyatt 1984: 158–60). Similarly, the empire included the state of Lan Na, which retained its own ruler but was otherwise clearly beholden to Bangkok. Rama I regarded these suzerain states equally as a part of his empire and, but for the vagaries of history, the shape of contemporary Thailand might still have included Cambodia or the Lao states, but possibly not Lan Na, which is now northern Thailand. Siam's border regions had always varied according to its political and military fortunes, but were more or less fixed in their current alignment by the establishment of two new competing empires, those of Britain and France, in the nineteenth century. France controlled Indochina, while Britain controlled Burma and the Malay Peninsula. Both wished to retain a buffer state, so as to avoid conflict (Fisher 1966: 149–56).

After a number of earlier attempts, by the middle of the nineteenth century France had occupied southern Vietnam and Cambodia, extending control of Cambodia to include the former Khmer heartland and long-held Siamese provinces of Battambang and Siem Reap. In 1860, upon the death of the Cambodian king, Duon, the successor to the throne, Norodom, faced a rebellion at home and fled to the court at Bangkok where he sought protection. Being assured of his throne, with the blessing of his Siamese master, he then faced pressure from the French, who now not only controlled Cambodia's access to the South China Sea through the Mekong, but also were clearly the strongest and most aggressive military force in what was to become Indochina. The French position was that they had inherited Vietnam's claim to dual suzerainty over Cambodia, a position that was never happily accepted by the Siamese court. In 1863 Norodom relented and accepted French 'protection', then set off for his coronation in Bangkok where the royal regalia was held. No sooner had he left, however, than the French raised the Tricolour over his palace at Udong, causing his abrupt return. The Siamese king, Mongkut, was unhappy about this change of political control, especially after having provided Norodom with protection in 1860. But there was little he could do to force a French withdrawal. In 1867, as a gesture towards placating the Siamese court, France gave to Siam the provinces of Siem Reap, Battambang and Sisophon in settling a treaty with them.

Having secured Cambodia, as a part of its control over Vietnam, France then sought to extend its control to other states that it claimed were suzerain to the court at Hue. A French expedition had already explored the Mekong north of Cambodia in 1866–68, through what was then Siamese territory. Having been slowed by the Franco-Prussian War of 1870, France renewed its efforts in the Lao territories under the pretext of Hue's suzerainty over Luang Prabang and Vieng Chan. Vietnam had briefly exercised suzerainty over these areas, but control had generally been retained by Bangkok, as was the case when the French confronted the Siamese in 1893. Auguste Pavie had been appointed vice-consul in Luang Prabang in 1886, and in 1887 ingratiated himself to the king saving him from attack by Ho bandits. In 1888 France occupied the T'ai *meaung* of the Black River Valley and in 1890 Pavie further spread French influence through the Lao region (Wyatt 1984: 202–3).

The Siamese responded by strengthening their military position at Nong Kai (opposite Vieng Chan), at Ubon and at Champassak. When two French commercial agents were expelled from the middle Mekong region, and the French consul at Luang Prabang died (of natural causes), France sought reparations in the form of the lands on the left bank of the Mekong. In April 1893, Siamese forces resisted French troops sent to take control of the region, leading to the death of a French officer. The French response was to send gunboats up the Chao Phraya River, forcing the defences at Paknam in a short engagement. The French ultimatum, including a naval blockade of Siamese ports, could not be resisted. The court at Bangkok was caught off-guard by this overt belligerence, and by Britain's refusal to become embroiled in the affair.

Siamese relations with Britain were only slightly less troubled than those with France. The court at Bangkok quickly recognised British military power, but in testing it came close to suffering a similar fate to Burma. When the throne of the previously suzerain state of Trengganu fell vacant upon the death of the local sultan in 1862, Siamese warships landed their claimant to that position. In response, a British warship shelled the local capital, Kuala Trengganu, encouraging the Siamese to abandon involvement in Trengganu affairs.

Britain and France sealed an agreement on the borders of Siam in 1896 by marking the Mekong River as the boundary between British Burma and French Laos, jointly guaranteeing the independence of that territory claimed by Siam drained by the Menam River system. This left western Cambodia open to further French claims and states on the Malay peninsula to British claims. In 1897 Britain and Siam reached a secret understanding that Siam would not construct a canal across the Isthmus of Kra (Wyatt 1984: 205). This had the effect of limiting Siam's capacity to develop its economy independently of the colonial powers. In 1904 and 1907 France no longer felt it had to placate the Siamese court and, noting that these regions did not drain into the Chao Phraya River system, retook possession of the three western provinces of Cambodia (Manich 1979: 198–200). While these losses irked the Thais' well developed sense of nationalism and imperial pride, it was their flexibility that helped to fend off possible war and preserve the state.

OPENING THE ECONOMY

Although Thailand has, since the beginning of the colonial period, remained politically independent, it was effectively economically colonised, especially by the British. Both Britain and Siam wished to avoid the sort of difficulties over trading relations that had led to the Second Anglo-Burmese War and Mongkut, notably, personally entertained the newly appointed British governor of Hong Kong, Sir John Bowring. Bowring had arrived in Bangkok in 1855 with a considerable display of importance, the backing of significant military power, and a thinly disguised threat to use force, if necessary, to protect British trading interests in Siam (Wyatt 1984: 183). Mongkut soon agreed to Bowring's request for the opening up of foreign trade. Import and export taxes were restricted to three and five per cent respectively, British subjects were allowed to reside and own land in Siam, and government monopolies (the basis of government revenue), except for opium, were abolished (Wyatt 1984: 183). As a consequence of the treaty, state revenues initially dipped slightly, but were soon restored by taxes on alcohol, gambling and a lottery, as well as opium, all of which fell outside the terms of the treaty. At least as importantly, Mongkut also negotiated similar treaties with the United States, France and numerous other states. The value in this lay in not being tied exclusively to Britain, as were India and Burma, or as Vietnam was tied to France. It was through playing off colonial powers against each other that Siam maintained its independence. Recognising these powers for what they were, Mongkut's strategy of acting as an equal, if a less powerful one, secured his state from the politically humbling circumstances that befell every other monarch of the region (Wyatt 1984: 184–5). It also had the added advantage of bringing Siam directly, rather than indirectly, into contact with and to begin to become a part of the (then) modern world.

MODERNISATION

Noting that the country had to adapt and change in order to stay apace with, or not be swallowed by, the growth of European colonialism, Siam embarked on a conscious program of modernisation. The reform program was begun by Mongkut after taking the throne in 1851 and was continued by his son, King Chulalongkorn (Rama V), who succeeded his father in 1868. Apart from the European examples, Chulalongkorn also watched Japan's development as a rapidly modernising state. Although there were vast differences between the two, Japan's top-down modernisation stood as a model for the Siamese king and influenced his own attempts at modernisation from above, albeit deeply modified by Siamese norms and requirements. Among other achievements, Chulalongkorn abolished slavery or corvee (compulsory state labour), attempted to modernise Siam's legal and administrative structures, and established a civil service.

To help strengthen Siamese identity in the face of so many challenges, and to conform to a European standard, in one of Chulalongkorn's last acts he required that all Thais have a Thai family name as well as a given name. This had the added characteristic of forcing ethnic Chinese in Thailand to assimilate.

When King Chulalongkorn died in 1910, Thailand was a very different place to that which had existed when he took the throne forty-two years earlier. The country had assumed its present shape, with minor rearrangements made during and after WWII. The five tiers of gradually diminishing authority that characterised earlier royal rule were gone, to be replaced by a bureaucratic structure modelled, in principle, on that of England. The 'wasteful and inefficient' rule of local elites was gradually being replaced by appointed officials, bringing the provinces more directly under the control of the centre. There had been resistance to these changes, resulting in rebellions in Pattani, the north-east and the north in 1902. But the old ruling families were eventually prised apart from the people who served as their generous source of income (Wyatt 1984: 212–14). A further legacy of Chulalongkorn was the enhanced role of the navy and especially the army in the affairs of the state.

THE ARMY AND THE END OF ABSOLUTE MONARCHY

King Vajiravudh (Rama VI) succeeded Chulalongkorn (Rama V) in 1910 and introduced (theoretically) compulsory education and other educational reforms. He also further 'Westernised' the state by making the Thai calendar conform to the European model. However, in 1912 a group of young military officers of mostly Sino-Thai ancestry attempted to overthrow the king in a coup. The inspiration for the coup attempt came from many factors: competition between the king's brothers for political power; the Chinese revolution of October 1911; the perceived injustices of the existing political system; and because of a perceived downgrading of the army in favour of the king's private 'Wild Tiger Corps' (Wyatt 1984: 225–6). The coup plot was foiled before it unfolded, but it was a sign that the army would play a very active role in Thai politics throughout the rest of the twentieth century.

The role of the Thai military was strengthened after the outbreak of the Great War (WWI) in 1914. The pro-Alliance sentiments of the government were finally tipped into action when the US entered the conflict in 1917, with Thailand choosing also to join the Allied cause. More than anything, though, Thailand did not want to be thought equivocal by the victorious Allies, and have its sovereignty thus threatened (Wyatt 1984: 230). More than anything else, maintenance of state sovereignty in a rapidly changing world was the key aspiration of the Siamese government.

Vajiravudh was a controversial king, because of social activities associated with his implied homosexuality, the distribution of power within the government and in significant part because of greatly inflated royal expenditure. After a long period of rapid social and economic change, including restructuring the system of government to resemble the British bureaucratic model more closely, Vajiravudh opposed further significant political change (Wyatt 1984: 231–3). Added to increasing economic instability caused by fluctuations in the price of Thailand's chief export, rice, not just the person but also the status of the office of the king was weakened. Then, in 1925, Vajiravudh died suddenly at the age of forty-four, leaving as his heir his half-brother and the youngest son of Chulalongkorn, Prajadhipok. Prajadhipok's reign 'both began and ended under clouds of criticism and unrest, dogged almost constantly by economic problems. Yet its denouement was profoundly political, involving no less than the end of the absolute monarchy and the ascension to power of segments of the new elite that had been growing since Chulalongkorn attained control of his administration in the 1880s' (Wyatt 1984: 234).

Prajadhipok inherited a high and disorganised level of state debt, which in turn fuelled conflict between ministers over budgetary allocations, stalled the process of government and caused a general loss of faith in the political system. Being both young and inexperienced, the new king was unable to control these problems. Having been educated in England and France, perhaps the one significant contribution that Prajadhipok did make was to raise discussion about a process of democratisation in 1927. At one level his plans for introducing such a process were too far in advance of his countrymen's desires. At another level, when events started to move out of his control, the king was too far behind those desires; they simply passed him by (Wyatt 1984: 235–7). When the Great Depression hit Thailand, from 1930 to 1932, the price of rice dropped by two-thirds and the value of land dropped to a sixth of its previous value. Siam also clung to the gold standard, which made the price of its rice more expensive than that of the competition on the international market, which further harmed its economy. Government spending was cut by a third, while cash incomes fell by an average of two-thirds.

Popular discontent was at an all-time high, and in the background was an old prophesy that after 150 years, on 6 April 1932, the Chakri Dynasty would end. Prajadhipok again raised the idea of representative government, rejected by his advisers, proposing a Constitution that was quite similar to that which was eventually adopted. While vacationing by the sea, on 24 June 1932, a small group of middle-level officers launched a swift coup. Bluffing or immobilising other military units around the capital, the 'Promoters', as they became known, consisting of forty-nine army and navy officers and sixty-five civilians, brought an end to absolute monarchy in Thailand (Wyatt 1984: 239–42; Steinberg 1971: 313–20; Kahin 1969: 15–21).

THE ARMY IN GOVERNMENT

The first constitutional governments of the 1930s were led by conservative, senior military officers. A provisional Constitution was established, a National Assembly of seventy members was appointed, and a smaller Peoples' Committee was drawn from it to act as a type of cabinet. Many of the senior figures in this government had held high office in the government of the last king. Under the auspices of a People's Party, the 'Promoters' sought popular support for their cause. Yet the civilian wing was relatively unsuccessful at attracting popular interest, while the military wing was busy consolidating itself in positions of power. It was this basic division, complicated by further internal factionalism, that led to a series of disruptions within the new government. A 'civilian' proposal for a socialist-type state was rejected by the conservative military group, who branded it as being like communism, even enlisting the support of the king to oppose it. The National Assembly, which was generally in favour of the plan, was prorogued and the architect of the plan, Pridi Phanomyong, went into temporary exile (Wyatt 1984: 247).

There was considerable discontent with the new government, and in 1933 a grandson of Chulalongkorn and former Minister of War, Prince Boworadet, led a regional rebellion that marched on Bangkok. The response to the rebels was organised by Lt. Colonel Phibun, who mounted a counter-attack in the northern fringes of Bangkok between 13 and 16 October. After intense fighting with heavy casualties on both sides, the rebel forces broke and retreated towards Nakhon Ratchasima. Realising his cause was lost, Boworadet fled to France and exile. A few months later, King Prajadhipok travelled to England for 'medical treatment'. From England he clarified the terms under which he could continue as monarch.

When he was refused a role in the appointment of members of the already undemocratic National Assembly, he abdicated in 1935. In his place, the National Assembly invited the ten-year-old son of Prince Mahidol, Prince Ananda Mahidol, then at school in Switzerland, to assume the throne (Wyatt 184: 248–9).

The government had promised a fully elected National Assembly when educational levels rose and, between 1933–34 and 1937–38, expenditure on education rose four-fold, while total government spending only increased by a third. This educational campaign raised literacy to over sixty per cent (for males alone over eighty per cent). Over the same period, the military budget also doubled, in part to defend Siam against perceived colonial threats and in part to defend itself against the greater war that appeared to be brewing. Added to this was the favourable impact that Nazi Germany, Fascist Italy, and in particular, pre-war Japan had on a large number of Siamese, especially in the military. From early 1932, younger army officers were in contact with their counterparts in Japan and militant nationalism was on the rise. At the same time, the economy began to improve, largely because the new government had taken power at the lowest ebb of the Great Depression (Wyatt 1984: 248–50).

In 1935, as Foreign Minister, Pridi Phanomyong (who had by then returned from exile) negotiated Siam's complete sovereignty. Following on from this wave of nationalism, Siam changed its name in 1939 to more accurately reflect what the Siamese called their state, Prathet Thai, rather than the name they were given by the outside world. The change of name had a further double purpose: it cemented the ethnic Thai as the 'national' group of the state, and had the literal meaning of being 'free',[5] which was useful in terms of anti-colonial/nationalist assertion at a time during the last throes of European colonialism. Although Thailand changed its name back to Siam at the conclusion of WWII, it reasserted its own identity, again under Phibun, in 1948.

WORLD WAR II

The Second World War was less painful for Thailand than for its neighbours. Fearing that Japan, preparing to consolidate its hold over Indochina, would forestall Thai attempts to reclaim border territory lost to France, it invaded western Cambodia and disputed Lao territories in November 1940. Japan intervened, forcing a settlement that gave Thailand the Thai side of the Mekong at Champassak in southern Laos, Sayabouri in north-western Laos, and Battambang and Siem Reap provinces in Cambodia. The Japanese ambassador requested passage for Japanese troops through

Thailand, but Phibun was touring the Cambodian provinces at the time and his Foreign Minister, Direk Jayanama, refused the request Phibun would probably have agreed to. The following day, 8 December 1941, coinciding with its attack on US installations in the Pacific, Japanese forces crossed into Thailand at nine points. Phibun arrived back the next morning and ordered a cease-fire. On 12 December Phibun signed a military alliance with Japan. This allowed Japanese troops to be stationed on Thai territory, from which they launched attacks against Burma and Malaysia.

There was no real choice in the agreement, although the pre-war tendencies of many in government were not uncomfortable with an alliance with Japan. In any case, this alliance reflected a continuation of the types of accommodationist policies that had allowed the country to negotiate its way through the colonial era. The ethic behind the decision was one of bending with the wind rather than breaking before it. Watching Japan's quick victories, Phibun expanded his alliance with Japan and, on 25 January 1942, declared war on the US and Britain. In 1943, Thailand invaded the Shan region of Burma and confirmed its incorporation into Thailand in a treaty with Japan in August of that year. Japan also returned administration of Kelantan, Trengganu, Perlis, and Kedah in northern Malaysia to Thailand (Wyatt 1984: 257–8).

The Thai ambassador to Washington, Seni Pramoj, refused to deliver Phibun's declaration of war to the US government, regarding it as not reflecting the wishes of the Thai people, and set about organising a 'Free Thai' movement. As the war began to go against Japan, the Thai government forced the resignation of Phibun as Prime Minister. The 'Free Thai' movement, supported by the US, operated out of Chongqing in southern China and from British bases in Sri Lanka and India. It had also infiltrated the Thai government and was, in effect, headquartered in the office of Pridi, who was acting as regent in the absence of the king[6] (Wyatt 1984: 258–9). With Japan's impending defeat, the National Assembly voted out Phibun and voted in Khuang Aphaiwong, who could deal with the Japanese, while Pridi became sole regent for his ability to deal with the Allies. Thus began a period of quick diplomatic transition.

THE POSTWAR PERIOD

In the last days of the war, Britain asked for reparations for its war costs, aggrieved at Thailand allowing Japan to use its territory to launch attacks against Burma and Malaya. It also announced it would claim back the four Malay states and appeared ready to invade Thailand. The 'Free Thai' movement worked more closely with the sympathetic USA, expressed a lack of Thai commitment to Phibun's declaration of war, noted that Thai troops had not actually engaged Allied troops in conflict, and offered to field a force of 50 000 'Free Thai' soldiers against the Japanese. The USA acted as an advocate for Thailand, against a less sympathetic British position. Upon the surrender of Japan, Pridi announced that Thailand's declaration of war was illegal and hence null and void, and repudiated all agreements made with Japan. Khuang Aphaiwong resigned as Prime Minister on the basis of his recent association with the Japanese, and the National Assembly announced its intention to ask Seni Pramoj to become Prime Minister on his return from Washington. Ending the conflict with France proved more difficult, as Thai sentiment ran in favour of retaining the provinces of Laos and Cambodia occupied during the war. These provinces were only restored in January 1947, after the residents had already voted in Thailand's 1946 elections (Wyatt 1984: 260–2).

Despite Pridi's People's Party winning a majority of seats in January 1946, the assembly elected Khuang, from the Democratic Party, as Prime Minister. With the majority not holding power, this situation could not last and, in March, Khuang resigned. Pridi drew up a new Constitution, introducing both an upper and a lower house, which came into effect in May 1946. Democratic prospects for the state began to look promising. But then the highest Thai court refused to proceed with a war crimes trial against Phibun, who remained popular and, along with the military, he was effectively exonerated for actions taken in difficult circumstances. Then, on 9 June 1946, the young King Ananda Mahidol was found dead in his bed, shot through the head. While the three chief material witnesses in the affair were quickly tried and executed, Pridi was popularly held responsible. In August he resigned as Prime Minister and left the country. The government began to flounder. Although Pridi returned, his links with Indonesian, Laotian and Vietnamese nationalists had him labelled as a communist sympathiser. Rumours spread about the death of the king and an impending communist revolution. On 8 November 1947, soldiers seized the government, appointed Khuang as caretaker Prime Minister to forestall international condemnation and began a program of persecuting leftists, especially Pridi's supporters. In elections in January 1948, Khuang's Democratic Party won a small majority in the National Assembly, but after three months Phibun and his 'Coup Group' forced Khuang's resignation, installing Phibun as Prime Minister. Thai politics was fractured and shallowly rooted. Neither Pridi nor Phibun were much liked or trusted, but Phibun had recourse to real force through the army, whereas Pridi did not (Wyatt 1984: 264–6; Wilson 1966: 24–6).

THE COLD WAR

Both Phibun and Thailand had to reinvent themselves politically in the postwar period, especially to regain the confidence of the international community. Seeking a new lead to follow, the postwar Phibun government modelled itself on the United States. The USA had three advantages as a new political model. The first was that it was the major power among the victorious Allies; the second that it had shown itself to be a friend of Thailand, whereas Britain and France had been hostile; and the third that it was emerging both as the world's dominant anti-communist force and as the world's dominant economy. The move towards becoming closer to the United States was seen in some quarters as diminishing the nationalist aspirations that Thailand had built up in the 1930s and 1940s. As such, it engendered a nationalist backlash within some sections of the military.

In the Cold War climate of the late 1940s and early 1950s, Thailand faced insurgencies in the predominantly Lao north-east, but more especially in the south, where both Muslim separatists and communists were active. Closer to home, however, were two attempted coups, the first in October 1948 and the second in February 1949. The first simply reflected dissatisfaction with Phibun within an anti-'Coup Group' section of the military. However the second was a plot by sections of the marines and navy to restore Pridi to power, resulting in three days of heavy fighting in Bangkok. Supporters of Phibun defeated the dissident forces and stepped up oppression of his opponents, executing many officials and politicians (Wilson 1966: 26). A façade of constitutional democracy was retained, but it was increasingly thin, with power transferred away from the National Assembly. On 29 June 1951, while on board a dredge ship being presented to Thailand by the United States, Phibun was taken prisoner by navy officers and held on the flagship, the *Sri Ayudhya*. Negotiations for a change in government broke down, there was heavy fighting in Bangkok, with more than 1200 civilians killed, and then the air force attacked the *Sri Ayudhya*. As it sank, Phibun swam to safety. Following this coup attempt, the navy was cut to a quarter of its previous strength and a further purge of perceived dissidents ensued. The suppression of this coup marked the rise in power of two chief rivals within the original 'Coup Group'. One of them was Major-General Sarit Thanarat (Wyatt 1984: 267–70).

The Thai economy improved throughout the 1950s, in part due to the demands for rice, rubber and tin stimulated by the Korean War, to which Thailand also sent a contingent of troops. The growth of manufactured goods also increased. In 1954, confirming its position within the US-led camp, Thailand joined the South East Asian Treaty Organisation and, compared to its neighbours, was viewed by the USA as powerful and stable. Compared to the insurgency-wracked Burma, the defeat of France in Indochina in 1954 by communist nationalists, a communist insurgency in Malaya and the success of Chinese communism, Thailand was indeed safe and stable. At another level, however, US involvement in the Thai military, as an anti-communist bastion, led to an increase in official corruption. It also tied the Thai military elite very closely to US foreign policy, which continued to jar nationalist sentiment.

THE RISE OF SARIT

In 1955, Phibun returned from a trip to the USA and Britain espousing the cause of democracy, allowing the registration of political parties and the democratisation of local governments. Phibun's group narrowly won the elections held in February 1957 but, despite his references to democratisation, 'only by blatant fraud, vote rigging, tampering, and coercion' did he secure his victory (Wyatt 1984: 274). They were the 'dirtiest elections in Thai history' (Wyatt 1984: 274). In response to the public outcry over these elections, Phibun declared a state of national emergency and made Sarit, now a Field Marshal, responsible for public order. Phibun's government continued to reel under further crises, in particular a drought in the north-east and a corruption scandal. Sarit publicly moved closer to the people. Then he and his deputies resigned from the cabinet. A group of appointed legislators also resigned and, as Sarit's popularity increased, he asked for the resignation of the government. Phibun attempted to have Sarit arrested, but Sarit was warned of the attempt and the next morning staged a quick and bloodless coup (Sulak 1991: 54; Wyatt 1984: 275). Thailand appeared to be incapable of escaping the domination of the army in the political process, and certainly the army seemed to believe that it had a legitimate role in keeping a watching brief over, and when necessary intervening in, the affairs of state. It was to be a self-perception a long time in changing.

As a political leader, Sarit was the archetypal military strongman. Although he claimed that he acted on behalf of 'the people', Sarit had little time for notions of democracy (Sulak 1991: 55). Under Sarit, in the face of a political deadlock, a critical media and labour strikes, on 20 October 1958 the Constitution was abandoned and martial law was declared. The National Assembly elected in early 1957 was dissolved and

an interim cabinet was appointed. Over the next five years, Sarit introduced a range of populist reforms, including ones on the 'law and order'
issues of prostitution, arson, opium, and public hooliganism. He banned
pedicabs as archaic and uncivilised, and he referred to virtually all of his
critics as 'communists'. Sarit's ideology, such as it existed, was to turn the
people's loyalty from the abstract notion of the 'state' to the person of the
king, whose executive officer was Sarit. In doing this, the king was
'restored to the apex of the moral, social and political order' (Wyatt 1984:
281). In a more positive concrete sense, Sarit also embarked on a program
of economic development, including bringing basic infrastructure such as
roads to rural areas and boosting education. And Sarit encouraged foreign
investment, which helped Thailand post growth rates of an average of 8.6
per cent a year from 1959 until 1969 (Wyatt 1984: 283).

In regional terms, Sarit accepted a high level of US military assistance, in proportion to non-military assistance from the late 1950s until
the late 1960s, as a means of boosting Thailand's capacity to defend itself
against revolutionary forces operating in Indochina. As a part of this program, the USA also used Thailand as its primary base for launching air
attacks against communist positions in Indochina. When Sarit died in
1963, he left behind a personal fortune of almost US$150 million, land,
houses, a second wife and more than fifty mistresses.

THE 1960S

Sarit was succeeded by his deputy, General Thanom Kittikachorn, who
had served as the stand-in prime minister in 1958. Thanom was a milder
military leader than Sarit, but never the less continued Thai politics along
military lines. Thanom's deputy was General Praphas Carusathian and
their political relationship was made all the closer by the marriage of
Thanom's son to Praphas' daughter. The Thanom–Praphas period was
noted for Thailand's increasing involvement in the Indochina conflict,
the continued modernisation of Thailand, and, finally, for the development of wide-ranging political debate (Wyatt 1984: 286).

The Indochina conflict was of special concern to Thailand and, pick-
ing up where Sarit had left the relationship with the US, during the
1960s Thanom and Praphas actively if quietly pushed Thai intervention
in the conflict in Laos. United States air bases were established in
Nakhon Sawan province, north of Bangkok, in Khorat, in the north-
east, and Nakhon Phanom. In the later 1960s, more than 40 000 US
military personnel were stationed in Thailand along with almost 6000

aircraft. Direct Thai involvement in the Vietnam campaign began in 1964, with an air force contingent going to South Vietnam, a naval contingent the year after and, between 1967 and 1969, up to 11 000 troops. Meanwhile, the US presence in Thailand increased the pace of 'Westernisation', at least in the most superficial sense of catering for US servicemen's interests (Wyatt 1984: 286–9). In response to its escalating involvement in the Indochina war, the Communist Party of Thailand, operating near and later from Laos and Cambodia and supported by North Vietnam, began a series of attacks in the north-east from around 1964. By 1967 the insurgency had spread throughout much of the north as well, and then into the south and eventually closer to the centre. 'By the early 1970s, the Thanom–Praphas regime faced a major security crisis' (Wyatt 1984: 290; see also Battersby 1999). In response, Thanom decided to go to the polls.

DEMOCRATISATION

In 1969, Thanom allowed elections for the National Assembly, which gave the government a majority and at least the façade of civilian rule. However, in November 1971, in response to increasing political dissent, Thanom dissolved the parliament, banned political parties and restored the military to its earlier dominant position. By this stage the military was increasingly factionalised and the government was no longer of the strong military type that had earlier dominated Thai politics. The government's response to student demonstrations in 1973, through expulsions from universities and arrests, led to mass protests, involving between 200 000 and 500 000 people. Thanom ordered troops in against the protesters, but the army began to disobey him. King Bhumibol supported the protesters and, on 14 October 1973, Thanom and Praphas resigned and fled into exile.

However, while the Army had been pushed from power in 1973, a bloody military coup on 6 October 1976 restored a right-wing military government. This military backlash was launched by a generation of Thai army officers known by the ubiquitous title of 'Young Turks', who had been blooded during the American War in Vietnam and who took a proactive view of their role as guardians of the state. It was this generation of army officers who came to dominate Thai politics (and military corruption) into the 1980s and 1990s and who, at the end of the 1990s, were only slowly being pushed from power by the government.

REBELLION

In the poverty-stricken and generally neglected north-east, a communist rebellion which had been underway since the late 1960s was particularly well supported following the 1976 coup. By the early 1980s, however, this rebellion was effectively finished. The failure of the pro-Chinese Thai communists was primarily due to the cooling of relations between China and Vietnam and Laos, which had provided much sanctuary for the rebels. The rebellion was also hampered by the loss of support from the pro-Chinese Khmer Rouge after Vietnam ousted them from power in Cambodia in 1978.

Although Thailand is a unitary state, it has numerous ethnic minorities, including Muslims in the south, Lao in the north-east (Isan) region, and numerous smaller hill tribes in the north and north-east. Many of these disenfranchised ethnic minorities supported the communist rebellion, particularly in the northern and north-eastern regions. Muslims in the south also engaged in separatist activities against the central government, although most attacks in the 1990s had ambiguous sources, with some observers believing the army was behind them to ensure its own perceived necessity.

In 1986, the government, led by General Prem Tinsulanonda, dissolved the House of Representatives after it voted against a royal decree to amend the Land Transport Act. The Thai people, and their political representatives, were beginning to show impatience with the continuing military involvement in political affairs. In 1988, Prem again dissolved the House due to disunity between and within political parties. Although majority votes within a number of parties had been carried, the parties themselves did not accept the votes, indicating that the undue influence the army continued to bear was no longer tenable. Although the position of the army in politics had been under challenge since the early 1970s, this event marked the end of the autocratic style of military rule. Prem allowed and even encouraged a gradual shift towards democracy, in 1988 stepping down in favour of a coalition government led by retired general Chatchai Choonhavan.

DEMOCRACY ESTABLISHED

However, factionalism and rampant corruption led to another military coup in 1991. By this time a significant middle class had become established, especially in Bangkok, and they and their student offspring were in no mood to continue supporting a non-reflexive military government. Spurred on by human rights and pro-democracy non-government organisations (Prudhisan & Maneerat 1997: 206), this led to public protests in May 1992, to which the army responded by shooting unarmed demonstrators. It was at this time that the king stepped in to support the protests, and, without that source of legitimation, the prime minister, General Suchinda Kraprayoon, resigned (SarDesai 1997: 262–4). With this effective defeat of the formal military in government, Thailand appeared to be on a course of liberal capitalist democracy. While retired military figures retained a high profile in Thai political life, they were too factionalised and spread across too many parties to present a united front for military interests (Wassana 1999b). This tendency was strengthened by the promulgation on 9 December 1991 of a new liberal Constitution confirming Thailand as a constitutional monarchy in that year. It was Thailand's fifteenth Constitution since 1932. This Constitution was amended again in 1997.

THE CONSTITUTIONAL STRUCTURE OF THE STATE

The Constitution established regular four-yearly elections for a 500-member House of Representatives, with 400 being from single-seat constituencies and a hundred from party lists, and a 260-member Senate. The number of members of the Senate was reduced to 200 in March 2000, providing a ratio of one senator to each 300 000 citizens. Senators were also restricted to two six-year consecutive terms in office. The Thai prime minister is usually but not necessarily an elected member of the House of Representatives and, similar to the British Westminster parliamentary system, leads the party or coalition of parties that enjoys the confidence of a majority of lower house members. The Prime Minister's 'council of ministers', numbering thirteen, may also include non-elected members. The lower house writes and approves legislation while the upper house votes on constitutional changes. Votes of no confidence in the government are taken by both houses voting together, which means that the Senate only requires a further forty-six votes to topple the government.

THE MONARCHY

For a constitutional monarchy, Thailand has a relatively active king. In most constitutional monarchies the monarch occupies the position of head of state but has little real input into the affairs of state. Thailand's King Bhumibol has tended to stay aloof from day-to-day politics, but has intervened directly at critical moments and has taken an active interest not just in day to day affairs of state but also in endorsing a strong role for himself. This intervention, for example in supporting an end to military rule in 1991, went a considerable way towards strengthening and legitimising the role of the king in Thai political life. The underlying philosophy of the king (and the 1991 Constitution) was that the monarchy and the people are as one, and that the people's interests are the king's interests (Hewison 1997: 61). This assumes that the king is familiar with the interests of 'the people', and logically also assumes that the people's interest is served by the maintenance of the monarchy. The alignment between the king and 'the people' is a relatively recent phenomenon. In the earlier period of King Bhumibol Adulyadej, he was a supporter of 'stability and order, authority and tradition, developmentalism, unity and solidarity, national chauvinism, and national security and anti-communism' (Hewison 1997: 63). Bhumibol was an 'activist' monarch, but he was conservative in his activism (Hewison 1997: 74).

Seen in this light, while King Bhumibol's intervention in state politics in 1991 was generally regarded as enlightened, it could also have been viewed as support for the ascendant private capital. It seemed that the military parties had already lost the initiative, especially in the face of public protests reflecting a range of social groups. When the king stepped in the public protests were 'legitimised' and General Suchinda stepped down as prime minister. New elections were held, in which a pro-democracy coalition led by Democrat Party leader Chuan Leekpai was put in government.

TRADITION AND AUTHORITY

Much of Thai society remains distinctly Thai and quite traditional, despite the economic development, especially of the greater Bangkok region, since the 1970s. Notions of 'big person–little person' (*phuu yai–phuu nawy*) still prevail and dominate not just the formal aspects of political life but also power relations within broader society. A further element of this idea of social hierarchy is reinforced by prescribed speech and manners. As such, in a formal sense, there are no equals at all,[7] although this assumption is perhaps more strongly asserted by those who perceive themselves higher in social ranking. The initial development of the 'big person' syndrome was a consequence of royal privilege, such as royal appointment or related association. Royalty remains broadly held as sacrosanct, in part due to tradition and in part due to the reconstruction of royalty in Thai political society following the coup of 1932, and under Sarit in the 1950s and early 1960s. As with other royal groups, when real power was diminished, symbolic power was enhanced, in many cases strengthening popular respect for monarchical figures and their families. The monarchy 'is now an important and now, arguably, a central institution and political actor' in Thai politics (Hewison 1997: 58). Thailand remains one of the very few countries in the world to retain *lèse-majesté*, in which insulting or criticising the royal family is a criminal offence, punishable by up to seven years imprisonment. Despite the criminal nature of insulting the royal family, many Thais regularly gossip about the royal families and their affairs.

Along with royalty, religion is also held to be sacrosanct. Around ninety-five per cent of all Thais are Theravada Buddhists, with Theravada Buddhism being the official state religion. A small minority of Muslims living in the four southern provinces of Yala, Narathiwat, Pattani, and Satun near the Malaysian border fell outside this officially defined version of being 'Thai' and, along with linguistic difference, often constituted themselves as unwillingly Thai. This led to a relatively mild security threat in the region, with a disproportionate response coming from the Thai military. Many of the northern hill tribes are also unwillingly constituted as 'Thai' and, in many cases, continue to identify themselves by ethnic association rather than as citizens of the larger state.

The notion of 'big person' was later expanded to include simple social rank defined by age, wealth, status, and personal and political power. In more contemporary terms 'big people' are much more widely dispersed among holders of real, practical power, including politicians and senior bureaucrats, army officers, wealthier businesspeople and so on. 'Small people', those without access to powerful positions, were usually deferential to 'big people' for reasons both real and imagined, including political threat or promise and the potential for loss or profit. Increasingly, as the Thai's sense of conspicuous consumption expanded in line with the country's economic development, money became the mark of a 'big person'.

A major division also exists between urban and rural dwellers, with Bangkok in some respects almost constituting a separate state to rural Thailand. Apart from the sheer fact of urbanisation, there are major wealth disparities between the people of the greater Bangkok region and the rest of Thailand, as well as disparities in government services. As noted at the time of the 2000 Senate elections, 'Thailand is still, no doubt, a tale of two democracies in which the middle and rural classes have conflicting expectations of politicians and government' (Crispin & Tasker 2000).

THAI MEDIA

Thailand's 1991 Constitution guaranteed freedom of the media, which was reflected in the country's generally unfettered and often high-quality news media. Thailand's newspapers were often the most informative and least restricted in SEA, while Thai television approximated Western television, including generally superficial news programming.[8] Similarly, Thai radio ran predominantly music-based programming formats, although there were some talk programs (which, like those elsewhere in the Western world, were often remarkably uninformed). The major exception was Thailand's national public broadcaster, Radio Thailand (Sathaani Withayu Haeng Prathet Thai), which ran quality local, national and international news, business, sport and news-related feature programming.

The Thai media often discussed critical or controversial issues, even though publishing permits could be suspended by the National Police Department for 'national security reasons'. As elsewhere, there was an element of self-censorship on some issues in the Thai media. Thailand's royalty was treated with the utmost respect, which was enforced by the legal sanction of *lèse-majesté*. This was most clearly illustrated, during the late democracy period, by a ban on the movie *Anna and the King*, which was a Hollywood remake of the film *The King and I* in 2000. The ban was justified on the grounds that it was an historically inaccurate portrayal of Thai royal history, but was seen by many as a bid to rein in the country's increasingly unrestricted media.

Of the print media, the English language press had perhaps the highest journalistic standards while the most popular Thai newspapers tended towards being tabloid and sensationalist. Better quality Thai language journalism existed, but was less popular than these other two categories of print media. As Thitinam has noted, however, the Thai media has not always been so relatively free and, under more oppressive governments, has acted more as a tool of state, reflecting government views rather than independent news (Thitinam 1997). Along with the Philippines, this shows the media acting as a clear barometer of the political climate, rather than directly influencing that political climate.

REINING IN THE MILITARY

By 1998, the government had begun to move to reduce the upper echelons of the armed forces, by instituting a policy of replacing only seventy-five per cent of retiring senior officers (Wassana 1998). However,

Thai soldiers continued to enjoy special legal privileges not granted to ordinary citizens, in particular the limited authority of police over soldiers, especially officers, who are suspected of committing crimes (Prakobpong 1998). This double standard was illustrated by a government crackdown on criminal activities within the army, which was officially described as the 'military mafia'. Four officers involved in such 'mafia' activities were given a 'stern warning' by the Bangkok and regional military police chief, Major-General Boonyoung Bucha. A source said the four included two major-generals, a cavalry colonel and a sublieutenant. The report went on to note that efforts to 'clean up' the military mafia had caused 'unease' among some officers who derived most of their income from illegal activities (Wassana 1999a). At the risk of slipping into cynicism, it seemed that giving 'mafia types' a 'stern warning', which caused them 'unease', did not reflect a serious attempt either to halt corrupt activity in the army or to treat all Thai citizens as legal equals. This was especially the case considering that an alleged motorcycle thief received somewhat more summary justice when he was shot dead by police (*Bangkok Post* 1999a).

Corresponding to this police 'crackdown', there was a series of bombings and bomb threats in Bangkok and elsewhere, some of which were directed against police in Bangkok. These were linked to Thailand's army. The primary link was that explosives found in one device, which was professionally constructed, were of the same type used by the Thai army (*Bangkok Post* reporters 1999; *The Nation* 1999b).

FROM MIRACLE TO CRISIS

While it had been performing admirably since the 1970s, from the late 1980s Thailand's economy grew rapidly, averaging more than ten per cent growth a year. Growth in the greater Bangkok region was phenomenal over this period, with both light and heavy manufacturing pushing the country to the forefront of industrial development. Meanwhile, Thailand's traditional export base, agriculture, remained strong, even though its returns were far lower than from manufacturing industry and led to what some observers referred to as a dual economy. This economic growth, aligned with a lack of foreign support, effectively ended the prospect of radical challenge to the government. Urban concerns focused more on democratisation and clean government, while rural concerns tended to focus more on adequate government support for infrastructure, including health and education and the decentralisation of industrialisation.

Thailand was seen as possessing one of Asia's miracle economies. As perhaps the most important measure of growth, between the mid 1970s and the mid 1990s, the number of people living in poverty in Thailand fell from around thirty per cent of the population to less than fifteen per cent. The face of Bangkok changed to reflect this new-found wealth, with skyscraper buildings dominating the skyline and more and more new cars clogging the already congested streets. New freeway systems and flyovers were built and wealth, long an indicator of social status, was conspicuously displayed. The World Bank, among others, attributed this 'miracle' to the 'sound fundamentals' of an aggressively export-oriented economy, openness to foreign investment, a high rate of savings and an increasingly highly educated workforce.

Yet at what seemed the peak of this economic boom, in the middle of 1997, Thailand's economy appeared to crumple, with the value of the baht falling by more than half on international money markets. After so many years of such strong growth, most people were taken by surprise. They should not have been, however, as the signs that the country's overheating economy had begun to boil over were increasingly obvious. While many orthodox economists claimed that, as with Indonesia, the economic crash could not have been foreseen, others were more critical in their analysis. Rowley (1999) noted that the crash of the Thai economy was not especially unusual for a capitalist economy, given the cyclical character of capitalism's boom and bust nature. Further, he also noted that in Thailand's case in particular, while its export industries had reached saturation point in their markets and that markets were in fact contracting, capital inflows had continued and credit had become almost dangerously easy to obtain. This easy and seemingly unstoppable flow of credit fuelled unproductive investment, especially in bidding up property prices, and was bled off into non-performing businesses or, indeed, into no businesses at all. As many businesses began to go bad, with their earnings no longer covering debts, more capital was borrowed to cover the shortfall. Corruption was behind much of this stage of the looming crisis, with good money being sent after bad through a series of pay-offs and kick-backs that benefited the individuals concerned but, ultimately, not their institutions or the broader economy. Then, after defaulting on repayments, the banks themselves began to look seriously exposed. The alarm bells started ringing, financial analysts re-assessed Thailand's 'miracle' economy and funds began to dry up. In a bid to increase foreign capital inflows and to make export industries more competitive, the Thai government floated the value of the baht on the international money market. Rather than dropping the value of the baht slightly and boosting exports, this had the effect of taking the floor from underneath the value of the currency, which slumped (see Rowley 1999).

The slump in the value of the baht exposed the seriousness of what was quickly shaping up to be a crisis, as most of the country's debts were denominated in foreign currencies, especially US dollars and Japanese yen. The slump in the value of the baht in effect increased this foreign denominated debt by the same proportion, making already unpayable debts impossible. Companies that had been able to meet their debt repayments under a steady baht suddenly found the size of their debt, in many cases, doubled. More than half of Thailand's finance companies defaulted on their own debt schedules.

The Thai prime minister, Chavalit Yongchaiyudh, resigned in November 1997, to be replaced by Chuan Leekpai. Chuan began to push through economic reforms, but pressure by influential businessmen meant that these reforms were increasingly abandoned or soft-pedalled into 1998. Then two of Chuan's ministers were forced to resign over corruption scandals, forcing Chuan into a new coalition government that reflected much of the 'old style' Thai politics which had been largely responsible for the economic crash in the first place. Prime Minister Chuan Leekpai expanded his governing coalition to include new members from the Chart Pattana Party, but many of them were political veterans who were identified with the old 'money politics'. While including the extra members in the coalition strengthened the government's position in terms of numbers, it also raised the spectre that, at a time when it needed to be clean and to be seen to be clean, it was not. The Chart Pattana Party, formerly a part of the Chart Thai Party, and the Social Action Party were also involved with military leader General Suchinda Kraprayoon, who had ordered troops to fire on unarmed pro-democracy protestors in May 1992. Chuan's reformist Democrats were, therefore, surrounded by politicians who were not averse to using money and power to shore up their political position, a style of politicking which Chuan had been keen to put behind Thailand (Tasker 1998). This situation was only slowly improving (for example, see Crispin 2000), with the Senate elections of mid-2000 being noted for their corruption, in particular in the Isan area where the ballot result was disqualified and the vote was conducted again.

As with all SEA states, corruption was endemic in Thailand. For example, 'buying' jobs or promotion was rife in Thai society, especially within the government service. This 'tradition' was widespread and relatively tolerated. However, along with other forms of corruption, this is officially unacceptable and, along with a relatively unfettered media, information on corrupt practices is widely available. Such corrupt activities have involved members of Thailand's government, but was most widely practised at an institutional level, where the processing of applications, favours in the letting of contracts and involvement in illegal business practises was common practice.

As with some other states, monopoly practices have been rationalised on the grounds of national interest and were a considerable source of corrupt activity. One example of this was a government move to end 'under the table' payments to the waterfront industry, which was intended to end bribes paid to get containers moving. The result of this crackdown was that container loading dropped from twenty to twelve units an hour at the Klong Toey port facility (*Bangkok Post* 1999b). At the same time, three government ministers had a censure motion put against them by the opposition for, among other things, activities that would usually be regarded as fitting the term 'corruption'. These included using development funds to build three private houses, irregularities in bidding for highway projects, and allowing close associates to benefit from government department auctions (*Bangkok Post* 1999c).

Despite its continuing problems, however, Thailand stood as something like a benchmark for good government, a strong economy, and a generally peaceful and tolerant people in what was an otherwise less perfect environment. Crossing the land borders into Thailand from Burma, Laos or Cambodia was regarded by many as a relief, and the sense of relative security was palpable. If Thailand had begun to seem a little dull to some Westerners, it was only because the country had become increasingly successful at its own process of Westernisation or, more accurately, modernisation.

NOTES

1   Of course, this sense of Thailand's economic 'irrepressibility' could have been superficial. But a couple of far more seasoned and critical observers of Thailand's economic development than I mentioned this to tended to agree on this point.
2   Thailand, Laos, China, India, Burma, Vietnam and Cambodia.
3   This method of royal execution was in common with that of Burma.
4   The exception to this was, of course, the British presence in neighbouring Burma, which was then just beginning to make its colonial presence felt to Thailand, and China.
5   This connotation derived from when T'ai people moved into the Menam valley, enslaving the local people, who were not 'Thai'. To be 'Thai' thereafter came to be associated with not being enslaved, or being free.
6   King Ananda had been at school in Switzerland, but did not wish to return to Thailand during the period of hostilities.

7   A parallel has been drawn with the use of language to embed hierarchy, in a similar manner to both Burma and Java. Yet in both Burma and Java not only have there been popular egalitarian (communist) movements but also the maintenance of social hierarchy through language is often otherwise resisted at a common level (see Berman 1998).

8   Channel 9 was the national public television broadcaster while Channel 5 was the military's broadcaster. Channel 7 was also owned by the military but was privately leased, while Channel 11 was owned by the Ministry of Education and featured educational programming.

7

Laos: The Land in Between

For a country that lies within the tropical zone, the frequently mist-shrouded highlands of Laos can be cold. Mountains rise sharply out of the valley floors far below, their steep, inhospitable sides pushing up through the clouds. Among these mountains are the various highland groups of Laos. In the region to the south of Luang Prabang towards Vieng Chan are many Hmong, a tribal group that arrived from southern China around the end of the eighteenth century. The Hmong had no traditional links with the other Lao ethnic groups—some 68 in all—and were disinclined to recognise the authority of the state. This led to conflict between the Hmong and the predominantly lowland Lao (Lao Loum) in the post-colonial state, a situation which was exacerbated by the United States using the Hmong as an independent military force against the communists in both Laos and Vietnam in the 1960s and 1970s.

Until 1997, the road between Luang Prabang, the old royal capital, and its historical rival Vieng Chan was unsafe as a consequence of Hmong attacks. These attacks were specially troublesome during the opium cultivation season, but tended to represent a more fulsome political security problem than that represented by just ordinary bandits, of which there were a few. But government control eventually extended over the mountainous regions in which the Hmong live. In 1997, government control was marked by the opening of a sealed road between the two former capitals. Not only did road transport become a regular, all-weather occurrence, but it also allowed government troops regular access to the remote regions. Under the guise of attempting to limit the environmental damage caused by swidden (slash and burn) agriculture,

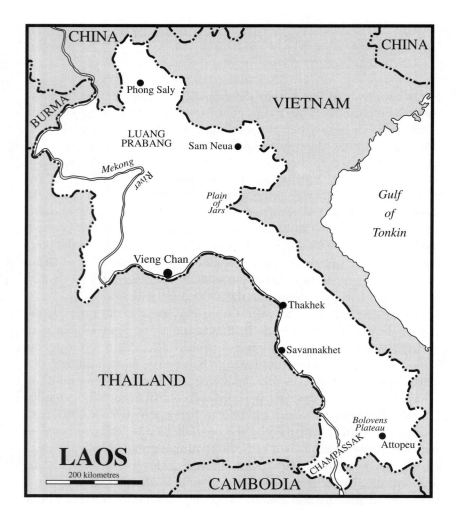

the Hmong were resettled into new villages along the side of the new, two-lane mountain highway. There, up in the clouds with regular cold rain, without access to adequate clean water and traditional sources of food, sickness set in and the mortality rate began to rise. According to one well informed source, in some of these new villages the death rate was as high as fifty per cent. After years of battling them, government concern over the fate of the Hmong was cursory, to say the least.

This chapter will look at the issues surrounding the various rivalries of Laos, which constitute further issues revolving around the formation of the state. Laos has a fragmented history, rising briefly under one glorious empire, then dissolving into petty squabbling states, re-formed only in part under French colonialism. Of special note will be the role of Laos in the Indochina conflict, covert USA intervention and internal political turmoil, and the coming to power of the communists and the end of the monarchy. It will discuss the earlier form of communist government and the later, more tolerant form of communism, which has become more accepting of Buddhism (though not proselytising Christianity), and has opened up to the global market economy. It will conclude by looking at ethnic and political opposition groups, government corruption (teak logging, opium production), and the role of the party in the state.

A LAND-LOCKED STATE

The country that is Laos, or more correctly the Lao People's Democratic Republic, is based on a broad linguistic and geographic identity that at once separates it from and unites it to its imposing Thai neighbour. The two dominant physical features that define Laos are the Annamite Mountains that run from the north to the south along its eastern edge, and the Mekong River. The Annamite Mountains are the easternmost arm of the ranges that descend to the south from the Himalayas and which, at the same time, are buttressed by the tectonic division of the western Pacific Ocean. The Annamites are the spine of the so-called Indochinese Peninsula, which holds Vietnam and Cambodia as well as Laos, and which cups Thailand to the west.

The other major defining feature of Laos is the Mekong River.[1] The Mekong rises in the watershed of the south-eastern Himalayas and spills down through Yunnan province in southern China, marking the modern boundary between Burma and Laos. It then continues, demarcating the central portion of the border between Thailand and Laos until entering northern Cambodia and finally exiting in southern Vietnam. The majority of the people of Laos live in the lowlands adjacent to the Mekong or in the nearby tributary valleys. Until the 1980s when roads started to be more widely constructed, the Mekong served as the main transportation route in Laos and, until the period between 1893 and 1907 with the final partition of the French colony which became Laos, it was also the focus, on both east and west banks, of the lowland Lao people. Indeed, the course of the Mekong River, which is steered southward by the Annamite Mountains, could be said to define Laos.

EARLY LAOS

The focus on the Mekong and the western flanks of the Annamite Mountains begs the question of the sense of community of Laos, and of its separation from Thailand. The Lao and the Thai, like Burma's Shan, the Lu of China's Yunnan and the Chuang of western Guangxi province, the Nung of northern Vietnam and other scattered groups, are of the T'ai language group.[2] The T'ai migrated south from these southern Chinese regions, probably ahead of the expanding Han Chinese influence, from the time towards the end of the pre-Christian period until the second half of the first millennium of the Common Era (Stuart-Fox 1997: 8). The first political communities established by these people were called *meuang*, a term which includes both personal as well as spatial relations, being a town or extending as far as a network of villages or towns under a single *chao* (lord) (Wyatt 1984: 7). One of the earliest known *meuang* was Meuang Thaen, now known as Dien Bien Phu, just across the border from northern Laos in Vietnam. Such *meuang* developed to include wider areas of authority, being in effect principalities and comprising the first identifiable states in the region.

The T'ai, though, were not the only inhabitants of the region. As the T'ai moved south they encountered existing Austronesian and Austro-asiatic speaking peoples, displacing them and driving them into the relative security of the mountains. The major group in this region called them-selves Lawa, or Lwa, which became Lao. According to Viravong, the name Lao was later applied by the T'ai outside the area of Laos to describe the T'ai inhabitants of that same region (Viravong 1964: 6–7). The original inhabitants of Laos, along with disparate groups that subse-quently followed and settled in remote areas, are the people who have come to form many of the ethnic minorities of Laos.

The development of early Laos cannot be understood independently of the development of the proto-Thai state, as the two crossed over and

were inter-linked in a number of ways. In this respect, early state formation reflected the *mandala* principle, whereby states had varying degrees
of control or autonomy that fluctuated and was poorly defined. In the
first instance, what was to become the Thai state was comprised of competing states that were either subsumed into or divided by the whole.
The early T'ai state of Lan Na typified this development. Lan Na, which
meant 'land of a million paddy fields', was centred on Chiang Mai in
northern Thailand but extended into what is now north-western Laos
and north-eastern Burma up to Yunnan in southern China, and was typical of this *mandala*-type development. A number of other small *mandala*-
type states are claimed to have existed in the region that approximates
what was to become Laos, along with more northern regions inhabited
by Lao people (Viravong 1964: 6–24). The dates of the establishment of
these small states is suggested to be as far back as the last years before the
beginning of the Christian Era, although evidence for this, especially in
the south (contemporary northern Laos), is slim.

The greatest threat to the development of such T'ai–Lao *mandala*-type
states came from two sources, the first being the rise of strong states in the
west of the region now known as Burma. The most powerful of these
Burmese states was centred at Pagan, which conducted frequent raids into
neighbouring territories. The second major threat came from the Khmer
empire based at Angkor, in the north-west of modern Cambodia. Indeed,
most of the Mekong Valley in what is now Laos was under Khmer control by 1200 CE (Wyatt 1984: 26). However, by the middle of the thirteenth century, the Mongol armies of Kublai Khan were consolidating
their control over the region and had overrun and occupied the last independent states of Yunnan by 1253, sweeping south-west to destroy Pagan.
The Mongols, moving down the Mekong Valley, also asserted their
authority over Angkor, although by this stage that once-great empire
was already in decline. Under Mongol-Yuan suzerainty, three major T'ai
mandalas became more formally established in the region. The first was
the T'ai-Siam mandala of Sukhothai, from 1438, which incorporated the
state of Ayudhya; the second the northern state of Lan Na; and the third
the state of Lan Xang, meaning Land of a Million Elephants, which was
centred on Xiang Dong Xiang Thong (later known as Luang Prabang)
(Stuart-Fox 1997: 9).

A Lao *meuang* had existed on the site of Luang Prabang since the land
was taken by Lao invaders from earlier settlers. It is probable that the site
had been a settlement of some importance, located as it is on the confluence of the Mekong and the Nam Khan rivers,[3] which provide fresh
water and transport and protect it from three sides. The 'kingdom' of Lan

Xang was believed to have existed from 1271, under a ruler entitled a *phraya* ('he who upholds'). However, other claims put Lao occupation of that site as far back as 757 CE (Viravong 1964: 25). Local claims to and some evidence of organised Mahayana Buddhist activity in the region in and around Luang Prabang appear to confirm this approximate date.

The development of the Lao *meuang* as a great kingdom is generally attributed to Fa Ngum, born in 1316 CE. Fa Ngum, a hereditary prince,[4] is said to have been expelled from the capital, possibly for attempting to seize the throne (Stuart-Fox 1997: 9). It has been claimed that Fa Ngum grew up and was educated as a prince at Angkor in Cambodia (Viravong 1964: 27). He is generally regarded as having established his credentials with the Khmer court of the day and to have been equipped with an army with which to invade his former home. Between 1349 and 1357, his armies conquered all of the region that was to be the empire of Lan Xang (Viravong 1964: 26–36). Fa Ngum was also credited with introducing Theravada Buddhism, then dominant in Cambodia, to the region under his control. The extent of the territory claimed by Lan Xang, at its height in the middle of the sixteenth century, extended to include modern Laos, the western periphery of modern northern and central Vietnam, north-eastern Thailand, and, through family rule in Lan Na, southernmost Yunnan and parts of what is now north-eastern Burma (Wyatt 1984: 82–7). However, the greatness of Lan Xang was soon challenged.

THE DIVISION OF LAN XANG

As a typical *mandala*-type state, the strength of the Lao state was determined by the strength of its ruler and the ability of the state to withstand external threats. In 1479, Vietnam invaded Lan Xang, sacking Luang Prabang, while in 1558, Chiang Mai fell to the Burmese, under whose control it remained for the next two centuries. In 1560, the capital of Lan Xang was moved from Luang Prabang to Vieng Chan, while Lao settlers moved further down the Mekong Valley to Champassak and on to the Khorat Plateau of north-eastern Thailand, shifting the geographic balance of power in the Lao world (Stuart-Fox 1997: 12). But all was not stable in the Lao world. In 1569, Burmese forces that had already sacked Ayudhaya and who had for the previous six years been attacking Lan Xang, moved on Vieng Chan, but withdrew due to lack of supplies. Burmese attacks continued, however, for the following six years. Lan Xang recovered and, under Xetthathirat, moved to invade Cambodia. There the Lan Xang army was soundly defeated and, during its retreat,

Xetthathirat disappeared, with the state being weakened through a series of disputes of succession.

From 1637, under Surinyavongsa, Lan Xang entered a period of relative tranquillity and prosperity, which was remarked upon by European visitors at that time. When Surinyavongsa died in 1694 he left no heir, his only son having been executed for adultery. The state quickly fell into internal squabbling, and between 1707 and 1713 divided into three smaller states approximating the natural division by rapids of the Mekong: Luang Prabang, Vieng Chan and Champassak. Each of these, over the next several decades, came under the sway of the new and increasingly powerful Siamese state. The Siamese state itself was subject to another Burmese expedition, with Chiang Mai falling in 1763, Luang Prabang in 1765, and Ayudhaya being sacked in 1767. When the Siamese state recovered and drove out the Burmese, it also asserted its control over the three Lao states.

Within the Siamese *mandala* state, the tributary states of Laos and Lan Na were independent in their day-to-day affairs, although this did not preclude the loss of authority of Vieng Chan over the Khorat Plateau, which increasingly (and accurately) recognised Siam as the dominant regional power. Within Vieng Chan, however, there was considerable resentment towards Bangkok and its offhand treatment of its suzerain states. In 1826, under Chou Anu (also referred to as Anuvong), Vieng Chan raised three armies and Champassak another, which crossed into the Khorat Plateau with the intention of reclaiming the region and, with Vietnamese support, uniting the Lao kingdoms and declaring Lao independence. Chou Anu believed that the Siamese would be too preoccupied with the British invasion of Burma to be able to respond, not knowing they had just concluded a treaty with the British. The Siamese responded, defeating the Lao south of Vieng Chan, putting the capital to the sack in mid May 1827 and forcibly resettling hundreds of thousands of its population on the Khorat Plateau. Even forty years later, Vieng Chan existed only as ruins (Ngaosyvathn & Ngaosyvathn 1998: 25). Chou Anu returned the following year, but his efforts were no more successful. Fleeing to Vietnam, he and his family were handed back to the Siamese. The Vietnamese emperor, Minh Mang, though holding suzerainty over Vieng Chan, was at pains to maintain peace with Thailand due to internal difficulties at home (Ngaosyvathn & Ngaosyvathn 1998: 105–8). In 1829, Chou Anu died from torture in custody in Bangkok. The result was that 'Not only was the Kingdom of Viang Chan erased from the map: so too was any remaining shadow of the mandala of Lan Xang' (Stuart-Fox 1997: 15; see also Viravong 1964:

114–31; Ngaosyvathn & Ngaosyvathn 1998). Only Luang Prabang retained any semblance of autonomy, paying tribute not just to Bangkok but also to the Vietnamese court at Hue and to Beijing. This was the state of affairs when France, under a doubtful assertion by the Vietnamese to suzerainty over Vieng Chan and the central region east of the Mekong, claimed a 'right of inheritance'.

LAOS UNDER THE FRENCH

In a series of manoeuvres between 1886 and 1893, France moved administrators and troops to the east bank of the Mekong. Thai and British opposition, however, generally limited French claims to the west bank. After minor clashes between French and Siamese troops and a confrontation with French ships in Bangkok, the French issued an ultimatum, which included formally ceding all territory east of the Mekong, all its islands and, in 1907, territory on the west bank in the north and south. In 1893, Siam agreed, creating the French protectorate of Laos from less than half the territory and perhaps a sixth of the population that could trace its descent from Lan Xang.

The northern demarcation of Laos from Burma was agreed upon in 1896 between the French and the British, who had annexed Shan State as a part of Burma. This created a boundary along the deepest points of the upper reaches of the Mekong, while a reduced Thailand was left as a buffer state between the main forces of the two colonial powers. Other boundary changes were more administrative. Huaphan, Xieng Khuang, and the Hmong-populated areas in the Plain of Jars[5] were returned from the French-administered Tonkin to Laos in parcels in 1893, 1895 and 1903. Stung Treng province was returned by Laos to French-administered Cambodia in 1904, while parts of the Central Highlands were returned to Vietnam in 1904 and 1905, and a small area of land in Xainaburi was returned to Thailand in 1907 (Stuart-Fox 1997: 26–7).

The original interest by the French in Laos was to establish a route along the Mekong to trade with southern China. However, it was discovered by them as early as the 1860s that the two sets of rapids and numerous other obstacles in the northern sections of the river made that an impractical goal. The French rationale for annexation then changed to one of rounding out their territories in Indochina and providing a potential base from which to launch the possible annexation of Siam. Yet the fear of conflict with the British, who had a well established economic presence in Siam, precluded the latter option. Having secured the territory, then, but having little practical use for it, the French adminis-tration tended to neglect Laos (Smith 1964b: 527–33). Infrastructure was almost non–existent, economic development continued at a very low level, education was underdeveloped, and even the local people were rarely able to develop administrative skills, for those positions were mostly taken by Vietnamese imported for the purpose. The French policy was to use Vietnamese both to work in Laos and to further popu-late it. This policy, which saw Vieng Chan and Thakhaek with an ethnic Vietnamese majority, was kept intact until as late as 1945 (Stuart-Fox 1996: 32). Despite various French attempts otherwise, perhaps the only real growth area in the Lao economy was the sale of opium, which was a government monopoly[6] (McCoy 1970: 81–6).

RESISTANCE AND REBELLION

Lao resistance to French occupation was at a relatively low level, but fairly consistent throughout the colonial period. Upland revolts began in 1896, peaked between 1910 and 1916, and continued, though declining in intensity, through to the 1930s. In the south, a revolt based on the Bolovens Plateau started in 1901, peaking in the following year when more than 7000 'rebels' attacked a French garrison at Kontum in Viet-nam. However, about 150 rebels were killed and the French retaliated by building a series of block-houses[7] around the edge of the plateau and burning most of the region's crops. While this broke most resistance, it was not until 1907 that the French launched a major campaign against the rebel leader, Ong Keo, forcing him to surrender and to swear loyalty to France. However, other rebel leaders escaped and even Ong Keo's submission was only short-lived. Ong Keo was killed in 1910, when he went to negotiate with the French in Champassak. One of his comrades, Komadom, continued to lead a small resistance movement, which gained renewed momentum in the mid 1930s. Komadom's movement was effectively ended when he was killed during a 'massive pacification campaign' in 1936[8] (Stuart-Fox 1997: 33–41).

A number of other rebellions broke out in the north in the early 1900s, and the most violent, from 1914 to 1916, actually removed French authority from a number of provinces in Laos and northern Viet-nam. In Laos, about forty T'ai and forty Chinese attacked a French gar-rison at Sam Neua, slaughtering the colonial troops stationed there and ambushing and repulsing troops from a neighbouring French garrison sent to relieve them. The rebels then retreated into Vietnam, where they fought two more battles, then returned to Phongsali province in northern Laos where, aided by local villagers, they captured nearly the whole province. After numerous inconsequential battles, the French finally organised more than 5000 troops from Hanoi who, after two months of fighting, drove the rebels into southern China. Three years later, the Hmong also revolted against the French. According to McCoy, these revolts ultimately failed because they were too splintered, failing to gain the support of other Lao minorities or, more importantly, the majority of Lao. As a small concession to proto-nationalist sentiment, the French allowed the establishment of an Indigenous Consultative Assembly from 1923. But this was no more than a token gesture towards disgruntled Lao. It was not until the Japanese interlude, which effectively began in 1940, that the Lao began to develop a cohesive sense of national identity (McCoy 1970: 87–92).

JAPANESE INVASION

Japan occupied Laos, and the rest of French Indochina, as a part of its alliance with the pro-German Vichy government in France in 1941. The main effect of the Japanese occupation of the region was that it enhanced a sense of pan-Thai irredentism, which led to Thai attacks on French shipping. Japan, supporting its Thai allies, brokered an agreement that saw France cede all its territories in Laos on the west bank of the Mekong (in Xianaburi and Champassak provinces). As a consequence, the Lao king, Sisavang Vong, threatened to resign, which would have further destabilised the French position in Laos and could have seen Thailand pressing for incorporation of the whole colony. The French responded by offering the king a number of concessions, including establishing the kingdom of Luang Prabang as a protectorate, including the provinces of Nam Tha, Xieng Khouang and Vieng Chan, and the granting of some political autonomy.

The French governor-general, Admiral Decoux, believed that if Lao nationalism was appropriately channelled it could assist in gaining the return of the lost territories. To this end, he appointed a colonial official, Charles Rochet, to encourage the development of Lao nationalist sentiment, especially among the lowland Lao (Lao Loum). The movement with which Rochet was associated achieved, among other things, the construction of 7000 schools, expansion of the poor health system, and the publication of the first Lao newspaper. While this new sense of national pride began to take hold among the Lao Loum, the highland

Lao were moved by other activities, in particular guerrilla warfare and the growth and sale of opium (McCoy 1970: 93–5). With the development of the conflict of World War II, Laos was cut off from much of its traditional sources of opium. Because of the social consequences for addicts and, more importantly, for government revenues, the French engineered the accelerated growth of opium by the Hmong, Yao and Tai tribes in northern Laos.

Competition for the lucrative opium trade engendered conflict between these tribes, which was exacerbated by the French, in 1944–45, arming tribal guerrilla bands against the Japanese. These conflicts produced 'permanent cleavages in Laotian society' (McCoy 1970: 97) which continued to plague the country into the twenty-first century. Probably the most significant 'cleavage' was among the Hmong, one clan of which was at the centre of the French campaign against Japan, and later the pro-independence Lao Issara, which was allied with another clan of Hmong. The military wing of the Lao Issara later transformed into the Pathet Lao,[9] while the former clan of the Hmong were armed by the US Central Intelligence Agency as a part of its covert war in Indochina.

Following a coup de force by Japan against the French in Indochina on 9 March 1945, on 8 April that year, at the behest of Japan,[10] King Sisavang Vong declared Laos independent. While France managed to return soon after, the idea of Lao nationalism had taken root, leading to an alliance of anti-French forces known as the aforementioned Lao Issara (Free Lao).

THE STRUGGLE FOR INDEPENDENCE

The situation among the small elite in the period leading up to and just after 1945 was complex, determined in part by ideology but in large part also by strategic alliances. With Japan, France, Thailand, China, and Vietnam all taking an active interest in Laos, the choice of available patrons based on who was perceived to be the best guarantor of power created multiple divisions, which were exacerbated by the shifting loyalties of some of the Lao elite (Adams 1970: 100, 105). When Japan surrendered in August 1945, its occupying forces fled south to escape the advancing Nationalist Chinese 93rd Division, hoping instead to surrender to the British. While the French assumed they would automatically resume control of Laos, premier, viceroy and soon to be head of a coalition independence committee,[11] Prince Phetsarath informed them they no longer had authority in Laos and that the independence that had been declared in April was still in force. On 15 September, Phetsarath took the further step of declaring the kingdoms of Luang Prabang and Champassak united.

No sooner had this declaration been made, however, than the king sent Phetsarath a telegram saying that he regarded the French protectorate as still in force. In response, a 'Defence Committee' was established, which on 12 October voted in a Provisional Constitution, formed a Provisional People's Assembly and nominated a Lao Issara government (Dommen 1965: 22). The pro-independence Prince Souphanouvong then made contact with leaders of the nationalist revolution of the newly proclaimed Vietnamese Republic. The Vietnamese leader, Ho Chi Minh, offered Souphanouvong 'all possible assistance' and gave him a guard of fifty Viet Minh soldiers for his return to Laos via Lao Bao (between Hue and Savannakhet). The importance of this alliance was illustrated by the fact that Ho also allowed Souphanouvong's escort to take with them 100 of the Central Vietnam committee's 240 rifles. Ho foresaw that Laos, and the pro-Vietnamese Lao nationalists, would later play a strategic role in the Viet Minh's war with the French. The group marched to the Mekong and then north to Vieng Chan, recruiting soldiers along the way, where it joined the Lao Issara government, with Souphanouvong being appointed Minister of Defence (Dommen 1965: 23).

Recognising their weak position, the Lao Issara sent a delegation to Luang Prabang to seek the support of the king, Sisavang Vong. The king duly agreed to place himself under the authority of the provisional government and stated that since the time of the Japanese surrender he had no secret agreements with any representative of the French government. This was intended to be a means of preserving, or enhancing, his authority. On this basis, the Lao Issara asked Sisavang Vong to assume the throne of a unified Laos under a constitutional monarchy. The French, however, had other ideas and, after a brief diversion to quell an uprising in southern Vietnam, sent troops north from Champassak. The Lao Issara offered resistance but, on 21 March 1946, the French occupied Thakhek, north of Savannakhet on the Mekong, which led to the pass just beyond Na Pe, east of Vieng Chan, and the primary communications route to the Viet Minh-controlled areas of north-central Vietnam. The French thereafter moved to control the towns, including Vieng Chan on 24 April 1946, while the Lao Issara operated from the countryside or from the security of the Thai side of the Mekong, under the protection of the sympathetic government of Pridi Phanomyong (Dommen 1965: 25).

It was from around this time that the United States began to take an active interest in the region. Initially agents from the Office of Strategic Services (OSS)[12] formed links with the Viet Minh, and opposed the

French re-occupation of Laos. However, while the US government took a broadly anti-colonial position in the immediate post-war years, recognising Laos as an independent state in 1950, its position began to harden along with the lines being drawn in the developing Cold War. What were essentially a series of wars of national independence in French Indochina were increasingly interpreted by the USA as 'communist aggression'. Following the outbreak of the Korean conflict, the USA adopted the French position of 'communist containment'.

A FRENCH 'UNION'

While still in the immediate postwar period, the French had secured an alliance with Prince Boun Oum na Champassak, heir to the defunct throne of Champassak, who was concerned about Vietnamese control of Laos. In exchange for being made Inspector-General for life, Boun Oum renounced his sovereign rights over Champassak. In 1946, under a nominal concession to Lao aspirations for independence, the French allowed elections for a Constituent Assembly. The assembly was given the task of drawing up a new Constitution, which would incorporate Laos as a part of the new French Union.[13] Meanwhile, Lao Issara attacks continued, increasingly assisted by the Viet Minh. The republic of Vietnam was also incorporated into the French Union, but tension between the limited scope of the supposed independence it offered and the aspirations of the Viet Minh soon led to conflict. The Viet Minh withdrew to the mountains and the French position against them hardened to one of no negotiation. The French further strengthened their position in Laos, in 1947, by having returned to Laos the territory ceded to Thailand during the period of Japanese occupation. But the Lao Issara increasingly recognised, following the Viet Minh experience, that little could be gained from negotiating with the French. The Viet Minh especially encouraged their ally, Souphanouvong, in this view.

The first Constituent Assembly sat in May 1947, but it was a feeble organisation with no real influence. In order to secure a quiet region at a time of their troubles with the Viet Minh, France granted Laos further concessions[14] in July 1949. Prince Souvanna Phouma and the king accepted the French proposal for the concessions, but Souphanouvong did not. In May 1949, with the support of the Viet Minh, Souphanouvong created a separate political front for his guerrillas, calling it the Progressive People's Organisation. In August the following year the organisation's name was changed to Pathet Lao. His split with the king was now irrevocable and Souphanouvong was removed from his ministerial positions in the Lao Issara government. In October that year, the Lao Issara formally disbanded, with its more pro-French members returning to Vieng Chan (Dommen 1965: 30–4), with Souvanna Phouma forming the first Royal Lao Government (RLG) in November 1951. Following French requests and its support for local governments, the USA agreed to give the RLG economic aid, which formed the basis of US economic involvement in Laos until the mid 1970s.

DEFEAT OF THE FRENCH

In response to continuing internal pressure for genuine independence, in 1953 the French government agreed to invite selected representatives to a new round of negotiations. The French agreed to greater autonomy for Laos, but the growing war for Vietnam's independence continued to pull at its vulnerable neighbour. What had started out as a 'police action' grew into a full-scale conflict, which the French neither understood nor, when they realised its scale and potential, wanted. Much of the conflict in Vietnam focused on the mountainous terrain in Vietnam's north-western Lai Chau Province, with the Viet Minh spilling over into and, in effect, invading neighbouring Laos. By 1953 the Viet Minh were routing the French and were within striking distance of Luang Prabang, though the attack did not materialise and the coming monsoon ended such potential plans. After the monsoonal rains, another column of Viet Minh crossed the Annamite Mountains and captured Thakhek.

Planning to thwart further Viet Minh advances, in November 1953 French paratroops reoccupied the valley of Dien Bien Phu, just across the Lao border in Vietnam, through which numerous Viet Minh had crossed from their mountain bases into Laos. By January 1954, the garrison at Dien Bien Phu was surrounded by Viet Minh. The Viet Minh commander, General Vo Nguyen Giap, sent a diversionary force towards Luang Prabang, which distracted French support while building strength around Dien Bien Phu. The French believed their entrenched and externally supported fortifications were the answer to Viet Minh attacks. But by August 1953, Dien Bien Phu was the only French base that had not been overrun by the Viet Minh. Inaccessible by ground and hundreds of kilometres from air support, the reinforced garrison was subject to severe bombardment by Viet Minh cannon and mortars in the surrounding hills. From the laying of the trap to its closure, there was never any doubt that the Viet Minh would claim the battle of Dien Bien Phu as its greatest victory (Dommen 1965: 40–3). That victory came to the Viet Minh on 7 May 1954, just days before a new round of negotiations with the French in Geneva, which ensured that the French position in Indochina was irretrievable.

Despite attempts by the Viet Minh to have the Lao guerrillas represented at the Geneva talks, the official Lao representative was not adequately supported by the Chinese or Soviet representatives at the talks and was not given official status. The agreement reached thus saw Vietnam partitioned at the 17th Parallel, with the Democratic Republic of Vietnam administering the north. But the agreement left Laos intact as a unitary, independent state under the Royal Lao Government in Vieng Chan, despite the presence of a substantial revolutionary organisation. Members of the forces of the Lao Resistance Government—the Pathet Lao—regrouped in the two northern provinces of Sam Neua and Phongsaly, prior to being integrated into the Lao army or demobilised. The practical effect of this and continued clashes between the RLG forces and the Pathet Lao, however, was to permanently allocate the two provinces to the Pathet Lao. This assured them of continuing north Vietnamese support and influence in Pathet Lao affairs. It also provided a base from which the Pathet Lao leadership could recruit from the country's minority groups.

US INVOLVEMENT AND POLITICAL CHAOS

In 1955, the US legation in Vieng Chan was raised to the status of an embassy and US involvement in Lao affairs increased. One effect of this was to bring into the country funds that increasingly destabilised the domestic economic base. Through the embassy, a US Operations Mission opened in Vieng Chan, providing a large proportion of the RLG's finances. This mission was staffed entirely by military personnel who engaged in training army officers and expanding the police force. It was a precursor to the later substantial CIA presence in the country (Stuart-Fox 1997: 89–93). Negotiations began in 1956 to bring the Pathet Lao within the RLG. Despite continuing armed clashes between RLG and Pathet Lao forces, this was achieved in November 1957. However, while this government of 'unity' was accepted by the 'neutralist' group[15] it was increasingly opposed by the conservatives, who were strongly encouraged by the United States, in particular from 1958 onwards (Stuart-Fox 1997: 99–134). What had heightened US concerns was that, in supplementary elections in May 1958, there had been gains made by leftist candidates.

This encouraged the United States to back the creation of a right-wing Committee for the Defence of the National Interest the following month.

CIVIL WAR

The view from the United States was, according to US President Eisenhower, that Laos, along with South Vietnam, was 'the present key to the entire area of South East Asia' (McNamara 1995: 35; see also 36–8). McNamara has since admitted the United States simply misunderstood the primarily nationalist motivation for ideological conflict. The Viet Minh did not, but exploited that sentiment. The suspension of US economic aid to Laos forced the resignation of Souvanna Phouma in July, leading to the formation of a right-wing government in August. Stuart-Fox regarded this event as marking a shift in power in Laos from the Lao National Assembly to the US Embassy, and irrevocably committing the country to conflict. 'The First Coalition Government was the last occasion when neutrality remained an option for Laos' (Stuart-Fox 1997: 104). In its bid to end what it correctly perceived to be a leftist threat to its control, the following government attempted to force the integration of Pathet Lao forces into the RLG army. The attempt was successfully resisted, so the government responded by arresting Pathet Lao leaders still in Vieng Chan. This precipitated a return to a more advanced state of civil war. By this stage, government authority existed only in so far as it could be enforced by military means, its legitimacy being effectively finished.

While the country's political situation was spinning out of control, King Sisavang Vong died, and was succeeded by his son, Savangvatthana, in October 1959. Within two months, however, real rather than symbolic politics reasserted itself with an attempted military coup. The coup failed due to mounting internal and external opposition, but it forced the resignation of the right-wing Phuy Xananikon government, to be replaced by a new government strongly influenced by the RLG army and police, and the US Embassy.

Laos in the 1960s was a strife-torn and divided place where elites, mostly aligned with a branch of the royal family, competed for authority. On 24 April 1960, 'blatantly rigged' national elections were won by rightists, with no Pathet Lao candidates returned, followed on 9 August by a Neutralist *coup d'état* led by Captain Konglae. A week later, on 16 August, the third Suvanna Phuma government was formed. But the rightists regrouped in Savannakhet to the south and marched north, attacking Vieng Chan from 13 to 16 December. Souvanna and the members of his government fled to Phnom Penh. Konglae and his troops retreated towards the Plain of Jars, where they made common cause with the Pathet Lao and the two forces jointly occupied the region (Stuart-Fox 1996: 43–4).

Faced with a situation in which neither side could achieve overall victory, and with international support from the USA and the USSR enforcing the stalemate, the Kennedy administration announced its support for the 'neutralisation' of Laos on 23 March 1961. This led to the Geneva Conference on Laos opening seven weeks later. The defeat of rightist forces at the Battle of Namtha in May 1962 sealed the uneasy balance, with the Second Coalition government being formed at the conclusion of the Geneva Conference on 23 June. The peace was fragile, however, and the assassination of Kinim Phonsena on 1 April 1963 signalled the de facto collapse of the Second Coalition government, with the two Pathet Lao ministers fleeing the capital. The outer shell of the government remained, however, despite several attempts to demolish it, because it suited all to maintain the pretence of 'neutrality' in light of the escalating conflict in neighbouring Vietnam. The practical fragility of the political environment was highlighted by an attempted rightist military *coup d'état* on 19 April 1964, followed the next month by a split between the Pathet Lao and the neutralists, with the former driving the latter out of the Plain of Jars. It was at this time that the USA began its bombing of Pathet Lao targets. On 31 January 1965 there was another attempted rightist putsch, but this was foiled.

If ideological conflict was not sufficient to tear apart Laos, the effective growth of warlords acting independently of the central government and the unrestricted greed of some sections of the elite seemed to complete the task. In January 1965, a group of rightist army officers seized the radio station in Vieng Chan and demanded an end to corruption and politicking in the army and improved conditions for soldiers and public servants. This led to fighting between police loyal to rightist army leader General Phumi Nosavan and soldiers loyal to the government. Government troops held the day and Phumi escaped to Thailand, leaving his own illegal economic empire to be carved up by greedy officers. Some officers took over the opium and heroin trade, tapping into the market of US soldiers in South Vietnam, others smuggled timber to Thailand or set up protection rackets, while yet others sold military hardware to the Pathet Lao. In October 1966, a dispute over an opium shipment led the Lao air force to bomb the army headquarters near Vieng Chan (Stuart-Fox 1997: 146–7).

Between the war and the outright corruption of officers, when Souvanna's government attempted to rein in the country's growing deficit in

September 1966, the budget was angrily rejected. Souvanna called new elections, which were held the following January. Souvanna was returned as prime minister of a 'neutralist' government, changing nothing of the increasingly corrupt society. 'By the late 1960s, corruption permeated all levels of Lao society' (Stuart-Fox 1997: 148–9).

By January 1968 the war in Indochina was not going the way the United States had hoped. North Vietnam and the Pathet Lao, renamed the Lao People's National Liberation Army (LPNLA; its political wing was the Lao People's Revolutionary Party or LPRP), took Nam Bak and Phu Pha Thi. The United States was keen both to destabilise the LPNLA and to secure the strategically important Plain of Jars. To this end in 1969, exploiting the divisions and antipathies between the various Hmong groups, the Central Intelligence Agency armed and trained a Hmong 'Secret Army'. In September, this 'Secret Army' took control of the Plain of Jars, but in February the following year, the combined Vietnam People's Army (VPA, also referred to as the North Vietnamese Army, or NVA) and LPNLA retook the region. But the Hmong continued to constitute a difficulty for the LPNLA and the VPA. By this stage Laos was inextricably drawn into the conflict in Vietnam. Arms and equipment were constantly being shipped down the network of tracks that was the 'Ho Chi Minh Trail', inside Laos and into northern Cambodia and north-western South Vietnam. In a bid to stem this flow, in February 1971 the Army of the Republic of Viet Nam (South Vietnamese Army, referred to as the ARVN) launched a major operation, Lam Son 719, in which 20 000 troops left Khe San along Route Nine heading towards Xepon in an attempt to cut the 'trail'. Souvanna declared a state of emergency and while Royal Lao Army troops mounted a diversionary tactic to the west, the real battle was fought by troops from the VPA. The ARVN assault was heavily defeated and allowed the VPA and LPNLA forces to consolidate their control over the entire Boloven region (Stuart-Fox 1997: 144).

THE LPRP TAKES POWER

By 1972, the United States was well advanced in its process of the 'Vietnamisation' of the regional war and was about to abandon its rightist Lao and Hmong allies. With reduced external support to the RLG, the LPRP was militarily dominant. With the rightists increasingly on the military defensive, elections were held for the National Assembly on 2 January 1972. The elections and negotiations for a cease-fire and a coalition government came into effect on 21 February 1973, with the Third Coalition Government being agreed to on 14 September 1973 and taking office on

5 April 1974. From this time on events began to move quickly. On 13 April 1975 the National Assembly was dissolved by royal decree, to the backdrop of the imminent fall of the republican government in Cambodia to the Khmer Rouge, which came just four days later. Saigon fell to the VPA two weeks and three days after the dissolution of the Lao Assembly. Public demonstrations orchestrated by the LPRP forced rightist leaders to flee Vieng Chan on 9 May. The 'Liberation of Vieng Chan' was formally proclaimed on 23 August along with a 'People's Revolutionary Administration' and the abolition of the Royal Lao Army and the police, which were replaced by newly formed workers' militia units. The coalition government under Souvanna was maintained, however, for more than three more months. In November the LPRP held local and provincial elections, around the same time clashing with the Thai army across the Mekong, which led to the closure of the border. With Thai support for resistance forces operating from across the Mekong, in a move to stabilise the political situation the LPRP forced the abdication of King Savangvatthana on 1 December. The following day the LPRP proclaimed the formation of the Lao People's Democratic Republic, formally establishing the power that had increasingly been theirs since the beginning of the year.

In power, one of the LPRP's first moves was to send approximately 10 000–15 000 people to re-education camps, some of whom remained there for up to thirteen years. The following year, heady with victory, the LPRP embarked on the socialist phase of its revolution. Between the LPRP's victory over its rightist opponents and the move towards creating a socialist state, thousands of Lao fled across the Mekong. Meanwhile, Hmong supporters of the 'Secret Army' who had been abandoned at the close of the war staged an uprising. Afraid that rightists would attempt to use the king as a symbol of opposition or even try to spirit him out of the country, on 12 March 1977 the LPRP arrested Savangvatthana, his wife and son, Vong Savang, and sent them to Vieng Xai for 're-education'. Vong Savang was believed to have died there of fever a year or two later (Sagar 1991: 130; Kremmer 1997: 195, 210). Because of fears of a Chinese attempt to seize the king, he and his wife were moved from Vieng Xai, near the Chinese border, to Sop Hao, where they were believed to have died in approximately 1980 (Kremmer 1997: 196, 211).

LAO SOCIALISM

An early and major move on the part of the LPRP government was to formalise its relations with the new Socialist Republic of Vietnam, through a twenty-five year Treaty of Friendship. It was at this stage that many observers believed that Laos was being turned into a Vietnamese satellite state. In practical terms, when Vietnam invaded Cambodia in December 1978 and China responded by invading northern Vietnam, Laos sided with Vietnam against China, despite sharing its northern border with China. While relations between Laos and Vietnam have remained close, Laos has subsequently gained more autonomy from its influential neighbour, especially in regard to its relations with Thailand and China. In 1990 the Chinese Premier Li Peng visited Laos, marking the formal warming of relations between the two countries.

The LPRP's moves towards socialism were put into practice with the program of agricultural cooperatives launched in May 1978. In the face of practical difficulties and popular opposition, the program of introducing cooperatives was suspended in July the following year. The LPRP also announced an interim three-year economic plan, although this did not produce any noticeable benefits. To this end, in December 1980 the LPRP's Central Committee endorsed a new economic policy and announced its first five-year plan to run from 1981 to 1985. Although by this stage the government of Laos was committed to the path of LPRP domination, its one link with the 'Neutralism' of the past ended with the death of Souvanna Phuma, aged eighty-two, on 10 January 1984 in Vieng Chan. It is worth noting that the types of policies pursued by the neutralists were later adopted by the increasingly pragmatic LPRP government.

One of the most noticeable aspects of the LPRP government has been, despite its close links to Vietnam, its policy of asserting Lao autonomy. In June 1985 Laos engaged in a short border conflict with its larger and far bigger neighbour Thailand over three disputed villages. Despite the potential cost to trade and the real problem Laos would have in sustaining a major conflict, it did not shy away from further conflict with Thailand from November 1987 to January 1988 over disputed territory in Phongsali province. The dispute was over the demarcation of the border between the two countries, based on tributary streams of the Mekong. In reality, local Thai generals had been engaged in lucrative but illegal logging in the area, which the Lao authorities disputed. With little official support from Bangkok, the relatively intense conflict was settled in favour of Laos and marked a significant assertion of a Lao sense of statehood.

In a different direction, one practical step in ascertaining exactly what, or who, comprised the state of the Lao PDR was the conducting of the first nationwide population census in March 1985. Given the ethnic diversity of Laos, the remoteness of many of its hill tribes and the lack of specific clarity about where the border actually lay in some parts of the country along its frontier with Vietnam, the census was a major feat. At last, the government of Laos had a formal idea of who its people were, where they were and what they did.

In line with political and economic developments in the Soviet Union, in 1988 Vietnam withdrew its remaining troops from Laos. In part this reflected a greater sense of Lao sovereignty and in part a desire to improve relations with Thailand, which had always been sensitive about a Vietnamese presence so close to its borders. This was an important gesture after the then recent border conflict. But driving the decision was a shift by the Soviet Union away from effectively propping up its allies, which greatly increased the cost of maintaining Vietnamese troops in Laos. Confident of its position (and limiting candidates to those either in or allied to the party), the LPRP endorsed the holding of the first elections for the Supreme People's Assembly in 1989.

ECONOMIC LIBERALISATION

Following the conventional centrally planned model for economic development, in 1986 the Lao government announced its second five-year plan. The economic reality at this time was that, starting from an already underdeveloped base, having suffered decades of war, having what little business capital that was available in the country leave after 1975, and the less than inspiring economic management of the LPRP from that time, Laos was one of the world's poorest countries.[16] As a consequence, no sooner had this second five-year plan been adopted than the LPRP began to move towards the idea of opening up the Lao economy. The acceptance of the 'New Economic Mechanism' introduced, tentatively at first, the free market to Laos. The LPRP also began to actively seek economic advice from the IMF, the World Bank and other donor agencies. Two years later, in 1988, the Lao government separated the central and commercial banking functions of the existing banking system. This complemented the development of a legal and institutional framework for economic and commercial activities, along with the institution of a range of taxes (amended the following year) to ensure a flow of revenue to the government.

In a significant move for the ascendency of economic pragmatists, in 1991 the leader of the LPRP (in its various guises) since 1955, Kaison Phomivan, was elected as the president of the LPRP and the state, while the Supreme People's Assembly endorsed the country's first Constitution. Despite him being the long-standing party leader, the election of Kaison reflected a move towards accepting market domination of the economy, which he and his faction had been pushing. But a year and a half after his election as president, Kaison died,[17] to be replaced by Nuhak Phumsavan as state president and Khamtai Siphandon as PM and president of the party, both of whom were seen as opposed to Kaison's economic liberalism. By this stage, though, the economic cat was already out of the ideological bag. The following month, in December 1992, elections were held for the renamed National Assembly. While the elections were open to all adult citizens, the choice of candidates was effectively limited to either LPRP members or candidates approved by the LPRP. Prior to the adoption of the new Constitution, between 1975 and 1991 the LPRP ruled by governmental decree and party directives. Power was centred in the Politburo and exercised in the name of the Council of Ministers. As a consequence of the adoption of the new Constitution, in 1991 the party secretariat was abolished and policy making was handed to the ministries, with party control of all state institutions being strengthened. This latter move was in response to the collapse of the Soviet Union, with which Laos was allied. Despite the adoption of a Constitution, law in Laos remained based on party dogma, with a significant input from Lao Loum tradition (having dispensed with colonial and royal law in 1975). There have also been some contributions to the legal code from the requirements of economic liberalisation. Laos had a total of forty laws, supplemented by further decrees and regulations.

By the early 1990s, the government had begun to move relatively quickly (at least compared to its original pace of development). In 1993 further economic reforms were promulgated and, importantly, an environmental protection law passed. Impetus for environmental protection came from NGOs and the international community, but also reflected a local awareness that, with so many other problems, the high quality of the physical environment was one advantage the country retained. For a country that has an internationally high proportion of forested area and faces pressure from logging and damming, such environmental protection was a major step in preserving the Lao environment. However, like most laws that have the potential to impede business, restrictions on logging have often been honoured more in the breach than in the observances.

As a symbolic gesture, the opening of the first bridge spanning the Mekong in 1994 marked the beginning of relatively easy access to Laos from Thailand. The Friendship Bridge, as it is known, was touted as a means for Laos to integrate more closely into the rapidly developing Thai economy. While there has been closer integration between Thailand and Laos since the bridge was opened, it has been less to the economic advantage of Laos and more to the advantage of Thai businessmen selling goods across the border. However, it did provide a direct road route from Vieng Chan, via Nong Kai on the Thai side of the Mekong, to Bangkok. One interesting response to a greater Thai presence, especially in Vieng Chan, was a concerted move to reassert Lao political and cultural independence. In this one could detect a faint echo of historical rivalries. Another significant move that marked the integration of Laos into the region was its acceptance in July 1997 as a full member of the Association of South-East Asian Nations. It was becoming increasingly clear that, though landlocked, Laos wished to become a regional participant. After hundreds of years of isolation, Laos was becoming less mysterious and more accessible to the outside world.

LIMITED POLITICAL DEVELOPMENT

National Assembly elections were again held in December 1997, with committed LPRP cadres dominating the conservative, party-oriented body. Reflecting the long-standing role of the army in political affairs, generals still held six of the nine Politburo seats in 1997 (Kremmer 1997: 212). As was noted in Laos in early 1999, the army existed before the party, so this was a natural extension of the army's political role. Accompanying the elections, there was also a minor ministerial reshuffle, especially in economic portfolios, which in a practical sense acknowledged high level economic mismanagement. Responsibility for foreign investment was split between two high-ranking officials, which was claimed would produce greater efficiency but was in reality intended to check corrupt tendencies of officials who were not answerable to others.

The changed economic policies in Laos began to produce results, with economic growth over 1991–96 at seven per cent, and real per capita growth increasing at 3.8 per cent. Growth dipped a little in 1997, being estimated at 6.5 per cent, but dropped to zero in 1998 as a consequence of the downturn in the Thai economy as well as a more general domestic malaise, and, to some extent, infrastructure bottlenecks unable to keep pace with economic growth. Investment from Thailand and South Korea, which constituted more than fifty per cent of foreign direct investment, had effectively dried up over 1997–98 and was slow in returning thereafter.

In the first half of 1998, foreign investment slumped by around sixty per cent compared to the same time the previous year. By the end of 1998, the trade deficit had worsened, the value of the Laotian currency, the kip, had slumped from 3900 to 4300 to the US dollar within the four weeks of December, and inflation hit 100 per cent (Pike 1999: 10). It soon fell further to 10 000 to the US dollar before settling in early 2000 at around 7500. As a consequence of the devaluation of the kip, Laos' balance of trade deficit grew to US$226 million over 1998–99, with the country importing approximately twice as much as it exported (*Indochina Chronology* 1999: 11–12). Inflation came back to around ten per cent, after peaking at 167 per cent in March 1999 (Lintner 2000). This meant that Laos continued to rely on foreign aid, which constituted around sixteen per cent of GDP, to remain functional.

While foreign aid was vital to Laos' economic survival, the country was approximately self-sufficient in terms of rice production, producing about 400 kilograms per person in 1999. Not surprisingly, agriculture accounted for more than half (51.3 per cent) of the economy in 1999 (*Indochina Chronology* 1999: 11).

Despite the liberalisation of the Lao economy to the point where it was in practical terms a free market capitalist state (if not an especially successful one), there was little sign of an organised civil opposition to the monopoly rule of the LPRP, while the overall influence of the party at the central level remained strong. While discontent among ordinary Lao people, especially in the larger cities and towns, was growing, it was largely limited to the very small and vulnerable middle class. As a part of the population that might want to encourage reform, this group was not sufficiently widespread or organised to have a meaningful impact on government.

By way of illustration, in a daring move in October 1999 a small group of teachers and students, led by a local lecturer, Thongpaseuth Keuakhoune, held a protest against the government in Vieng Chan. However, the protest was quickly dispersed and Thongpaseuth and others were taken into custody (Lintner 2000), with ten people still being held six months later. A further forty-six Protestant Christians were also being held without trial as a consequence of their work for the Lao Evangelical Church (*Indochina Chronology* 1999: 11–12). The protest was regarded as a sign of both external and domestic pressure on the government to reform. However, the brittle control held by the government meant that it was deeply reluctant to offer change, lest it lose its grip on power.

All electoral candidates continued to be vetted by the party-controlled National Construction Front. In 1992 proponents of a multi-party political system were jailed. One died in early 1998 and two were still in jail in early 2000. Opposition to the government was also difficult to organise as the country's intellectual elite remained small and transparent. Although politically dominant, the LPRP tended to work in the background, setting overall policy directions. There also continued to be some distrust by the older, conservative party members for younger, often tertiary educated officials. Despite its grip on power, there were increasing concerns at the elite level that the LPRP had been weakened by economic change and by the passing of its revolutionary generation. At the local level, where most people actually live, there was a growing perception that party units were failing to provide a lead for grass roots development.

THE ARMY AND BUSINESS

For administrative purposes, Laos is divided into provinces, each of which falls into one of three broad military regions. These military regions are formally based on geographic distinction, but in practice conform to business enterprises operated by the army. Given its history of preceding the LPRP, the army operates relatively independently of the government, although it strongly influences the government. Also, like a number of armies that trace their origins to (self-sustaining) revolutionary activity, the Lao army subsidises itself through independent and joint venture business activities, meaning that it operates somewhat independently of government policy other than the regional commanders contributing to that policy. Business ventures included logging, shipping (with a port facility in Vietnam owned and operated by the Lao military), shoe manufacturing, and so on. This in turn exacerbated a slight sense of warlordism that pervaded Lao political life. For example, until early 1999 there were immigration checks between each province, which not only kept note of where people were going (or where they had been) but also acted as a security measure against anti-government groups.

In a variation on the enterprising business theme, official corruption was fairly widespread throughout Laos, with government and military leaders skimming off percentages of business takings, arranging cosy deals for family members and 'clients' (that is, of patron–client relationships). Corruption also existed at lower levels of officialdom, with payments of bribes helping to ensure that what should be procedural matters were appropriately looked after.

Many aid donors have insisted on institutional checks to clean up some aspects of profit skimming, given Laos' officially parlous economic position, and this has in turn led to some steps towards doing away with the worst cases of corruption. Some ministers and their staffs have been removed, although they still hold positions of power and are not entirely excluded from possibilities of making money. Much of the middle level of government management is run by technocrats, who are in some cases foreign trained (mostly in USSR/Russia). However, their policy advice, which was basically sound, tended not to be heeded by the older, revolutionary generation. That is, government decisions on economic policy tend to be taken according to the concerns of the older leadership rather than reflecting rational economic decision making. This was a particular source of frustration to both aid agencies and foreign investors, the latter having shown a marked disinclination to continue business dealings in Laos.

ARMED OPPOSITION TO THE LPRP

In the period after the revolution, there was a threat of small-scale insurgency by Lao rightists and Thai mercenaries operating out of north-eastern Thailand. However, as American interest in mainland SEA diminished so too did this threat. In the north-east of Laos, however, those Hmong who supported Vang Po's 'Secret Army' and who did not escape launched a rebellion against the central government. The scale of this rebellion never threatened the LPRP, but it continued to make unsafe a large area of northern Laos, including the area within 100 kilometres of Vieng Chan. Even as this was being written, there was still a significant area south-east of Luang Prabang that was considered unsafe, although the Lao military appeared to be tightening its grip on the region. In the first half of 2000, a series of bombings upset the usual calm of Vieng Chan and, although no one claimed responsibility for them, an attack on a government post at Pakse in Champassak province in July 2000, in which five guerrillas and one government soldier were killed, was publicly linked to a revitalised wing of Vang Pao's Hmong guerrilla group.

The government likened the rebellion to banditry and to some extent this was an accurate characterisation. However, the continued existence of two separate (and antithetical) Hmong military groups with overtly political agendas undoubtedly constituted more than just simple banditry. The provinces still under threat at the beginning of the twenty-first century included Luang Prabang, Xieng Khouang, Vieng Chan, and Saysomboun special zones. Apart from the bombings in Vieng Chan and that attack at Pakse, Hmong military activity was, however, increasingly restricted to Xieng Khouang. Sporadic skirmishes continued in this mountainous province despite deployment of significant numbers of troops. The government acknowledged the problem, but would not specify the casualty rate, which was probably around fifteen or twenty people a year being killed as a consequence of hold-ups and incidental fire.

In general, though, anti-government activity was less overtly ideolog-ical than it was an assertion of local independence. There has never been a close formal relationship with the non-Lao Loum groups and the upland Lao and many non-Lao Loum continue to regard the policies of the lowland government as little more than an interference in their affairs. While this was particularly the case with regards to the Hmong, it could also be said to apply to many of the other ethnic minorities that inhabit Laos. The assertion of local independence tended to occur around the same time as the opium harvest and transshipment from the northern regions. The opium harvest was down in 1998, to 126 tonnes, from 140 tonnes in 1997, in part due to drier conditions.

A major issue of contention between the Lao government and the Hmong was, not surprisingly given its international opprobrium, the cul-tivation and sale of opium. Given that there was a certain level of official involvement in the opium and heroin trade, helping Laos maintain its position as the world's third largest illegal opium producer after Burma and Afghanistan, it was not at all clear whether the government's stated opposition to opium cultivation was genuine. As in Burma, it was quite likely that local military officers involved in the drug trade were simply trying to put their competitors out of business. A further related issue was that of the transshipment of heroin from Burma through to Cambodia and Vietnam. The nature of the linkages between Burma and Laos were not clear, but again it seemed that there was a significant degree of official involvement. This was especially so in relation to the transshipment to Cambodia and Vietnam, where political and military links were close.

The government was engaged in a campaign of relocation of Hmong villages to areas on or close to major roads. The ostensible purpose for this was to introduce the Hmong to cash cropping to stop swidden (slash and burn) agriculture. The Lao government does have an active policy of protecting (or attempting to protect) the natural environment, and it was believed that the growing population had made the relatively destructive swidden agriculture ecologically unviable. Government policy on the environment was reflected in logging in areas that were in the process of being flooded for dams, rather than more general log-ging, so there appeared some consistency to this program. However, the relocation of the Hmong also brought them under closer government supervision and control.

Beyond problems with some of the Hmong community, there were also security problems in Champassak province, bordering Cambodia. Here, however, armed activity was more genuinely believed to be related to banditry rather than politics. Elements of disbanded Khmer Rouge from Cambodia who had turned to banditry appeared to be working with some Lao nationals in the poorly policed areas of southern Laos and northern Cambodia.

LAO TOLERANCE

The government checks that were especially noticeable in the more troubled parts of Laos were not especially oppressive of ordinary people. There was, almost as a matter of course, a certain brusqueness and arrogance that seems to come with wearing a uniform. But there was no overt intimidation and the Lao I saw in the presence of army or police officers, in 1998 and 1999, unlike in a number of other developing countries, did not appear to be in the least cowed. There was, it seemed, an unstated belief that most people, or at least most Lao Loum, would behave towards each other with a degree of tolerance and respect.

In part this tendency appeared to stem from the predominant influence of Theravada Buddhism on everyday life (Evans 1998: 49–70), which was manifested in Sangha (Buddhist clergy) involvement with and support for ordinary people and the government's explicit respect for Buddhism and the Sangha. Having said that, Theravada Buddhism appears to have less of a benign influence on officialdom in Burma and Cambodia, so it alone does not stand as sufficient explanation. In part, too, there was not inconsiderable support for the government on the part of many ordinary Lao Loum. This did not necessarily imply that many Lao would not like to have a more direct say in the policies of their government. But it did indicate a degree of popular support for the Lao government, in terms of its nationalist credentials and its more general developmental policies. Perhaps more importantly, though, was that many Lao do not have a particularly well developed sense of political consciousness. That is, if the Lao government allowed most people to live without interfering too much in their daily lives that seemed to be reasonably well accepted.

The Lao government's broad sense of acceptability also stemmed from the loosening of its formerly fairly strict, orthodox Leninist policies that derived directly from the Communist Party of Vietnam and before that from the Soviet Union. Since the Soviet Union has ceased to exist and Vietnam has, since 1987, moved towards opening its economy, Laos too has moved towards a less centrally planned economy. This was, in any case, something of a joke in a society that was very significantly subsistence-oriented and in which illicit cross-border trade was a fact of economic life.

The international community, too, had a very significant impact on Laos. Thailand was in the process of attempting to reassert its economic, if not political, hegemony over Laos while the international aid agencies had a very significant presence in Vieng Chan. Vieng Chan was beginning to take on some of the feel (and the money) of being a smaller sibling to the mighty, bustling Bangkok. But an official and unofficial sense of Lao propriety tended to curb the greater excesses of the Thai capital. However, development outside Vieng Chan and a few other major towns appeared to be so limited it was almost non-existent. Village life was hardly touched by 'development'.

At a local level, political society was still organised at village level, with the village headman being the principal political representative and arbitrator between ordinary people and medium echelons of government. The village headman held his position as a consequence of bi-annual elections and, short of losing consensus support, could be expected to maintain that position until he was no longer able to fulfil its functions. However, there were examples of village chiefs losing their positions because they had attempted to enrich themselves and their families through their position, so there was a degree of accountability for ordinary Lao people. The village chief was virtually always a member of the LPRP, so there was a direct connection between the party and community life.

Family and village life was further organised by mutually reinforcing communal values, which tended to be typical of societies which were in transition from being agrarian-based and pre-modern to urbanised. Even in the larger urban centres, the fundamental administrative unit was still based on the village, or local community, so the model pertained across the state and not just to villages as such. Transgression of village rules could result in expulsion from the village, although redemption and forgiveness was a marked characteristic of such situations.

At the more overtly political level, the 'government intelligence' network was extensive. That is, with everyone knowing more or less what everyone else is doing, there was little scope for anti-social, much less anti-government, behaviour. Similarly, although the law is technically quite strict in a number of matters, in fact its application is fairly lax. It depends more on whether or not there is a belief that a person has acted outside the bounds of socially acceptable behaviour rather than whether any actual crime has been committed. Of course, this did allow considerable scope for abuse, especially with reference to relatively low-level corruption. But in general there tended to be pretty much a live and let live approach to formal social organisation.

In part at least, the increasingly relaxed approach of the government was a reflection of the ordinary Lao people themselves, for whom authority was not to be taken too seriously (and so has difficulty in asserting its authority).

In some senses this typified political life in Laos. Authority was an historical necessity, but tended not to be too oppressive, at least since the paranoia associated with running a state for the first time faded in the later 1980s. The government relaxed, incrementally; once-closed borders were re-opened and ordinary Lao citizens were allowed to get on with their lives. In so far as the LPRP maintained any Marxist credentials, it was more as a government in which public welfare (and some self-enrichment) was a priority. The ethical values of Theravada Buddhism, of tolerance and respect, were pervasive and managed to knock off the harder ideological edges. But perhaps underlying all of this was the usually open, receptive and forgiving nature of most Lao people (see Evans 1998). In the final analysis, unless a government wishes to oppress its own people it must ultimately come to reflect their values. This slowly but increasingly appeared to be the case with the government of Laos.

NOTES

1   This name is actually redundant, as 'mae' is the Thai word for river, while its actual name is the Khong, hence Maekhong.

2   The T'ai languages, which are to some extent mutually intelligible, are largely monosyllabic and tonal.

3   Like the Thai word 'mae' (as in Mae Khong), the Lao word 'nam' (as in Nam Khan) means 'river', so the English use of the term in this context is formally redundant.

4   Viravong claims Fa Ngum to have been the twenty-third in a continuing line of royal descent.

5   The Hmong had begun to move into the Plain of Jars region between 1820 and 1840, continuing the southward drift from southern China over the next several decades.

6   While some opium was grown and sold in Laos, until 1939 most of the opium from which the government derived its income was imported from India (Stuart-Fox, pers. comm. 1999).

7   The French use of block-houses, or small fortifications, was retained until the early 1950s, when they proved ineffective against the highly organised Viet Minh.

8   Interestingly, Komadom's son, Si Thon, who was captured by the French during the 'pacification' campaign, was in 1970 vice-chairman of the Pathet Lao for the southern hill people.

9   Pathet translates from Lao as 'land' and the name Pathet Lao is held to mean 'Land of the Lao' (Martin Stuart-Fox, pers. comm.).

10 Towards the end of WWII in the Pacific, Japanese forces encouraged the declaration of independence by occupied former European colonies, in large part as a means of slowing the Allied advance.

11 The coalition represented the Committee of the People, the Lao-Pen-Lao (Laos for the Lao) and the Committee for a Free Laos.

12 The OSS was the forerunner of the Central Intelligence Agency, which was later very active against the successors to the more leftist, military wing of the Lao Issara, the Pathet Lao.

13 The Indochinese Union included Laos, Cambodia, Tonkin, Annam, and Cochin-China; the last three states comprising Vietnam.

14 These were towards creating greater internal control over day-to-day matters of government, although leaving in the hands of the French the crucial areas of foreign affairs, defence, monetary policy and customs.

15 The neutralist group, led by Prince Souvanna Phouma (half brother to Souvanna Vong), was ideologically positioned between the Pathet Lao and the conservatives, and opposed to involvement by both North Vietnam and the USA.

16 Laos is now 125 on a listing of 163 countries with a per capita GDP of US$400, which places it above Vietnam at 139, which is just ahead of Cambodia.

17 Evans (1998: 24–40) notes that Kaison's death resulted in a high degree of traditional ancestor worship, leading to the 'Cult of Kayson'.

8

Cambodia: 'The Dancing Country'

In western Cambodia, from Siem Reap near the ruins of the fabled Angkor complex to Sisophon, the dirt track that passes for a highway lurches and judders over pot-holes and mine craters, passing over the twisted, mangled wreckage of bridges blown up by the Khmer Rouge. There are not five metres of this track that are not in desperate need of repair. In the wet season, the road is almost impassable. Funding made available for its repair and upgrade was constantly siphoned off by corrupt government officials and contractors, and no work was done on it for years. Soldiers were stationed at posts, little more than thatched bamboo and palm frond shelters, at regular intervals along the road, demanding bribes to let traffic pass. The bribes became so routine that drivers hardly even slowed down to thrust cash into the soldiers' hands. Travelling over this 'highway', one was so constantly thrown about that it was locally called 'The Dancing Road'. Its damaged condition, which was already poor before the ravages of war took their toll on it, and the monumental corruption that precluded any major repair, stood as something of a metaphor for Cambodia itself.

At the beginning of the twenty-first century, Cambodia entered what was its most stable political environment in decades. The Cambodian People's Party (CPP) and the National United Front for a Neutral, Peaceful, Cooperative and Independent Cambodia (FUNCINPEC) had entered into a reasonably stable coalition government under the prime ministership of Hun Sen. Following the death of Pol Pot, the last of the Khmer Rouge leaders had either surrendered or been captured, with three of them living in amnesty in their western redoubt at Pailin, while

THAILAND

LAOS

● Siem Reap

Battambang
●

Tonle
Sap

River

● Pailin

Mekong

Phnom Penh ●

VIETNAM

Svay Rieng ●

Gulf of
Thailand

CAMBODIA

200 kilometres

South
China Sea

their troops had joined the government army or returned to civilian life. Even the millions of land mines, which continue to plague Cambodia, were slowly being cleared. Cambodia's belated inclusion into the Association of South-East Asian Nations in May 1999 and its readmission to the United Nations in November 1999 appeared to confirm, at least on the surface, that the country was on a sound political footing.

From another perspective, however, Cambodia continued to carry the legacy of decades of war. It had the highest amputee rate in the world, due to war and landmines, virtually no real industry outside subsistence rice cropping, very poor infrastructure, and little money to improve it. Most worryingly, there was also a level of official corruption that was breathtaking in its scope and audacity, while the country's human rights record remained poor. Meanwhile, the average income of an ordinary Cambodian was less than US$300 a year.

Yet ahead of the 1998 elections, there appeared little doubt that the Cambodian People's Party (CPP) government of Hun Sen was employing the fullest extent of its institutionalised power to swing popular support behind it. In simple terms, the CPP not only had the advantage of being in government, it also had the full use of government resources for its party political purposes. Of the thirty-eight opposition parties, only FUNCINPEC and the Sam Rainsy Party stood any chance of securing a sizeable block of votes. There was also much discussion about a pre-election deal having been done to ensure that even if the CPP did not achieve a simple majority it was well placed to form a coalition with smaller, pro-CPP parties. This was 'democracy', Cambodia-style.

This chapter looks at Cambodia's history as an empire and thereafter as a regional battleground. It notes the rise and fall of the Khmer empire, and the country's subsequent status as a subject of regional hegemonies, which led to it becoming a French protectorate. After examining the French period and the Japanese occupation, it will then look at its period under Prince Norodom Sihanouk, in terms of his moving the state towards being a personal fiefdom, its 'neutralist' policies in relation to regional conflict, eventual US involvement, and the rightist coup. This then leads to the rise of the Khmer Rouge and its policies that flowed from 'Year Zero', the period of increasing fratricide/genocide from 1975 to 1978, and the eventual Vietnamese invasion of December 1978. Further, this chapter will look at the establishment of the state's puppet government and its US/UN-backed opposition, the Vietnamese withdrawal, UN-sponsored elections, and the two-party government that left the Khmer Rouge on the outer. It will then consider the fragmentation of the UN-brokered government, alliances with remaining Khmer Rouge, the outing of the 'First Prime Minister', Hun Sen's consolidation of power, Pol Pot's 'house arrest' and death, and the 1998 elections and their aftermath.

OLD CAMBODIA

The contemporary Cambodian nation is effectively the remnants of the once powerful Khmer Empire, which at its peak during the twelfth and thirteenth centuries ruled much of what is now Thailand, Laos and Vietnam. Cambodia's origins lie in the fertile Mekong basin as the state of Norkor Kuork Phlouk, or Norkor Phnom (translation: 'King of the Mountain'), referred to by contemporary Chinese as Funan,[1] which dated to about the first century BCE. Prior to that, a mixture of prehistoric peoples and Khmers are known to have lived in the region as far back as 4000 BCE (Rooney 1994: 21). This state was located primarily in the region of the Mekong River to the north of present day Phnom Penh and Tonle Sap (Great Lake). The establishment of Funan, from around 100 BCE, corresponded with the introduction of Indianised culture into the region, most probably from Java, and included the widespread adoption of Hinduism and, later, the use of written Sanskrit. Sanskrit acted to divide the elites from ordinary Khmer-speaking people. It was about this time that patron–client social relations were established in the region (MacDonald 1987: 34–6; Chandler 1983: 11–18; Coedes 1966: 1–2). Funan, which may have been just one local state among many (Rooney 1994: 23), shifted from predominantly dry rice agriculture to wet rice agriculture as late as 500 CE. Chandler noted that while the state of Funan existed and was a precursor state to Cambodia, it was decentralised, being based on an 'aggregation of leaders' and a 'multiplicity of centers' (Chandler 1983: 19). It was a despotic state, but not an integrated despotic state (Chandler 1983: 25).

Khmer Funan suzerainty extended over most of present-day Cambodia, as well as parts of Thailand and the Mekong delta region of Vietnam. However, by the seventh and eighth centuries, its power had declined and it was replaced by a conglomeration of small principalities known to the Chinese as Chenla, located in Cambodia and southern Laos, which was also a Khmer state. Chenla was divided into 'Water Chenla' and 'Land Chenla', the former located near the Mekong Delta and the latter along the Mekong south of modern Laos (MacDonald 1987: 37–40). The greatest Cambodian empire rose in the area near the north-western tip of Tonle Sap, taking its name Angkor from the Sanskrit term *nagara* (city).[2]

From the late eighth century for about a hundred years, Cambodia was ruled by the Sailendra Dynasty of Java. The end of Javanese suzerainty in the ninth century led to the unification of the Khmer people and the establishment of the Khmer Empire under Jayavarman II, who had returned from Java to proclaim the unity and independence of the Khmer state (Coedes 1966: 2–3, 73–83; Rooney 1994: 25). This new empire was centred on Angkor Thom and, during its peak in the twelfth century, extended its borders in Laos to the north, to the South China Sea in the east, and to the Bay of Bengal in the west. On the scale of regional empires, the Khmer Empire established sophisticated administrative structures, built a network of roads and government outposts throughout its territory, and established cities and towns reflecting its cultural and political domination across a vast area. Its master work, however, was the building of its capital, just north of modern Siem Reap, in north-western Cambodia. The complex of temples, walls, reservoirs, moats, bridges and other structures that remain at the Angkor site are equal to the most impressive ruins in the world, covering a vast area and reflecting levels of technology, artisanship and artistry unknown in Europe at that time. It is instructive that the ancient Khmers did not live in the stone structures that remain, which had a religious purpose, but in wooden buildings that have long since disappeared. The walled city of Angkor Thom contained hundreds of thousands of people and was a cosmopolitan centre, attracting visitors from India, China and the whole of SEA.

Upon the death of Jayavarman VII, the empire began to decline. It is believed Angkor's decline was a result of internal rebellions, disregard for economic maintenance, and the introduction of Theravada Buddhism, which preached salvation of the individual through his or her own efforts, rather than the hierarchy of Hinduism or Mahayana Buddhism (which preceded Theravada Buddhism). The rise of the Thais to the west also wreaked havoc upon the state, and the capital at Angkor Thom was too close to the new Thai power to ever really be safe again (Herz 1958: 15–16; Chandler 1983: 67–70). By the middle of the fourteenth century the state was weak enough for the neighbouring Thai to invade and capture the city, first in 1353 and again in 1430–31. The following year the city was abandoned (see MacDonald 1987: 34–63).

When Angkor was abandoned, what remained of the elite shifted southward into the safer lower Mekong Basin, and Cambodian social structure, perhaps responding to a smaller population, became less exigent and more diffuse. Theravada Buddhism became the state religion, enshrining an ideal of egalitarianism (for men, at least) in a society that retained its hierarchical trappings. Angkor itself was soon forgotten. By about 1650, Cambodia had become one of many small, self-sufficient, relatively isolated Buddhist kingdoms that dotted the landscape of SEA between western Burma and Vietnam.

This seemingly idyllic situation darkened when two strong, expansionist and competitive kingdoms came into being on either side of Cambodia. Vietnam had increasingly expanded southwards, at the expense of Champa, until the latter ceased to exist. Champa had sent pleas to the Cambodian court to seek assistance against the Vietnamese in 1471, but Cambodia was at this time preoccupied with internal squabbling and the threat of Thailand to the west (Herz 1958: 42–4). The decline of Cambodia thereafter was not a foregone conclusion and there were brief moments of glory that marked the period between Angkor and the arrival of the French. For example, when the Burmese invaded Siam in 1556, the Cambodian king, Barom Racha, took advantage of the situation to also invade Siam the following year, and again in 1559 and 1562 (Herz 1958: 44–5). But in 1587, the Siamese got their own back, storming the Cambodian capital at Lovek and razing it to the ground. To the south-east, in the 1620s the Nguyen Dynasty of southern Vietnam had established itself at Saigon, eventually consolidating control over the previously Khmer Mekong Delta and effectively cutting off Cambodia from its access to the sea. Cambodia's regional decline was thus now guaranteed.

Until France established its protectorate in 1863, Cambodian kings and regional rulers tried to avoid being dominated by either Thailand or Vietnam, mostly by offering a degree of suzerainty to both. They sought the patronage of their 'enemy's enemy', alternating between Thailand, whose Buddhist (and patron–client) culture was familiar, and Chinese-influenced Vietnam, which had a markedly different social make-up based to a large extent on Confucian thinking (which in theory promoted a bureaucratic hierarchy based on merit). Rivals for the Cambodian throne would seek help from the enemy of the incumbent, which exacerbated factionalism among the Cambodian royalty along pro-Thai or pro-Vietnamese lines. The stakes in such factionalism were high and the costs in Cambodian lives and territory were enormous.

By the 1830s, most of the kingdom of Cambodia was a satellite of Vietnam, with the Vietnamese putting King Ang Chan on the throne in 1833. Meanwhile, two north-western provinces, including the one containing the ruins of Angkor, had been ceded to Siam. Years of warfare between Thai and Vietnamese armies devastated Cambodia. In this period, anti-Vietnamese feelings began to be identified, in many Cambodians' minds, with half-formed notions of nationalism. Vietnam and Thailand, for their part, developed the idea that Cambodia was not a sovereign country but a place, inhabited by inferior people, that could be exploited or 'protected' at will. In the 1840s, between Vietnam and Thailand, the state almost disappeared, although a popular anti-Vietnamese rebellion broke out in 1842 (Herz 1958: 52–4; Chandler 1985: 99–116). Siam, meanwhile, attempted to reassert its authority over Cambodia, offering sanctuary to the Cambodian king when a rebellion against him broke out, and in 1862 sending him back to Cambodia accompanied by Siamese troops. In 1863, frightened of his neighbours and under direct pressure from the French governor in Saigon, who noted that he could claim suzerainty over Cambodia as heir to Vietnamese suzerainty, Cambodia's King Norodom 'asked' for French protection, which was a rare example of voluntary colonisation (Herz 1958: 57–60; Chandler 1985: 117–36; Osborne 1973: 13–19). Not surprisingly, the French were seeking the request. There were subsequent revolts against the French, in 1866–67 and 1885–87, while the boundaries of Cambodia were renegotiated. To placate the Siamese, Siem Reap, Battambang and Sisophon were handed to Siam (but later returned to Cambodia, in 1904 and 1907) (see Tully 1996: 41–112). In 1884, King Norodom handed over internal administration of Cambodia to the French. While the period of French colonialism did little to enhance Cambodia's development as a state, if France had not intervened, Cambodia, divided between Thailand and Vietnam, would have ceased to exist.

THE FRENCH PROTECTORATE

The period between the establishment of a French protectorate in 1863 and 1941 was marked by encroaching French control over the king and his ministers. However, French rule also strengthened the king's symbolic position, both by the ministers retaining a high estimation of the king and by the style of Norodom's successor, his half-brother Sisowath. Succeeding to the throne in 1904, Sisowath did not clash with the French, as had Norodom. Indeed, Sisowath was later castigated by supporters of independence as having been too acquiescent to the French. As a consequence of Sisowath's close collaboration with the French, and their support of him, during a quiet and untroubled period of Cambodia's history, there was an even greater opportunity for 'the king's symbolic prestige to be enhanced' (Osborne 1973: 21). This set up a situation where, should he wish, the king's symbolic prestige could be used to gain temporal political advantage. Sisowath's reign ended when he died in

1927, and he was succeeded by his son, Monivong, who reigned from 1927 until 1941. The period from 1904 until 1941 has, not incorrectly, been identified as 'the years of colonial calm'. There was some anti-French dissent during this time, but it did not amount to a threat to the state (Osborne 1973: ch. 3).

During World War II when Japanese forces occupied all of Indochina, French administrators[3] stayed on in Cambodia, as they did in Vietnam and Laos. To counter claims for independence, the French chose a nineteen-year-old prince, Norodom Sihanouk, to be king when his grandfather, the reigning monarch, King Monivong, died in 1941. The French assumed that Sihanouk would be pliant in their hands, which turned out to be a mistake. Having occupied Cambodia in 1941, Japan handed the western border provinces back to its ally, Thailand, but gave Cambodia independence in 1945. Sihanouk assumed the role of prime minister as well as king, and appointed his own, largely conservative, cabinet. However, a coup launched by the strongly nationalist foreign minister, Son Ngoc Thanh, led to the arrest of all pro-French ministers. Sihanouk resigned and Thanh made himself prime minister (Kiernan 1985: 48–9). In a tense political environment and without recourse to a parliament, one Cambodian faction called for occupation by the British forces then in Saigon, which they did with French and Indian assistance. French administration returned to Cambodia soon after (Smith 1964a: 607). Thanh was arrested and charged with treason, being exiled to France.[4] But as a concession to mounting claims, the French allowed political parties and the first of Cambodia's five constitutions was announced in 1947.

Between 1950 and 1954 Cambodia's move towards independence operated on two levels. On one level there were above-ground political parties that agitated for independence, dominant among which were the Democrats, who favoured the French model of government and independence as soon as possible. There was also the more conservative Liberal Party, which advocated the education of the Cambodian people and, in the interim, a close relationship with France. A third party, the Progressive Democrats, was also conservative but quickly faded from significance. The Democrats were the best organised of the parties and quickly asserted their dominance of the elected political system (Chandler 1985: 176–8; Osborne 1973: 43–4). The political primacy of the Democrats and their generally anti-royalist tendencies worried King Sihanouk.

At a more underground level, supporters of the exiled Son Ngoc Thanh took to arms to form the non-communist Khmer Issarak (Free Khmer), which launched attacks against the French administration in 1946–47 with support from the Thai government. A change in government in

Bangkok, conflict with the pro-communist Vietnamese nationalist forces, the Viet Minh, and an amnesty offered by the government quickly halved these rebels' numbers. To the east, Vietnamese opposition to French occupation also became involved in the resistance movement against France in Cambodia, under the umbrella of the Indochinese Communist Party (Kiernan 1985: 117–68; Chandler 1985: 183; Smith 1964a: 616). By 1952, these guerrillas controlled perhaps a sixth of the Cambodian countryside (Chandler 1985: 183). However there were tensions between the Vietnamese and the Cambodian guerrillas. From around this time, at the beginning of the 1950s, a group of young Cambodian students were forming themselves into a 'Marxist Circle' in Paris, which was to become the nucleus of the Cambodian Communist Party when it rose to military and political prominence in the 1970s. They included Saloth Sar, Ieng Sary and Son Sen (Kiernan 1985: 121–4).

In 1952 Son Ngoc Thanh, now back in Cambodia, fled to the north-west, from where the Khmer Issarak resumed their attacks on the government, sometimes co-operating with pro-Viet Minh guerrillas but often not (Corfield 1994: 14–15). By 1952 about two-thirds of Cambodia was no longer in government hands. Sihanouk launched an attack against guerrillas in the north-west in September 1952 and, on the strength of its claimed success, in mid 1952 dismissed the Democrat government (Smith 1964a: 614). With this he proclaimed martial law, assuming power as prime minister and appointing his own cabinet. In January 1953 the Democrats responded by refusing to pass his budget, which he answered with the dissolution of the Assembly and the arrest of several Democrat assemblymen. The next month, Sihanouk travelled to France to seek the country's independence as a part of his 'Royal Crusade for Independence'. It was not granted and Sihanouk complained to an international audience about France's intransigence. He then went into a self-imposed exile, first in Bangkok, then in Battambang, to highlight the French position.

At this time, in mid 1953, the war against the Vietnamese nationalist Viet Minh was going badly for France and its government was increasingly worried about the declining security situation in Cambodia. In order to reach a settlement in Vietnam, the French began to look at cutting their ties to Cambodia (Kiernan 1985: 140–64). Then, unexpectedly, in October France agreed to grant Sihanouk authority over Cambodia's armed forces, judiciary and foreign affairs, effectively granting the country independence (although it did maintain most of its economic interests in Cambodia until the early 1970s).

Sihanouk claimed to have won this independence single-handedly, which was only partly correct. His public tactics had pushed the French, but more so the French position was influenced by the Viet Minh. In any case, the achievement of independence was enough to briefly end Son Ngoc Thanh's opposition to Sihanouk and to curtail the Khmer Issarak as a threat to the state. Sihanouk then abdicated the throne and, claiming a mandate as a consequence of independence, started a national political movement, the Sangkum Reastr Niyum (People's Socialist Community), intended to smother Cambodia's political parties. Despite its name, there was little about Sihanouk's new party that reflected conventional social- ist ideas. By 1955 the Democrats, unable to counter Sihanouk's claims of having achieved independence for the state, had effectively ceased to exist. When elections were held on 11 September 1955, the Sangkum Reastr Niyum won every seat in the National Assembly, allowing Sihanouk to run Cambodia as a personal fiefdom, imposing consensus on 'his children' while attempting to modernise the country.

CAMBODIA AND THE USA–INDOCHINA CONFLICT

Unfortunately for Cambodia, and despite attempts to placate the United States (Caldwell & Tan 1973: 91–7), Sihanouk's nominally socialist program and his neutral foreign policy were not acceptable to either his pro-USA neighbours or to the United States itself. In the late 1950s, Son Ngoc Thanh and the Khmer Issarak were revived by the United States and its Thai allies to destabilise the neutralist Sihanouk (Caldwell & Tan 1973: 99). An attempted right-wing coup in 1959 was foiled, although South Vietnamese incursions into Stung Treng Province came soon after, followed by allegedly CIA-backed attempts by South Vietnamese agents to assassinate Sihanouk. These latter moves had the effect of strengthening Sihanouk's distrust of the US and its South Vietnamese allies (Kiernan 1985: 187). As fighting intensified in Vietnam, Sihanouk chose to enter into secret alliances with the Viet- namese communists, allowing them to use Cambodia's eastern provinces bordering Vietnam for supply routes from the north and to base themselves in (Osborne 1973: 110). Sihanouk believed that by reaching such agreements, he would stop the Vietnamese communists from assisting in the escalation of the insurgency against his own gov- ernment. He feared that such an escalation would, in turn, invite inter- vention on the part of South Vietnam and the US and its allies. As well as making secret deals with the Vietnamese communists, Sihanouk also sought economic and diplomatic help from China and France, who were sympathetic but not able to offer any real protection to his gov- ernment from either the insurgency or the pressure from the USA and South Vietnam.

Cambodia's economy, once strong and self-sufficient in food, began to suffer as harvests were drawn onto the black market and then into South Vietnam (Osborne 1973: 7). This deprived the government of revenue from export taxes, as well as beginning to cause hardship through food shortage and price rises. Government spending, meanwhile, continued to grow (Corfield 1994: 30–6). By the mid 1960s, the country was spinning out of control. In large part Cambodia's increasing involvement in the Vietnam conflict was in a fundamental sense the cause of the country's problems. But it also appeared that Sihanouk was less focused on the country's internal affairs, to the extent that he often appeared out of touch with the day-to-day reality of life in his country. By the late 1960s, Cambodia was spinning out of his control. In this period, the Cambodian communist movement, which had almost disappeared, regrouped under Vietnamese guidance, led by Saloth Sar, who fearing persecution had fled Phnom Penh for the jungle in 1963 (Chandler 1992: 64–7, 1994: 4). Saloth Sar became better known after 1976 by his nom de guerre, Pol Pot.

CAMBODIA DRAWN INTO VIETNAM'S 'AMERICAN WAR'

The mid 1960s had seen the leftist anti-government movement quieten, primarily in response to the Vietnamese communists' agreement not to destabilise Cambodia in exchange for access to Cambodian territory and Sihanouk's logistical support. But pressure from Cambodia's conservative element was also mounting, making this policy increasingly difficult to sustain. In response to the United States bombing campaign of North Vietnam, its landing of combat troops in South Vietnam on 8 March 1965 and, most importantly, continued air attacks within Cambodian territory, on 3 May 1965 Cambodia severed diplomatic relations with the USA. In an attempt to counter pressure from the right, for the 1966 elections, Sihanouk decreed that the electoral process would only play a part in designating candidates for the Sangkum (Assembly) and that he would also participate in choosing candidates. After deciding that while the right was troublesome his main threat came from the left, Sihanouk moved to bolster the right, increasing their numbers in the Sangkum. But rather than placate the right, their ascendancy in the Assembly only enhanced their already developing ambitions for political control.

Despite his friendly actions towards North Vietnam and covert material support for Vietnamese guerrillas operating from Cambodia, by 1967 Sihanouk was losing control of his government's operations against Vietnamese and Cambodian communists operating on Cambodian territory.

As a result, conflict re-emerged between the Cambodian communists, by now popularly known as the Khmer Rouge (Red Khmers), and the government. From around this time, Sihanouk tried to mend relations with the United States, but it appears that the decision both to reject Sihanouk and to widen the Vietnam conflict to include Cambodia had already been taken in Washington (Corfield 1994: 53–79; Caldwell & Tan 1973: 177–91; see also Norodom Sihanouk 1973).

At this time there were also signs of re-emerging hostility between groups of Cambodian communist rebels and Vietnamese belonging to both the Democratic Republic of Vietnam (DRV) and the National Liberation Front (NLF) of the South (see Kiernan 1985: 73–6, 87). Disputes between the Cambodian and Vietnamese communists ranged over a number of issues. These included the Vietnamese approach of first winning the conflict in Vietnam and then pursuing the struggle in Cambodia, and of wishing to generally retain friendly relations with Sihanouk for strategic reasons. They also perceived themselves to be at differing stages of political development[5] and having varying responses to and support from the Chinese Communist Party (Kiernan 1985). But probably most important in the distinctions between the Cambodian and Vietnamese communist guerrillas was the age-old antipathy of the Cambodians towards the Vietnamese, which, for alleged allies, frequently spilled over into battles between units of the two groups.

A COUP, A REPUBLIC, AND AN ESCALATING WAR

After more than two years of cross-border incursions to attack guerrillas at their bases, and in a bid to disrupt DRV military supply lines into South Vietnam (Kiernan 1985: 285–6, 306, see 307), on 17 March 1969 the USA began the first of its many 'secret' bombing raids along the Vietnam–Cambodia border. The bombing raids had three consequences: the first was to further destabilise Sihanouk; the second was to push both Cambodian and Vietnamese fighters further into Cambodian territory; and the third was to bolster popular support for the Khmer Rouge. By this stage, with support from the USA, and given Sihanouk's inability to control events at home, real power in Cambodia had passed from Sihanouk to Defence Minister General Lon Nol and the conservative Prince Sirik Matak. Responding to the developing situation and formalising what was already in practice the case, in 1970 a bloodless, pro-American coup removed Sihanouk from power while he was in France for medical treatment. His successor was Lon Nol. Sihanouk learned of

the coup while on his way to Beijing, where he established his government-in-exile.

Lon Nol's coup can be seen as being in support of US strategy in the
region (it was widely believed to be strongly backed by the CIA, and
received immediate US support). But it was also an expression of a long-
standing tussle between Sihanouk, being both royalist and neutralist, and
the successors to the conservative, republican Son Ngoc Thanh. The
name of the state was changed to the Khmer Republic and the monarchy was abolished. Yet the Lon Nol government was riven from within
by factional disputes and lurched from crisis to political crisis (Corfield
1994: 52–183).

With Sihanouk no longer leading the government, Cambodia's neutralism was ended and the country's communists could step up their anti-
government activities without worsening the DRV's strategic position.
This escalation of anti-government activity was taken under the guise of
a new alliance between the Khmer Rouge and Sihanouk in exile. This
alliance was known as the National United Front of Kampuchea
(NUFK), although in practice it was dominated by the Khmer Rouge.
Indeed, it now suited the DRV to have the Cambodian guerrillas actively
engaged against their pro-American government. In this, DRV troops and
their counterparts from the NLF, the Viet Cong (VC), were also actively
engaged in military operations against the Cambodian government.
These forces operated with Khmer Rouge troops, especially in the eastern provinces, as well as independently. Also, the DRV and VC troops
launched numerous campaigns from Cambodian territory into South
Vietnam (for a more detailed discussion of DRV–NLF–Khmer Rouge
relations, see Kiernan 1985: ch. 8).

For the USA, the war in Vietnam was still the main game, while conflict in Cambodia became what was widely referred to as a 'side-show'.
Conflict between the Lon Nol government and the Khmer Rouge
quickly developed into a full-scale civil war. By 1972, the Khmer Rouge
fielded a force of 200 000 fighters and controlled almost half of the
country, with the Lon Nol army being only a little larger (Kiernan 1985:
345). In response to this, and in particular to the use of Cambodian
territory by DRV and VC troops, the USA intensified its bombing
campaign, especially in eastern Cambodia, disrupting civil society and
plunging much of the country into famine and primitive conditions
(Kiernan 1985: 349–57). Once a country well able to feed itself, Cambodia's government descended into reliance on US aid. Having been
aided by the Vietnamese communists, which they resented[6] (Chandler
1992: 147–50), and with widespread rural support, the Khmer Rouge

entered Phnom Penh and toppled Lon Nol on 17 April 1975.[7] The state was reinvented as Democratic Kampuchea[8] (Corfield 1994: 184–233).

CAMBODIA UNDER THE KHMER ROUGE

Inspired by a more purely agrarian version of Mao Zedong's collectivised Cultural Revolution, a sense of utopianism, and being progenitors of a peasant-based revolution without recourse to modern (or sufficiently literate) bureaucracy or technology, the Khmer Rouge cleared the cities and began a campaign of producing food and manufactured surpluses (see Chandler, Kiernan & Boua 1988). The Khmer Rouge cut itself off from foreign assistance (except from China) and, allied to its work campaigns, the consequences were horrendous, with hundreds of thousands dying from starvation and illnesses (the latter exacerbated by there being no doctors or medicine). Arbitrary violence had already become a trademark of the Khmer Rouge (as it had with other Cambodian political and military groups), with disobedience being judged as treason punishable by death[9] (see, for example, Kiernan 1985: 375–80, 384–93; Chandler 1992: 128–39). Cambodia's small educated class was either killed in the period 1975–78, or fled.

Eventually the Khmer Rouge began to turn on itself, in particular the central group in Phnom Penh began turning on its members in the eastern zone who were believed to have been excessively influenced by Vietnam (Vickery, in Chandler & Kiernan 1983: 128–30, 1985: 330–7; Kiernan 1993: 192). As the Khmer Rouge program of producing surpluses led to economic failure, tens of thousands more who questioned the policy direction were purged from the party ranks and murdered (Kiernan 1985: 392). As the purges began to take hold, Khmer Rouge soldiers and commanders in the east began to desert, fleeing across the border into Vietnam (Kiernan, in Chandler & Kiernan 1983: 136–211). Cambodia's total death toll, from disease, starvation and murder, between April 1975 and December 1978/January 1979, is variously estimated at up to 2 000 000, from a population of 6 000 000. It was one of the worst genocides in modern history (see also Kiernan 1996).

In 1978, for reasons that had to do with historical animosity, ideological conflict, probably to divert attention from internal problems (Kiernan 1985: 393), and possibly the sanity of its leadership, the Khmer Rouge launched a series of border attacks against the recently unified and battle-hardened Vietnam. The border disputes had begun in 1975 over Vietnamese claims to islands in the Gulf of Thailand, which had been formalised by the French during the colonial period. These claims were not accepted by Cambodia and, under the Khmer Rouge, there were now moves to have the islands returned (Chanda 1986: 12–13). There was also the lingering animosity over that part of south-eastern Cambodia that had been incorporated into Vietnam some 200–400 years before. So much a part of the Khmer 'nation' was this region of Khmer Krom that it was considered normal by the Khmer Rouge that Brother Number Two, Ieng Sary, was born not in Cambodia but in this Vietnamese occupied territory. Similarly, ethnic Vietnamese living in Cambodia were increasingly persecuted, with large numbers being killed from 1975 until the Khmer Rouge was effectively finished as a military force in much of the country in 1979.

VIETNAM'S OCCUPATION

In December 1978, fronted by members of the Khmer Rouge who had escaped across the eastern border, the Vietnamese army struck hard and fast, within days pushing the Khmer Rouge to the western edges of Cambodia and into Thailand (Chandler 1992: 150–68; see also Evans & Rowley 1990: 85–126). Vietnam installed a former Khmer Rouge officer, Heng Samrin, as president and head of the Kampuchean People's Revolutionary Party (later renamed the Cambodian People's Party, the CPP) while its army, supported by the Soviet Union, formally occupied the country until 1989. Cambodia was again renamed, this time as the People's Republic of Kampuchea. Heng Samrin had joined the revolutionary movement in 1959 in the south-eastern province of Svay Rieng[10] and had been engaged in anti-government activity from that time. Heng Samrin was no doubt close to his Vietnamese allies, and was among those that the central Khmer Rouge had attempted to purge in the late 1970s. Heng Samrin's protégé was a young officer by the name of Hun Sen, who had first engaged in revolutionary activity as a student but who had fled to the guerrilla movement during a crackdown in 1967. He returned to Cambodia with the Vietnamese forces, being appointed Foreign Minister in 1979 and becoming Prime Minister in 1985. Both Heng Samrin and Hun Sen were graduates of Vietnamese military training, and the fighters in their zone were regarded as the most successful within the Khmer Rouge (Kiernan 1985: 310–12).

The period of Vietnamese occupation was characterised by a coalition in opposition to Cambodia's new government and the Vietnamese.

The dominant group in the coalition was the Khmer Rouge, who operated from the hills and border regions in the north-west and west of Cambodia. Another group, based on Lon Nol's republican government under the leadership of Son Sann, also participated in the coalition but identified themselves as explicitly non-communist. A third group loyal to Sihanouk, later to form the basis of the royalist party FUNCINPEC, also participated in the coalition against the Phnom Penh-based government. This coalition styled itself the Coalition Government of Democratic Kampuchea (CGDK) (see Kiernan 1985: 32–3). The CGDK received most of its support from China, but some also came from the United States and Thailand.

Throughout the 1980s, a pattern emerged of wet season CGDK attacks against the Vietnamese and the PRK government, and dry season offensives by the Phnom Penh government's forces and the Vietnamese army. Although the government and Vietnamese forces tended to dominate, much of the west and north-west of the country was under the control of the CGDK, while guerrilla activity made much of the rest of the country unsafe. Refugees streamed to the Thai border, paddies were left fallow and mines were planted so extensively that large sections of the country, especially in the west, were unable to be used for any purpose at all. In a move that was designed to pressure Vietnam into leaving Cambodia, the United Nations recognised the CGDK. Technically, Pol Pot resigned the leadership of the Khmer Rouge in 1979 and disbanded the Khmer Rouge as a communist party in 1981. However, the Khmer Rouge retained its organisational structure and Pol Pot remained as its actual leader until shortly before his death in early 1998.

Soviet support for Vietnam began to decrease from 1985–86, in light of its own economic difficulties, and Vietnam was tiring of supporting an army in Cambodia when it was more interested in its own national development. From the early 1980s, and more noticeably towards the end of the 1980s, Vietnam began a staged withdrawal from Cambodia, with the intention of 'Cambodianising' the on-going civil war (Kiernan 1993: 192–4). Sensing the opportunity to press home the military advantage that Vietnam's withdrawal offered the CGDK, the attacks on the Phnom Penh government forces intensified after Vietnamese troops withdrew from Cambodia formally in September 1989 (Kiernan 1993: 209–19). To help relieve the Phnom Penh government's embattled army, special Vietnamese forces were employed in 1990 and 1991, but their presence was temporary and all Vietnamese forces and advisers were permanently withdrawn in 1991.

THE UN AND ELECTIONS

With the withdrawal of Vietnam, the way was clear for the UN to work towards a resolution of the Cambodian conflict. Until Vietnam had withdrawn, the UN was diplomatically restricted from working in Cambodia and in any case was unlikely to have been receptive to a request for such intervention.

Moving towards an internationally brokered settlement, in 1990 the four parties to the conflict formed the Supreme National Council (SNC). Sihanouk was invited to return as head of the Supreme National Council, though as the SNC failed to exist in a real sense he did not do so at that time. Events moved towards a resolution and, on 23 October 1991, the parties to Cambodia's conflict signed the Paris Peace Accord to form an interim coalition government to rule, ahead of national elections. One important aspect of this agreement was that it ended external support for the various parties to conflict in Cambodia, forcing most of the combatants to seek a genuine settlement (Kiernan 1993: 220–31).

To ensure that elections went ahead as planned, the United Nations established the UN Transitional Authority in Cambodia (UNTAC), its largest ever peacekeeping operation. This authority oversaw the establishment of the interim coalition government and monitored the ceasefire, started to regroup armed units of the different parties and disarm them, repatriated 300 000 refugees from the Thai border, and organised general elections (Berry 1997). While the Khmer Rouge was a signatory to the Paris Accord, it refused to comply with its conditions, including regrouping in specified areas and disarming. It later also refused to participate in the elections, although its attempts to cause disruption were unsuccessful (Kiernan 1993: 232–46; Chanda 1986: 386–9).

With twenty political parties registered, elections were held in May 1993. For a country that had never previously experienced genuinely free elections,[11] the UN-supervised elections were a remarkable achievement, with a voter turnout in excess of ninety per cent. There were some reported irregularities, but on balance they were so minor as to not to bring into dispute the outcome of the elections.

The National United Front for a Neutral, Peaceful, Cooperative and Independent Cambodia (FUNCINPEC) gained enough votes to make it the single biggest party, but did not achieve the two-thirds of seats in the Constituent Assembly[12] as required under the Paris Peace Accord. Even though it held more seats than any other party, it failed to exert the political power that would ordinarily be assumed to be due to it on the basis of the elections, as a consequence of the CPP's continued entrenchment in the institutions of state. The failure of any party to secure a two-thirds majority of the assembly led to killings and threats by elements of the CPP who failed to accept defeat. But with a political stalemate, Sihanouk (who from 24 September 1993 again assumed the status of king and head of state) pressured FUNCINPEC into joining a coalition with the CPP. In September 1993, with little reference to the Constituent Assembly, a 'power sharing' coalition between FUNCINPEC and the CPP embracing the principles of constitutional monarchy and, at least nominally, liberal democracy was produced. Sihanouk had agreed to stay outside the fray of day-to-day politics, so his son, Prince Norodom Ranariddh, as head of the royalist FUNCINPEC became 'First Prime Minister' and Hun Sen was appointed to a theoretically junior role, as 'Second Prime Minister'. The cabinet contained sixty-seven posts distributed among sixty-five individuals, thirty-three of them CPP members, while Hun Sen was in practice the more powerful of the two 'Prime Ministers'.

STATE STRUCTURES

On the face of it, Cambodia had a formal political process that should have ensured the relatively smooth running of the state. The state was now established as a constitutional monarchy, with the king as head of state without exercising any executive authority. During his absence or incapacitation, the chairman of the National Assembly (which was then a unicameral parliament), the CPP's Chea Sim, acted as head of state. The National Assembly itself comprised 120 members elected from twenty-one provinces, with a Council of Ministers (cabinet) formed by the government. In a practical sense, the two-thirds of seats required for forming government under the new Constitution meant that virtually all elected governments would be coalitions.

At a provincial level, where most Cambodians lived, local governors preside over provincial governments. Provincial governors and chiefs of districts were appointed by the (First) Prime Minister using a quota system. Chiefs of communes and village headmen were directly elected by their constituency.

Cambodia's judicial system, formalised at that time, was based on three tiers: the regular court, the Appeals Court and a Supreme Court. Judges were to be appointed, promoted and dismissed by a Supreme Council of the Magistracy, consisting of a representative of the Minister of Justice, the President of the Supreme Court, the President of the Appeals Court, and three elected judges, each with a five-year mandate. The Council was supposed to be chaired by the king, but as of mid 2000 had not been convened. A Constitutional Council was intended to interpret the Constitution and laws passed by the National Assembly and, after it was formed in July 1998, comprise nine members who have a nine-year mandate. Three of the members were to be appointed by the king, three by the National Assembly and three by the Supreme Council of the Magistracy.

Despite the theoretical separation of powers between the executive and the judiciary, the 'courts are subject to influence by the executive, and there is widespread corruption among judges, virtually none of whom receive a living wage' (US Department of State 1999a). The composition of the courts was also widely regarded within Cambodia as favourable to the CPP, while the courts also require Ministry of Justice and relevant departmental permission to prosecute civil servants, including members of the police force. A 'culture of impunity' was allowed to flourish in Cambodia, especially among government officials. For example, police and soldiers were implicated in a spate of kidnappings in 1999 and 2000, while Hun Sen's wife, Bun Rany, was alleged to have ordered the killing in 1999 of Hun Sen's lover, the dancer Piseth Pilika. Both Hun Sen and his wife rejected the allegations (some believe Bun knows too much about his past) and charges against Bun Rany were not expected to be laid.

In 2000, Hun Sen acted against 'corrupt and incompetent' members of the judiciary, 'responding in part to critics who said that Cambodia was incapable of mounting a fair and credible trial of the surviving Khmer Rouge leadership without UN participation' (Faulder 2000).

THE NEW POLITICAL SYSTEM IN ACTION

For the first two or three years after the establishment of the Coalition Government in 1993, political processes in Cambodia ran relatively smoothly. But the potential for long-term political stability in Cambodia was upset by further factors. The first was that, with two 'Prime Ministers' from two parties, neither of which trusted the other, there were in effect two bureaucracies running the government. This was both expensive and unwieldy, and led to considerable administrative friction and, consequently, instability.

As a political exercise, this arrangement offered the establishment of a coalition sufficiently divergent that most Cambodian people were formally represented, ensuring its de facto political legitimacy. This, in turn, allowed it to begin the arduous task of rebuilding Cambodia's shattered economy and civic infrastructure. The Khmer Rouge chose to remain outside the coalition, but would probably not have been accepted in its existing form by the CPP in any case, given its history of atrocities in the period 1975–78. The situation where the Khmer Rouge stayed outside the government caused two problems, one internal and the other external. The internal problem was that the CPP's unwillingness to incorporate the Khmer Rouge into the new political process—a situation exacerbated by the Khmer Rouge's own intransigence—led to conflict between the CPP's leader, Hun Sen, and the Khmer Rouge's erstwhile partner, Norodom Ranariddh. The problem that was external to the government, but that deeply concerned it, was that after 1993 the Khmer Rouge under Pol Pot and Ta Mok launched a new insurrection against the government.

In reality, Hun Sen was never going to genuinely share power with Ranariddh, which events came to prove. There were initial attempts at doing so, but Hun Sen harboured too much suspicion of Ranariddh, as a former colleague of Pol Pot, to want to allow him to exercise real, independent power. Further, Ranariddh's capacity as a leader was in some doubt, a fact acknowledged even by senior members of his own party.[13]

Beyond this, with the state relatively secure and operating under a moderately stable government, and with China and Thailand agreeing to no longer support the Khmer Rouge,[14] and with offers of amnesties by the government, the guerrilla organisation began to disintegrate. The disintegration of the Khmer Rouge was not in itself a problem. What was problematic was how units of Khmer Rouge soldiers were courted by FUNCINPEC and the CPP. The timing of the disintegration of the Khmer Rouge approximated, and to a large extent was a contributing factor to, the deterioration of relations between CPP and FUNCINPEC functionaries in the coalition government, and between Hun Sen and Ranariddh. With the CPP 'tainted' by its association with the traditional enemy, Vietnam, and FUNCINPEC similarly afflicted by association with the Khmer Rouge, both sides continued to genuinely believe that the other had been a traitor to the nation's cause.

THE DEATH THROES OF THE KHMER ROUGE

The edges of the Khmer Rouge had been breaking away for some time, but the pace of disintegration accelerated in 1996 and into 1997. The most significant blow came in 1996 when the Khmer Rouge's second-in-command (and Pol Pot's brother-in-law), Ieng Sary, defected to the government with 10 000 troops. Ieng Sary already occupied Pailin in the west of Cambodia and troops under his command had clashed with troops under the command of Pol Pot and Ta Mok. In exchange for his defection, Ieng Sary was given effective warlord control over Pailin. The disintegration of the Khmer Rouge was compounded by its structure as an organisation of quasi-autonomous groups led by regional warlords. As the strategic situation of the remaining Khmer Rouge became more desperate, the various groups began to act more independently. It was only a matter of time before individual leaders began to make their own deals with the government (Thayer 1998a).

The disintegration of the Khmer Rouge was played out in the idiosyncratic style of that notorious organisation. Upon learning that fighters had entered into negotiations with Ranariddh in order to defect, Pol Pot ordered one of their leaders executed in March 1997. That was Pol Pot's long-time friend and 'Defence Minister', Son Sen, his wife, nine children, and three other family members (Schanberg 1997). By this stage, Pol Pot was clearly losing control of the organisation and, in a bid to save themselves, the remaining senior leadership arrested Pol Pot. He was put through a show-trial for the killings and sentenced to life imprisonment. This split at the most senior levels of the Khmer Rouge led to rebellion within the ranks, with the Khmer Rouge's senior military leader Ta Mok taking Pol Pot as his prisoner, and several hundred loyal soldiers, further into the jungles of Anlong Veng in Cambodia's north-west. By April 1998, Ta Mok suggested that he could hand over Pol Pot in exchange for his own freedom. But on 15 April 1998 Pol Pot, who had long been sick,[15] died (Thayer 1998b). No autopsy was carried out on his body. No one knows whether he died of heart failure, as claimed, whether he committed suicide before being handed over to government authorities, or whether, the proposed exchange for freedom deal being rejected, Ta Mok decided that Pol Pot had outlived his usefulness and killed him.

The rest of the Khmer Rouge leadership followed the remaining members by taking up government offers of amnesty or, in rare cases where they did not surrender, being captured (or handed over). In December 1998, Nuon Chea and the former head of state of Kampuchea from 1975 until 1979, Khieu Samphan, returned to Cambodia from Thailand[16] and were in the interim granted an effective amnesty. This was despite widespread calls both within and without Cambodia for a trial to account for their involvement in Cambodia's killings. People on the street were saying they wanted the former Khmer Rouge leaders to be tried, even if it meant re-opening the old conflict. 'I want peace,' said one young Cambodian who had been a small child when he and his family were sent to the fields in 1975. 'But I also want justice. Without justice there is no real peace.' Nuon Chea was later identified by Deuch, the former chief of the S-21 (Tuol Sleng) interrogation centre in Phnom Penh, as being primarily responsible for the vast numbers of killings conducted at the prison (Camnews 1999).

Hun Sen hedged on the idea of a trial, saying that the parts of the international community that were calling most loudly for a trial, including the United States, Thailand and China, had themselves been complicit in support for the Khmer Rouge (Smith, S. 1999). There was also concern that opposition and foreign observers would push for the prosecution of the defendants on the basis of their more recent activities or their political position, rather than their crimes after the fall of the Khmer Rouge Government but before acceptance of amnesties. To the Cambodian people Hun Sen said that a trial could re-open the now ended conflict with the remaining Khmer Rouge. The pair and their families then left Phnom Penh for Ieng Sary's stronghold of Pailin.[17] Around 2000 troops loyal to Ta Mok formally joined the Royal Cambodian Army in February 1999, and just a few days later Ta Mok was arrested near the Thai border, his Thai hosts apparently having handed him over to Cambodian authorities.

THE 1997 'COUP'

As the Khmer Rouge's regional groups began to surrender, both FUNCINPEC and the CPP saw the opportunity to bolster their own forces with new, ex-Khmer Rouge recruits.[18] The scramble to secure these recruits created a sense of insecurity that led, in July 1997, to an armed showdown between CPP and FUNCINPEC forces in Phnom Penh. This brief conflict between the two groups saw both sides trying to settle old scores. With the CPP clearly having the upper hand, the outcome was dubbed by some observers as a 'coup' on the basis that Ranariddh had been 'First Prime Minister'. The death toll from the conflict exceeded 100, and Ranariddh and his key supporters fled the capital for either overseas or to the hills of the north-west. More than 60 000 other Cambodians also fled for the border areas near Thailand.

This event appeared to horrify the international community,[19] which had invested so much in the peace agreement of 1993, and consequently led to Cambodia losing its seat in the United Nations and being cut off from multilateral and some bilateral aid. This loss of income plunged the country into economic crisis (Boyce 1998) (at about the same time as a differently inspired economic crisis was hitting the rest of SEA), and challenged the viability of the now CPP-dominated government. To overcome Cambodia's international credibility problem and to help restore aid flows—and acknowledging that they were due in any case— Hun Sen announced that elections would be held in July 1998. Initially, FUNCINPEC and the Sam Rainsy Party[20] said they would not contest the elections, primarily because the lead time was too short for them to adequately organise. However, Hun Sen countered by saying that if he postponed the elections the international community would not believe that he seriously intended them to go ahead. The opposition groups eventually relented and thirty-nine parties contested the polls in an atmosphere of intimidation and occasional violence.

With control over the electoral system and dominating political life at the village level where the vast majority of Cambodians live, the CPP won a little more than half of the total vote. FUNCINPEC won the next biggest percentage of the vote. The CPP-dominated police in the provinces were active in removing signs for FUNCINPEC and the Sam Rainsy Party, which caused considerable concern. The government claimed that it did not direct such action, but the other parties claimed this followed direct government policy to use its institutional force to hamper the political process. More positively, the former Khmer Rouge bases were included in the political process and the Khmer Rouge was finally, formally finished. More negatively, Khmer Rouge remnants retained their warlord status in the provinces and, while the electoral process took place, it did so under the watchful eye and doubtful impartiality of the Khmer Rouge forces newly integrated into the CPP.

THE 1998 GOVERNMENT

International observers announced that the 1998 elections were a 'valid reflection of popular will', without going so far as to say they were 'free and fair'. The CPP received a slight majority of seats. In November 1998, FUNCINPEC agreed to form a coalition government with the CPP, after much complaint about the fairness of the electoral process, and under pressure from Sihanouk to resolve their differences for the sake of the country. In this government, Hun Sen became Prime Minister, Ranariddh took the powerful position of Speaker of the Assembly, and ministries were distributed between CPP and FUNCINPEC members, with the CPP holding a slight advantage. As a compromise and to placate political functionaries who had lost out in the election, there was also an agreement to establish a Senate, to be headed by Chea Sim.

FUNCINPEC also had the physical security of its members guaranteed against CPP attack as an inducement to join the CPP in the coalition government. The coalition secured for Cambodia's government its seat in the UN and began to see a return of multilateral aid. The CPP's clear dominance of the new government and the formal absence of the Khmer Rouge provided for a higher level of potential stability than the 1993 coalition government.

POVERTY

Cambodia is a poor country. The potential for it to provide for its own basic material needs has been well established. This is reflected in the fact that the agricultural sector still accounts for almost half of total economic output, about eighty-five per cent of employment and more than ninety per cent of exports. But the turmoil and destruction that has been a legacy of the three decades to the end of the twentieth century reduced most of the population to economic levels below that of their neighbours to both the east and the west. Per capita income was just US$290, with the vast majority of the population subsisting at a much lower level than this. Absolute poverty was variously estimated at around forty per cent of the population, with eighty per cent of all Cambodians living in the countryside. Until 1996, Cambodia's macroeconomic performance had started to improve, especially in relation to its pre-1993 levels. Inflation was below ten per cent and growth was at a healthy 6.5 per cent, even though foreign aid accounted for around forty per cent of the government's revenue.[21] However, the violence and looting associated with the ousting of Prince Norodom Ranariddh and his supporters from the coalition government by the CPP in July 1997 led to a rapid decline in Cambodia's economic fortunes. Growth was down to zero while inflation, projected to be five per cent, was over fifteen per cent. More importantly, though, about US$100 million in foreign aid (and IMF representation) was suspended along with Cambodia's seat at the United Nations.

Beyond domestic political impact on the economy, the loss of its Eastern Bloc trading partners (a gap that was not filled by Western investors) and the economic crisis in Thailand in 1997–98 further hampered Cambodia's trade and investment. Having noted that, the country's black economy operated perhaps more strongly than ever during this period, indicating a weakness of the state to control internal markets and foreign exports and limiting its ability to raise taxes for urgent infrastructure projects. The profitable gem mining and timber exporting fiefdom around the former Khmer Rouge stronghold of Pailin (Puy 1998), in western Battambang province near the Thai border, was indicative of the central government's inability to adequately exercise control over the state.[22]

Yet if Cambodia is materially poor, based on anecdotal evidence and voter registration figures, there seemed to be a level of political consciousness that was most unusual for a developing country. Certainly the population was directly affected by overt political developments from the late 1960s onwards. But the 1990s brought to Cambodia a realisation that some sort of representative political process was achievable, in theory at least, and that all Cambodians could and should take an active role in the political process. This active political life has been manifested in the plethora of political parties that have sprung up since the 1993 UN-brokered elections. By the time of the 1998 elections, the arrangement of those parties might have changed, but there appeared to be at least as strong a commitment to the electoral process by the people if not by the country's political leaders.

HUN SEN AND THE CPP

The Cambodian People's Party, increasingly dominated by the person of Hun Sen, directly controlled not just the party of the government but also the administration of government. In most cases, there was no distinction between the party of the government and the institutions of the state, which meant that an impartial political process was impossible. It also meant that the government could use the organs of state to facilitate the electoral process to its own advantage. Yet even with such a massive advantage in all forms of official life, the high rate of voter turnout in the 1993 elections and the seemingly high level of political awareness in 1998 meant that Hun Sen and the CPP were far from the favourite choice for most voters.

Within the CPP, there was growing disillusionment with Hun Sen's personalisation of power. There were Hun Sen primary schools, the Hun Sen Park in Phnom Penh and even Hun Sen's initials, in Khmer, printed opposite the CPP logo on electioneering T-shirts. Hun Sen's wife, too, was increasingly taking on the role of public benefactor, appearing at official functions as a powerful person in her own right. Hun Sen derived much of his personal power from manipulating the CPP, disposing of his enemies (both figuratively and sometimes literally) and promoting his supporters. Supporters were looked after through a patronage system, by which they were rewarded with positions of power and the potential for corruption. The party itself was funded by Chinese owned businesses, which arranged lucrative logging and other contracts, the proceeds from which were directed towards the party and individuals, rather than towards the state. There was also reported to be a high level of official or military support for the transshipment of heroin from Burma and Laos through Cambodia to its sea ports at Kampong Som and to the islands close to the Thai border.

The lack of official accountability that accompanied this situation reflected what was probably close to a genuine perception that the state and the party were, in effect, one and the same, and that the party was exemplified by its leader. In this way, traditional streams of patronage and favour have come to replace even nominally accountable government. The Leninist structure of the CPP, inherited from Vietnam and in turn from the former Soviet Union, placed primary political responsibility in the hands of the party's 'vanguard'. The logic of this process is that, as the pyramid of power narrows towards the top, power is concentrated in the hands of an individual leader. In other Leninist systems this has given rise to the cult of personality, such as of Lenin, Stalin, Mao Zedong, Ho Chi Minh, Fidel Castro and various lesser political luminaries. This concentration of power, however, fits neatly into traditional Cambodian conceptions of power, which is concentrated at the 'exemplary centre' of the political *mandala*. In this sense, Hun Sen brought together the logic of the traditional with the modern, in both cases managing to largely sidestep popular accountability. The processes of democracy, for Hun Sen, remained superficial.

Dissent within the party was muted by the Vietnamese Party's insistence that the CPP not divide,[23] that party loyalty is more important than the niceties of decision-making by committee, and by Hun Sen's personal military following. His personal bodyguard and officers loyal directly to him, and the troops they command, easily comprised the single most powerful force in the country, and most Cambodians recognise the efficacy if not the legitimacy of rule through the exercise of military power. Formal education may still be quite limited in Cambodia, but practical political education has been well entrenched. There may be groups or individuals who also command some military loyalty, but this at best means only a defensive measure against the omnipresent Hun Sen military group.

THE PRINCE AND HIS PARTY

Prince Ranariddh, on the other hand, was an ineffectual political leader. He insisted on being solely responsible for decision-making within FUNCINPEC, but was not capable of running such a political organisation single-handedly. FUNCINPEC was comprised of numerous different factions, few of which regarded Ranariddh as the best or most desirable political leader. However, Ranariddh was able to draw on his status as the son of the king and, beyond the urban areas where CPP control was more muted, in a countryside that still venerates the king as almost god-like, Ranariddh still attracted considerable popular support despite a sometimes oppressive CPP presence.

FUNCINPEC, however, was comprised of individuals who, as associates of royalty, by and large preferred not to mix with the peasants at village level. This fundamentally compromised FUNCINPEC's ability to function outside the urban areas (themselves almost entirely comprised of people who until 1978–79 had no urban experience—Phnom Penh is populated mostly by ex-country folk). Added to still appallingly low levels of education and a lack of professionalism at senior levels of government, Cambodia was caught in a situation where collapse and turmoil were just a step away. The international community, which had a high presence in, and impact on, Cambodia, remained, largely through historical guilt and a sense of needing to resolve a site of former superpower conflict and external interest (USA/USSR/China/Vietnam/Thailand/France).

Perhaps one of the lingering problems of Cambodia is that its people, in so many respects gentle and quiet, have been acculturated to accept violence. Through being brutalised, many were also desensitised. Seemingly random violence was relatively common—more so than circumstances would seem to provoke—while a desire for revenge against former Khmer Rouge leaders was palpable among most people. Of course, having lost so much and so many, such a desire was not unexpected. But many wanted it even if it meant the return of war. One foreign aid worker who specialised in teaching local dispute resolution said that the automatic response to an insignificant dispute was to raise the odds above that of the opponent. What might start as a disagreement over a small purchase could end, through aggressive one-upmanship, with guns being used. Whether at the level of the national–political or the local–personal, violence in Cambodia seemed to be the common fall-back response to confronting situations.

NOTES

1   Early Khmer has the sinicised Funan as 'bnam', or contemporary 'phnom' (hill or mountain) (SarDesai 1997: 23). The state of Funan was linked to Javanese rulers, the later Javanese name 'Sailendra' also meaning 'king of the mountain' (See also McCloud 1995: 91).

2   The word *nagara* also corresponds closely with the Malay word *negara*, meaning 'state', and probably reflects not just the Sanskritisation of Cambodia but also the influence of the Javanese Sailendra Dynasty in the early days of Angkor.

3   The Vichy government of France was allied with Nazi Germany and, by association, with Japan at this time.

4   Son Ngoc Thanh was exiled to France, rather than executed, as a measured response to his popularity within Cambodia.

5   The Cambodian party tagged itself as 'communist', indicating what it regarded as its more complete political development towards the goal of communism, while the Vietnamese party tagged itself a 'workers' party, indicating that it was still in the process of developing towards a communist goal. Central figures in the Cambodian party took this as a literal distinction between the two political organisations, marking themselves out as politically more developed, or superior.

6   By 1973 the Khmer Rouge was attempting to drive out the Vietnamese communists (Kiernan 1985: 357).

7   Ieng Sary noted that Khmer Rouge and Vietnamese communists had clashed as early as 1972 (Kiernan 1985: 275).

8   It is perhaps a small distinction, but the state of Democratic Kampuchea was technically a new state, given that none of the institutions of the former state survived. However, it did occupy pre-existing state boundaries and citizenship of one was transferred to 'citizenship' of the other.

9   The Khmer Rouge had always had a relatively harsh policy towards dissidents and other enemies, but from 1973 began to actively execute prisoners of war and others deemed to be untrustworthy.

10 Svay Rieng is also sometimes known as 'the Parrot's Beak', for the way it protrudes into Vietnam to the north-west of Ho Chi Minh City. It was an area much influenced by the Viet Minh.

11 The elections of 1947 and 1951 were moderately free but effectively meaningless, as France retained political control of the country.

12 The National Assembly was formed in September.

13 This is based on conversations with FUNCINPEC officials.

14 Although the Thai government had long denied such support, Ta Mok was known to have a house and business interests in the Thai provincial city of Surin. The last of the Khmer Rouge leaders did not leave (or were not expelled from) their bases in Thailand until early 1999.

15 It was widely believed that Pol Pot had malaria and perhaps other illnesses. However, while he was clearly enfeebled at this time, there is no evidence of any formal diagnosis.

16 The Thai government denied they had been living in Thailand, but they arrived in a Thai-registered car and younger members of their families could speak little Khmer but appeared to speak Thai fluently (Agencies 1999).

17 At the beginning of 2000, it seemed that the pair would eventually be put on trial.

18 Attempts by the opposition leader (and former FUNCINPEC member), Sam Rainsy, to the high moral ground in the 1998 elections were compromised by his party also accepting Khmer Rouge members, in his case Colonel Chhuk Rin, the regional leader who was responsible for the kidnapping of three Western tourists from a train in 1994. Chhuk handed the three over to his superior, Nou Paet, who later had the tourists executed.

19 At least an element of that 'horror' was presented as a means of asserting a sort of moral political standard, not against the coup but against the CPP's Marxist background.

20 Not surprisingly, based around the person of former FUNCINPEC member Sam Rainsy.

21 Almost US$2.3 billion had been pledged by the international community to Cambodia for the period 1992–95, though much of this was related to the UN-sponsored elections.

22 The area around Pailin was controlled by Ieng Sary, the Khmer Rouge's former second-in-command until his defection, with his troops, to the CPP in 1997. The arrangement to secure his defection was that he would continue to run the region as quasi-independent, including its lucrative gem and timber exports to Thailand.

23 The VCP retains the status of 'elder brother' to the CPP and is influential in the party's strategic affairs.

9

Vietnam: The Little Dragon

The two young men had their eyes riveted on events at the front of the bus and they were shaking. First impressions can never account for the complexity of a more complete reality. But in Vietnam, that such ordinary people should be so terrified of what was otherwise a relatively non-dramatic situation illustrated that agents of the state exercised extraordinary personal power. This was the personal face of totalitarianism.

The bus from Savannakhet in southern Laos had stopped a couple of kilometres short of the Vietnam border, in the middle of the area of what used to be the old Ho Chi Minh Trail, where a number of Vietnamese got off and walked into the undergrowth. Others on the bus thought little of it, except that there did not appear to be much but scrub around. The bus then pulled into the border post of Lao Bao and, after about four hours of drawn-out checking of passports, visas, baggage and contents in the cool, early morning highland drizzle, the bus and its passengers were allowed through into Vietnam. It was when we reboarded the bus that we realised a couple of bags had been left on board and that they belonged to the men who had previously got off the bus on the other side.

A few kilometres along Route Nine, just inside Vietnam, the bus again stopped, and the men who had got off before the border reboarded the bus. They had mud on their feet and trousers, and it seemed that they had crossed over the border at a point well removed from the official entry. Another five kilometres up the road, an immigration/police motorcycle outfit with flashing lights and wailing siren followed by another police motorcycle stopped the bus. One of the men who had reboarded the bus climbed through a window and began to run, but was

CHINA

Hong R.

Dien Bieu Phu

Hanoi

Gulf of
Tongking

HAINAN

L A O S

Vinh

THAILAND

South   China
Sea

Hue

CAMBODIA

Mekong R.

Saigon

Gulf of
Thailand

VIETNAM

250 kilometres

quickly caught. The immigration police began a check of identity papers of those on the bus. This was when the two men began shaking with fear. Unable to stand the tension, one, then the other, stood and offered themselves to the police. They and a number of other men were taken off the bus and, after about fifteen minutes, reboarded handcuffed to each other. The bus continued on to the old Lang Vei Special Forces Camp, which had once been one of a series of outposts established by the American military across the southern edge of the so-called 'demilitarised zone' (DMZ), but which was now occupied by the Vietnamese military. Here eight men and the bus driver were led away to the camp. It seemed that the men who had crossed the border illegally had been working in Thailand and were returning home. Certainly they had considerable possessions with them, which were also taken to the army base. After about half an hour, the bus driver and an officer returned, then shook hands. The bus journey continued along Route Nine past some of the most infamous sites of the American War: Khe Sanh, Dakrong Bridge, the Rockpile, Ca Lu, Camp Carroll, Cam Lo, Con Thien, Dong Ha, Gio Linh, and Cua Viet, just north of the Ashau Valley. All along here were extensive road works, part of an effort to provide a better link between Thailand and Laos and the port facility at Danang.

It was perhaps not a typical introduction to Vietnam, and the mood was most definitely one of oppression and fear, backed up by so many pointed reminders of the conflict that came to shape much of contemporary Vietnamese society. But this is the way it happened, in mid 1998, and it did create a sense that the Vietnamese administration was relatively efficient, overly bureaucratic and somewhat oppressive. If it was not a good omen, though it was not one that lasted.[1]

Arriving at the old imperial capital of Hue, by contrast, was an exercise in delight. The city is very attractive, situated alongside the Perfumed River and focused on the old citadel. There is a sense of former colonial ambience in much of the architecture, while the streets are filled with bicycles and scooters, with well-dressed people going to and fro. Hue was perhaps not exactly indicative of life in Vietnam, as the road workers and many villagers elsewhere did not look as prosperous. But Hue had considerable charm and an ambience and a feel that had more to do with preserving local culture within the context of a developing economy than it did with a totalitarian one-party state. Of course, appearances can be deceiving, but Hue was a breath of fresh air compared even with Vieng Chan (Vientiane).

The army also featured prominently, at least in road works and on television. The American War may now be further away than most Vietnamese are old, but its legacy persists in many ways. The defoliated areas still struggle to regrow, unexploded ordnance still takes its toll on hapless people in the countryside and tourism, now a thriving industry, capitalises on tours of the major sites of conflict. But, more importantly, the army has earned itself an honourable place in Vietnamese society. There is quiet though considerable pride in the fact that the nation was able to defeat the might of the USA. With a longer term view of history, there also remains a continuing sense that a viable defence force is necessary to protect the state against the dangers that could again threaten its existence. Of course, having become so institutionalised, the bureaucracy that is the army no doubt wishes to perpetuate itself. But this does not take away from the fact that it has earned and continues to hold an important place in the life of the state.

This chapter on Vietnam will briefly note the evolution of the nation/state as it expanded from southern China into the present-day territory of Vietnam, noting its internal squabbles, its history of conflict with (and influence of) China and adventures into neighbouring countries, and, prior to colonisation, its division into three states. From this point evolved the period of colonisation, Japanese occupation and the anti-colonial war, with the subsequent creation in 1954 of the two zones and, eventually, two states. This then leads to US/allied involvement in Vietnam and the period of withdrawal and subsequent collapse of the South and subsequent reunification. At a time when much outside interest dropped off, this was the start of significant internal upheavals, including the devastating 1975–79 droughts, economic mismanagement and the persecution of ethnic Chinese, war with and invasion and occupation of Cambodia, and the consequent Chinese invasion. The 1980s saw greater consolidation and the introduction of *doi moi* (economic renovation), followed by the collapse as an entity of Vietnam's main ally, the USSR. This chapter will go on to consider Vietnam's continued economic liberalisation alongside the maintenance of the effectively non-participatory one-party state.

ORIGINS OF THE STATE

Vietnam has the oldest continual history of any SEA state, being able to trace its lineage back more than 2000 years. Relics have been found from the Neolithic period and bronzes have been found in the Red River Delta region dating from the middle of the second millennium BCE (Nguyen 1993: 7–19). Legend has it that the first Vietnamese state of Van

Lang, in the Red River Delta region, existed from 2879 to 258 BCE. Probably, though, reality rather than legend puts Van Lang, under the Hung Dynasty, as being established around 500 BCE. The overthrow of this kingdom by northerners, and the merging of the states of Tay Au and Lac Viet, created the state of Au Lac in 258 BCE that, although it only lasted fifty years, marked the beginning of a clearly defined Vietnamese history (Buttinger 1968: 19–20; Nguyen 1993: 16–18). The capital of Au Lac was about 20 kilometres from modern Hanoi.

It was from around this time, in the third century BCE, that the people of what is now northern Vietnam began overseas trade with China and parts of what was to become Indonesia. A regional Chinese official, Trieu Da, taking advantage of the collapse of the Ch'in Dynasty in 208 BCE, founded the state of Nam Viet, which included the Red River Delta to almost the centre of the modern state, and parts of southern China. The people of Nam Viet were Viets from the lower Yangtze Valley who increasingly mixed with the local Austronesians, as reflected in the development of their language (which includes monotonal Mon–Khmer and multi-tonal T'ai elements). The Chinese referred to these people as the *Bach Viet* (the Hundred Tribes), which consisted of a number of ethnic groups including the Lac Viet, descendants of the Au Lac and Nam Viet groups. The state of Nam Viet lasted for almost 100 years, until the rise of the Han Dynasty, in 111 BCE, which crushed the independent Nam Viet and, apart from brief uprisings, ushered in more than 1000 years of Chinese rule. It was this period that left a lasting impression on Vietnamese culture and marked it as distinct from the cultures of its SEA neighbours.

It was from around or just before the Chinese occupation of the Red River Delta region that a new, Malayo–Polynesian state began to develop near Hue in what is now central Vietnam, spreading to approximately between the 12th and 17th Parallels. This was Lam Ap, a precursor to the Indianised state of Champa, which came to vie with Vietnam to the north for regional supremacy, and remnants of which can still be found in this area of Vietnam, in central Cambodia and in southern Laos. The southern Lao state of Champassak[2] is the most obvious nominal reminder of the state of Champa, while a Cham community of up to around 100000 people continues to live separately from their fellow countrymen in Cambodia.[3] The early Vietnamese state was expansionist and clashed repeatedly with its neighbours, especially Champa. But it also came into conflict with states further afield, including Nan Chao in what is Yunnan in southern China, and with the Javanese and Malay states of the southern archipelago.

Following the Han invasion, distinctly Chinese characteristics inherited by the Vietnamese included the removal of the old, purely feudal system of social and economic relations, and its replacement with a new bureaucratic and administrative structure based on education, a standardised written language and examinations. The ethos of Confucianism[4] became dominant, and Chinese technical advances and agricultural methods were passed on to the Vietnamese. There were constant efforts on the part of the Chinese to 'Sinicise' the Vietnamese, and they readily adopted Chinese ideas. Early Vietnam had a political social system akin to China's, where it had 'the mandarinate; the examination system; and the moral precepts embodied in Confucianism. Absolute authority in principle emanated from the emperor, who held the mandate of heaven as the representative of divine power on earth, similar to the celestial sovereigns of China' (Jumper & Normand 1969: 377–8).

However, while the organisational forms of the Chinese were embedding themselves, the Vietnamese also maintained and even strengthened their own self-identity. In part the reason for this was geographic: the coastal region of Vietnam was relatively separate from the mass of China. But it also seems that the Vietnamese had, even by the end of the Nam Viet state, more than 2000 years ago, established an assertive cultural identity that continues to the present day (Buttinger 1968: 26–9). It is claimed by at least some Vietnamese that they are a people adept at copying forms from other cultures and applying them even more rigorously than the original. But this same claim also posits that it is only the outward characteristics that are copied, while the driving force for adoption remains distinctly Vietnamese.

VIETNAM'S EARLY ASSERTION OF INDEPENDENCE

The first recorded revolt by the Vietnamese against China was in 39 CE. Although there had been progress of a type under Chinese rule, there was also widespread discontent by indigenous lords who saw their power disappearing, as well as among peasants over high levies imposed by resident Chinese bureaucrats. The occasion of the revolt was in response to the killing of a Vietnamese lord, intended as a warning by the Chinese to other Vietnamese lords. The lord's widow, Lady Trung Trac, and her sister led other lords and their vassals against Chinese forces guarding the governor's residence. The success of this attack led to the establishment of an independent state. But within two years the Chinese counter-attacked and the two sisters committed suicide by drowning. The death of the two sisters marked the formal end of Vietnam's feudal system and the beginning of almost a millennium of Chinese political hegemony (Nguyen 1993: 25–6; Buttinger 1968: 30–2). Buttinger notes three characteristics of the new Chinese-created dominant class. As a consequence of acquiring land, it became semi-feudal; it was semi-mandarinal (officialdom being largely based on education); and it was culturally Chinese, despite a growing input from ethnic Vietnamese. 'Its culture was Chinese, and it kept on being replenished with Chinese appointees, many of them refugee intellectuals' (Buttinger 1968: 32).

The collapse of the Han Dynasty in 220 CE created a loosening of political control throughout the empire, including in the southernmost region. Vietnam (the state then being based on the Red River Valley) asserted its practical independence under its governor, Che Sie (187–226 CE). Che Sie paid tribute to China and when the Han Dynasty formally dissolved, Che Sie paid tribute to the Wu, based in Nanjing in southern China. Upon Che Sie's death, his son attempted to assert his right of succession. However, the Wu decided against the succession, defeating Che Sie's son in battle, killing him and reasserting foreign control (Nguyen 1993: 25–9; Buttinger 1968: 32–3).

The next successful attempt at asserting independence came with Ly Bon, who in 542 briefly broke Chinese domination of Vietnam. Although a member of Vietnam's ethnic Chinese elite he, like others, had become 'Vietnamised'. While the revolt he led was successful, it lasted little longer than that led by Trung Trac some half a millennium earlier. Political tension clearly existed between Vietnam and China and Vietnam had a well established national identity, but it was unable to assert its independence in any permanent way. One of the factors that militated against change was the wholesale adoption of Chinese agricultural techniques. With a Sino-Vietnamese elite and Chinese overlords benefiting from this system, social and political relations remained relatively static (Buttinger 1968: 35). It was more than 300 years before Vietnam's peasants felt sufficient disenchantment with this state of affairs to join with their local ruling class, in what was perceived as a shared cause, to again throw off Chinese political domination.

In 939 CE, after a series of bloody encounters, the Vietnamese finally pushed the Chinese armies out of the Red River Valley and secured the country's independence. With the exception of the period 1407–27, when China re-asserted its authority, Vietnam remained an independent state until 1883. The initial years of Vietnam's independence were less than secure and danger was omnipresent. Yet, after an initial period of relative instability, Vietnam established a stable and efficient system of government, united under a hereditary monarchy and administered by a central government. Between 1010 and 1400, Vietnam had only two dynasties, the Ly and the Tran, each lasting close to 200 years. Apart from continuing to ward off potential threats from the north, and the corruption and decay to which hereditary rule is prone, Vietnam was also successful in fending off challenges from the south. The nearby Khmer empire for a time threatened to swallow the whole of mainland SEA. But more immediately, the successor state of Lam Ap, Champa, jostled for control of the region, with Vietnam relegating Champa to a tributary state in 1312. Within fourteen years, however, Champa had freed itself and in 1371 invaded the Red River Valley, while ethnic T'ai insurrections, in particular in parts of what was to become Laos, further weakened the state. Yet after having successfully resisted the Mongol armies of Kublai Khan, Vietnam succumbed in 1406–07 to attacks by a huge army under the Ming dynasty. This period under Ming rule was oppressive and exploitative in the extreme (Nguyen 1993: 30–63).

Led by Le Loi, a newly resurgent and more fully developed Vietnamese nationalism asserted itself during the ten-year struggle to end this Chinese interregnum, effectively completed by 1427, with the last Chinese garrison at Hanoi falling the following year. This victory over the Chinese cemented the notion of Vietnamese national unity. The Le dynasty, related to an earlier, brief, ruler, was thus founded, remaining in power for the next 350 years. It was under the Le that Vietnam expanded southwards, at the expense of Champa by 1471, and eventually also of parts of the decaying Khmer empire. Vietnam grew from an inverted geographic triangle centred on the Red River in the north to close to its current shape of 'two rice baskets on a pole'. In particular, the south grew quickly, providing land for the growing Vietnamese population and, by beginning to move into the Mekong Delta where swamps were replaced with rice paddies, supporting a new and growing primary economy.

The first hundred years of the Le dynasty was marked by generally strong government. But the following 250 years were marked by 'political ineptitude and moral debasement, feudal impertinence and usurpation of royal powers [often marked by political assassination], occasional vain efforts to secure economic stability by aiding the peasants, and bloody civil strife' (Buttinger 1968: 47). Civil war rent the country twice, in the early 1500s and again from the late 1500s, only ending in a 100-year truce between north and south. It was this period of separation between the two population centres, and the minor cultural and linguistic differences that arose from this time, that gave rise to some claimed legitimacy for the division of Vietnam from 1954 until 1975. Though the circumstances were entirely different, some sense of distinction between the two halves remained, and was exacerbated by the later French influence. The civil conflict in the latter 1500s also saw, for the first time, European powers playing a role in regional affairs, first with the Portuguese siding with the ruling Nguyen in the south, from 1535.[5] Portuguese involvement in the south, which dominated Western trade with Vietnam, in particular assisted with counterbalancing the competing northern and southern forces. From 1636, the Dutch sided with the Trinh in the north. However, the new and increasing source of strength to the south was its more complete expansion into the Mekong Delta, until then a part of Cambodia.[6] And, from 1680, another new European power had started to make itself known to Vietnam: France.

The Portuguese had initially attempted to convert the Vietnamese to Roman Catholic Christianity. But after their main (French) protagonist, Alexander of Rhodes, was barred from both the north and the south in 1630, when his Portuguese superiors failed to act decisively on the matter, he turned to France. Thus began the arrival of French priests in Vietnam, under the French-directed Society of Foreign Missions. Merchants followed soon after. What was usually low-level conflict between the Vietnamese administrators and priests continued, which was later to provide a useful pretext for expanding French involvement. French interest in Vietnam was initially limited to religious proselytising, with a little trade on the side. But the French soon had reason to expand their interests. The Treaty of Paris in 1784, which ended the American War of Independence, required France to cede most of its Indian territories. As a result, and still seeking bases on the route to China, it developed a stronger interest in Vietnam, encouraged by the individual interests of soldiers and regional administrators (Buttinger 1968: ch. IV).

THE TAY SON REBELLION

The situation in the north of the country remained chaotic from the late seventeenth to eighteenth centuries. Rebellions were frequent and often only barely suppressed. Famines were common, exacerbating rural unrest, and populist leaders repeatedly challenged the authority of the Trinh rulers. The situation in the south was similar, but perhaps made even more parlous by near-constant warfare with both the north and with Cambodia, into which the south was expanding. The effects of misrule in the south were to some extent alleviated by the opening up of the new lands in the Mekong Delta. But away from the delta, regional life was almost impossible (Nguyen 1993: 97). In 1771, in the village of Tay Son in the north of the southern part of Vietnam, three brothers launched an insurgency that quickly spread to other provinces.

The three brothers, Nguyen[7] Nhac, Hue and Lu, presented themselves as defenders of peasants, but soon gained the support of wealthier merchants. In 1775, with the Nguyen lords on the defensive, the Tay Son rebels Nhac, Hue and Lu, joined with the Trinh rulers from the north to defeat the remainder of the Nguyen army. Victory in the south was completed in 1776, with only one Nguyen prince, sixteen-year-old Nguyen Anh, managing to escape to the western area of the Mekong Delta. Here he proclaimed himself 'King of Cochinchina' and harassed the new Tay Son rulers. In 1778, Nguyen Nhac proclaimed himself king, establishing his capital at Do Ban in Binh Dinh province. Nguyen Anh attacked, but was eventually pushed back by Nguyen Nhac's brother, Nguyen Hue. Nguyen Anh then called on the Thai monarch for assistance, who sent him 20 000 soldiers and 300 vessels. In 1784, in support of Nguyen Anh, the Thai army invaded the western part of the Mekong Delta, but was ambushed on the My Tho River by Tay Son forces under Nguyen Hue. Nguyen Anh managed to escape the Thai defeat, being rescued by the Bishop of Adran, Pigneau de Behaine, whom he asked for assistance in restoring him to the throne. Events in France precluded immediate assistance, but French interest was aroused. The Trinh rulers in the north had by this time decided to move against the Tay Son Nguyen. Riding high on success against both Nguyen Anh and the Thais, the Tay Son turned against the Trinh. The Trinh court was at this time in crisis, with factions competing for power. The Tay Son forces under Nguyen Hue quickly marched from Hue to Hanoi in what has been referred to as a 'brief but brilliant campaign' (Buttinger 1968: 71).

Nguyen Hue placed a Le descendant, Le Chieu Thong, on the throne of Hanoi. But Chieu Thong schemed against the Tay Son, was found out, and called on assistance from China. In 1788, the Qing ruler, Kien-lung, sent a force of 200 000 to reconquer Vietnam. The Tay Son Nguyen brothers divided Vietnam into three: Cochin-China in the south, Annam in the centre, and Tonkin in the north, with Nguyen Hue proclaiming himself king in Hanoi, under the name Quang Trung. He then arranged a campaign against the Qing troops, defeating them in a series of battles culminating in the occupation of the Qing stronghold of Thang Long. 'In six days, the Tay Son troops had advanced 80 kilometres and defeated a 200 000-strong army. This was the greatest victory in Vietnam's history' (Nguyen 1993: 104). China reconciled itself to recognising the Tay Son Nguyens.

No sooner had the Tay Son Nguyens secured Vietnam than the Nguyen prince, Nguyen Anh, recaptured much of the south with unofficial French financial aid and mercenaries. In exchange, Nguyen Anh ceded to France the port of Tourane (Danang) and the Poulo Condor (Con Dau) Islands, as well as the right to free trade in Vietnam to the exclusion of other European nations. While Nguyen Hue was a great military tactician and politician, his brothers were not as skilled. The death of Nguyen Hue in 1792 and his brother Nguyen Nhac in 1793 led to squabbling within the Tay Son camp, weakening it considerably. From 1790 Nguyen Anh's forces battled the Tay Son forces indecisively. But the final fall of the city of Quy Nhon in 1800 tipped the balance in favour of Nguyen Anh. Hue fell, then Hanoi. In 1802, Nguyen Anh proclaimed himself emperor of a united Vietnam, under the royal name of Gia Long (Nguyen 1993: 106–8).

EXPANDING FRENCH INFLUENCE

Despite Pigneau's assistance to the new emperor, Gia Long, Vietnam turned against Europe generally and France in particular. Gia Long's successor, Minh Mang, became even more hostile, largely in response to European expansion in Asia, and in 1825 he issued an imperial edict charging that Roman Catholicism was a 'perverse religion', which had been 'corrupting the hearts of men' (Buttinger 1968: 73). Between 1833 and 1838, seven missionaries were executed for their work. This reflected France's more general failure in its attempts to gain a commercial and diplomatic foothold in Vietnam. After a period of European consolidation and considering English, Dutch, Spanish, and Portuguese colonisation of the region, France again looked at Vietnam. Using the pretext of the sentence of death upon a French priest, under Minh Mang's edict, and the requirement of freedom of religious practice, two French warships attacked Tourane in 1847. The attack was not officially sanctioned by France, but was later supported by influential missionary leaders in Paris (Buttinger 1968: 77–9).

Along with priests working against the government both within Vietnam and in France, Minh Mang's successor, Emperor Tu Duc, believed he had little choice but to fight the foreign missionaries and Vietnamese Roman Catholics. The actively pro-Roman Catholic France of Louis-Napoleon and the increasingly interventionist position of diplomats, military men and priests led, in September 1856, to a further attack on Tourane. However, the attack was poorly coordinated and resulted in no change but to further anger the Vietnamese government against the Roman Catholics. The following year, France revised its policies on the region and decided to enter the colonial race. In September 1858, the French fleet in the Far East took Tourane. However, an attack on the imperial capital at Hue was thwarted through a lack of appropriate craft, wet weather and sickness among the French marines. The commander of the expedition therefore decided to attack Saigon,[8] taking it in February the following year. The garrison left at Tourane was withdrawn in March 1859, meaning that the focus of the French presence in Vietnam would from then on be in Saigon and the south.

In response to English advances in Burma and China, France renewed its efforts in Vietnam, with the region between Saigon and Cambodia falling to fresh French troops in 1861, with the Mekong Delta falling the following year. After resisting as much as possible, Emperor Tu Duc sued for peace, giving France possession of the three provinces adjacent to Saigon and the island of Poulo Condor, and opening three further ports to trade. This agreement also allowed French warships up the Mekong to Cambodia, barred Vietnam from ceding any part of its territory to another power, allowed missionaries freedom of movement, and reimbursed France 4 000 000 piastres for costs expended in the conflict. Tu Duc was playing for time, for the French to weaken and for his own position to strengthen, especially against rebellion in the north (Buttinger 1968: 84–9). However, after the French had become established in Cochin-China, their policy of expansion throughout the rest of the region (including into Cambodia in 1867) was largely driven by the resident governor.

France's expansion throughout the rest of Vietnam was not without difficulty. After the establishment of the colony of Cochin-China and a protectorate over Cambodia, France consolidated its position there before looking towards the north. It was also distracted by the Franco-Prussian War of 1870, through which Napoleon III lost his throne, France lost the territories of Alsace-Lorraine, and, for a brief moment, the Communards of Paris took the city. With the French government inwardly focused, the French in Indochina acted independently, especially under Admiral Dupre, the governor of Cochin-China from 1871, who was abetted by the trader Jean Dupuis and Francis Garnier, a bright and energetic young promoter of French imperialism. In 1873, Dupuis, who had been trading arms in China, sailed up the Red River to Yunnan with a new supply of arms, returning with a cargo of tin. He was barred from taking salt on a second journey; as not only was exporting salt illegal but the local authorities were also trying, belatedly, to keep foreign shipping out of the Red River Delta. Dupuis responded by taking 150 heavily armed Asians and twenty-five Frenchmen, occupying a section of Hanoi, hoisting the French flag, and then appealing to Saigon for help. Dupre responded favourably to Dupuis' request by sending Garnier to Hanoi with full military and political powers in 1873. Garnier unilaterally opened the Red River to international trade, replaced customs tariffs with rates linked to Dupuis and others, and, eventually, shelled and stormed the citadel, following up with attacks on all the important towns and fortifications between Hanoi and the sea. However, on 21 December 1873, Garnier was killed outside Hanoi. Paris informed Dupre not to pursue the occupation of Tonkin and later sacked him, while Dupuis lost his ships. The French gain was to consolidate its conquests in the south, with a new treaty signed in Hue on 15 March 1874. Just after the death of Emperor Tu Duc, the French in Vietnam renewed their assault on the north in 1883, this time with the full support of their government, and Hue capitulated after being shelled soon after. The Treaty of Protectorate, which put an end to the independence of Vietnam, was signed on 25 August 1883. The bloody 'pacification' of the north took another twelve years (Buttinger 1968: 91–8).

THE COLONIAL PERIOD

The first years of full-scale colonialism were marked by a disintegration of the Vietnamese emperorship. Tu Duc had died without leaving an heir, so the palace factions divided. One group continued their resistance to the French, while another group worked with them. Tu Duc's successor, Du Duc (1883), was himself quickly succeeded by Hiep Hoa (1883), who in turn was succeeded by Kien Phuc (1883–84). Palace coups, dead emperors and unsubtle French involvement gave the court at Hue a farcical aspect. A fourteen-old-boy, Ham Nghi, was the next emperor (1884–85), fleeing the court and resisting the French from the mountains. He was betrayed, captured and exiled to Algeria. The next time the French took fewer chances, appointing their own emperor, Dong Khanh (1885–89).

France used a 'top down' method of local administration by a governor-general, usually supported by career colonial officials, who facilitated the economic exploitation of the primarily agrarian Vietnam for direct metropolitan profit (Jumper & Normand 1969: 384–5). The French, as colonial administrators, undertook some public works in Vietnam, including construction of the Saigon to Hanoi rail line, port facilities, irrigation and drainage works, and branches of a government bureaucracy. However, to fund these activities, the colonial government heavily taxed peasants, ruining the rural economy. It also controlled the monopoly on the sale of alcohol, salt and opium.

French investment in Vietnam was initially centred in the mining sector, in the areas of anthracite coal, tin, tungsten, and zinc, with plantations soon coming on stream in tea, coffee and later rubber. Conditions for Vietnamese workers in these mines and plantations were appalling, with one Michelin rubber plantation recording that between 1917 and 1944, of its 45 000 indentured labourers, 12 000 died from disease and malnutrition. As rural Vietnamese became poorer, the ownership of land became more concentrated, with 2.5 per cent of the population in Cochin-China owning forty-five per cent of the land. In contrast to most Vietnamese having traditionally owned land, by the 1930s more than two-thirds were landless.

THE GROWTH OF NATIONALISM

Against this background, it was not surprising that many Vietnamese people, steeped in a tradition of fending off external conquerors, began to organise themselves into armed opposition. When Emperor Dong Khanh died, he was replaced by a ten-year-old boy, Thanh Thai (1889–1907). However, by the time Thanh was eighteen, he too was plotting against the French, which resulted in him being deported to the Indian Ocean island of Reunion until 1947. His son and successor, Duy Tan (1907–16) was also a teenager when he plotted, with poet Tran Cao Van, a general uprising against the French in Hue. The poet was beheaded and the young emperor was also exiled to Reunion. Duy Tan was succeeded by the compliant Khai Dinh (1916–25), who was followed by his twelve-year-old son, Bao Dai, at that time studying in France.

Vietnamese nationalism was alive and well, if frequently rooted out and broken down by the French. Many Vietnamese nationalists looked to China and Japan as their role models for resistance to a European power, especially after Japan's defeat of Russia in 1905 and the success of Sun Yat Sen's Nationalist revolution in 1911. In 1911, a poor young peasant of strongly nationalist inclinations (Salisbury 1971) from Nghe An Province near Vinh, named Nguyen Sinh Cung, joined a ship running between Haiphong and Marseille. After seeing much of the French colonial world, in 1917 he disembarked in France, moving to Paris where, in 1921, he enrolled in the ninth cell of the French Communist Party. Nguyen Sinh Cung later went under a number of names, becoming famous in Vietnam as Nguyen Ai Quoc. Apart from joining the French

Communist Party, he also joined the Russian Communist Party and was for a time probably also a member of the Chinese Communist Party. In 1925, as Nguyen Ai Quoc, he founded the Vietnam Revolutionary Youth League (VRYL), being a precursor to the Communist Party of Vietnam (Dang Cong San Viet Nam), founded in 1930, and later the Indochinese Communist Party (ICP), from which grew the three communist parties of Laos, Cambodia and Vietnam.[9] Like its founder, as a revolutionary organisation, the VRYL and the ICP were necessarily secretive. The founder of, and inspiration for, the communist movement in Indochina was later known to the rest of the world as Ho Chi Minh.

By contrast, a largely middle-class nationalist party, modelled after Sun Yat Sen's (Nationalist) Guomindang, was founded in 1927.[10] Named the Viet Nam Quoc Dan Dang (VNQDD), it infiltrated the French garrison at Yen Bai manned by Vietnamese troops and attempted an uprising in 1930. The French responded with an air and then ground attack, killing many and capturing thirteen of the group's leaders, who were later guillotined. A few, however, escaped to Yunnan Province in southern China. The Yen Bai uprising was clearly ill-planned and was not supported elsewhere in the country, although it made a great impact both within Vietnam and France. The ICP responded by organising peasants into a 'hunger march', ending at Vinh. Large estates were shared out during the march and people's councils were established. Already the Vietnamisation of communism had begun, with the new councils being called *Xo-Viets*, a nationalist twist to the Russian 'Soviet' (Lacouture 1969: 56). There were strikes and uprisings, but the biggest, in 1940, was brutally crushed by the French, almost breaking the communist party. It was from this time that Ho Chi Minh decided on a new course of action.

THE FRENCH WAR

When France fell during WWII in 1939, Vietnam's pro-Vichy administration was recognised by the Japanese, maintaining a tenuous balance—with Japan having military occupation—between the two colonial forces. It was in this environment, in 1941, that Ho Chi Minh launched the armed wing of the VCP, the Viet Nam Doc Lap Dong Minh Hoi, better known as the Viet Minh. The Viet Minh actively fought against Japanese occupation, receiving Chinese and American support for their efforts. Based on a claim to nationalist credentials, the Viet Minh was relatively successful against the Japanese and, at war's end in 1945, constituted a major military force in the north of Vietnam. Towards the end of the war, Japanese forces ousted the French and, as they had done else-where in an attempt to slow the advancing allies, prompted Emperor Bao Dai to proclaim Vietnam's independence.

This 'independence' was, however, weak and the Viet Minh began an insurrection and elected a National Liberation Committee headed by Ho Chi Minh, which was tantamount to a provisional government. 'The truth is,' Ho Chi Minh said, 'that we have wrested our independence from the Japanese, not from the French' (Ho Chi Minh 1994: 55). They moved into the power vacuum in the north and central regions but had difficulty bringing a united front to the southern groups, which was dealt a final blow by the occupation of British troops as a consequence of the Potsdam Conference. The British armed French prisoners who then staged a coup in Saigon. The French formally returned to the south in 1946. In the north, the Chinese had occupation and forced some modifica-tions on the new National Assembly (Jumper & Normand 1969: 392–3).

In 1946, the Viet Minh signed an agreement with France recognising the Democratic Republic of Vietnam (DRV—what became known by most of the world, from the mid-1950s until the mid-1970s, as North Vietnam) belonging to the Indochinese Federation and to the French Union (see Buttinger 1967a: 344–51 on the inclusive nature of the DRV government). The three provinces of Vietnam—Tonkin in the north, Annam in the centre and Cochin-China in the south—were to unite as French troops gradually withdrew. In turn, the DRV promised not to oppose the arrival of French troops sent to relieve the Chinese. However, in negotiations there were two sticking points: the definition of a 'free state' within the French Union, and the status of Cochin-China (Buttinger 1967a: 379–83). The situation deteriorated and in November 1946, fighting broke out in the port city of Haiphong. This quickly esca-lated into a full scale war 'accomplishing for the Viet Minh what it had been unable to achieve on its own—the rallying of Vietnamese of all political beliefs to the Viet Minh banner in the struggle against French colonial rule'. The anti-colonial conflict was marked by 'extreme vio-lence and cruelty' on the part of both the French and the Vietnamese. Fighting covered virtually the entire country for almost eight years, lead-ing to significant and often severe suffering throughout the rural popu-lation (Jumper & Normand 1969: 395).

The point on which the war turned was that the Viet Minh adopted guerrilla tactics as outlined by China's Mao Zedong, while the French stuck to fixed position military tactics. France's deteriorating military sit-uation led to negotiations on one hand and calls to the United States for air strikes on the other. By 1954 there was a military stalemate in the south. In the north, however, the French believed they could win a decisive victory over the Viet Minh. Using the establishment of 'block house' fortifications throughout the highland region, the French had been able to suppress local anti-French activity. However, the size and organisation of the Viet Minh was more than they had counted on. Having established themselves in a series of connected fortifications around the town of Dien Bien Phu, which was far removed from their lines of supply, the French engaged the Viet Minh. The Viet Minh, however, surrounded the French positions and, from the hills, bombarded them with cannon and mortar carried in pieces through the mountains. In the final attacks the linked fortifications fell one by one. The French were completely defeated. The fall of the French garrison at Dien Bien Phu in 1954, upon which the conflict finally centred, forced the French to agree to a provisional division of Vietnam at the Ben Ha River, near the 17th parallel. The intention was to separate the hostile forces, with elections to be held in 1956 to unify the country. Over the next three years, more than 300 000 refugees fled to the south (see Karnow 1991: 203–39; also Buttinger 1967b). Conditions later became so harsh in the north that Vietnamese even fled to China, which was itself no liberated, tolerant state.[11]

At one level 'The Vietminh leaders intended to accomplish in a few years that which in more advanced nations had taken decades' (Buttinger 1968: 418). The state rebuilt itself from virtually nothing to a level of industrial capacity capable of conducting further warfare. However, the price of this rapid industrialisation was severe. Personal liberties were deeply restricted, food was closely rationed and dissent was not tolerated (Karnow 1991: 240–2). From 1954 until 1990, in North Vietnam and, after reunification, throughout the country, the supply of rice was restricted through the use of coupons to thirteen kilograms per person per month. Meat was restricted to 200 grams at the same ratio. Food was available on the black market, but had to be secretly eaten, lest one be 'denounced' to police. Agriculture was collectivised, which in some provinces led to mass starvation. In Hanoi, there was almost no physical change, apart from bomb damage, between 1954 and 1990. Those who had money hid it, and what was deemed to constitute 'excessive' property was confiscated—no one was supposed to be able to afford it, hence it must be illegal. Secret denunciations instilled fear into ordinary people and the jailing of alleged dissidents became the primary means of quelling dissent.

In part because of the concern over the seemingly repressive government of the Democratic Republic of Vietnam and, more importantly, because of French and American financial and military aid to the south, the south was encouraged to establish a counter-government, that of the Republic of Vietnam. Emperor Bao Dai, effectively a (deeply corrupt) puppet of the French, appointed the staunchly anti-communist Ngo Dinh Diem as Prime Minister. With two governments, one communist and the other anti-communist, plans for the elections faded as the southern government backed away from its commitment. The government of the newly proclaimed Republic of Vietnam, under Diem, was intent only on building up its own political base and, it hoped, managing to keep at bay the far better organised communists. It was clear at the time that if elections had been held the communists and their sympathisers would have won an absolute majority throughout the country. In the south, the plan was to divide the country in two.

THE AMERICAN WAR

The USA became involved in Vietnam because it regarded the rise of communism there (and elsewhere) 'not as nationalist movements—as they largely appear in hindsight—but as signs of a unified communist drive for hegemony in Asia' (McNamara 1995: 31, also 106; see also Hammer 1966 and Smith 1968 by way of illustrating the misconceptions of the time). In this respect, the involvement of the USA in Vietnam (and elsewhere) was a manifestation of the Cold War, in particular aimed at stopping the spread of communism in SEA. The southern government, led by Diem, quickly established a military foundation, initially allying itself with and then eliminating local sect/warlord chiefs by 1959, while DRV sympathisers in the south stored their arms and laid low. France withdrew military aid from the Republic's government, with the USA now fulfilling that role. However, Diem's government was notoriously corrupt and oppressive, enriching itself while alienating the very peasants it would have had to rely on to combat communism. 'By 1960 it had become obvious that Diem was not using American aid to woo his people' (Buttinger 1968: 433). While the initial policy of the government of the DRV was to wage a 'political struggle' against the government of the south, under Diem's repression of political opposition this was seen as being unable to achieve this goal. The policy of the north towards the south changed in 1960, no longer relying on just 'political struggle', but moving to the new phase of 'armed struggle'. The first manifestation of this was the establishment of the National Liberation Front in the south, created to launch a guerrilla campaign against Diem's government. From the perspective of the communist party, which had steered the anti-French struggle, its continuing campaign against the government in the south and its American supporters was not a separate campaign, but 'two phases of the same fight' (Chanoff & Doan 1996: 30; Karnow 1991: 264–85; Young 1991: 60–74).

Rebels in the south became more active, being countered in 1962 by the establishment of the US Military Assistance Command, Vietnam (MACV). It was becoming increasingly clear that Diem's leadership alone would be enough to drive most of the population of the south into the hands of the communists. In response, in 1963 Diem was overthrown and killed in a US-sponsored military coup (McNamara 1995: 51–87; see also Karnow 1991: 293–327; Young 1991: 95–104). Rid of Diem, the civil war in the south escalated, involving more and more US advisors[12] and then, on 3 August 1964, committing combat troops,[13] with air and naval support, and including US allies in the region. The north also committed North Vietnam Army (NVA) troops at around the same time. In 1965 there were 25 000 US troops in Vietnam. The north was targeted for air attack by the USA and openly engaged in the conflict. The government of South Vietnam, in the meantime, propped up by the United States, was notable for its repression and corruption.

By 1968, after having taken the option of escalation when facing 'a fork in the road' (McNamara 1995: 169–206), there were half a million American troops in Vietnam. The public rhetoric of the time was that the USA and the Army of the Republic of Viet Nam (ARVN) were 'winning' the full-scale war that the conflict had become. American briefings and body counts acted to reassure those outside that the battle to contain communist expansionism was being won. In truth, it was not about 'communist expansionism', and it was not being won.

When Ho Chi Minh died in 1969, the party leadership was taken over by Le Duan, leading a more ideologically strict faction of the CPV. 'Le Duan inherited power, but not Ho's wisdom and flexibility, the Vietnamese said ruefully' (Sheehan 1994: 15). Already an austere, authoritarian state, the Democratic Republic of Vietnam became more ideologically rigid and less concerned about addressing the practical requirements of its people. In large part, this retreat to conservatism was engendered by the deprivations of the war, and to a lesser extent by a lack of vision. At one level the effect was to strengthen the armed effort against the government of the south. At another level, though, it set up a division between hard-line conservatives and more reformist-oriented members of both the CPV and its Central Committee. This division was the primary political issue affecting Vietnam at the beginning of the twenty-first century.

The turning point of the war is generally regarded as the Tet[14] Offensive, starting on 31 January 1968, when attacks by the Viet Cong—communist guerrillas in the south—and the North Vietnamese Army

(NVA) penetrated a number of targets in over a hundred cities and towns, including the US Embassy in Saigon. It was the turning point not because it was a great military success—in many ways it was the opposite—but because it showed that, at a time when the American and ARVN forces were supposed to be so clearly in control, they were not. The public realisation of this effectively broke the will of the United States to continue with the war and, without this support, it ended any chance of the Republic of Vietnam surviving (Young 1991: ch. 11).

At one level, the Tet Offensive was intended to be the final push to end the war. In reality, though, the cost to the NVA and the Viet Cong was so great that, after losing around 32 000 troops and virtually all the military objectives they had temporarily gained, they needed to regroup, take stock of their horrendous losses, and consider alternative strategies to the conflict. The American army lost around 1000 troops in the Tet Offensive and the ARVN around 2000 troops. The battle for the hill-top fortification of Khe San just south of the 17th Parallel, which started a few weeks earlier, cost a little less than a further 500 American lives and around 10 000 troops from the NVA.[15] It was clear that one sudden push would be insufficient to topple the ARVN and the government of the Republic of Vietnam. Notably, as with much of the rest of the American War in Vietnam, it was the civilian population that bore the brunt of the fighting. Within the three weeks of the Tet Offensive, around 165 000 civilians were killed and a further 2 000 000 made homeless (Maclear 1981: 202–23).

Public opinion in the USA was turning against the Vietnam War and Richard Nixon was elected president in 1969 on a promise to reduce American involvement in the conflict, encouraging Asian states to become more self-reliant for defence. This was a double-edged plan, though. While ground troops were gradually withdrawn, the USA escalated its bombing campaigns in the north and extended them into eastern Cambodia (see Engelbert & Goscha 1995: 58–100). In 1971, secret information was made public about how the US government had systematically lied to Congress and the American public about its involvement in Vietnam. In the spring of 1972, the NVA launched a new offensive across the 17th Parallel, bringing forth a further wave of bombing of the north. Peace talks that had been underway in Paris finally reached a conclusion during this period, being signed by the combatants on 27 January 1973. In recognition of American desire to extract itself from Vietnam, the Paris peace talks did not mention the approximately 200 000 NVA troops still south of the DMZ (see Karnow 1991: 638–84).

In January 1975, the NVA launched a massive attack on the 17th Parallel, contravening the terms of the peace agreement. The Army of the

Republic of Vietnam made what it called at the time a 'tactical withdrawal', which soon turned into a rout due to disorganisation and widespread desertion. A massive offensive in the south finally toppled its government, with the thirty-year-long war of independence ending on 30 April 1975 (Young 1991: chs13, 14; Maclear 1981: 313–49).

The Socialist Republic of Vietnam was formally proclaimed in July 1976, setting in train a process of reunification. The cost of this war to the Vietnamese had been a little less than a quarter of a million ARVN troops killed, NVA and Viet Cong deaths at around a million, and civilian deaths at approximately four million. More than 300 000 Vietnamese were never accounted for. According to Vietnam's ambassador to the UN, Ha Van Lau, as many as fifteen million people were killed or injured in the conflict (Maclear 1981: 351). A quarter of a century after the war ended, there were still many reminders of its horror in the twisted and burned bodies of those the war touched but allowed to survive.

AFTER THE AMERICAN WAR

In the south, 're-education' programs, the collectivisation of agriculture, severe economic difficulties, generalised political repression, and extensive corruption in the years after the war engendered considerable local bitterness. The country was in physical ruin, with virtually all the infrastructure of the north destroyed in bombing raids while the south had also been bombed, mined and saturated with poisonous chemicals. Mutual suspicion and hatred ran deep. Foreign aid, which would have alleviated many of its difficulties, was limited and Vietnam was diplomatically isolated. Pushing forward for socialism at any cost, the party collectivised agriculture in the south in 1978, along the lines of that already achieved in the north, while free trading of any goods or services was effectively abolished. Following the old Soviet model, Vietnam attempted to push through heavy industrialisation, but succeeded in only producing highly subsidised, inferior quality products that had no market. By the late 1970s, with no incentive to produce, rice production had plummeted. A string of natural disasters compounded the problem and the shortage of rice was so severe that starvation became a real problem in the Red River Delta and the central provinces.

The limited foreign aid that Vietnam still received, mostly from the Eastern Bloc countries, was in terms of value largely in the form of military hardware. This was especially so when tensions began to mount between Vietnam and Cambodia over the persecution of ethnic Vietnamese in Cambodia and increasingly frequent attacks against Vietnamese villages across the border. In December 1978, in response to these attacks, the Vietnamese army invaded and occupied Cambodia, fronted by a small number of Khmer Rouge who had fled the terror of Pol Pot's Cambodia. The invasion was a military success, with the Vietnamese forces occupying the eastern and central provinces within weeks. However, the invasion led to a formal break with China, which supported the Khmer Rouge, and the invasion of northern Vietnam by China in February 1979. The Chinese attack caused considerable damage and loss of life in the northern region of Vietnam, but the battle-hardened army of Vietnam repulsed the Chinese army, inflicting on it severe losses (Evans & Rowley 1990: ch. 5). The cost of the war in Cambodia was high and was added to by the conflict with China. More importantly, Vietnam's continuing presence in Cambodia led to the country's few Western donors, such as Japan, cutting off remaining aid. Vietnam's economy thus slid into ruin.

ANTI-ETHNIC CHINESE PURGES IN 1978–79

With Vietnam's long history of intimate association with China, the country's Chinese community had managed to coexist in relative tranquillity. Many Chinese married Vietnamese and often the distinction between the two groups became blurred. But, as with the rest of SEA, many Chinese, especially those who had arrived during the colonial period, maintained close-knit communities. This was no more so than in Cholon, the Chinese city adjacent to Saigon and now an integral part of the greater Ho Chi Minh City. As elsewhere, while many Chinese were involved in the struggle for reunification, a very significant number did not get involved. Indeed, many continued to develop their businesses, again as they had done throughout the region.

At the time of reunification in 1976, Vietnam's ethnic Chinese presented the government with a particular problem. There was considerable reluctance by the ethnic Chinese in the south either to close their businesses or to bring them under state control as a part of the government's 'anti-capitalist' campaign of 1978. Further, in Cholon, what had been an area effectively independent of the rest of the city was brought strictly under Communist Party control. These two moves generated considerable resentment on the part of the Chinese, prompting protests and minor clashes with authorities.

Further, Vietnam's relations with China had gone from warm to cool to chilly throughout the period of the American War (Karnow 1991: 653–4), as China first attempted to assert some degree of control over the CPV. By 1978, China had moved closer to the United States and was clearly hostile to the Soviet Union, which was Vietnam's main ally. The Chinese in Vietnam, though having been there for several generations, were perceived as potentially disloyal. This reflected their continued identification as Chinese rather than Vietnamese, and the Chinese tradition of regarding its overseas Chinese people as still being of 'dragon blood', that is, loyal to the Chinese homeland. This problem has also arisen in a number of other SEA states. The Vietnamese Government responded by actively encouraging, through negative rather than positive incentives, Chinese to leave Vietnam for China. The situation with the Chinese became significantly worse as tensions rose between Vietnam and China, especially with China's attack in 1979. The ethnic Chinese in Vietnam were increasingly perceived as a potential 'fifth column' and were harassed because of this.

Between the economic difficulties faced by Chinese businesspeople in the south and the harassment they received throughout the country from the government, many Chinese decided it was time to leave. Along with a number of Vietnamese who had suffered under the change of government, the small but steady stream of refugees that had been coming out of Vietnam since before the reunification became a flood in 1978. Over a period of several years, but especially in 1978–80, around 545 000 ethnic Chinese and Vietnamese poured out of Vietnam. The main method of leaving was by fishing boats or small ferries. These marginally seaworthy craft were not built for the open seas, nor were they able to withstand the attacks of pirates who operated from the coast of Thailand through to the eastern parts of the Indonesian, Philippine and Malaysian archipelago. It has been variously estimated that half or more of those 'boat people' who left Vietnam never reached their destinations. In some other cases, where they did reach their destinations, especially among the later departures, they were eventually repatriated.

HUMAN RIGHTS ISSUES

As a part of its hangover from following a rather older-styled Soviet model of political organisation overlaying a base of neo-Confucian moralism, Vietnam has a history of strictly enforced responses to dissent. In the period following reunification in 1975, 're-education' was a euphemism for punishing citizens who had either been too active in support of the Government of the Republic of Vietnam or who had opposed elements of the new political and economic style that accompanied reunification. Tens of thousands of people were held in special camps for months or years, often without trial and usually forced to undertake hard labour. The property of many of those who were believed to have collaborated with the Republican government was confiscated. Many skilled workers from the south who were eventually released found that they could no longer practise their profession. It was not uncommon to find cyclo (three-wheeled-bicycle) drivers in Ho Chi Minh City who had once been teachers, doctors or dentists, now eking out a living with this most menial work. Others were denied residence permits, which limited access to official services, including employment, attending school or owning property.

Religious freedom, too, was constrained. Both lay people and senior leaders of the Unified Buddhist Church of Vietnam (UBCV) were variously harassed and arrested, including some of those who assisted in bringing about the downfall of Ngo Dinh Diem in 1963. Their crime was not submitting the UBCV to the control of the CPV. In 1981 an 'official' Buddhist church was formed by the government. To the end of the 1980s, protests by Buddhist monks at what they believed were inappropriate government policies led to numerous arrests and detention without trial for more than four years. Roman Catholic and sect leaders fared little better under a government which regarded religion as, at best, misguided, and certainly as an overt political threat (Nguyen 1994).

ECONOMIC 'RENOVATION'

The economic styles of the north and south had always been different. The north was industrialised around Hanoi and Haiphong, but was otherwise relatively impoverished. The policies initiated by the CPV after 1954 encouraged a Soviet-style economic development, while the destruction caused by the subsequent war destroyed the region's infrastructure. The south had opened up two centuries before, drawing in immigrants to its new land, prospering, and eventually supporting a larger population. It was also in the south that the French first made their deepest impact on Vietnamese society and it was through there that most French investment flowed. Between 1954 and 1975, first the Viet Cong and then the government of the Republic of Vietnam instituted a small-holder land ownership policy, the former as a means of redistribution, the latter to thwart the appeal of the communists among rural peasants. By 1975, small landholdings in the south were common, and many such small landholders were relatively well off, especially compared to both their time under the French and, more importantly, compared to their counterparts in the north (Beresford 1988).

In 1982, during the depths of economic failure, Nguyen Van Linh was elected general secretary of the CPV. Nguyen was a northerner who had spent the French and American wars fighting in the south and who had earlier been voted out of the Politburo for taking a qualified position on the introduction of pure socialism. As general secretary, Nguyen pulled Vietnam back from its headlong rush into socialism and began to introduce what became known as *doi moi*, interpreted as (economic) renovation, but literally translating as the 'new way' (Vu 1995: 17–30). The policy of *doi moi* marked a significant change in Vietnam, with only three of the thirteen members of the Politburo from 1982 remaining. However, while Vietnam spent the mid 1980s moving towards liberalising its economy, it did not begin to liberalise its political structures. Those who believed that political liberalism should accompany economic liberalism were purged from the party, while outspoken opposition was punished by jail or, in extreme cases, death. A conservative, Pham Hung, was elected prime minister in 1987 and, when he died a year later, was succeeded by Do Muoi, who was also regarded as a conservative.

While Vietnam liked to boast later that it led the Soviet Union into economic liberalisation, *doi moi* was most effectively put into practice in 1988–89, at about the same time the Soviet Union was undergoing massive economic and political upheavals. As the Soviet Union reassessed its own parlous economic state, it began to reduce aid to Vietnam radically, which, along with international economic isolation, led Vietnam to disengage from Cambodia. By the late 1980s, party general secretary Nguyen Van Linh had begun to show clear liberal political as well as economic tendencies, although the primacy of the party has never been open to meaningful challenge. In so far as political reform was on the agenda, it was to be based on the premise that the party would remain the leading political force (see CPV 1991). At the same time it was granted that there should be greater inner party democracy, that the party should operate within the framework of the law, and that the government should be guided by it rather than subordinate to it (Nguyen 1993: 400–5).

Vo Van Kiet, a 'managerialist', succeeded Do Muoi as prime minister, who himself succeeded Nguyen Van Linh as party general secretary. Non-party candidates were allowed to stand in the 1992 National Assembly elections, taking eight per cent of the vote. However, all non-party candidates were first approved by the Vietnam Fatherland Front, a party organisation. The 1992 Constitution removed some of the more revolutionary rhetoric from the 1980 Constitution, opening the way for Vietnam's new 'open door' economic policy. The National Assembly, formerly a rubber stamp for the Council of Ministers, now had enhanced powers of legislation and oversaw government activity. Vietnam's president has the power to recommend dismissal of the prime minister to the National Assembly and to act as commander-in-chief of the armed forces.

Despite fluctuations as a consequence of regional economic imbalances, economic development appears to have proceeded at a considerable pace in Vietnam. Inflation, for example, which was once the major scourge of the Vietnamese economy, was brought down to 17.5 per cent in 1992 and just 3.8 per cent by 1997. By 1999, however, it was up again to 9.1 per cent as a consequence of the regional economic downturn, while the inflationary effect was even greater in the area of food, at 21.3 per cent in 1998 (Ha 1999). Economic growth in 1998 was, remarkably, faster than any of the other ASEAN economies at 5–6 per cent. However, Vietnam's economic growth was not reflected in job creation and tended to fluctuate. By 1999, Vietnam was heading towards a longer period of low growth. At least in part, the apparent inability of Vietnam to consistently develop, beyond the knock-on effect of the regional economic downturn, focused on the state's decentralised decision making process, in which an agreement in one sector of the government did not necessarily translate into action in another. Fforde also recognised an ideological reluctance to fully accept what was touted as free market mechanisms, which corresponded to other models of economic development in the region (Fforde 1999).

In spite of its economic downturn, there remained a profusion of motor scooters and television sets, both of which were in abundance. Indeed, during the 1998 Football World Cup, it seemed that virtually every Vietnamese home was lit by the muted glow of a television screen at night, the electronic light reflected off the faces of rapt viewers. Even in the more remote districts, television sets and often video cassette recorders were standard fare. It was only in the poorest, most basic of thatched huts that such items were found less, although even here there could be seen an occasional aerial rising from the dried palm fronds. Motor scooters likewise outnumbered bicycles by about ten to one, and overall the common level of material development was at least on a par with that of Indonesia, which had long been claimed as one of the region's economic success stories. For most people, according to a United Nations report on Vietnam, the economy continued to improve (Tu 1999).

THE POST-UNIFICATION STATE

Although it existed in various historical guises, modern Vietnam can be said to date from the reunification of the country in July 1976. Vietnam is a centrally controlled state, although Ho Chi Minh City, of which Saigon is the heart, challenged Hanoi for pre-eminence, particularly in the economic sphere. Vietnam is a socialist state governed by people's representatives who are elected at a local level. Although there were some limited pro-nationalist non-communist parties in post-1975 Vietnam, they either have been outlawed or have otherwise been effectively incorporated into the communist framework. The Communist Party of Vietnam remains effectively the party of state, with no distinction between party ideology and state ideology and all state institutions, including the military, being beholden to the party. Government policy is set by the Politburo, a thirteen-member executive elected by the party Central Committee at approximately five-yearly intervals, with the party secretariat directing government policy on a day-to-day basis. Of the thirty-four-member cabinet, thirty members are also members of the Central Committee. Of the 395-seat National Assembly, 92 per cent were held by the CPV.

Shifting towards a new, capitalist economy, Vietnam introduced a Value Added Tax (VAT) at the beginning of 1999. The introduction of a VAT sent two signals, the first being that the government was moving away from a 'progressive' taxation system to a flat tax system, where the tax burden fell proportionately more heavily on the shoulders of the poor. The second signal was a recognition that a conventional income tax was not working in Vietnam, with too many people working outside the formal economy and generating invisible income, both as farmers selling surplus, artisans selling services for cash, or in the wider black economy.

From having been the austere capital of the DRV, change began to take place in Hanoi from around 1990, which has drawn mixed responses from its citizens. Most people were happy about the improved material conditions (if they could afford them), but there remained many misgivings about the loss of traditional culture and architecture.

In 1999, bud-lighting illuminated Hanoi's main streets at night, lending the city an air of prosperity and gaiety, even if many of the lit symbols were hammers and sickles. Billboards warned of the evil of AIDS throughout the country, rather than the evils of capitalism. After decades of somnambulance, while perhaps not as brash as Ho Chi Minh, Hanoi was clearly a booming city. Even the Hilton Hotel chain had established a hotel in the city, giving an ironic twist to the American War prisoner-of-war camp named the 'Hanoi Hilton'.

In Ho Chi Minh City, the pace of life and development was very slow and opportunities were few between 1975 and 1990 (see Sheehan 1994). Since 1990, though, the city has streaked ahead in terms of economic development and population growth, attracting immigrants from around the country and developing a substantial manufacturing base.

Left apart from the other major centres of Vietnam, Vinh, a major port city south of Hanoi, was bombed to rubble during the American War for its role as the major point of transshipment to the Ho Chi Minh Trail. It has since been completely rebuilt, even if mostly in Comecon[16] architectural style (which looks forty years out of date when new and deteriorates at a rate to give its architectural style further apparent authenticity). An uninspiring city in so many respects, Vinh has a dilapidated grace that comes directly from its people; slightly reserved and unaffected, but warm and courteous. But perhaps what Vinh most represents is the huge personal and economic cost to the Vietnamese of the attempt to halt 'international communism' in communism's supposed bid for 'world domination'. In the final analysis, a city like Vinh forces the question: would communism have more quickly come to show its 'human face' had capitalist countries not so violently attacked it? The answer to such a question will never be known, and fading old 'Cold Warriors' still argue that those times were different. Perhaps the contest for 'world domination' really was the main agenda. But then again, it is also possible that, after initially confusing communism with Russian political culture, the ideological response of hegemonic vested interests in Vietnam lost sight of the fact that, if left alone, most people and governments just wanted to get on with looking after themselves.

THE ARMY

As for the government, unlike some other SEA states, by 1999 it was notable by its absence. In each town or village there would be one building that was clearly for government administrative purposes, but there were no more than in any other country that has a town hall or municipal office. Police, similarly, were not thick on the ground, though an occasional police patrol could be spotted in the inner city area of Saigon at three o'clock in the morning. As for the army, there were groups here and there of young soldiers near army bases, but their profile was not high and for the most part they seemed no more out of place than would young recruits in towns adjoined to military camps in the United States. Perhaps, in part, this relatively low profile and seemingly high level of acceptance of the Vietnamese army by ordinary Vietnamese stemmed from the fact that it was quite genuinely a defence force, and an original part of the contemporary political process, rather than a paramilitary police, as in Indonesia.

The purpose of the army is to defend Vietnam and, to a lesser extent, to assist in the development of public works. The army maintained a central role in the life of the CPV as well as the government, a legacy of the army's original political as well as military role. Because the army was very much a creation of the party and the army's leaders were, originally, also the party's political leaders, the army and the party remain effectively two parts of the same organisation. While this has meant an active role for the army in political affairs, it has also meant that there has been no significant army–party friction, as is the case in many other countries in which the army is a dominant political feature (Turley 1988: 197–202).

As well as continuing its influential role in civil affairs, the army also maintained a substantial grip on the economy, participating in at least fifty-six joint ventures and wholly operating at least 200 other businesses. In 1998 army businesses generated US$609 million, in part through its timber concessions, off-shore oil services and helicopter transportation (Balfour 1999). Perhaps for those who attempt to challenge more directly the authority of the government, Vietnam remains an oppressive place. But the truth is that the presence of the government is not high and most people seem fairly free now to get on with their lives. The main distinction, perhaps, between Laos and Vietnam was one of national style and levels of economic development, rather than any fundamental distinction about the degree to which the government engaged directly in the lives of ordinary people.

POLITICAL 'RENOVATION'?

On 3 January 1999, Vietnam's Communist Party chief, Le Kha Phieu, pledged openness among the country's leadership and said that tolerance of 'more acceptable bounds of criticism was on tap for the new year'. It was, however, a short-lived resolution and outspoken General Tran Do was the first major figure to pay the price of this inconsistency. Do, a lauded revolutionary-turned-government-critic, had claimed that the party was riddled with corruption and had lost touch with the masses. As an interesting comment on the gap between 'the masses' and the VCP, membership of the party rose by 106 000, or 3.18 per cent, over the previous year, which was the biggest increase since economic reforms were introduced in 1986 and lifted numbers to a record 23 000 000. It was widely believed that the rise in party membership reflected the increased opportunities for employment and other forms of profit-taking for party members, which were not open to ordinary members of the public.

Corruption was so widespread in Vietnam and of such concern that there were public protests against corruption in Thai Binh in 1997.

For his criticism, Do was expelled from the Communist Party, ironically the day after Le's announcement on 'openness'. His offence was to call for democracy, free elections and an end to corrupt, state-controlled economic planning. A reshuffle of the Communist Party's Central Committee soon after placed conservatives and the military back in the ascendency over reformers (DPA 1999). Reflecting that shift, some members were disciplined for excessive liberalism. The CPV soon passed a new resolution to punish members who persisted in disseminating views or documents counter to the party line (Reuters 1999b). The split within the top ranks of the CPV between reformers and conservatives was such that respected leaders such as former Prime Minister Vo Van Kiet and Deputy Prime Minister Nguyen Manh Cam were vilified as working for Washington in an unsigned letter circulated to party members. How this translated in practice was that, with the leadership of the CPV unable to agree on basic economic issues, it had IMF loans deferred for two years, while foreign investment dropped to around a quarter of its 1996 high of US$1.8 billion (Keenan 1999).

It would be inaccurate to claim that Vietnam's current problems are solely a result of its history of post-colonial conflict. Each state makes its own decisions and the American War in Vietnam did finish, in its extended, puppet-government sense, twenty-five years before the end of the twentieth century. This was enough time for the CPV to move on. However, the attitudinal responses of sections of the CPV reflected not just corrupt self-interest, although that was surely there as well, but also a deeply conservative and defensive position in regard to change that sprang out of a profound sense of insecurity. It is suggested in holocaust literature that it takes three generations before a people can begin to move on from an historical trauma. Among Vietnam's leadership, most are still of the first generation.

NOTES

1   A later crossing at the mist-shrouded 734-metre-high border post of Cau Treo, approximately south-west of Vinh, was marked by a surly Vietnamese immigration official taking small (about US$0.50) but consistent bribes from both Lao and Vietnamese citizens to validate passports for entry. Truck drivers paid appreciably more.

2   The Chams of Pasak.

3   Chams are identified as separate from both the Cambodians and the Vietnamese by their language, which is related to Indonesian, and their adoption of Islam, as opposed to Buddhism.
4   As outlined in the section on 'Asian Values'.
5   This was just 24 years after the Portuguese conquered the Islamic Malay trading city of Malacca.
6   This area is still known to the Khmers as Kampuchea Krom and many ethnic Khmers born there have played a role in postwar events in Cambodia. Many Khmers still hold grievances over the loss of this region to Vietnam.
7   Nguyen is a very common name in Vietnam.
8   Saigon, now Ho Chi Minh City, was originally a small Khmer town.
9   The Communist Party of Vietnam was the original communist party in the region, later expanded to become the ICP, which in turn later devolved into three separate parties.
10   There was also a Constitutionalist Party in Cochin-China founded by wealthy, French-influenced Vietnamese. While it was a pliable organisation it was successful, but, when, after 1930, it began to assert a more independent line, it quickly declined as French support evaporated (see Cook 1977).
11   Since the early 1990s, the population flow has gone in the other direction, with people moving from southern China to the liberalised economic zones in Vietnam's north.
12   Lacouture (1968: 245) claims there were 50 000 USA military 'advisers' in Vietnam in 1964.
13   The troops began landing, first at Da Nang, from 8 March 1965.
14   Vietnamese New Year.
15   It is an insight into American thinking at the time that the battle of Khe San was regarded by American planners as being the NVA's attempt to restage the pivotal 1954 battle of Dien Ben Phu against the French. In response, the US military command poured a huge amount of materiel into the base to fend off the mounting attack. The US commander, General Westmoreland, even believed that the Tet Offensive was designed to distract attention from Khe San. In hindsight, it seems that Khe San was intended to distract attention from the build-up for the Tet Offensive.
16   Council for Mutual Economic Assistance, the former Soviet Bloc economic trade group.

Part III

10

Malaysia: Inclusion and Exclusion

As a former British colony, and having at least the external appearance of a constitutional parliamentary democracy, Malaysia shocked the world in November 1998 when the recently sacked Deputy Prime Minister and Finance Minister, Anwar Ibrahim, was photographed in police custody with a black eye. The charges against him at that time included sexual misconduct and attempts to corrupt the course of justice, the former of which was dropped during his initial trial. As it transpired, Anwar had been beaten up by the chief of police, who later resigned over the incident. A doctor's report five days after the incident said that Anwar was lucky not to have been killed by the beating. His appearance in public with the black eye was a week after the event, when his condition had started to improve.

Here was a picture of a repressive government using violence against one of its own who had fallen foul of his leader. The public protests at the time were seen by some observers as a 'pro-democracy' movement, although this reflected wishful thinking on the part of the observers rather than any political reality. But what it did show was that Malaysia's aggressive Prime Minister, Dr Mahatir Mohamad, retained power through dubious means. The notion of Malaysia as a democracy, which it had not functionally been for at least two decades, was irretrievably gone.

This chapter on Malaysia will briefly outline the pre-colonial history of the region, with particular reference to Malacca and the role of archipelagic and wider international trade, as well as the growing influence of Islam. It will then consider the increasing impact of colonialism, which culminated in British domination of the peninsula and de facto control

over the northern parts of Borneo, and the delineation of the Malay world along Dutch/British/Spanish imperial lines.

Facing the decolonisation process, this chapter will then consider the political balance between ethnic Malays, Chinese and Indians, the maintenance of Malay political hegemony and subsequent control of the political process, economic imbalance, and the New Economic Policy of 'positive discrimination'. Of particular importance is the centralisation of power within the main government party, the United Malay National Organisation (UMNO), and the curtailing of the judiciary and media. It will conclude with an examination of the idea of the Malaysian government as both authoritarian and responsive to some political pressures.

PRE-COLONIAL MALAYA

What was to become Malaysia has had a diverse historical existence, its limited unity being based on the spread of 'Malays' throughout the Malay Peninsula and, to a far lesser extent, along the coastal regions of the island of Borneo.

The Malay Peninsula was populated by Malayo–Polynesians at around the same time that they moved into the rest of the archipelago (in the early years BCE) where they displaced the original aboriginal inhabitants. However, most of this migration to the peninsula came not from the north, but from Sumatra. It was from the Sumatran kingdom of Meleyu that the peninsula and the state derive their names. More mountainous and less suitable to the wide-scale rice cultivation that developed especially in Java, the original states of the Malay Peninsula developed along river banks and estuaries. They were small and largely cut off from one another, often existing as much from piracy as from trade or agriculture.

The Malays who currently live on the Malay Peninsula and on the north coast of Borneo supplanted the original inhabitants, who survive in small numbers in the upland areas of the peninsula and predominantly along and inland from the northern Borneo coast. While in some cases Malay immigration dates back more than a millennium, much of the migration to the west coast was over the last few centuries up to the twentieth. The major sources of immigrants were Sulawesi to the east and, more importantly, various ethnic groups from Sumatra to the west, but included Javanese, Riau Malays and Arabs (and Arab-Malays) from Aceh. Both the Bugis of Sulawesi and the Minankabau of Sumatra established states on the Malay Peninsula and its nearby islands, and the political system, dominant religion (Hinduism, Buddhism and Islam), culture, and language prior to the colonial period derive from Melayu–Jambi and, before that, from Sri Vijaya (Turnbull 1989: 1–98). Immigration from Sumatra to the Malay Peninsula continued until World War II, with a trickle following after that.[1] Sumatrans assimilated easily, having a common language and culture, with the Javanese and Banjermasi having a little more difficulty (Turnbull 1989: 192).

The major contributing factor to Malaysia's political profile of this flow was in the traditional hierarchical forms the many immigrants brought to the peninsula. Perhaps less formal than in Java, there was never the less a greater sense of deference towards traditional leaders shown by them than by members of Malaysia's non-Malay communities.

Some larger states did develop in the region, although they were frequently indistinguishable from the larger regional empires of Java and Sumatra. Notable exceptions included the state of Johore and its trading city of Singapura (see the Singapore chapter) and the Islamic city–state of Malacca.[2] Malacca, as a free port, was exceptionally well placed to take advantage of shipping between India and China. At its peak, during the fifteenth century, it was probably the world's busiest and perhaps richest trading port, and the Sultan of Malacca commanded the loyalty of numerous minor sultans throughout the rest of the peninsula (Coedes 1968: 246).

EUROPEANS ON THE PENINSULA

The peak of Malacca's fortunes coincided with the development of European trade and adventurism. The first of Europe's explorers, the Portuguese, seized Malacca in 1511, leading to an exodus of the city–state's Muslim traders. Perhaps more than any other event, it was this dispersal of Islamic traders throughout the region which did most to spread and cement Islam as the dominant regional religion. However, the rise of Portuguese influence was soon challenged by the Dutch, who captured Malacca in 1641. The more restrictive trading practices of the Dutch, in which they both demanded a monopoly on certain aspects of trade and heavily taxed others, sealed Malacca's fate as a great trading city.

BORNEO

A little later than Malacca's rise to prominence, another Islamic Malay state also grew in northern Borneo: the Sultanate of Brunei. By the sixteenth century, Brunei had established itself as a major coastal state, claiming control over an area extending from Borneo's western reaches across its north and down the eastern coast. So broad was its control that the island itself derived its name from this state.

However, the establishment of coastal towns and claims to political authority did not often match the reality of control. The inland tribes of proto-Malays, the earlier inhabitants of the island, only rarely acknowledged the authority of the Sultan of Brunei and, being out of reach of his limited and thinly spread forces, continued to exist more or less unmolested. As they moved down river in search of more productive lands on which to practise their traditional shifting agriculture they increasingly came into conflict with the still small populations of coastal Malays. From time to time the inland tribes would cooperate with the coastal Malays (and visiting Chinese) for the purposes of trade and piracy, but there is little evidence to suggest that the inland tribes ever regarded this arrangement as anything more than a temporary convenience. Certainly the inland tribes were frequently in revolt against the sultanate or its representatives and the history of the region indicates that Malay control was limited to a few relatively small coastal pockets. This was the situation when the British adventurer Charles Brooke arrived in northern Borneo in 1839 (discussed in the section on Brunei).

While this situation of cooperation and conflict between the Proto and Deutero Malays dominated the northern coastal region to the west of what is modern Brunei, the north-east corner was a different situation again. While the various Sultans of Brunei claimed that corner of the island, so too did the Sultans of the Sulu Archipelago. For the majority of the inhabitants of the region, however, this was fairly meaningless, as they tended to live in small communities on the tops of the district's spectacular mountains, apart from conflict, cut off from each other and from the coast. The village headmen might have nominal loyalty to the Sultan, but they did not exist as part of a unified polity (Bedlington 1978: 44–6).

NORTH BORNEO

The first British contact with North Borneo was in 1761, when an agent for the East India Company concluded a treaty with the Sultan of Sulu to establish a trading station at Balambangan in return for protection from Spanish claims. However, due to chronic piracy by the Bajaus of the coastal and Sulu region[3] and mismanagement the station was abandoned in 1775. British attention later moved to the island of Labuan in Brunei Bay, in 1846, in return for British assistance in suppressing the still endemic piracy. Labuan was initially administered by the Brookes of Sarawak, but became a part of the Straits Settlements in 1907.

American interest out of Hong Kong came with a concession in 1865–66 for small scale cropping. But the real move came in 1877–78, when a mixed group of British and Americans (plus one Austrian) obtained grants for approximately 46 000 square kilometres of territory from the Sultans of both Brunei and Sulu. Aware of local competition and in an era of rapidly expanding colonialism, the British government granted the company a royal charter in 1881, creating the British North Borneo Chartered Company. Over the next twenty years, the company expanded its holdings by annexing semi-independent territories of Brunei, sometimes by force. Conflict with indigenous inland peoples of the region was occasionally a problem, but much less so than in Sarawak.

North Borneo expanded its agricultural development and encouraged Chinese settlers, while regional Malays (especially from Java) also moved to the region, both groups settling and intermarrying with local people. Sandakan on the east coast became the capital of North Borneo, and the company was in effect the government. The model this colonial government followed was similar to that of Sarawak under the Brookes, although its resources were thinly stretched and most of the possession remained undeveloped and unexplored.

The discovery of oil in the region established North Borneo's economic fortunes, but it also acted as a magnet for the Japanese army at the onset of hostilities in WWII. To deprive the Japanese of facilities, the towns of North Borneo were bombed into rubble during the conflict, requiring extensive reconstruction in the postwar years. The territory was renamed Sabah upon its incorporation into the Federation of Malaysia in 1963.[4] Sabah and the other northern Borneo state of Sarawak were given a quarter of all the seats in the new federal parliament, even though they only held 15 per cent of the federation's population.

THE BRITISH ON THE PENINSULA

Britain's first colony in what is now Malaysia was established at Penang, which was founded as a British post in 1786. The settlement of Penang followed a search by the British for a naval station from which to service its trade between India and China, and from which to counter growing Dutch influence and later French expansion. While other sites had been considered, Penang was chosen because of its strategic value, being near the head of the Malacca Straits, and because, in 1771, its then ruler, Sultan Muhammad Jiwa of Kedah, was prepared to cede the territory in exchange for defence support. The agreement between Britain and Kedah was formalised with Muhammad Jiwa's son, Sultan Abdullah Mukarram Shah. As a consequence of a dispute over payment for the island, Britain reduced the amount payable to Abdullah (Spanish $6000 p.a., down from a requested S$10 000 p.a.). This was superseded in 1800 by a further Treaty of Peace, Friendship and Alliance, which included a further payment (S$10 000 p.a.) for the adjacent land on the peninsula, which became Province Wellesley. British defence support, though, was not given to Abdullah in his time of need.

Although the cosmopolitan population of Penang expanded quickly, the station was uneconomic and was only retained as a base for the British navy as a consequence of its conflict with France, with two brief interludes, from 1793 until 1815. Following French occupation of the Netherlands, Britain occupied Dutch possessions in the region, taking Malacca in 1795 (and the Moluccas in 1796 and Java in 1811). Despite agreeing to the return of Dutch possessions in 1814, Britain began to develop commercial interests, primarily in tin, on the Malay Peninsula. In 1819, against Dutch wishes, Thomas Raffles reached an agreement with the chief of Singapore to establish a trading station. Due to difficulties with succession to the local sultanate, the agreement remained intact until the Treaty of London in 1824. Under this treaty, in exchange for its possessions in Sumatra and all islands south of Singapore with the Dutch, Britain received Malacca and retained Penang and Singapore. It was this treaty which delineated the British sphere from the Dutch, and which was to define modern Indonesia from Malaysia.

The present shape of Malaysia was settled in 1909, when Britain extended its 'protection' to the four northern states of Kedah, Perlis, Kelantan, and Trengganu, which had been suzerain to Thailand. Also in that year, the other Malay states, apart from Johore, were joined under a common federal legislative council. Although suggested to the sultans as a means of lessening British control, the high commissioner, who presided over the council, assumed more authority. The sultans were effectively relegated to advising the council.

ETHNIC COMPOSITION

Probably the single most important political issue in Malaysia is that of its ethnic composition. A little more than half of the country's population is ethnically Malay, approximately 35 per cent is ethnic Chinese, with the remainder being largely of South Asian (Indian, Pakistani and Sri Lankan) descent. This ethnic mix has proved at times to be explosive, with the ethnic Malays, self-styled as 'sons of the soil' (*bumiputras*), being largely excluded from the process of economic growth in the state. This in turn has reflected the agricultural orientation of the Malays, which was encouraged by a land reservation scheme begun in 1913, intended to protect them from the rapidly expanding, land-intensive rubber industry. The industrial focus of the Chinese, first in mining and later in commerce, followed their recruitment into largely Chinese owned and operated tin mines and later into support services. Indians were recruited by the British primarily to work on rubber plantations.

One consequence of the British colonial policy of educating ethnic South Asians to work in the lower echelons of the bureaucracy, at the point at which they intermarried with Malays, was the growth of a small, locally born non-aristocratic intellectual elite. Able to claim a Malay heritage but with access to a British-based education, these Indian–Malays were among the first to consider alternatives to British rule and to provide intellectual guidance in terms of national development. Malaysia's long-serving Prime Minister Dr Mahatir Mohamad, who is of mixed Malay and Indian descent, is a case in point.

Another small subgroup is the Portuguese–Malays who continue to live in and around the area of Malacca. Although Malay in language and custom, they are not officially accepted as Malays by the state. A small number of original aboriginal inhabitants of the peninsula, the *Orang Asli*, live in small communities in the highland regions, effectively outside the Malaysian mainstream.

To a considerable degree, resentment of the Chinese by Malays, and to a lesser extent of Indians as well, is based on two criteria. The first is the enhanced economic status of the Chinese relative to the Malays. The second is a consequence of the relatively recent arrival of the Chinese on the Malay Peninsula. What was perceived as relative indifference by Malays towards the Chinese changed early in the twentieth century, when it seemed that the Chinese would begin to outnumber Malays. Differences between the Malays and Chinese were centred on language and religion, the Chinese being predominantly Confucian or Buddhist and speaking one of the dialects of southern China as their first language. The Malays, on the other hand, were largely Muslim and spoke a version of what was to become Bahasa Malayu.

In 1927 alone, 360 000 Chinese landed in Singapore, and by 1931, for the first time, a census showed that non-Malays actually outnumbered

Malays, by 2 230 000 to 1 930 000. Tensions were exacerbated, from 1929, by the impact of the Great Depression, which severely limited Malaya's exports of rubber and tin.

The Chinese received their first taste of official disapproval with the appointment of Sir Cecil Clementi as governor in 1930. He quickly banned the Chinese nationalist party, the Guomindang (established in 1925), and fragmented the Chinese-dominated Malayan Communist Party (MCP, set up in 1927)[5], while also withdrawing government grants from Chinese schools, censoring the vernacular press, and imposing the first restrictions on immigration (Turnbull 1989: 205–6). At the behest of the sultans, from the 1930s Malays were also actively promoted as the only suitable candidates for the civil service. Labour grievances among the Chinese fed into the growth of the MCP throughout the 1930s. In 1937, in response to Japanese incursions into China, the MCP established the politically open Overseas Chinese Anti-Japanese National Salvation Association (OCAJNSA).

It was not until the 1920s that a modern nationalist movement began on the Malay Peninsula, influenced by the Reform Islam movement and culminating, in 1926, in the first Malay political organisation, the *Kesatuan Melayu Singapura* (Singapore Malay Union). This was followed, in 1937, by the formation of the *Kesatuan Melayu Muda* (Union of Malay Youth), which sought to achieve speedy independence from Britain. Both organisations appealed to the educated and rising Malay middle class, in particular those frustrated with colonial education policy and their employment prospects.

Based in Siam (Thailand), the Japanese occupation of the Malay Peninsula in 1942 was quick, with Allied forces falling back ahead of the Japanese advance. Isolated, Singapore was surrendered to Japan forces, dispelling forever any idea of British superiority. In their panic ahead of the Japanese advance, however, British forces accepted an offer from the MCP to organise an ethnic Chinese militia, especially from the OCAJNSA, which was named the Malayan People's Anti-Japanese Army (MPAJA).[6] Shortly before Singapore was surrendered, a number of the MPAJA were in position on the Malay Peninsula, where some managed to escape capture (*A Short History of the Malayan Communist Party*[7] 1955: 15).

Survivors of the MPAJA fled to the jungle, from where they continued guerrilla operations against Japanese forces. By 1943, Britain was assisting the MPAJA by arming and helping to train them, in preparation for the planned Allied invasion. By 1944, the MPAJA attracted new recruits, including non-communists. However, the MPAJA leadership intended to use the final showdown after the defeat of the Japanese to establish a communist republic in Malaya (*A Short History of the Malayan Communist Party* 1955: 16–17; Turnbull 1989: 227–8).

THE 'EMERGENCY'

Upon the surrender of Japanese forces, the MCP did assume authority until the return of the British. The 'open' section of the MPAJA dis-armed, but a 'secret' group, of about 4000, hid its arms, while the MCP enjoyed legal status. The MCP engaged in union activities until a 'State of Emergency' was declared in June 1948, after the murder of some plan-tation managers who had been involved in a violent industrial dispute. The MCP immediately went underground, and its 'secret' and much of its 'open' sections embarked on an armed struggle, marked by terrorism and a guerrilla campaign. This campaign was initially based on relatively indiscriminate violence, but from 1951 became much more selective. Perhaps the most effective outcome of this change in strategy was the assassination in October 1951 of the British High Commissioner of Malaya, Sir Henry Gurney.

The two long term consequences of the 'Emergency' were the delay in organising independence for Malaya, and the introduction of the Internal Security Act (ISA), under which 'suspects' could be held with-out charge or trial. The ISA and the related Sedition Act and Official Secrets Act were later used by the 'democratic' governments of both Malaysia and Singapore to silence and jail critics and members of oppo-sition parties (Crouch 1996: 79–84). As a military venture, the commu-nist rebellion failed partly because of the inadequate arms, training and numbers of the MCP's armed wing (from 1949 called the Malayan Races Liberation Army or MRLA). The British strategy of cutting off access to Chinese communities from the MRLA[8] also contributed to the failure of the rebellion. The critical factor in the failure of the insurgency was the lack of support for the MCP from much of the Chinese and most of the Malay population.

By the late 1950s, the MCP's insurrection had tapered off to become a localised annoyance, restricted primarily to the area near the Thai border. The last MCP guerrillas did not formally end their struggle until 1989 and even then agreed only to a cease-fire rather than surrender. A few ancient and fading comrades were still living in the remote and rugged jungle-covered mountains just over the Thai border at the end of the twentieth century. Despite the cease-fire, the border remained tightly sealed and Malaysian army units were conspicuous along the border area. The MCP continued to receive some support from the clearly delineated ethnic Chinese community which lived in southern Thailand.[9]

With the 'Emergency' increasingly under control, in June 1955 Britain held elections in Malaya for a local parliament. Of the ninety-eight members, fifty-two were elected and forty-six were appointed. The elections resulted in Tunku Abdul Rahman becoming Chief Minister and the counter-insurgency campaign being directed by the new Malayan government rather than the British government. Malaya was formally granted independence on 31 August 1957.

FORM OF GOVERNMENT

With its British parliamentary legacy,[10] the Federation of Malaysia began life in 1959 as a liberally oriented federated constitutional monarchy. Malaysia has a bicameral federal parliament, with sixty-eight members of the *Dewan Negara* (Senate), twenty-six of whom are elected from the state legislatures and forty-two of whom are appointed by the king and have a six-year term. The Dewan Rakyat (House of Representatives) has 180 directly elected members each with a five-year term.

The monarchic aspect of Malaysia's Constitution is novel, in that the 'monarch' (*Yang di-Pertuan Agong*) is elected every five years by the State Sovereigns' Conference of Rulers on a rotational basis. In practice, this means that the State Sovereigns take turns in assuming monarchical duties, except where they decline the offer. The inspiration for this model was the Malay Minangkabau state of Negri Sembilan, whose four territory chiefs elected a *Yang di-Pertuan*. Negri Sembilan was originally a confederation of nine states (as its name implies) (Groves 1962: 271–3). The status and privileges of the State Sovereigns were increasingly eroded in the last two decades of the twentieth century as more power became concentrated in the federal government. This has most obviously been so in the case of the prime minister, in this case Mahatir Mohamad. There are also thirteen state governments, nine of which have hereditary rulers as their head.

The three major communally based parties of Malaysia were founded in 1946. They are the United Malays National Organisation (UMNO), the Malaysian Chinese Association (MCA) and the Malaysian Indian Congress (MIC). Together these parties continue to dominate the coalition of government, first known as the Alliance and, from 1974, as the *Barisan Nasional* (National Front), or BN. In its latter guise, the coalition further consolidated its grip over Malaysia's political system. Numerous smaller parties also exist, including the BN members Gerakan Parti Pesaka Bumiputera and Sarawak National Party. A number of parties also exist exclusively at state level. The smaller parties either tend to be co-opted into the coalition in order to address their concerns and buy off their supporters, or are generally relegated to the political margins. Although a coalition, the BN works as a party in its own right, with internal elections, its own Constitution and common policies for all the member parties.

One means by which UMNO and the BN assured itself of retaining power was through the 'gerrymandering' of the electoral boundaries, by which electorates favouring the government are smaller and therefore greater in number. The biggest electorate was approximately five times the size of the smallest electorate, with the smallest electorates tending to be among the rural Malay areas (Rawana 1999). Another means of ensuring UMNO/BN dominance was through the exclusion of opposition candidates on minor technical grounds. One example was the failure of a potential candidate to write 'none' on an electoral registration form where it referred to 'aliases', as well as employing other means of control and intimidation (Crouch 1996: 58–64). This has created what has been referred to as an 'hegemonic party system', 'in which opposition parties are legal but denied—through pervasive electoral malpractices and frequent state coercion—any real chance to compete for power' (Diamond, Linz and Lipset 1989: xvii, quoted in Crouch 1996: 6).

Through its support from the three major parties, its ability to co-opt smaller parties, and various means of manipulating the electoral process, the BN controlled the federal government with a two-thirds majority. This allowed it, if it so desired, to change the Constitution at will. The BN also controls the state governments, with the exception of Sabah in 1985–86 and 1990–95, and Kelantan from 1990. These state governments were exceptions to the BN rule primarily as a result of specifically local issues, including the political advantage or disfavour accorded to local political personalities.

In all, the electoral system in Malaysia gave a less than fair chance for genuine opposition to contest the government. The electoral system 'was so heavily loaded in favour of the government that it was hard to imagine that the ruling coalition, as long as it remained united, could be defeated in an election' (Crouch 1996: 75). In one analysis, the process of 'modernisation' or industrialisation, rather than leading towards greater liberalism, could in fact have the opposite effect. This was because the mechanisms of state which had to be employed to achieve the greatest potential growth were, by nature of their application, authoritarian

(O'Donnell 1973). However, it is also clear that within a system that privileges one ethnic group over another and functions on the basis of 'patronage', that is cronyism, authoritarianism is also likely to be employed to retain those privileges.

THREATS TO THE STATE

The Federation of Malaysia came into being in 1963, bringing together the states of the Malay Peninsula, Singapore, Sarawak and Sabah. However, the new federation faced two immediate problems. The first was strident opposition to the creation of the federation by Indonesia, and to a lesser extent by the Philippines. The second problem was the incorporation of the overwhelmingly ethnic Chinese city–state of Singapore. In short, Singapore's ethnic make-up made it an uncomfortable fit for a new state that was politically dominated by ethnic Malays (Crouch 1996: 17–20). The Singaporean Chinese also tipped the ethnic balance away from Malays towards Chinese and Indians, which was unacceptable to the traditional Malay elite, while the wealth of Singapore focused Malaysia's economy towards the Chinese city and away from the more even racial demography of the peninsula.

To exacerbate this problem, Singapore's leader, Lee Kuan Yew, insisted on retaining the title of 'prime minister' after federation, demanded aspects of autonomy from the rest of the federation, and was considered too leftist for the conservative Alliance government. But what really annoyed the Malay leaders was when he launched his People's Action Party (PAP) on the mainland to contest the federal elections. Its call was for a 'Malaysian Malaysia', which was intended to signal to the Malay political elite that the ethnic Chinese wanted more of a say in federal affairs, effectively challenging their political pre-eminence. As a Chinese-based party, it opposed the Malaysian Chinese Association, which worked in coalition with UMNO as a part of the *Barisan Nasional*. The perception at the time was, not inaccurately, that the PAP was a vehicle for Lee Kuan Yew's wider political aspirations and that he hoped, through extending Singaporean political machinery to the peninsula, to challenge for Malaysia's prime ministership. His hopes to this end were dashed when Singapore left the federation in August 1965 (see Singapore, chapter 13). Following the split, the PAP on the peninsula was renamed the Democratic Action Party (DAP). The DAP remained Malaysia's primary opposition party, latterly in alliance with the *Partai Islam SeMalaysia* (PAS) (Pereira 1999).

Further afield, the growth of Filipino nationalism led that country to make a claim for the 'return' of the state of Sabah and, upon federation, its objection to the existence of the new state of Malaysia on the grounds of Sabah's inclusion. The claim was based on the inclusion of the Sultanate of Sulu into the Philippines state, and Sulu's former links with the territory of north-east Borneo (Tarling 1998: 115–16; McCloud 1995: 199–200, 292; Harrison 1966: 262). However, this claim was primarily diplomatic and the Philippines never actively threatened the existence of the new federated state.

The greatest threat to the Federation of Malaysia came from Indonesia, when its president, Sukarno, announced his active opposition to the new state. This 'Confrontation' (*Konfrontasi*) was primarily diplomatic, although from 1963 units of Indonesian troops disguised as local volunteers did land on the Malaysian Peninsula and attacked across the border from Kalimantan into Sarawak (Tarling 1998: 115; SarDesai 1997: 269–71). Units of the MCP began operating in Sarawak from 1963, receiving support from the communist-influenced Indonesian government. The communist insurgency in Sarawak operated somewhat distinctly from the MCP on the peninsula and had its origins among ethnic Chinese activists.[11] It was brought under control in two phases, in 1973–74 and 1989–90. Malaysia was able to fend off the threat of Confrontation (and the MCP) with the assistance of British, Australian and New Zealand troops, who were active in Sarawak. However, the Indonesian threat did directly challenge the legitimate basis of the establishment of Malaysia as a separate and sovereign state.

A further challenge to the maintenance of the federation came from within Sarawak and Sabah. While the local Islamic Malay populations were keen to join the federation, the Chinese and indigenous communities were less supportive (Sario 1999). Indeed, these groups refer to Peninsular Malaysians as *semananjung* (literally 'peninsular', although with a pejorative connotation), which highlighted the difference and consequent political sensitivities for the Peninsular Malays. Most of the opposition to federation was, and still is, based on the allocation of income. Both Sabah and Sarawak contribute more to the federal government than they receive, which many in those states consider 'unfair'. The terms 'fairness', 'justice' and 'equality' were commonly used, often by the indigenous peoples, when talking about their grievances against the federal government.

Similarly, the ethnic Chinese of east Malaysia claimed theirs was a better region because of the greater proportion of Chinese to Malays.[12] While there are significant cultural gaps between the Chinese and indigenous peoples, they view each other with much greater equanimity than the Malays. Some of the bases of understanding between them revolve around their mutual antipathy towards the local Islamic Malays, as well as towards Peninsular Malaysia more generally. Politics in Sarawak has been more plural and fluid than in Peninsular Malaysia, with indigenous groups (combined representing the largest potential voter block) represented by a number of organisations. As with the politics of Malaysia more widely, the Alliance and the *Barisan Nasional* after that have wielded considerable influence over which parties are included in the coalition and which are kept, or pushed, outside (Cramb & Dixon 1988: 11). Further, also reflecting peninsula politics, a small elite allied to the government has tended to control the political process of the state, and the 'land, timber and minerals' from which it draws its significant wealth (Cramb & Dixon 1988: 11–12).

DOMESTIC TENSIONS

Tensions between the ethnic Malay and Chinese populations, which culminated in race riots in May 1969, contributed to modifying Malaysia's earlier more liberal orientation (Crouch 1996: 24–7). The following year, internal factional battles within the UMNO led to the downfall of Tunku Abdul Rahman as prime minister, to be succeeded by the more 'nationalist' pro-Malay Tun Abdul Razak. Following the 1969 riots, internal security laws were strengthened, and, to redress Malay grievances about economic disparities, the government introduced its New Economic Policy (NEP) in 1971. Among other things, NEP legislation was intended to break down the Chinese commerce/Malay labourer dichotomy by shifting a greater proportion of corporate wealth into Malay hands (Crouch, 1996: 24–5; 37–8; Goldsworthy 1991: 53).

Until the mid 1980s, the *Barisan Nasional* coalition worked well. However, by 1986–87 there were tensions over the increasingly authoritarian style of both UMNO and the prime minister, Mahatir, as well as within the Malaysian Chinese Association (MCA). This was exacerbated by a downturn in Malaysia's economy, including higher unemployment and increased bankruptcies, following on from an international recession and a related rise in ethnic tensions.

Hussein bin Onn became prime minister in 1976 following the death of Tun Abdul Razak. Onn's prime ministership was noted for its relative moderation and consolidation following the turmoil of 1969. However, while Onn's leadership was regarded as moderate, he still had to preside over a difficult period, including internal UMNO scandals caused by the beginning of the Malay elites' push towards entrepeneurial activity (Shamsul 1999: 5). Onn's deputy prime minister was Mahatir Mohamad, who had previously been education minister and had presided over putting down the student protests of 1974 which were led by Anwar Ibrahim.

In early 1981, the prime minister, Onn, was hospitalised and underwent heart surgery, leaving the country in the hands of his then deputy, Mahatir Mohamad. Onn formally resigned on 16 July, and Mahatir was elected as UMNO party president and hence as prime minister. While the election of Mahatir was fairly straightforward, there was a bitter factional struggle for the deputy prime ministership between the education minister, Satuk Musa Hitam, and the finance minister, Tungku Razaleigh Hamza. Razaleigh had challenged Mahatir for the deputy prime minister's position, so there was already an antithetical relationship between the two. Mahatir backed Musa, who won the party ballot. The poll was repeated in 1984, with Musa again winning, this time with a slightly increased majority (Case 1996: 152–60; Rinn-Sup 1984: 210–15).

The 1984 poll was complicated by the arrival of the former Muslim youth leader, and perceived Islamic moderate, Anwar Ibrahim. Anwar had been detained for almost two years from 1974 under the ISA for organising student demonstrations. However, Mahatir soon came to recognise Anwar's political usefulness and set up the youth organisation which Anwar headed. In 1982 Mahatir asked Anwar to stand for election. Anwar was immediately appointed deputy minister in the Prime Minister's department and in 1983, after being elected to head UMNO Youth (and automatically becoming a vice-president of UMNO), was made Minister for Youth, Sports and Culture. Anwar's rapid rise caused tensions between Mahatir and Musa, which spilled into the open in 1986, leading to Musa's resignation as deputy prime minister. There were earlier signs of tensions between the two, in particular over Razaleigh's continued position in the cabinet. The split between Musa and Mahatir was far less ideological than it was personal (Case 1996: 152–83).

As if this was not enough to destabilise Malaysia's political environment, a further major division within UMNO centred on the party's long-standing commitment not to emphasise ethnic issues. One faction of UMNO, self-styled as champions of the Malay cause, challenged the more conservative faction (which also said it represented the Malay cause). In part these tensions within UMNO reflected unease with the Chinese community, notably through its two main political representatives, the MCA and the DAP. Within the Chinese community, there were tensions over the strong performance of the DAP in the 1986 elections, following deep concerns over senior MCA figures being implicated in business scandals involving the $1.5 billion collapse of Chinese-based deposit-taking cooperatives. About 600 000 ethnic Chinese were affected by the collapse. Tensions between the MCA and UMNO were also heightened after an MCA convention declared that all of Malaysia's inhabitants were of immigrant stock and, consequently, none should claim themselves as natives and label others as immigrants. There was also concern over the potential to undermine the use of Chinese language in Chinese schools, which was played upon by the DAP with the support of the MCA (Crouch 1996: 106–8).

Then, while Mahatir was abroad, several UMNO leaders decided to stage a public rally as a demonstration of Malay unity. The rally was expected to bring together hundreds of thousands of Malays, which had the potential to spark off an uncontrollable protest or riot. But Mahatir returned and called off the rally, giving approval under the Internal Security Act (ISA) for police to arrest a total of 119 dissidents between late October and mid November 1997. Among those arrested were ten members of parliament from the DAP, five members of the Chinese education movement, eight members of the MCA, and five members of Gerakan. Only three members of UMNO were arrested, one of whom was believed to have been detained for unconnected reasons. The three UMNO arrestees were supporters of Razaleigh, who was at that time fomenting a challenge to Mahatir's leadership of UMNO. A number of other arrestees were equally as prominent in Malaysian society. Seven DAP members and five Chinese education movement detainees were among those jailed for two years. The UMNO, MCA and Gerakan members were quickly released (Crouch 1996: 106–13).

In order to attack Mahatir, Musa settled his differences with Razaleigh and the pair challenged Mahatir and his new favourite, Ghafar Baba, for the leadership and deputy leadership of UMNO. Baba was a millionaire businessman who owed much of his wealth to government patronage. Like most states that have a history of one-party domination, there have been numerous reports of high-level corruption, interpreted as 'patronage', in Malaysia, with lucrative government contracts going to UMNO associates. Baba was but one example of this system at work (Shameen 1998a; Crouch 1996: 35, 38–43, 54). The issues of nepotism, crony-capitalism, non-transparency, and corruption were raised at an UMNO Youth meeting in June 1998. Mahatir responded by warning party members not to make accusations about such issues (Hiebert 1998). However, while such corruption (or 'patronage') clearly existed

(Shameen 1998a), it was not nearly at the level of neighbouring Indonesia, or perhaps even of Thailand.

Mahatir and Baba narrowly defeated Razaleigh and Musa in the party elections of 1987. In the wider elections, Mahatir's candidates for vice-presidential positions came first and third (the latter position being taken by Anwar), while a Musa supporter came second. Of the twenty-five positions on the party's Supreme Council, the Razaleigh-Musa faction won eight positions. Following his re-election as leader, Mahatir took the opportunity to purge cabinet of remaining Razaleih-Musa supporters.

As a consequence of the split between Razaleigh-Musa and Mahatir-Baba, about half the party was opposed to Mahatir, although both factions remained deeply divided within themselves. In a bid to continue the struggle against Mahatir, Razaleigh's group launched a challenge against the legality of the elections, which resulted not in new elections but in UMNO being declared a technically illegal organisation. Mahatir reorganised UMNO into UMNO *Baru* (New UMNO), while an opposition group set up UMNO Malaysia. The battle was for the loyalty of UMNO's 1.4 million members, and the party's assets. It also marked a shift in party style and future policy direction. While UMNO *Baru* increasingly won over the loyalty of old UMNO members, it was not until Mahatir enticed Musa to defect that he truly won his battle. Razaleigh's response was to establish a new party, *Semangat '46* (Spirit of '46), referring to UMNO's founding year (Crouch 1996: 114–21; Case 1996: 184–214).

HOBBLING THE JUDICIARY

The declaration of UMNO as an illegal organisation was a major setback for Mahatir and showed that while he was increasingly master of his environment, there remained some important elements of the state outside his control. As a consequence, there were a series of overtly political moves that caused perhaps even more concern, in particular in international terms, than the UMNO split. In 1988 Mahatir sacked the judge responsible for organising the hearing of an appeal of the Razaleigh-Musa challenge, Lord President of the Supreme Court, Tun Salleh Abas. The ostensible reason was 'gross misbehaviour', but the real reason appeared to be Abas' unwillingness to allow a backroom deal to be done on the appeal which favoured Mahatir. A further five Supreme Court judges who supported Abas in Mahatir's attack on him were also suspended.

The Malaysian Bar Council was deeply disturbed by this overt attack on the independence of the judiciary and weighed in, supporting Abas and the five suspended judges. It also brought contempt proceedings against the acting Lord President, who headed a tribunal hearing a case against Abas. The government retaliated by evicting the council from its offices in the High Court building. New and more sympathetic judges were appointed to the Supreme Court and it eventually ruled on the original UMNO case, providing the Mahatir group with the opportunity to reform UMNO as a stronger, more cohesive and more Mahatir-loyal UMNO *Baru* (Case 1996: 201–14). 'We used to be a very democratic organisation,' said one former UMNO official. 'Now the members can't do anything without Kuala Lumpur telling them to go ahead' (Burger & Bogert 1988). In all, Mahatir's challenge to the courts seriously hobbled the independence of the judiciary and blurred the basic democratic tenet of separation of state and judicial power. It also brought both the party and the state more directly under Mahatir's personal control.

FREEDOM OF SPEECH AND THE MEDIA

There were some human rights concerns over political opposition and indigenous peoples and the media was fairly tightly controlled, with UMNO controlling (although no longer directly owning) the country's two largest newspaper groups and one commercial television station (as well as the government television station). Free speech was generally tolerated and the political atmosphere, while limited, was not very repressive for most people.

In terms of the mass media, it has been subject to both direct and indirect government control, through ownership, licensing and bans. Malaysia's most influential newspaper, the *New Straits Times*, was owned by UMNO until 1993, after which it was bought by four newspaper executives who were close to Anwar Ibrahim. The two newspapers of the *Utusan Melayu* group were also owned by a group of UMNO leaders, while the newspaper *The Sun* was started in 1994 by Tan Sri Vincent Tan, who has close links to UMNO. Another paper, *The Star*, was once owned by a former Chief Minister of Sabah, who was a close personal friend of then Prime Minister Tunku Abdul Rahman. It was later bought, in 1977, by Huaren Holdings, which is largely owned by the MCA. Because of its sometimes pro-Chinese views and a column by the former prime minister Abdul Rahman, the licence of *The Star* was suspended for several months in 1987. When it reappeared in March 1988, Abdul Rahman's column had been dropped.

Another means of control over the media was through criminal charges being laid over the 'malicious' publication of 'false news'. Under such an offence, the publisher, printer, editor and author (journalist) are all liable, as in a defamation case. The closure of papers has been used relatively sparingly, although in 1987 during a period of considerable political unrest within UMNO over Mahatir's leadership style, three newspapers were temporarily closed, returning to print in a more subdued form.

More recently, two prominent newspaper editors, from *Utusan Malaysia* and *Berita Harian*, resigned after what was understood as pressure to run anti-Anwar Ibrahim stories. There were also reports of pressure being brought to bear at the independent television station TV3. An UMNO leader from Johore said that both editors had been appointed with Mahatir's approval, but their independent line on Anwar led to their resignations (Sangwon 1998).

Malaysia was also considering introducing limits on the circulation of non-Malaysian media, along the lines of Singapore's foreign media restrictions, in an attempt to control negative reporting. This applied in particular to the trial of Anwar Ibrahim. Publications referred to for possible restriction included the *Far Eastern Economic Review* and *Asiaweek*.

THE FALL OF ANWAR IBRAHIM

Shamsul (1999: 4–9) has noted that the introduction of the NEP in 1971 eventually led to a realignment of traditional Malaysian politics away from a focus on security (exemplified by the ISA), the 'ethnic bargain' (which retained Malays in power), and development planning which included an 'economic bargain' which complemented the 'ethnic bargain'. The shift was towards entrepreneurialism by Malay elites on one hand, and a divergent focus on social justice on the other.

Upon becoming Prime Minister, Mahatir pushed the entrepreneurial aspect of Malaysian development with a passion, allocating the task of social justice to his deputy. Shamsul suggests that this led to the development of a grass-roots based 'new politics', of which then Deputy Prime Minister Anwar Ibrahim was increasingly seen as the head. Such 'new politics' was suggested to include a range of non-communal, non-class-based social and environmental issues that had previously been left off the traditional or entrepreneurial agenda (Shamsul 1999: 9).

While an undercurrent of increasing authoritarianism has prevailed under Mahatir, the sacking and jailing of Anwar Ibrahim offered a stark reminder of how quickly benign authoritarianism was able to turn malignant. After entering politics in 1982, in 1983 Anwar Ibrahim and his supporters swept into power in UMNO. In 1993 Anwar took the deputy Prime ministership with his supporters taking the Youth and Sport Ministry, Education and Chief Ministership of Selangor state.

Having started as Mahatir's favourite and, for a long time, the heir-apparent, Anwar was sacked by Mahatir on 2 September 1998. Anwar's sacking came at a time when Malaysia's economy was convulsing as a consequence of the regional economic crisis. This situation had not been helped by intemperate remarks by Mahatir about conspiracies by the international financial community generally and by a Jewish money trader in particular to wreck the Malaysian economy. Then Mahatir imposed controls on the repatriation of profits from Malaysia and the exchange of the Malaysian ringgit which, in the shorter term, further alarmed the international financial community. As Finance Minister, Anwar was not consulted on any of this and clearly a rift had developed between the two men (Skehan 1998b; see Fan 1999). An article by Anwar on the Filipino nationalist Jose Rizal in *Asiaweek* (21 June 1998) which mentioned 'dictatorship', 'graft, abuse of power, profligacy and the like', 'years of self-deception' and 'a new tyranny' was a major signal that something was seriously amiss between the two (Fan 1999: introduction). It appeared that Anwar was beginning his push to replace Mahatir as Prime Minister. By August it had become clear that there had been an irretrievable falling out between Mahatir and Anwar and there was speculation that he could be removed from office (Shameen 1998b: 2).

The sacking just a few days later immediately led to an upsurge in public support for Anwar, with demonstrations calling for Mahatir to resign. Following on from the 'pro-democracy' protests in Indonesia, protesters began calling for '*reformasi*' (reform) (Skehan 1998c). Anwar hinted that he might soon be charged in order to remove him as a focal point for opposition to Mahatir. One view of events was that a change in Malaysia's leadership was becoming increasingly inevitable and, indeed, Mahatir said in 1998 that he intended to retire soon and that Anwar would succeed him. He reiterated his comments about retiring during Anwar's trial, but changed his successor to the new Deputy Prime Minister, Abdullah Badawi. While Anwar was seen to be patiently waiting for Mahatir to step down and, he hoped, hand leadership to him as his deputy, Anwar's supporters became impatient and began pushing the issue. It was the tension created by this push that led to Mahatir first establishing grounds for sacking Anwar and then doing so, following up quickly with having him charged under criminal law. Mahatir said, during the period of the trial, that he could not condone having a deputy who had allegedly committed the crimes of sexual misconduct and corruption, which necessitated his removal from office. After Anwar was arrested, the protests became larger and more vocal, with tens of thousands of protesters calling for Anwar's release and Mahatir's resignation. On 24 October, the protests turned violent as police and demonstrators clashed in the streets of Kuala Lumpur.

The sacking of Anwar was interpreted by non-Malay Malaysians as a 'family dispute', meaning it was a matter to be sorted out within the Malay community. As a consequence, while non-Malay Malaysians looked on with considerable interest, it was not a dispute they wished to involve themselves in.

Although there had been considerable speculation about a leadership challenge and Mahatir had mentioned Anwar as his eventual successor, Anwar was not in the throes of mounting a leadership challenge when he was sacked. Anwar was thereafter unable to put together an opposition political organisation once he was charged with criminal offences. However, there was considerable support for Anwar, particularly from urban middle class Malays, who were the most active group within UMNO. UMNO did not openly fracture, but the Anwar issue deeply divided the party (Choong & Arjuna 1998).

ANWAR'S TRIAL

Anwar noted during his trial that the charges against him were a consequence of his 'major differences' with Mahatir, in particular over economic policy in response to Malaysia's economic crisis (*Daily Express* 1999a). This evidence was disallowed by the trial judge. Apart from the legal campaign, Mahatir also launched a two-pronged attack on Anwar which effectively found him guilty before he had been tried. In a conventional judicial system, these comments would be regarded as *sub judice*, that is as an interference or having the ability to sway the independent affairs of the court. 'I interviewed the people he sodomised, the women he had sex with, the driver who brought the women to him,' Mahatir told a news conference. 'They told me this in the absence of the police or anybody else ... They denied being forced and they told me they were telling the truth. Several of them even said this man was not fit to become leader' (Baker 1998; also Stewart & Alford 1998).

Such comments were not only subsequently denied by some of those Mahatir 'interviewed', they were also prejudging the trial. Further, Malaysia's tightly controlled media also ran a series of stories on Anwar which recounted in full Mahatir's claims against him as well as details of the charges. Along with a booklet entitled *50 Reasons Why Anwar Can Not Be Prime Minister*, which was anonymously circulated at a party congress in June 1998, Anwar was clearly being set up as the victim of a well-orchestrated smear campaign. A number of witnesses later said that they had been forced to lie and that their allegations against Anwar were not true.

The local media disclosed allegations against Anwar outside evidence presented in his court case. Mahatir also made several announcements that Anwar was clearly guilty of the charges, even though the court case was continuing and that charges to which Mahatir referred were dropped.

Initial signs that the trial of Anwar would reflect Mahatir's wishes occurred when Anwar was refused bail. Given that the charges against him did not imply a threat to anyone else, the only reason he could have been refused bail was if his freedom during the trial could have drawn his supporters together. A further indication of how proceedings did not conform with conventional procedures was when the trial judge, Augustine Paul, disallowed what would have been the submission of conventional evidence in the defence. He also refused to allow the trial to be adjourned even though Anwar was required to give evidence at a Royal Commission of Inquiry and could not attend his own trial. The Royal Commission was investigating the cause of Anwar's injuries while in police custody (*New Straits Times* 1999).

Anwar told the Royal Commission that while he was blindfolded and handcuffed he believed that he had been assaulted by the chief of police, Rahim Noor. He said he heard the distinctive sound of Noor clearing his throat. Anwar was hit seven times during the assault and was bleeding from the nose and mouth. He later lost consciousness (Wong 1999). Noor said he assaulted Anwar because Anwar had insulted him. Anwar was examined by doctors three days after the assault. Noor resigned from his position in December 1998 and was convicted of assaulting Anwar.

Anwar ended up facing four counts of corruption for allegedly using his former position to (unsuccessfully) order police to quash charges of sexual misconduct that had been levelled against him. There was also another count of corruption, although the sexual misconduct charges were dropped during the trial, which itself was a highly unusual procedure. Judge Paul said the sexual misconduct charges need not be established to prove the corruption charges.

While in prison during the period of his trial, Anwar began communicating with another jailed DAP member of parliament, Lim Guan Eng, who 'sits in a dingy cell with only a ventilation hole in the ceiling. His crime: asking why a powerful government politician was not detained in a statutory rape case'. The reference was to Abdul Rahim Tamby Chik, a 'Mahatir loyalist' (FEER Yearbook 1997: 164) and former chief minister of Lim's home state of Malacca. Lim had previously been jailed for eighteen months when Mahatir 'cracked down' on the Opposition in 1987 (Roy 1999).

Within Malaysia's Constitution and under its parliamentary system, there remained scope for wider political change, even if it remains a theoretical rather than a practical alternative. The groundswell of support for Anwar following his arrest and detention began to bring together some of the potential opposition to Mahatir's grip on UMNO. Such a coalition faced two major obstacles, however, even if it could succeed in toppling Mahatir. The first obstacle was that beyond opposition to Mahatir, there was little to bind the factions together. The second, related, point was that while he was regarded as a symbol of opposition to Mahatir's political excesses, Anwar was only a recent convert to a more inclusive political format. His grass-roots support base was growing and his links to a number of NGOs expanded his reach. But Anwar's core support base was not outside the Islamic Malay community and he could therefore have been expected to look after his strongly Islamic *bumiputra* support base, ultimately to the detriment of non-Islamic and non-ethnic Malays. In any case, on 14 April 1999, Judge Paul sentenced Anwar to six years in jail, effectively ending his political career for at least the foreseeable future. Part of the significance of this sentence was that it was far in excess of any previous sentence for a similar offence (usually about two years) and that it did not take into account the nine months Anwar had already spent in prison, which is against the British legal convention upon which Malaysia claims to base its own laws. More importantly, though, it showed that Mahatir would not hesitate to use whatever means he believed necessary to quell genuine opposition to his rule.

MAHATIR'S FIRST POST-ANWAR TEST

The first political test for Mahatir in the wake of the start of the Anwar trial came with state elections in Sabah. Although not a federal election, the *Barisan Nasional* of Sabah is a regional branch of the federal *Barisan*. The election was interesting for two points, the first being that it acted as a measure of the developing political style of the *Barisan Nasional* more generally. A long-standing complaint in Sabah has been over the terms of its incorporation into the Federation of Malaysia. Many

Sabans, along with many Sarawakans, have expressed a sense of disunity with Peninsular Malaysia, and very often ethnic Malays have only just been tolerated by both the indigenous people, the Chinese and their mixed-race descendants.

Responding to reservations by the opposition *Partai Bersatu Sabah* (United Sabah Party) about Sabah's continuing links with the federation, the Deputy Prime Minister and Home Affairs Minister, Abdullah Ahmad Badawi, threatened the opposition. He said the government 'may have to act' as a consequence of what it called 'fanning anti-Federalist sentiments that arouse feelings of hatred towards Peninsular Malaysia and the Federal Government' (Sunar 1999). The PBS was in particular disfavour with the government as it had left the *Barisan Nasional* in 1990, and achieved state government in Sabah in 1994.

A second indication of the deeply patronising tone of Malaysian politicking was in a public statement by a sitting candidate to a challenger. 'As an older brother, I advise [Dayang] Maimuh not to challenge me,' said Kahar Mustapha, the *Barisan Nasional* member for Banggi. 'Maimuh is only wasting her time because the people in Banggi have already decided who to support in the coming state polls' (*Daily Express* 1999c). There was also a tendency for sitting government members to criticise 'ungrateful' voters, who were expected to show 'loyalty' to the government. Sabah's Deputy Chief Minister, Joseph Karup, told local community leaders not to 'collaborate with the Opposition' or 'anti-federal elements'. Karup described people who did so as 'traitors': 'as they forgot that the infrastructure and basic amenities they currently enjoyed were through the efforts and initiatives of the Barisan Nasional leaders' (*Daily Express* 1999b). Clearly the use of such language, including the terms 'directive' and 'traitors', introduced a degree of partisanship that did not reflect the idea that governments carried out their time in office as a public duty, and indicated a linkage between voting and rewards.

The *Barisan Nasional* took the elections very seriously, spending a lot of money on campaigning. Local people noted that there were more than the usual amount of *Barisan Nasional* flags fluttering from many homes and other buildings throughout the state. The elections were contested by a large number of small parties including ethnic-based parties, many of which were linked to the *Barisan Nasional*, as well as the *Barisan Nasional* and the PBS. While the *Barisan Nasional* won the Sabah state elections, it did so with a considerably reduced majority, indicating that the antics of Mahatir in what was increasingly seen as the political persecution of Anwar were having a detrimental effect on his legitimacy as leader.

THE 1999 ELECTIONS

While the Sabah elections were an initial post-Anwar test, the elections of November 1999 clearly delineated the fall-out from the affair. The BN won the elections, with 148 of the 193 available seats. But UMNO lost nineteen seats to PAS, reducing its total to seventy-four. PAS also captured the state of Trengganu while making further advances in the state of Kelantan, which it already held. In Mahatir's home state of Kedah, PAS had eight federal seats to UMNO's seven. Four UMNO ministers lost their seats as a consequence of the shift in UMNO's fortunes. Anwar's wife, Wan Azizah, won Anwar's seat in Penang representing the newly formed Keadilan (Justice) party. The DAP won ten seats, but appeared to be in long-term decline (Alford 1999: 7). The damage inflicted upon UMNO, notably in the northern, Malay 'heartland' seats was worrying to UMNO strategists and reflected a high level of disapproval for Mahatir's leadership style.

What was also of interest in the 1999 elections was that Malaysia's ethnic Chinese community fell more strongly behind the MCA and the BN, reflecting what was said to be a deep concern over the rise of a more fundamentalist Islamic political orientation. The formal alignment of the DAP with the PAS for the 1999 elections no doubt contributed to Chinese voter support for the MCA.

The mixed showing of the BN generally and of UMNO in particular confirmed Mahatir's decision to retire from the prime ministership. While Mahatir had publicly anointed Abdullah Badawi as his successor as UMNO president and prime minister, Razaleigh Hamza indicated that he would challenge for the succession. Who won this contest was less important than the divisions it demonstrated within UMNO. Razaleigh could probably have counted on less than a third of the votes from UMNO members for himself, but angry Anwar supporters could have shifted a further third of the party behind him (Elegant 2000; also Singh & Ranawana 2000). This meant that somewhere close to half of the members of UMNO, perhaps more, were not prepared to accept Mahatir's candidate and, consequently, were rejecting his style of rule. It was far from the end of UMNO, although in the heated rhetoric of the time, one Razaleigh adviser claimed that 'UMNO is dying'. 'If UMNO loses power, we tell division heads, there will be no MPships or money, you will lose everything, you will be a pariah. People will hate you' (Elegant 2000).

One thing the election results did show was that for there to be a credible alternative to Mahatir, and to UMNO, the opposition against him had to be united. To date they have not been and this division has been a significant factor in the opposition's weakness. While UMNO remained united and could count on the loyalty of the MCA and the Malaysian Indian Congress (MIC) it was not likely to be removed from office, despite the varying positions of the minor parties. The variety of controls ranged against the opposition, from media restrictions to electoral rorts, also limited the real possibility of political change. Despite his prickly character, there is little doubt that Mahatir was a master strategist and made UMNO and the BN stronger, if at the expense of their original more flexible orientations. A question remained, however, over their future after Mahatir.

NOTES

1 Following in this tradition, there was a renewed flow of migration from Sumatra to the Malay Peninsula in the wake of Indonesia's economic crisis from mid 1997.

2 Most of the inhabitants of Malacca had converted to Islam following the conversion of Raja Kasim (later known as Sultan Muzaffar Shah), who took the throne from 1446.

3 The Bajaus and the related Illanuns were 'by nature and education undisciplined robbers, searovers and freebooters' and under the leadership of one Mat Saleh 'gave the Directors many uneasy moments' (Evans 1922)

4 The background to Sarawak is included in the section on Brunei.

5 The Malayan Communist Party was originally established under a front organisation, the Nanyang General Labour Union, in 1926, and under the name Nanyang Communist Party the following year. Nanyang is the Chinese term for the 'South Seas'. The Malayan Communist Party was formally established in 1929.

6 This was in exchange for the release of political prisoners. Four MCP groups totalling 165 men were trained by the British before the fall of Singapore on 15 February 1952 (Comber 1995).

7 This was a 'confidential' government document, so its author (probably an MI6 intelligence agent) was not identified.

8 This 'systematic resettlement of Chinese squatters in New Villages' (*A Short History of the Malayan Communist Party* 1955: 23) was later adopted, with less success, by the United States in its 'Strategic Hamlets' program in South Vietnam.

9 The Chinese community in Thailand has largely blended with the Thais. However, in the less clearly defined region of southern Thailand there is a greater Islamic Malay population, which the Chinese remain quite separate from, hence their more clearly defined local identity.

10 There has also been the suggestion that the universal suffrage and elected position of the leaders of Negri Sembilan also acted as a model for the federation of Malaysia (Groves 1962: 270).
11 This assertion is based on material publicly available at various historical sites in Kuching, Sarawak.
12 Based on private conversations in Kota Kinabalu, Kuching, and Sibu.

11

Brunei: Floating on Oil

Brunei is an interesting anomaly in the make-up of SEA, being a tiny sultanate that could not afford to exist if not for its very considerable supplies of oil and natural gas. Because of this, Brunei chose to stay outside the Malaysian Federation, even though apart from its sea border it is entirely bounded by Malaysia. However, Brunei has a similar history to the other sultanates that came to comprise Malaysia, and, because of its geography, history, and ethnic composition, will be considered within this section on Malaysia.

Formally known as Negara Brunei Darussalam, Brunei is located within the Malaysian state of Sarawak in the northern part of the island of Borneo.[1] Its earliest population is believed to have come to the island around 2000 BCE. These Proto-Malays lived predominantly inland, along the island's many significant rivers and, in some areas, in the mountains. Chinese traders are known to have visited the north coast of Borneo in particular from early in the Common era, trading manufactured goods such as pottery and later metalwork for jungle produce. Immigration to Borneo probably continued at a low level from the earliest times, as waves of migrants leaving the mainland and western archipelago drifted eastwards, many ultimately settling in the Philippines. The north coast of Borneo was, therefore, an early trade and migration route.

Deutero-Malays began to make a noticeable impact on coastal Borneo from around the eighth and ninth centuries CE, as regional states began attempting to assert their trading and political hegemony over the region. The sea-based trading state of Sri Vijaya, located near modern Pelembang in southern Sumatra, was the first regional power to

BRUNEI

50 kilometres

Brunei Bay

Bander Seri
Begawan

MALAYSIA
(SARAWAK)

South
China
Sea

lay claim to Borneo's coast, and therefore to its interior. From this time until the rise of a domestic sultanate, coastal Borneo received increasing, though still relatively limited, numbers of Malay immigrants. It was upon this predominantly Malay population that the first local power was based, the remnant of which exists today as Brunei.

Brunei rose to prominence as a Malay state between the fourteenth and sixteenth centuries, exercising political control over much of coastal Borneo, the Sulu Islands and parts of the southern Philippines. During the fifteenth century, Brunei rivaled Malacca as the leading regional power, though the two states traded amicably. However in 1511 Malacca fell to the Portuguese and from then onwards growing Portuguese and Spanish, and later Dutch and English, influence in the region limited Brunei's influence to Borneo's northern coast. Mostly as a consequence of Dutch intervention in the regional spice trade and the growth of sea trade with China, local seamen took to piracy, which had long been considered a viable way of making a living. Success made these pirates 'bolder and more insolent' (Runciman 1960: 17–25). Between the power of the local sultan and the high level of piracy, European attempts at establishing bases in Borneo met with little success.[2] The British contented themselves with establishing a new base at Penang while the Dutch also abandoned Borneo, in the face of greater economic difficulty and conflict with Britain over their involvement in the American War of Independence.

In 1811, Thomas Raffles led the British occupation of Java and, under the conditions of its occupation, Britain renewed its commercial and political interests in north Borneo, through the East India Company. This interest was piqued when Raffles was informed that pirates from 'Serawa' (Sarawak) had taken a British ship, in response to which, by 1813, Raffles had secured the entire coast of the island except for the north-west tip. However, under the new agreement, British control was intended to be relinquished in 1816 when the Netherlands would resume their regional control. The north coast of Borneo, however, fell outside the terms of this agreement[3] (Runciman 1960: 34–41). Raffles later wrote of the potential of Brunei, and one of his readers was James Brooke. Brooke had been born in India in 1803 and, after being educated in England, returned to India as an officer, where he was noted for his bravery and initiative. However, he was wounded in battle, ending his military career. After a long recovery and one failed venture, but with a well-developed sense of the potential of 'the Far East', Brooke took his own ship to Singapore in 1839, and thence to the Sarawak River in the western part of what was then Brunei (Runciman 1960: 45–55).

Brooke ingratiated himself with Brunei's Sultan by helping to suppress revolts by inland Dayaks[4] (predominantly Iban), who were noted for 'a weakness for "lifting" human heads from their owner's shoulders—purely as a matter of sport and prowess, partly as a matter of religion' (Evans 1922). In return for suppressing the revolt, in 1841 Brooke negotiated his first gift of land from the Sultanate of Brunei. Unable to control piracy in the region, the Sultan ceded two further parcels of land, to adjoin Sarawak (Runciman 1960: chs II–VI). A formal treaty with Britain in 1847 provided for the development of commercial links and the suppression of piracy, which had continued as a regional problem. Brooke thereafter administered Sarawak as 'rajah' and the state remained under the direct control of his family for three generations, until its occupation by Japanese forces in WWII.

As an erstwhile part of Brunei, Sarawak underwent slightly unusual colonial development under Brooke and his successors. James Brooke was unable to attract British interest in colonising the region and indeed his actions in setting himself up as rajah were generally not well received in London. Brooke's entreaties to England to establish a 'company' there, which would in effect administer the region and allow Brooke the opportunity to develop his private commercial interests without the burden of territorial administration, were also unsuccessful (Reece 1988: 22–5). James Brooke's nephew, Charles Brooke, took local administration more firmly in hand, building both the physical and the administrative structures of state. It was this nephew who more fully developed the natural resources of the state and who encouraged fixed rather than shifting cultivation as a source of the state's economy. He also strongly encouraged Chinese settlement, through gestures as diverse as assisted passage to nominal leaseholds for plantations of cheap opium. He encouraged mining, for antimony, coal and mercury, and later oil (Reece 1988: 26–30). Between Charles Brooke's development and the Japanese invasion, Sarawak underwent little further development, although it had secured for itself a future that was by now irretrievably separate from that of the Sultanate of Brunei.

SABAH

Sabah, part of which had also been a part of Brunei's territory, was ceded to the British North Borneo Company, which was chartered in 1881. All three states became British protectorates in 1888, with Brunei negotiating its own treaty. From 1906, under the protectorate Brunei's sultan was 'advised' by a British Resident on all matters except local custom and religion. When the state of Malaysia was granted independence in 1959 and Sarawak and Sabah moved to join the federation (formalising the arrangement in 1963), Brunei chose to stay apart, and, in three stages, achieved full independence. Because of the piecemeal way in which northern Borneo was carved up during the colonial period, Brunei came to exist in two closely located but physically separate parts (Turnbull 1989: 155–70, 283–5; Bedlington 1978: 257–9).

Britain was pressured by the United Nations to grant Brunei's independence, but the Sultan and his son argued against it, fearing either being swallowed by Malaysia or succumbing to internal dissent. In 1959 Brunei was given a larger measure of internal domestic rule, in 1971 full internal sovereignty, and in 1984 full political sovereignty, including responsibility for its own external affairs and defence.

Brunei did briefly flirt with a representative form of government, holding its first and last elections in August 1962, in which the Partai Ra'kyat (Peoples' Party) won an overwhelming majority. The main platform of the Partai Ra'kyat was the incorporation of Sarawak and Sabah into Brunei as a united state (Parmer 1969: 308). However, the Sultan refused to allow the convening of the Legislative Council, and in response, on 8 December 1962, the party's armed wing, the North Borneo National Army, launched an armed uprising against the Sultan, Sir Omar Ali Saifuddin.

The cause of this uprising has been variously interpreted. One view is that the uprising was a sideshow in Indonesia's looming *Konfrontasi* (Confrontation) with Malaysia, with the anti-government rebels being supported by Sukarno's government in a bid to bring North Borneo into a Greater Indonesia. The revolt was in fact used as a pretext for Indonesia's launching of the *Konfrontasi*. Another view was that the anti-government rebels were communist-inspired, being linked to the Malayan Communist Party (MCP), which had been engaged in the 'Malayan Emergency', a communist insurgency, throughout most of the 1950s. These two views have been suggested as having a common cause, with the Indonesian Communist Party (PKI) being sympathetic to the CPM. However, a third view is that Brunei's rebels were genuine democrats who were opposed to the proclamation of Brunei's Constitution in 1959, claiming it allowed too much power to remain in the hands of the Sultan, who exercised it by not allowing the convening of the Legislative Council. Under British advice, the Sultan declared a state of emergency in 1962, the Constitution was suspended, the Partai Ra'kyat was proscribed, and, with the assistance of the British military, the Sultan quelled the revolt. Brunei has been governed under this 'state of emergency' since that time.

The revolt in Brunei was a major factor in the Sultan deciding that Brunei would not join the Malaysian federation. Other factors that have kept Brunei apart from Malaysia included a claim by the Sultan of Brunei, in 1970, that on historical and religious grounds he had sovereignty over the neighbouring Malaysian towns of Limbang, Lawas and Trusan. Anti-Malaysian sentiment was furthered when fifty-nine Partai Ra'kyat members, who had been imprisoned without trial since 1962, escaped to Malaysia, where they were given asylum and allowed to establish a political office. In 1975 the party issued a manifesto in which it called for the establishment of an elected government under a constitutional monarchy (Bedlington 1978: 265–8).

According to the official *Brunei Darussalam in Profile*: 'Brunei's political system rests on the twin pillars of the country's written Constitution and the tradition of Malay Islamic Monarchy. These two facts dominate both the formal political life of Brunei and its government ethos' (1988: 21). In this sense, Brunei is one of the world's very few remaining monarchical states, with its sultan being the twenty-ninth in one of the oldest continual monarchical lines in the world. While this would imply an autocratic style of rule, *Brunei Darussalam in Profile* also claims that a further characteristic of Brunei's political structure is its adherence to the rule of law, the system of which is primarily based on English common law, and the independence of the judiciary. However, as the Constitution is in a state of indefinite suspension, the Sultan rules by decree. To help ensure that there is no further threat to the monarchy, the Sultan maintains a well-equipped standing army and employs a battalion of retired Gurkha soldiers for both state and, presumably, personal defence. Singapore also bases an infantry battalion in Brunei for these reasons (Leifer 1995: 4).

After experimenting with slightly differing systems during each stage of its move toward full independence, Brunei's Sultan, Hassanal Bolkiah, assumed the position of Head of State, Supreme Commander of the Royal Brunei Armed Forces, Minister of Defence, and Minister of Finance. The Sultan retains full executive authority. Since 1984, Brunei has had a cabinet style of government, with its eleven members appointed by the Sultan, including one brother, Prince Mohammed, as Foreign Minister and another, Prince Jefri, who was Finance Minister until 1998. The Brunei Solidarity National Party came into existence in 1985, but has only a few hundred members. Government employees—about half the workforce—are not allowed to belong to a political party (Mitton 1998: 32).

Prince Jefri was banished from Brunei by the Sultan in mid 1998 after his private Amedeo Corporation, the largest in Brunei, was found to have significant debts. According to one account, the debts amounted to US$16 billion (Spillius 1998; AP 1998), although that figure was reduced to a more manageable US$3.5 billion when the company was formally wound up in July 1999 (Mitton 2000b). In February 2000, Prince Jefri's assets in Britain were frozen and the prince was officially said to have made 'improper withdrawal and the use of substantial funds from the Brunei Investment Agency' (BIA) (Mitton 2000a). The BIA was said to have controlled more than US$30 billion when Jefri took over, but less than US$20 billion when he left in 1998.

Despite having scope for what was claimed as financial irresponsibility, seemingly as a consequence of a lack of representation or public accountability, Brunei's political system was still claimed to 'provide for a degree of reciprocity in the relationship between subjects and Monarch' (Brunei Darussalam 1988: 24–5). The pending trial and open manner in which Prince Jefri's affairs were handled was seen by many as a move towards greater accountability. However, others viewed it as more of a family feud, noting that he was highly unlikely to see the inside of a jail.

Perhaps the main reason this otherwise constrained political system works is because of the country's wealth from oil and natural gas. With just 300 000 people (about two-thirds of whom are ethnic Deutero-Malay), Brunei enjoys a high per capita income of US$17 900 (in 1996), while the Sultan was reputedly the world's second richest man (behind American computer magnate Bill Gates). Because of this income, until the end of the twentieth century Brunei had a unique social welfare system, with free education and full health care benefits, along with no taxation. However, a 40 per cent slump in the price of oil in 1998 put pressure on Brunei's government to put the rest of its economic house in order.

Brunei had an active anti-corruption unit and a relatively good human rights record. However, according to Amnesty International, Brunei has seven prisoners of conscience who had been held without charge or trial, in four cases for more than twenty-eight years and in one case for fourteen years. Brunei's penal code is relatively harsh, and lashings were common for many offences (Amnesty International 1990: 51–2).

NOTES

1   The name 'Borneo' is a European derivation of the name 'Brunei'.

2   Being on the sea route from India to China, Alexander Dalrymple was sent from Madras to Borneo in 1759, making an agreement with the sultan of Sulu in 1761 to exchange trade for defence cooperation. A trading post was thereafter established on Balambangan island, off the northern tip of Borneo, in 1773 (Turnbull 1989: 89).

3   The agreement gave to the Dutch all islands south of Singapore, but was ambiguous about that part of Borneo north of Singapore.

4   It should be noted that these Proto-Malay people do not call themselves 'Dayaks', but rather use their tribal names (Iban, Penan, Kayan, Baram, Kenyah, etc). As with so many other smaller ethnic groups, they were given that name by their primary oppressors (in this case Deutero–Malays).

12

Philippines: Oligarchic Democracy

'Chinky Eyes'. It would be fairly safe to say that nowhere else in Asia would you see such a name. Yet in the Philippines, home to an unusual, sometimes bizarre, cultural mix, the Chinky Eyes Cab Company does not seem out of place. Nor does 'Manila's Finest' emblazoned across the door of police cars, in far more prominent letters than the word 'police'. That the term 'finest' was initially coined as an ironic comment on a corrupt American police force seems to have been lost in this usage. Such cross-cultural misinterpretations, malapropisms and manglings abound in the Philippines.

If at the social level this is colourful but not important, at the political level misconstruing cultural signifiers has led to a very particular political style. Underscoring this seemingly literal interpretation of many aspects of popular American culture is a background steeped in the traditions of Spanish colonialism. The former is most clearly seen in the Philippines' political process, which is at least superficially modelled on that of the United States, although notions of authority, power, legitimacy and natural justice (or lack thereof) derive from the colonial Spanish. The latter finds reflection in the maintenance of large land holdings associated with politically powerful families, the construction of a politically and economically under-developed *campesino* peasant culture, and the embeddedness of Roman Catholicism. Between them is the role of what is at least nominally a democratic society.

This chapter will look at what has been referred to by some as Asia's honorary Latin American state. In some senses, the Philippines is closer to its Latin American colonial cousins than it is to South-East Asia. This

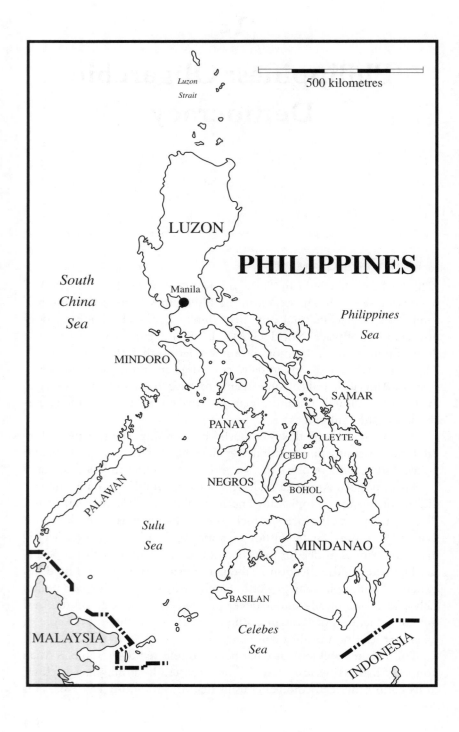

allusion refers to the Spanish imperial history of what was otherwise a Malay society functioning at relatively simple levels of political development. This Spanish heritage had the similar Latin effect of leading to the establishment of a landed mestizo elite and the structural disenfranchisement of ordinary Filipinos.[1] It also had the effect, as it did in large parts of Latin America, of breaking down local cultural traditions. While some pre-colonial traditions remain, such as family loyalty and patron–client relations, much of Filipino culture is built up or borrowed from elsewhere, often poorly understood, and leads to the types of interpretations noted above. This was later manifested in the country's newly emerging post-colonial political structure, which reached its height of corruption and repression under Marcos.

The chapter will also consider the Islamic influence in the southern Philippines, and disputes within the southern islands in particular, indicating the somewhat arbitrary nature of the state. As with some other SEA states, nationalist–communist influenced guerrilla action against the Japanese occupation was manifested in the Huk rebellion and, later, the New People's Army (NPA). The rise of the NPA paralleled the rise of Marcos and the imposition of dictatorship and attendant crony corruption and kleptocracy, which led to US-sponsored political change. This chapter will then note the (military-backed) rise of Corazon Aquino, which leads to the structure of the current political form. It will conclude with an examination of the Philippines' post-Marcos return to oligarchic 'democracy'.

At the beginning of the twenty-first century, the Philippines was enjoying a period of relative political harmony. Political unrest continued in the south, with the Muslim based Moro Islamic Liberation Front (MILF) and the fragmented remains of the communist New People's Army (NPA) continuing their struggles against the government. But in mainstream Philippine political life, the elected government did not face any major challenges from within or from its own military. Mainstream politics tended to be driven more by personality than by ideology or, indeed, by policy.

BEFORE THE SPANISH

The history of the islands now known as the Philippines is to a large extent unclear prior to the arrival of Islam. No records were kept and archeological remains are few. The Philippines were populated through a series of waves of migration, first by Negritos and then, after the loss of land bridges, by Nesiot peoples whose descendants now occupy the inland regions and still practise shifting cultivation, predominantly of maize rather than rice. The last wave of immigrants were the Malay peoples who began to arrive in the region from the last few centuries BCE, and whose migration probably continued, as an extension of their spread throughout the region, to colonial times. Contrary to some claims, it is highly unlikely that the Sri Vijaya or Majapahit empires, of Sumatra and Java respectively, ever extended more than occasional trade to this region (Fisher 1968: 698–9). Chinese traders, however, had been resident in the Philippines from around 1000 CE (Nelson 1968: 22–6).

The overwhelming religious influence of the region was animist, rather than the Indianised religions that became dominant further to the west. This was in large part due to the more western SEA states adopting these religious structures to better suit the hierarchical administrative requirements of their larger, more sophisticated political societies of the Indonesian/Malay archipelago. From a more cultural perspective, two prevailing influences included an 'obligation to avenge harm or insult to a member of one's family' and patron–client relations. This latter aspect neatly dovetailed with Spanish feudal traditions (Wurfel 1988: 2–3, 25, 34).

From around the fourteenth century, Islam had come to the coastal areas of southern Luzon, Mindanao and in particular the Visayas via northern Borneo, Palawan and the Sulu Archipelago following its spread throughout the Malay world. With Islam came some attempts to set up similar forms of government, such as under a *datu* (chief or lord) and the more Indianised *rajahs* (kings) in a manner similar to that to the west of the Philippines. But without a suitable political base upon which these more elaborate structures could build, even the arrival of Islam did not fundamentally alter the simple and local style of political organisation, as there was no pre-existing state upon which it could found these institutional structures. And despite following some of the political styles originating elsewhere in the Malay world, the impact of Islam was in most cases superficial, allowing the succeeding Spanish to imprint their own colonial culture so effectively (Fisher 1968: 699–70). Had Islam had more time to implant itself the Philippines might have become an Islamic society, as had its cousins to the west. But the proselytisation of Islam was interrupted by the arrival of the Spanish and their at least equally aggressive proselytising Christian missionaries.

In the interim, political life in the Philippines continued as it had done since time immemorial, with only a local form of government, the *barangay*, which was a kinship group approximating a village. The political structure of a *barangay* comprised a *datu* who presided over a community of free men, serfs and slaves. Sometimes such *barangays* would come together in a federation, but such alliances were brief and localised (Wurfel 1964: 680). With *barangays* unable to form lasting coalitions, there was no centralised governmental structure ruling over any large area. As a consequence, there was also no political elite of note, nor was there a court culture from which Filipinos might have drawn a political tradition. Without such a unifying tradition or a commonly accepted set of political values there was no sense of a greater identity or national cohesion. This lack of national cohesion was reflected in the more than eighty distinct linguistic groups (eight of which comprise 90 per cent of all Filipinos) (Wurfel 1988: 27) that make up the population of the contemporary state.

This lack of a broader history upon which nationalism might have been built had two, inter-related consequences. The first was that the Philippines has had a strong external focus and was highly susceptible to foreign influence, based on its links with Chinese traders, Malays and Arab Muslims, the Spanish, and later Americans. The second consequence was that the sense of nationalism that did develop in the Philippines was largely derivative, reflecting a feeling of cultural insecurity, and taking ideological and cultural cues from its colonial masters (Steinberg 1982: 33–5). This latter aspect has negatively impacted on ordinary Filipinos, whose every-day indigenous reality, as opposed to and outside the country's foreign-influenced elite, has relegated them to the margins of public influence.

THE SPANISH ARRIVE

The archipelago was claimed for Spain by Ferdinand Magellan when he and three of his original five ships landed at Cebu in search of spice in 1521, having crossed the Atlantic Ocean, sailed south of Tierra del Fuego, and crossed the Pacific. After stopping at Guam, they sailed on to the Philippines, arriving on 28 March. After befriending a *barangay* chief, Magellan became involved in a local conflict and was killed in battle on the small island of Lapu-Lapu, opposite Cebu, on 27 April 1521. With depleted crew, one of his ships was burned and the other two headed back for Spain, in opposite directions. Only one ship managed to return, via the Cape of Good Hope, with just eighteen of the original 270-person crew. This was the first vessel to circumnavigate the globe. Magellan's voyage was an early expedition of exploration to the region, and, despite other attempts, it took another fifty years for Spain to extend its control to the Philippines.

Even the Philippine islands themselves were originally not recog-
nised by the Spanish for what they were, but for what they might lead to,
such as trade and religious conversion in China and the Spice Islands.
These ideas were discounted as impractical at about the same time as
Spain's colonial greatness began to wither. The Philippines, named after
Philip of Spain, was an extension of Spain's South American colonial
expansion and its last outpost to the West (rather than the usual sense of
European colonialism that posited Asia as the 'East'). Its trade and administration was largely via Mexico and its early administration, particularly
at junior levels, was often by those of mixed Spanish descent who were
born in the Spanish colonies of the Americas. It was these 'creoles', who
often stayed on and married locally, who came to constitute the developing dominant economic class of the Philippines.

COLONIAL SETTLEMENT

In 1565, Legaspi established the first permanent Spanish settlement in
the Philippines, in Cebu, being attracted to that area both because it lay
across the main Pacific trade route with China and because it was the
focal point of the islands of the Visayan Sea. However, prompted by Portuguese activities in the Moluccas, Legaspi shifted to Panay, in 1569, and
then quickly to the small Muslim stronghold of Manila in 1570. Manila's
chief advantage was its fine harbour, which was well sheltered from
typhoons, and the large and rich area of low-lying land nearby. Within
two years he had made Manila the centre of administration for the
whole archipelago. Not only did Manila soon overtake Cebu as the main
Spanish settlement but also, primarily because of Chinese trading con-
tacts, it quickly, if briefly, became the main trading port in eastern Asia. It
was from Manila that Spain set out to consolidate control of the coastal
regions, while Augustinian friars began to convert local inhabitants to
the Roman Catholic faith. This proselytisation was particularly zealous,
according to Wurfel, to make up for the disappointment of not finding
spices or gold (1988: 4). Due to the superficiality of Islam in the north
these friars met with considerable success. But in the south, in Palawan,
Sulu and Mindanao, Islam was too deeply entrenched, while Spanish
responses to Islam were predicated on their bitterness over the 'holy
wars' against the Islamic Moors of Spain (Wurfel 1988: 4). An attempt in
1596 to establish a settlement near Zamboanga in Mindanao was driven
out by local Muslims three years later. These Muslims, referred to by the
Spanish as 'Moros',[2] retained their independence until midway between
the nineteenth century, when steamships put the advantage in favour of

the Spanish, and the early twentieth century, more than a decade after American troops arrived (Fisher 1968: 700; Wurfel 1964: 681).

Economic development was late coming to the Philippines. Its early economy relied on Manila as a transshipment port for the silk trade with China. However, cut off from direct contact with Spain due to an old agreement with Portugal not to sail via the Cape of Good Hope, the emerging group of Filipino merchants was unable to influence Madrid to look favourably on the colony's economic development. Instead, in order to secure their domestic business interests, Spanish silk merchants forced the Spanish government to impose limits on the Philippines' galleon trade. Assuming no galleons were lost, the trade left to them was just enough for the Spanish community of Manila to survive (Steinberg 1982: 35). This limited galleon trade also precluded opening up trading relations with other SEA ports, which limited the ability of Manila to grow as a regional trading centre. It further acted to distract the resident community from other forms of internal economic development. 'The ease with which the colony could survive created a kind of torpor and, for better or worse, kept the foreigners [creoles]—except for the priests—isolated and uninvolved' (Steinberg 1982: 35). The strict limits to trade were also often demonstrated more in the breach than the observance, leading to the development of a culture of corruption. This was exacerbated by a more general lack of distinction between public welfare and officials' private benefit, 'a confusion that survives today' (Wurfel 1988).

From the early nineteenth century, the Philippines' primary export economy came to rely on plantation crops such as sugar, coconut and tobacco. This agricultural development was managed under the 'hacienda' style of economic progress, which was directly borrowed from Spain's American colonies and which reflected the still feudal state of social and economic relations persisting in Spain itself. Under this system, labourers lived and worked on a large, family-owned estate, invariably in highly exploitative circumstances. The inequities of distribution of land ownership exaggerated the already marked divide between the creole landowning and administrative elites and indigenous Filipinos. This in turn has had repercussions for Philippine politics up to the twenty-first century, with a marked division existing between those who are descended from or married into landowning families, and those who are landless peasants and, increasingly, urban workers. It also, according to Hutchcroft, gave rise to what was to become a powerful political elite whose interests lay outside concern for the state (1998: 25–6).

With the successful revolt of Spain's American colonies, starting in 1808, and with transshipment thereafter having to be undertaken directly from Spain via the Atlantic and the Pacific Oceans, the Philippines was even more cut off from its colonial master (see De Comyn 1969). After 1813, with the ending of the papal decree on the division of the world between Spain and Portugal, the galleons traded directly with Spain via the Cape of Good Hope, a move that matched a gradual relaxation of trading restrictions on the colony. In terms of dominance of trade, however, by 1879 the Philippines was being referred to, in economic terms, as an 'Anglo–Chinese colony flying the Spanish flag' (Hutchcroft 1998: 24). A wave of liberalism in Spain introduced the education decree of 1863, which saw primary education introduced for children from seven to twelve years of age. Many similar decrees were either not implemented or withdrawn as Spanish politics fluctuated between liberalism and reaction. During 1810–13, 1820–23 and 1834–35, the Philippines was represented in the Spanish parliament but was at other times excluded. This heightened the sense of injustice that was beginning to prevail among the Philippines' elite. The opening of the Suez Canal in 1876 further facilitated contact between Europe and the Philippines, with greater trade between the two. But, politically more importantly, Philippine-born students were beginning to arrive to study at Spanish and other European universities. It was from these students, chafing under an increasing sense of injustice, that the nucleus of the first nationalist movement, known as the 'Propagandists', was formed. These 'Propagandists' did not want revolution or independence, but formal incorporation as a province of Spain (Wurfel 1964: 684).

AMERICAN COLONIALISM

The 'Propagandists' movement was misunderstood by the colonial Spanish and its leaders were imprisoned and their property confiscated. As such, it failed. A popular rebellion broke out around Manila in 1896, eight decades after almost all of Latin America cast off the remnants of declining Spanish power. After months of fighting, the now revolutionary army retreated to the hills (Benitez 1954: 274–82). While initially not successful, this rebellion coincided with a similar revolt in Cuba, in which the USA intervened in 1898, bringing the USA and Spain to war. A US naval squadron destroyed the Spanish fleet in Manila Bay, ending Spanish colonial rule (Benitez 1954: 286–90).

The USA brought back to the Philippines rebel leader Emilio Aguinaldo, who proclaimed Philippine independence in June 1898. However, through collusion between US armed forces and the departing Spanish colonial authorities, Manila was surrendered to the USA and not the Filipinos, with the Philippines being ceded by Spain to the USA for US$20 million. When the USA did not grant independence to the new republic, fighting broke out between the US occupying forces and the Philippine army. Although Aguinaldo was captured in 1901 and swore allegiance to the USA, a sporadic guerrilla campaign continued for the next ten years. Perhaps this movement for independence was not successful, having only succeeded in transferring sovereignty from one colonial master to another. But, notably, it was the first revolt of an Asian people against their colonial masters.

Under US colonial rule, democratic institutions were introduced and Filipinos increasingly took over political and bureaucratic positions. English-language education was also extended throughout the country. However, the social and economic structure was little changed. Spanish civil law was retained, which did not include a jury system, but the American influence added the writ of *habeas corpus* and of civil marriage. The existing judicial structure was also capped by a US-style Supreme Court in 1899, the first Chief Justice of which was a Filipino. 'By 1912 half of the judges of the first instance were Filipinos; in 1926 only two out of fifty-five judges were American' (Wurfel 1964: 687).

In 1907, the Philippines received its first elected government, the first country to do so in SEA. The electoral franchise was restricted, however, by property ownership (Wurfel 1988: 10) and the ability to speak either English or Spanish. The pre-existing American-dominated eight-person commission which operated as both the legislature and the cabinet of the governor-general was reconstituted as the upper house of a bicameral legislature. The lower house, the Assembly, comprised eighty members elected from single-member districts. For a bill to be enacted as law, it had to be passed by both houses. In 1916, the Jones Act abolished the commission and allowed for a twenty-four-person Senate, twenty-two members of which were elected from eleven districts and two of whom were appointed to represent non-Christian areas. The electoral franchise was broadened to include all literate males. Throughout this period, the US-appointed governor-general retained the right of veto over legislation, which thereafter required the ratification of the US president. Further, all laws concerning public land, currency, immigration or tariffs required the US president's signature, while the US Congress retained the right to annul any Philippine law.

LOCAL POLITICIANS

From its foundation in 1907, the Philippines' dominant political party was the elite-based Nacionalistas, which controlled both houses of the legislature until the Philippines was made a self-governing Commonwealth in

1935. Full independence was planned for 1946. However, the American focus of self-government involved a somewhat contradictory policy. In the first instance, political power was to be gradually handed over to those capable of administering it, and in the second instance the USA helped to build an economic base upon which a democracy could rest. Self-government meant rule by those Filipinos who were sufficiently educated and that meant they were almost exclusively from the landed elite (see Wurfel 1988: 10–11). That elite, however, was unwilling to give up its economic privilege, a position that had been enhanced by the Payne-Aldrich tariff of 1909, which hampered industrial development but stimulated agricultural exports (Hutchcroft 1998: 27; Wurfel 1988: 9). Agrarian reform was, even from the early 1900s, not a program that would be undertaken with any meaningful success. Indeed, the number of tenant farmers doubled between 1900 and 1935 and, in response to this growing iniquity, there were three small rebellions in central Luzon during the 1920s and 1930s (Sturtevant 1976: 141–255). Thus elite domination of politics also ensured the retention of a quasi-feudal economic system, which both hampered economic growth and, eventually, engendered considerable political backlash. With the goal of preserving the economic *status quo* (Hutchcroft 1998: 65–70), the focus of the Nacionalistas was therefore less on the legislative than on the more broadly defined, less obviously threatening, and more patriotic goal of independence. The legislative program was thus dominated by the executive, which placed direct political power in the hands of a small group (Constantino 1975: ch. XVII; see also Lande 1968: 92–129; Friend 1969: ch. 4).

Despite the outward democratic appearance of the Philippines political life, the country's mestizo elite cemented its control over the electoral process. The initiative for independence, though cheered on by the elite, actually came from the USA. There were some moves towards agrarian reform, expanded education and infrastructure development under Manuel Quezon's presidency in the late 1930s. However, Japanese occupation of the Philippines in 1941 and the Japanese declaration of independence for the Philippines two years later interrupted this plan. The Japanese were not widely welcomed, even initially, in the Philippines as they often were in other Asian colonial states, as the achievement of independence was not guaranteed by the Japanese but forestalled. The Philippine elite, though, remained largely intact during the war and a good many of its administration worked under the Japanese, including two-fifths of the Congress and most of the Senate. An associate justice of the Supreme Court, Jose Laurel, was appointed president in October 1943, with the power of absolute veto over the Congress and the ability to enter into unilateral agreements with foreign powers. He was, in practical terms, a Japanese puppet. Meanwhile Quezon, as president of the government in exile, died in the United States in August 1944, to be succeeded by vice-president Sergio Osmena (Stanley 1974: ch. 2).

THE REPUBLIC OF THE PHILIPPINES

The Philippines political system is based on the US model, where the president holds executive power and works with, or against, a bicameral legislature. As with the USA, at least in principle, the judiciary is independent of the executive arm of government. The Philippines also enjoys a free and unfettered media, which is in principle a cornerstone of a democratic society. This system has been in place, with the exception of the later Marcos period, since the Philippines achieved full independence in 1946.

Although collaboration with the Japanese became the major post-war political issue, the commander of the US forces in East Asia, General Douglas MacArthur, freed his friend Manuel Roxas, who had served as a minister in the Laurel administration. This act both confused the issue of collaboration and helped launch Roxas on his post-war political career. With independence looming, in early 1946 Roxas was elected as leader of the Liberal wing of the Nacionalista Party, ahead of the elections in April to form a new government for the Republic of the Philippines. Roxas and what had become the Liberal Party (Wurfel 1988: 97) won by a slim majority after a big spending campaign. In July 1946, the Philippines was proclaimed a republic. As president, in 1948, Roxas granted amnesty to all those indicted for treason as a consequence of their collaboration (though not for people also found guilty of murder, rape or theft). After a minor change to the Constitution and a public vote, the Philippine ratified an agreement to allow free trade between the Philippines and the USA for eight years from the date of independence. The Philippines maintained close relations with the USA in trade until 1974. In exchange, the USA agreed to pay war damages to the Philippines, which provided the Roxas administration with much needed funds to fight an escalating insurgency.

A DEEPENING DIVIDE

In 1942, a peasant group that had been demanding land reform in the 1930s reformed as the Hukbo ng Bayan Laban sa Hapon (Anti-Japanese Peoples' Army), abbreviated in Tagalog (the common language of Luzon) as 'Hukbalahap'. The 'Huks' were active in the guerrilla war against the Japanese. Although initially regarded as allies by the USA, leaders of the communist-influenced Huks were imprisoned by the Americans in 1945, while US military police assisted private Filipino landlord armies in restricting leftist political activity, most notably for land reform. Clashes between Huks and police became more frequent and an attempted cease-fire in 1946 failed. The Huks formally (although not actually) disbanded in 1946 in order to contest the coming elections. Under the name of the Democratic Alliance, six Huks were elected to the Philippines Congress. However, Roxas barred them from assuming their seats (Wurfel 1988: 101), with assassination squads killing two of them (Monk 1990: 8). Meanwhile, approximately US$2 billion worth of economic aid from the USA was largely siphoned off by Roxas and the rest of the political elite, prefiguring the type of corruption which would become better known from the mid 1960s until the mid 1980s (Seagrave 1988: 126). Although they did not present an electoral threat, Roxas declared the Huks illegal in March 1948 and refused them participation in the elections of the following year. Roxas died the month after the declaration. Roxas' successor, Quirino, offered the Huks an amnesty in 1948 but the effort failed on both sides and quickly led to all-out conflict.

The three-sided elections of 1948 were noted for their use of guns and money, and a high level of fraud and intimidation, which secured a 52 per cent majority for Quirino. 'The way in which the Liberal regime achieved power substantially affected the way it exercised power, that is, corruption bred more corruption' (Wurfel 1964: 700). Foreign exchange reserves and treasury funds declined markedly, government employee salaries went into arrears, public projects were stopped, and, not surprisingly, the public lost faith in the government. In February 1950, the Huks changed their name to the Hukbong Mapagpalaya ng Bayan (People's Liberation Army) and called for the overthrow of the government. The USA stepped in to assist the Philippines government sort out its economic problems, in large part with a grant of US$250 million. The Philippines government failed, however, to adopt a land reform program which had been drawn up by American adviser Robert Hardie (see Monk 1990: ch. I, II, III). Ramon Magsaysay was appointed as Secretary of National Defense and rebuilt the Philippines armed forces. Magsaysay's army ensured that the 1951 elections were relatively honestly administered, boosting his popularity. In 1953, at the instigation of the United States, Magsaysay resigned his position, joined the Nacionalista Party and was elected president with a two-thirds majority in the elections of that year. Despite being regarded as a great nationalist leader,

Magsaysay only came to power with the direct support of the United States (Smith 1958: ch. 4, 5).

The Magsaysay government did not achieve all its goals. For example, the Agricultural Tenancy Act was 'mangled', which meant that those who worked the land continued to have little or no ownership of or control over it (Wurfel 1988: 15, 167). But it did inaugurate the beginning of a relatively unfettered trade union movement, cleaned up customs and foreign exchange dealings, and reduced corruption. Most importantly, however, between holding out the promise of reform to disaffected land labourers and embarking on an active military campaign with the help of the United States, Magsaysay managed to end the Huk rebellion in 1954 (Smith 1958: ch. 6, 7). The USA had continued its high level of military interest in the Philippines after independence and maintained its close association until 1991. In 1991, an increasingly well-developed sense of Philippine nationalism manifested itself in high rent for American military bases, in particular the Clarke Air Force Base and the Subic Bay Naval Base. Along with an increasing tendency for the USA to put into effect its 'Guam Doctrine' of withdrawing forces west of that island, it finally decided to end its long, direct military involvement in the Philippines.

Magsaysay's personal popularity was still high when he was killed in a plane crash in 1957; his funeral procession was lined by hundreds of thousands of mourners. His death led to a four-cornered presidential election, which was won by the late president's Vice-President, Carlos Garcia. While Garcia's victory appeared in one sense to promise a continuation of Magsaysay's trajectory, because of divisions within the Nacionalista Party, which saw younger members break away to form the Progressive Party, it actually put power back into the hands of the party's 'old guard'. This in turn led to a high level of spending on the elections, and flowed on into the Garcia administration with unprecedented levels of corruption. Garcia also refused to liberalise import controls, which supported new local manufacturers. As a result of his support for local capital, Garcia's administration 'may have marked the zenith of the national bourgeoisie's influence within the political elite' (Wurfel 1988: 16). Garcia's presidency was blessed with a divided opposition, at least until the elections of 1961 in which the Progressives merged with the Liberal Party. In that campaign, corruption was the major political issue. Wurfel notes that in the eight years between the election of Magsaysay and Macagapal's victory in 1961, spending on presidential campaigns rose tenfold and senatorial campaigns nearly as quickly, although congressional campaigns only sixfold (1988: 100).

From the American occupation until the late 1960s, the Philippines had witnessed sporadic uprisings and rebellions. None, apart from the Huk rebellion, was ever likely to directly challenge the government. But they did indicate a deep-seated sense of untenable oppression among the country's rural poor, and even its urban poor (see Sturtevant 1969). The outcome of conservative agrarian legislation, and a structural failure to implement land reform programs, was the 'proliferation throughout the archipelago in the 1960s of all those pernicious institutional practices which had triggered the Huk rebellion in the 1940s' (Monk 1990: 84). This laid the groundwork for further radical rebellion in the late 1960s.

MARCOS

Ferdinand Marcos was born in 1917 in Ilocos Norte, the illegitimate son of Ferdinand Chua, who was from the wealthiest family in the region: 'Of the top ten Chinese clans in this inner group of forty billionaire families, Ferdinand's (Chua's) clan ranked number six' (Seagrave 1988: 14, see also 22–3). While Chua never openly acknowledged Marcos as his son, he did financially assist him, including his education. In 1939 Marcos graduated with a law degree. At the same time, he was charged with murdering Julio Nalundasan, who had defeated Marcos' nominal father, Mariano Marcos, in his bid to be elected to the Congress for Ilocos Norte. The conviction for this crime was overturned in 1940, with the assistance of President Jose Laurel, to whom Marcos became indebted as one of his 'clients'.

Marcos was in officer school for the Philippine army when war broke out in the Pacific in early 1942. Although there were many stories of Marcos' heroism from the war period, these were almost entirely invented. Marcos was captured by the Japanese in August 1942, and released soon after. After the war, he was elected to Congress for Ilocos Norte in 1949, the same seat occupied by the person he was alleged to have killed. Elected to the Senate in 1959, he became Senate president in 1962. Marcos stood against the incumbent Diosdado Macagapal in the 1965 elections, winning with money and nationalist slogans.

Marcos had promised to end rice shortages and importation, to reduce graft and corruption (punishing those who had enriched them-selves in office), and to implement faster land reforms. Like his predecessor, in office Marcos fulfilled none of these promises (Monk 1990: 84). Under Macapagal but more so under Marcos, during the 1960s, the Philippines had begun to shift its economic foundation from import substitution, where local industry was protected from external competition, to an export-oriented economy, which exposed local businesses to greater external competition. The purpose of this change was to drive down the value of the peso and to enhance the profitability of primary commodity exporters, who were almost entirely dominated by the traditional landed elite, but which also included major multinational corporations (Hawes 1987: ch. 1; Bello, Kinley & Elinson 1982: ch. 5). This led to a division within the Philippines elite group, and 'opened the floodgates of popular political participation by peasants, workers, students and intellectuals' (Hawes 1987: 37).

At around the time these 'floodgates' were opening, a different set of floodgates opened—those that paid US$50 million for Marcos' 1969 election campaign. In line with this unprecedented pork-barrelling, the corruption and maladministration of his government only worsened (Monk 1990: 87), while protest against a perceived loss of legitimacy grew (Wurfel 1988: 38). As demonstrated by his campaigning technique, Marcos had been a keen political operator and used every facet under his control to continue his tenure in office (Infante 1980: 10–11). Pressure had been building for land reform (Wurfel 1988: 17), but even Marcos' 'espousal of land reform in 1971–72 must be interpreted in terms of his determination to outbid and outmanoeuvre all possible rivals for political supremacy and not in terms of a sober and responsible philosophy of statesmanship' (Monk 1990: 90). By the beginning of the 1970s, however, Marcos' grip on power appeared to be slipping. In the end, the continuation of the Philippines' exploitative agrarian policies and continuing Islamic unrest in Mindanao gave him the excuse he needed to continue his rule unimpeded (Infante 1980: 11–12).

DICTATORSHIP

Taking into account the corrupt practices used to win office, including the election of Marcos to the presidency, the Philippines political elite had alternated in power in a relatively stable fashion. But in 1972, nearing the end of his second term, Marcos knew that, under the eight-year (two-term) limit on the presidency, he was about to leave office for good. So, citing the threat of 'subversive forces', in reference to the Islamic and communist rebellions, he imposed martial law. In doing this, Marcos did not just impose a more strict control over those areas in which the rebels were believed to be operating, he also closed the Philippines' Congress, subordinated the judiciary to the executive, and engineered the ratification, by a show of hands, of a new Constitution that gave him permanent tenure in office (Hawes 1987: 13; Infante 1980: 12–16). 'In retrospect the proclamation of martial law appears to have been produced by a convergence of three growing conflicts: between power-holding elites and increasingly discontented masses, between foreign investors and economic nationalists, ... and within the power elite, between Marcos and his two most potent competitors, Benigno Aquino and "sugar baron" Euginio Lopez' (Wurfel 1988: 21).

Marcos' control was complete. For the next thirteen years[3] the Philippines underwent effective one-person rule, supported by violence and exercised in an arbitrary manner. It was, in a practical sense, a dictatorship. With no recourse to an electoral contest, the Philippines suffered looting by Marcos and his cronies on a hitherto unprecedented scale of tens of billions of dollars. By the early 1980s, even the elites that had supported Marcos and who had profited so richly from his patronage had begun to reconsider their position (Wurfel 1988: 235–40). What had started out as yet another example of elite rule on behalf of their own economic interests soon became plunder of the economy from the centre, with presidential clients ('cronies') being secondary beneficiaries of the economic rape of a state no longer even protected by its own self-serving elite (for example, see Hutchcroft 1998: 111–15, 136).

By the end of 1985, the Philippines had the lowest per capita income of any of the ASEAN states, in particular contracting rapidly between 1982 and 1985. In the 1950s it had been the highest. External debt was almost equivalent to the gross national product and was three times the value of exports. The country was in the grip of economic crisis (Jayasuriya 1987: 80). In part this was a result of a fall in world commodity prices, but also reflected poor economic planning and wildly excessive corruption. Marcos' kleptocratic rule had begun to alienate even the economic elite. In part they were themselves beginning to suffer from Marcos' unrestrained greed, and in part they reasonably feared the flow-on effect of the sort of radical and even popular backlash which Marcos' rule was beginning to engender.

In 1983, the usually conservative Roman Catholic Bishops' Conference vigorously and unanimously criticised Marcos for the excesses of his government and for using political violence (Wurfel 1988: 279). From 1972, as Archbishop of Lubrense, Jaime Sin had been a critic of Marcos, albeit a mild one. Sin was made Archbishop of Manila in 1974, and, while agreeing to tone down his criticisms of Marcos, 'continued to visit jails, detention camps and asylums, to which many political prisoners had been sent'. Among those Sin stayed in regular contact with was Senator Benigno Aquino, by correspondence when Aquino was later in the United States (Lyons & Wilson 1987: 33–4). In 1984 Sin publicly embarrassed Marcos by calling on him to release all political prisoners. In 1981 Sin claimed that Marcos was deliberately attempting to silence the church from speaking out on matters of Roman Catholic morality. The following year, a number of churches were raided by the military, and some priests were charged with having links to the NPA. In 1986, Sin was a prime activist in bringing tens of thousands of people onto Manila's streets to call for the resignation of Marcos.

OPPOSITION

Long averse to being brought into the Philippine 'nation', and chafing under the relocation of Christian migrants to traditionally Islamic lands, Islamic separatism in Mindanao developed a militant character in the 1960s (Wurfel 1988: 28–31, 154–60). The armed wing of these Islamic separatists, the Moro National Liberation Front, was becoming increasingly aggressive, while the armed wing of the Communist Party of the Philippines (CPP), the New Peoples' Army (NPA), established in 1969, had become a military force to be reckoned with. The CPP/NPA drew on disaffected peasants, urban poor and radical students, but could trace its lineage back to the same support base as the Hukbalahap rebellion. The primary difference was that while the Huks were communist-inspired, the CPP/NPA was directly influenced by the radical version of communism outlined by China's Mao Zedong during the period of China's Cultural Revolution (Weekly 1996: 35).

The Philippines' elite was also increasingly horrified at Marcos' unrestrained abuse of power, offending even their easily assuaged sense of propriety. The Philippine economy was beset by the linked problems of an inefficient local industry, unsustainable levels of government foreign borrowing for often highly dubious projects, and myriad forms and levels of official corruption. The political mechanism over which Marcos presided was, along with the economy, rapidly crumbling. Even Marcos' political guarantor, the United States, had become heartily sick of his unrestrained excesses.

THE END OF THE MARCOS PERIOD

It was against this backdrop that Marcos' foe and former Philippine senator Benigno Aquino, who had since 1980 been living in exile in the United States, returned to the Philippines. Aquino was from a provincial dynasty in Tarlac, north of Manila (Seagrave 1988: 14) and, as a son of a former cabinet member, was a member of the Philippine economic elite (Wurfel 1988: 205). Despite his post-mortem sanctification, Aquino was not a liberal reformer and, like many of his class, favoured authoritarian political methods. Aquino was elected to the Senate in 1967, and by 1972 even he had told journalists that if he ever became president he would declare martial law, as Marcos was later to do (Wurfel 1988: 18).

If Aquino was, like Marcos, a conventional representative of the elite, he was no less seen by Marcos as an enemy, in the traditional manner of politics being about elite competition rather than policies. It was in this context that there was an attempt on Aquino's life and those of his Liberal Party colleagues, in a bombing at a rally at the Miranda Plaza in 1971. With the backing of the country's wealthiest family, the Lopez clan, it had been expected that Aquino would win the 1973 presidential elections (Wurfel 1988: 18).

Unfortunately for Aquino, when Marcos declared martial law in 1972—a move that was in principle favoured by Aquino—he was one of the first picked up, the following year being charged with subversion and murder (Wurfel 1988: 206–7). In 1977 Aquino was sentenced to death, a sentence that was probably not intended to be carried out, given the disquiet it would have caused among the Philippine elite. In 1980, Aquino was beset by a serious heart complaint and was sent to the United States for heart surgery. Marcos had feared he would be blamed if Aquino died in the Philippines. Aquino recovered from a triple by-pass operation and remained in the USA until 1983.

Aquino's return to the Philippines on 21 August 1983 was a direct challenge to Marcos' increasingly shaky grip on Philippine politics, as by this stage Aquino was openly supported by the USA. Upon alighting from his plane after landing at Manila airport, Aquino was shot dead on the tarmac. The alleged assassin was gunned down on the spot in an attempt to cover up the source of the order for the assassination. But the attempt to infer responsibility for Aquino's death on the lone gunman was feeble, it subsequently being attributed to General Fabian Ver, who was Marcos' long-time confidant and, from 1981, military chief of staff. Ver had previously been a policeman, head of Marcos' personal security, and director of the National Intelligence and Security Authority. His relationship with Marcos had extended to assisting Marcos in having an affair with an actor, bombing the Liberal Party headquarters in 1981, and arranging the killing of one of the doctors involved in Marcos' failed kidney transplant in 1982. After the killing of Aquino, Ver was tried for the crime but acquitted, although the Supreme Court ordered a retrial. But before the retrial could take place, Philippine politics turned critical (Corfield 1998).

Aquino's death galvanised the non-violent opposition particularly among the middle and business classes, with the USA distancing itself from Marcos and aligning itself with Aquino's widow, Corazon. In the face of mounting criticism over Ver's putative involvement in Aquino's assassination, Marcos called presidential elections to be held in February 1986, assuming that he would prevail. With widespread voting irregularities, including the discovery of ballot boxes full of marked papers before the election and hacking into computer records to alter the voting tables, Marcos did win the election. But the vote was seen as a sham by the opposition, the USA, and finally a large section of the armed forces led by the Defence Minister Juan Ponce Enrile and deputy chief of staff, General Fidel Ramos. As pro-Marcos troops attempted to locate and destroy pro-opposition radio stations, the troops' communications were scrambled by the American forces that had initially set them up. Although Ver ordered a commando helicopter-borne assault against the rebel soldiers based at Camp Crame, once inside the camp the commandos defected. Hundreds of thousands of protestors packed the streets around the camp and troops sent against them joined them instead. In response to this overwhelming show of antipathy, accompanied by Ver, Marcos fled to Hawaii, where he remained until his death in 1989 (Lyons & Wilson 1987). Corazon Aquino's legitimacy as the succeeding president was not challenged. Although she moved to restore civil liberties and put into place a new Constitution with controls on the power of the president, the Philippines social and economic structure was left basically intact. A promised land reform program, not surprisingly, failed to materialise in any significant sense.

One of the most important immediate effects of the accession of Corazon Aquino to the presidency was the lifting of controls over the news media. Under Marcos, the news media was repressed and had become, in effect, a public relations tool for his government. Under Aquino, a long suppressed sense of exuberance sprang forth. In a similar manner to reflecting other aspects of American culture, the media almost immediately took upon itself the role of outspoken critic of all that was wrong and unjust. Newspapers flourished and restraint and taste were cast aside in a headlong rush towards 'freedom of speech'.

One of the lasting benefits of this change is that a culture of free expression appears to have deeply and perhaps permanently permeated Filipino society. The few serious commentators writing for the Filipino press were as acute in their observations, as trenchant in their criticisms, and as sharply analytical in their commentaries as any in the world. But they were few, and they were generally little read and even less regarded. Most newspapers quickly reflected a lack of constraint in garish headlines,

318 Southeast Asia: A Political Profile

graphic images, and salacious stories that more paralleled gossip than news. This appeal to a lowest common denominator is the price paid for a relatively unfettered news media around the world. In the Philippines, with only a limited understanding of the role of the media in an open and plural society, the lowest common denominator was quickly reached and fully exploited. Serious news and commentary, while existing, was relegated to the margins.

DISSENT WITHIN

After Marcos fled, Enrile was not accorded the senior position he coveted and set himself up in opposition to Aquino, while Marcos used his financial reserves and the remnants of personal loyalty to urge the armed forces to overthrow Aquino, which resulted in a series of attempted coups in 1986, 1987 (which came close to success), 1988 and 1989. The attempted coups generally and the 1987 attempted coup in particular, made worse by mounting NPA activity, shook public confidence in Aquino's government (SarDesai 1997: 224–5). The 1989 coup attempt, which appeared to be otherwise succeeding, was quashed with the aid of US war planes from the Clarke Field air base. The main group behind the coup attempts was the Reform the Armed Forces Movement (RAM), which later became known as the Revolutionary Alliance Movement (RAM).

Like many other aspects of the cultural life of the Philippines, the Armed Forces adopted a variation of the American sense of collegial loyalty, which was reflected in the RAM. This sense of duty to each other did not sit well with the armed forces' duty to the state. One of the leading figures of the RAM, Colonel Gregorio 'Gringo' Honasan, was a Scarlet Pimpernel type of figure, after orchestrating the 1987 attempted coup, on the run but thumbing his nose at the government, often through the media. Honasan was later pardoned and stood for the Philippines Senate, being elected Senator. At the end of the 1990s, Honasan was still antagonistic towards the government, threatening the state with dire consequences should thirteen RAM members charged with killing a union leader be convicted.

REVOLUTIONARY DISSENT

In the south, the island of Mindanao continued as a deeply troubled area for the Philippines government, being a hotbed of communist and

Islamic rebellion. By the end of 1992, Corazon Aquino had moved politically to the right, to assuage opposition complaints that she was too liberal, and with little real reform (including land reform) having taken place she lost much of her popularity. Probably the most important aspect of Aquino's presidency was that at the end of her term, when Fidel Ramos was elected president in 1992, power was transferred peacefully, indicating a sustained return to democracy. Ramos succeeded in forming a pro-government coalition in congress, appealing to the country's economic creditors and achieving a 'cessation of hostilities' with the MNLF and, briefly, with the NPA.

The MNLF reached its cease-fire agreement with the Manila government in 1996. As a consequence, the MNLF's leader, Nur Misuari, became the provincial governor in southern Mindanao. Having reached an accommodation with the government, the MNLF's place on the battlefield was taken by the Moro Islamic Liberation Front (MILF), led by Salamat Hashim, who had broken with the MNLF in 1977. The main difference between the two groups was that the MNLF accepted a degree of regional autonomy along with the promise of extra funds for local infrastructure projects, which four years later were still only partially forthcoming. Misuari said that billions of dollars promised by the Philippines government for a new airport, an irrigation project, reafforestation, and other smaller projects had instead materialised as millions of dollars. In contrast, the MILF demanded total independence. 'The only way to solve the problem permanently is to give the Bangsa Moro people independence,' Hashim said. 'They believe that the homeland of the Bangsa Moro people was annexed illegally and immorally' (Hashim 2000).

The MILF claimed 120 000 fighters, although more sober estimates put the real figure at closer to 12 000 members under arms, with an active support base of perhaps another 50 000 (Davis 1998). The MILF admitted to receiving funds to help them establish a *bangsamoro* (Islamic homeland) from international Islamic terrorist, dissident Saudi millionaire Osama bin Laden until 1997 (*Philippines Star* 1999). Other global Islamic communities were also claimed to contribute to the MILF's coffers. It also claimed that 1000 of its fighters had battle experience in Afghanistan against the former Soviet Union.

The Ramos presidency was basically a period of consolidation. While some divisions within the elite of Filipino society remained, the sharp divisions that characterised the early part of Aquino's presidency were absent. In large part, this was achieved by restoring many of the privileges to the Marcos era cronies, and treading softly on their prosecution. While Ramos quelled a significant part of the rebellion in the Philippines, his successor, Joseph Estrada, was not nearly as adept at either diplomacy or, it seemed, economic management.

Under Estrada, in early 1999, the Philippines government began to make noises about reaching some sort of settlement of the rebellion, perhaps including a type of regional autonomy for Mindanao. However, Estrada soon wrecked that discussion by grandstanding with a 'policy' of 'no negotiation'. The MILF, on the other hand, demanded 'full autonomy' for a region that remains within the island of Mindanao upon which the majority of the population is not Muslim (being around four million of a total of twenty-one million). The MILF's military chief, Al Haj Murad, said that as a consequence of the failed negotiations, the conflict would spread beyond Mindanao. However, the MILF's ability to carry out attacks beyond the island would have been limited to terrorist rather than full-scale military activities (*Borneo Post* 1999). Just ahead of a visit to Mindanao by Estrada in February 2000, MILF guerrillas blew up two buses on board a passenger ferry at Ozamiz City, killing forty-five people, along with a number of other similar attacks (Lopez 2000a). In response, Estrada ordered the further escalation of attacks against the MILF. A separate, smaller but more extreme Islamic group, Abu Sayyaf, also stepped up its campaign in the late 1990s and into the next decade. In early 2000, the group was responsible for numerous kidnappings, including twenty tourists from a Malaysian resort island off the east coast of Sabah, retreating to the island of Basilan, off the coast of Mindanao. This indicated, if nothing else, that the traditionally dangerous waters between the Philippines and Malaysia had not yet come fully under state control. A Filipino author noted that 'Islamic Mindanao' was 'the lynchpin of border security in the ASEAN region', indicating at least in part why the government in Manila felt it could not let go of the province (Mastura 1999).

THE NPA

Following the collapse of international communism and the purges within the NPA in which numerous comrades and supporters were executed, the guerrilla army's numbers shrank and it broke into several effectively independent factions (for example, the Revolutionary Proletarian Party). Operating at a peak strength of around 26 000 armed guerrillas in 1987, the combined strength of the remaining forces was around 6000 in 1999.

A large part of the reason for the decline in the strength of the NPA was a purge conducted in 1985, while the leaders of the Mindanao branch of the NPA[4] were in Manila to help decide the next phase of the revolution. Informed that there were spies operating within the NPA, local commanders took the process into their own hands, arresting and killing almost a thousand, mostly loyal, NPA members. Although this process was halted as soon as the horrified leaders returned from Manila, the effect of the purge was to leave the Mindanao branch shattered, its strength declining from 9000 to 3000 within nine months. The CPP also lost over 50 per cent of its mass base. In response, the 'ferocious' criticism of the Mindanao purges by the CPP's leader, Jose Maria Sison, further weakened and dispirited the party (Abinales 1996).

In part, however, the decline in support for the CPP/NPA also stemmed from the fact that, until 1986, there was effectively no discussion about ideology within the CPP/NPA, which in itself contributed to the Mindanao party crisis (Weekly 1996: 35–7). But more importantly, with the end of Marcos and the (largely unfulfilled) promise of land reform, many party supporters were drawn back into mainstream political society. Most of their continuing military activity from the communist-based groups appeared to be on the islands of Negros and Mindanao. 'Sparrow forces' of urban guerrillas conducted a sporadic terror campaign, including political assassinations, in Manila up until the early 1990s. Attempts at negotiating a 'peace accord' between the government and the National Democratic Front, the 'umbrella' organisation for the former CPP/NPA, floundered again under Estrada's 'tough-guy' intransigence.

HOLLYWOOD IN CONTROL

The influence of the United States continues to be at least superficially dominant, particularly among the Filipino elites. For example, Filipino authority figures such as the police ape their American counterparts, or at least the television versions of them, but have a different sense of responsibility, perhaps in part because of the continuation of a colonial Spanish idea of machismo. Guns carry a powerful social message and are firmly linked to the public prestige of those who possess and display them.

Similarly in politics, much of the form of a Hollywood version of that function is there, but the rationale for that form seems almost entirely disconnected. Looking at it another way, the Philippines wholeheartedly embraced 'fast food', not recognising its junk status elsewhere. As a metaphor, perhaps much of the public element of Philippine political life could find a parallel in this adoption of 'fast food'.[5] Even the Philippines president, Joseph Estrada, was a 'B' grade actor turned 'B' grade politician, first as a regional mayor and then as Vice-President (*Asiaweek* 1998a). Estrada's popularity, which was early on at an historical high for a Philippine president, did not reflect his policies, or lack thereof. The lack of policy debate ahead of his election was 'extraordinary' and the election itself was described as 'probably the worst in the country's history' (Easton 1998). Estrada reverted to the time-honoured tradition of pork-barrelling, guaranteeing favours for his supporters ('clients') and himself being beholden to his own patrons. But the Philippine voting public's fascination with and admiration for empty rhetoric delivered in what was perceived as authentic Hollywood style won Estrada the day. In this sense, the Philippines seemed like a country unaware of itself, other than as a mangled reflection of a superficial USA. If the country was burdened by a separatist and revolutionary movement, an appallingly high crime rate, and such dire poverty, it was hardly surprising if alienation was its cause.

The biggest long-term threat to Philippine political stability remains economic, as the roots of the NPA and the MILF will remain strong while income and land distribution remains so uneven. To counter this, in 1997 the economy of the Philippines did begin to look as though it was improving, with only a small rise in per capita GDP but lower inflation (5.1 per cent) and a positive balance of trade for the first time in many years. But by 1998 the 'Asian crisis' had also hit the Philippines and both investment and exports dropped off, returning the country to its more usual parlous position.

A self-confessed economic illiterate, Estrada seemed to have few concrete plans for developing the Philippine economy. 'Estrada's critics say he shows several weaknesses: lack of direction on the economy, inertia in pushing through economic reform bills, a tendency to coddle cronies and an erratic governing style' (Tiglao & Vatikiotis 1999). His public pronouncements on finally sorting out the legacy of the Marcos era seemed even more doubtful. Officially, work on the Marcos legacy was going ahead, and after thirteen years, the Presidential Commission on Good Government (PCGG) appeared to be moving towards preparing for the final confrontation with the Marcos family. This followed the failure of the government to reach an acceptable agreement with the former president's family over their ill-gotten wealth. The PCGG had already tracked down some of this money——about US$520 million—in two Swiss bank accounts under six pseudonyms. Billions more were still to be accounted for. There was never any doubt that Marcos was an enormously corrupt political leader, but eventually his widow, Imelda, in effect, confirmed it. She was quoted in a local Philippines newspaper as saying that her husband had bought large parcels of shares in major Philippine companies. Investigating these share holdings, the Philippines senate was told by Mrs Marcos that her family could be worth as much as US$13 billion.

Estrada said that his government was nearing the end of talks with the Marcos family regarding this fortune. A significant proportion of the funds was expected, after negotiations with the government, to be left in the family's hands (Reuters 1999a). Marcos' son, Ferdinand Marcos Jr, was elected governor of Ilocos Norte, the Marcos family's home province, in 1998, indicating that they were far from defeated. It may have helped that the Marcos family supported Estrada's campaign, and was regarded as his friend (Tiglao 1998b).

While this rhetoric of the PCGG and Estrada, with his professed concerns for the Philippines poor, assuaged some, the reality was that many of Marcos' cronies were 'likely to escape virtually unscathed from charges of ill-gotten wealth, as long-running cases against them flounder in the courts' (Tiglao 1998a). Indeed, not only were the 'cronies' continuing with their business interests, they were also establishing new and close relations with Estrada, indicating that some things in Philippine politics do not change. For example, the most notorious Marcos crony, billionaire Edouardo Cojuangco, headed up Estrada's political party, Laban ng Masang Pilipino (Fight of the Filipino Masses). Other cronies had also escaped prosecution, including Jose Yao Campos, who owned the largest pharmaceutical company, United Laboratories, and real estate. Roberto Benedicto, who had the sugar monopoly under Marcos, under Estrada owned a major hotel and bank, Traders Hotel and Traders Royal Bank. Enrique Razon, who was considered the 'boss' of Manila's port, retained the International Container Service and also owned the newspaper, *The Manila Standard*. Lucio Tan had also retained his Fortune Tobacco company and Allied Bank. These were just some of those who benefited under Marcos' corrupt rule and who had maintained much of their fortune after his political demise (Lopez 1998; Tiglao 1998a).

On 19 January 2000, the head of the Philippine Stock Exchange, Perfecto Yasay, claimed that Estrada had told him by phone to exonerate Dante Tan, who was being investigated for stock manipulation. Tan was a friend of Estrada's (Saludo & Lopez 2000). A nun who was famous for her work with the poor in the Philippines, Sister Christine Tan, claimed that US$10.5 million intended for the poor went to projects headed by Estrada, his wife Maria Louisa and their son, mayor of suburban San Juan, Jinggoy Estrada, along with other officials. This left just US$1.6 million for the charity's intended beneficiaries (Lopez 2000b). Even in the Philippines,

Estrada's emptiness could not be hidden forever and, by late 1999, the popularity rating of the Philippines' most popular president ever had slumped (Crowell & Lopez 1999).

In the Philippines, it seemed that not much had changed. The elites remained entrenched, the rich remained rich, though with some small redistribution of wealth, the Philippines remained a poor country, and ordinary Filipinos reflected that in the poverty of their lives. The deep institutionalisation of what is basically feudalistic/hacienda power appeared to be the greatest legacy of the Philippines history as both a Spanish and an American colony.[6] When Filipinos, as a nation, were required to deal with complex issues, when aping the surface aspects of another culture were found to be inadequate, where others might draw down on a deep local cultural reserve, they found virtually nothing. The *tabula rasa* that the Spanish found, or more accurately created, left the Philippines hollowed out, lost for values and without a past of its own to draw on. The superficial reflection of this Spanish–American influence was interesting, in a 'colourful' way, and at times oddly comical in its malapropisms. But more importantly, and more deeply, the underlying reality of Philippine political society was and remains genuinely tragic.

NOTES

1   The similarities between the Philippines and, in particular, a number of Central American countries are considerable. These range from the structure of land ownership, to the disparities between rich and poor, to the lifestyles of the elites, to oligarchic structures, and to the problems all of this engenders.

2   That is, Moors, after the Islamic invaders of Spain from Morocco.

3   Marcos was re-elected as president in 1981, against what was in effect a non-existent opposition.

4   The Mindanao branch of the CPP/NPA arose largely in response to the depredations caused by the influx of the Philippines armed forces in response to MNLF rebellion.

5   'Hamburgers' are probably the single most popular food in the urban areas of the Philippines. However, these 'hamburgers' are usually just fried minced pork in a sweet bun.

6   Again, this can be seen in Central America, where USA influence has been pervasive.

13

Singapore:
The Corporate State

The Sunday shoppers bustled back and forth in the heat and humidity of the equatorial afternoon. The setting was Orchard Road, once a fashionable colonial boulevard but now the city state's best known shopping precinct, flanked by high-rise buildings and shopping malls of the type to be found in any modern city. Outside perhaps the busiest mall, Centrepoint, was a tall young man, conservatively but typically dressed in black lace-up shoes, pressed trousers and an open-necked white shirt selling books, exhorting passersby in a quiet voice, '*To be free.* Learn about Asia's struggle for human rights. *To be free.* Read about Singapore's longest serving political prisoner.'[1] The following Wednesday afternoon, the young man, Chee Soon Juan, secretary general of the Singapore Democratic Party, was led off to jail, sentenced to twelve days imprisonment during which time he would be in solitary confinement for twenty-three hours of each day. He was also banned from standing for Singapore's parliament for five years.[2] His wife had their first child while he was in prison, although he was not informed of the birth or the health of the mother and child until his release. His crime, the second same offence within two weeks, was to speak in public without an 'entertainment permit'.

The circumstances of Chee Soon Juan perhaps best reflect the state of contemporary politics in Singapore. Here is a state that is clearly successful at the economic level, having lifted its citizens out of developing country status within three decades. Yet the price of the material advance has been the institutionalisation of a political organisation which is more efficient and precise in its suppression of dissent than perhaps any other

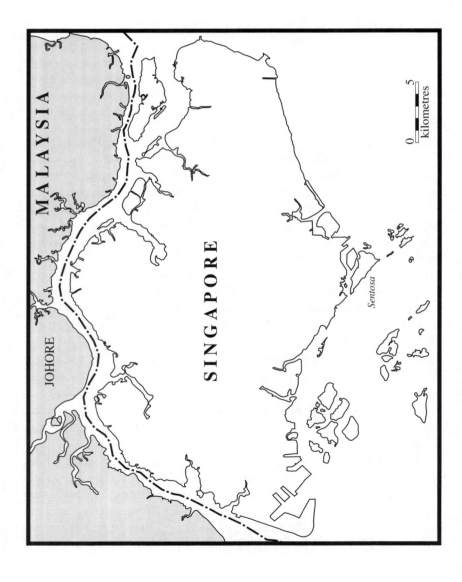

in SEA. According to Chee Soon Juan, although Singapore derives its political institutions from Britain, it offers 'not the rule of law, but rule by law'.[3] Having said that, most Singaporeans appear to be well satisfied with their lot, perhaps reflecting the effect of a successful process of hegemony and because all they want is a materially prosperous life. For those less satisfied, Singapore is a daunting place.

This chapter will examine Singapore as a corporate city state, which is dominated by an authoritarian one-party political system lightly masquerading as parliamentary democracy. In particular, it will outline the pre-colonial and colonial origins of Singapore and its post-colonial politics, both on its own terms and *vis-à-vis* Malaysia, with particular reference to the People's Action Party (PAP) and its continued domination of the political process. It will then note the economic policies of the state and how these have worked to build a backward entrepot centre into one of the world's leading per capita GDP states. Attention will then be paid to the reconstruction of Singapore's political identity as an explicitly non-liberal, non-Western polity, and the political adoption of (particularly constructed) 'Asian values'. It will conclude with an examination of the process of political exclusion, especially the use of the courts to demolish what little opposition there is, and the possibility for genuine political succession when Lee Kuan Yew finally leaves the political arena.

EARLY HISTORY

Singapore's pre-British history is not clearly recorded, although it is known that the island was at different times home to at least a couple of Malay polities. Chinese records referring to the island, known by them as P'u Luo Chung, date back as far as 231 CE, although that information is incomplete and suggests a lack of direct knowledge. In the eleventh century, the then flourishing empire of Sri Vijaya based in south-east Sumatra established an outpost on the strategically placed island they knew as Tumasik. One version of events has it that it was during a visit by a prince of Sri Vijaya, Sri Tri Buana. He sighted an animal that he confused with what was to Malays a mythical lion. Suitably impressed, Sri Tri Buana decided to settle there and found a kingdom, naming the island Singapura (Lion City). A substantial city was located in the area of colonial Singapore, which was noted by the Portuguese explorer Affonso de Albuquerque. It was, he said, 'a big town with a large population'. However, by the time de Albuquerque reached Singapore, he could only make his assessment based on the remaining ruins (Flower 1984: 5–6).

Another story notes that, as a consequence of conflict with the Majapahit empire of Java at the beginning of the fifteenth century, the ruler of Singapura, Paramesvara, fled to the mainland, founding the city of Malacca (Coedes 1968: 245). If not for its destruction at that time, Singapore might have become the great trading centre that Malacca came to be. Instead, it became home to 'sea gypsies' and a place of execution for the victims of pirates (Flower 1984: 7). The status of Singapore remained more or less unchanged until the arrival of Raffles, who is credited as the founder of the modern city state.

The island was a possession of the Sultan of Johore when Raffles first identified it as the location for a British outpost. Raffles was then in his prime, having risen quickly in the service of the East India Company, helping establish the colony at Penang and having been given the governorship of the Dutch East Indies during the Napoleonic Wars. He was knighted as Sir (Thomas) Stamford Raffles and, before returning to SEA, wrote a paper emphasising Britain's longer-term interests in trade with China. This included the necessity of occupying one of the strategically placed islands at the mouth of the main trade route of the Malacca Straits: either Riau or Singapura. The Dutch quickly claimed Riau, narrowing the choices. Raffles then headed for Singapura, landing there on 29 January 1819.

BRITISH PERIOD

Acting outside official British policy, Raffles entered into an agreement by which he would pay 3000 Spanish dollars a year in rent to the local Sultan, Had Wa Hakim. However, real authority over the island lay with the Sultan of Johore, who owed nominal allegiance to the Dutch. Raffles knew that the Sultan of Johore, who was allied with the Dutch, had seized the sultanate in dubious circumstances. Raffles had the legitimate heir, Tunku Long, returned to Johore and restored him to the throne, encouraging his acceptance of the position with a payment of 5000 Spanish dollars a year. Raffles then sealed a treaty with the new Sultan and left his second-in-command, Colonel William Farquar, as Resident and Commandant of Singapore. Raffles designated Singapore a free port, which was to have profound long-term implications.

The Dutch were, of course, furious with Raffles' move, claiming that Singapore was a part of Johore, which was in turn a dependency of the Dutch territory of Malacca. However, Dutch blustering was unable to be enforced, as Holland was then in a weakened military state *vis-à-vis* Britain. Britain itself was unable to negotiate the situation, as news of the occupation only reached there in September, by which time Chinese, Malays and Bugis traders were swarming into the new colony, seeking respite from Dutch limitations on trade. It was a classic *fait accompli*. When Raffles' superiors found out about the move they were disturbed, but traders were delighted. Official opinion quickly moved in behind commercial opinion.

By the 1830s Singapore 'acted as a magnet for the region's trade' primarily as a result of its free trade policy (Turnbull 1989: 100). Already attracting the local shipping trade, it increasingly attracted shipping from Europe, India and China, in the latter case mainly after the East India Company's monopoly was abolished. Further trading links were initiated in the following decade with southern Vietnam, Siam and northern Borneo. Between 1824 and 1868, Singapore's trade increased by more than 400 per cent, being valued at £59 million. As a trading state, its economy progressed in bursts, but the development of the steamship and the opening of the Suez Canal in 1869 established Singapore's central role in international trade. As Britain's main base in the 'Far East', Singapore was also vital to British imperial interests.

SINGAPORE AS CHINESE

Singapore was initially ruled from Bengal as a part of the British Empire in the 'East', but the Indian Mutiny proved the inappropriateness of this distant link. The 'Straits Settlements', including Singapore, Penang and parcels of land on the Malay Peninsula, were given self-rule in 1857. From around the 1860s, Singapore was the central point for the organisation of ethnic Chinese business interests throughout SEA—what has been referred to as the Nanyang[4] diaspora—and by the 1880s, the island had firmly established itself as the prime trading city in the region. It had become the headquarters for a number of shipping companies, businesses and trading agencies, and was central to financing and servicing the mining and agricultural industries in the Malay states (Turnbull 1989: 180). The sentiment in Singapore by this stage was that the city's success was 'self-engendering [and] that they were riding on a wave of destiny which could only lead them on to fulfilment. It was a moment of great excitement and self-esteem' (Flower 1984: 145). In a number of important senses, this sentiment has been reinvented in contemporary

Singapore. Singapore's government and, through its tight and pervasive control of information processes, its people, are again adept practitioners of the politics of self-congratulation.

As Nanyang, Singapore retained close links with China, and its ethnic Chinese population continued to consider themselves Chinese rather than Singaporean. Although there were domestic issues to unite or divide the local population, the issues which commanded the high ground of ethnic Chinese attention in Singapore were those which prevailed in China. The rise of the Republican movement in China spurred parallel interests among Singaporean Chinese, with a Chinese revolutionary group established in Singapore as early as 1906 (Bedlington 1978: 58). The establishment of the republican Guomindang (or Kuomintang, KMT) government in China in 1912 saw the founding of KMT branches in Singapore soon after. When the KMT finally managed to impose government on all of China, under Chiang Kai-shek in 1927, the first of Sun Yat Sen's *Three Principles of the People*, the indivisibility of Chinese people (and the rejection of foreign control), gave impetus to a Singaporean Chinese proto-nationalism. Although there was considerable anti-imperialist and nationalist activity in India, Indians in Singapore did not form themselves into political parties at this time. In part they were perhaps quietened by the failed mutiny of an Indian regiment stationed in Singapore in early 1915 (Turnbull 1977: 128–30). Similarly, ethnic Malays did not form themselves into formal political organisations in Singapore, not least because of the 'outsiders' overwhelming numerical majority. While politics—and trade—developed, so did Chinese language education, stressing Chinese culture and ignoring indigenous culture. Although this was to have been expected, it began to shape Singapore as an overwhelmingly and somewhat formal Chinese city (Turnbull 1977: 133–4).

The purge by the KMT against the Chinese Communist Party in China caused a similar split in Singapore. In 1929, the International Committee of the Communist Party (the Comintern) recognised the founding of the Nanyang Communist Party (NCP). The NCP and its related branch on the northern peninsula, the Malayan Communist Party, were based in the trade unions, among teachers and leftist intellectuals. The KMT appealed to more conservative and affluent Singaporean Chinese. Both parties received considerable impetus from Japan's attack on China in 1937. This rise in Chinese nationalism, reflected in the political activism of KMT and NCP/MCP branches, caused the British colonial government to suppress these organisations (Turnbull 1977: 134–7).

THE JAPANESE INTERLUDE

Launching from Thailand in December 1941, Japan's imperial forces struck down the Malay Peninsula in a manner that the British forces there could not comprehend. Singapore had been established as a major military base, but the view had always been that any threat to it would come from the sea. It was, the British presumed, safe from attack through the Malay Peninsula. As history shows, they could not have been more wrong. In less than three months after launching the beginning of their attack on Malaya, Singapore was surrendered to the besieging Japanese army. This event was significant for a number of reasons, but perhaps mostly because it marked the beginning of the end of imperial power in SEA and, consequently, the first step towards the dismantling of colonialism more generally (Turnbull 1977: 173–88).

The response of the Japanese towards Singapore's population was, by and large, brutal. After their experiences in China, the occupying force did not trust the ethnic Chinese and rooted out suspected opposition with great ruthlessness. Malays, on the other hand, were initially treated significantly better and were increasingly moved to occupy administrative posts, while some Indians also saw an anti-British advantage in cooperation with the occupying force. However, the use of Indians and Malays, as well as Chinese and prisoners of war, in slave-labour conditions shattered whatever bond might have been established between the great majority of both Chinese and non-Chinese Singaporean residents and the Japanese. Despite this treatment of local people, what was perceived to be collaboration between many Malays and the Japanese on the peninsula sparked anti-Malay violence in the immediate post-war period, which influenced ethnic Chinese thinking in Singapore. The split between the Malays and the Chinese, long submerged under a colonial policy of political representation for the Malays and economic development for the Chinese, broke through the surface. Singapore was not as affected as the peninsula but, as a predominantly Chinese city, it was regarded with suspicion and some hostility by politically organised Malays on the peninsula thereafter (Turnbull 1977: ch.VI).

POSTWAR SINGAPORE

Following the war, Britain moved relatively quickly towards establishing Singapore as an independent state. However, there was perceived to be problems from the beginning. Singapore was not regarded as materially viable apart from the mainland states, yet because of its overwhelming Chinese make-up it was regarded as being difficult to integrate. The former view came close to holding true, while the latter most certainly did. In order not to upset the ethnic balance within Malaya, Singapore was initially created as a separate Crown Colony, in April 1946. In this, the governor was supreme administrator and was supported by an appointed executive council and legislative council (Bedlington 1978: 199).

To ensure that Britain did not dawdle on the issue of independence, the Malayan Democratic Union was formed by a group of middle-class intellectuals while interred by the Japanese during WWII, officially launching itself on 21 December 1945. Its program was to end British colonial rule and to join Singapore and Malaya in a united state (Shee 1985: 3). Until the Malayan Communist Party (MCP) launched its armed revolt in 1948, the Malayan Democratic Union (MDU) and the MCP worked together. Lee claimed that the MDU was in fact just a political front for the MCP (Lee 1998a: 88–9). Meanwhile, other areas of political development proceeded apace. The Progressive Party was launched on 25 August 1947 (Josey 1970: 2–3). Britain had announced that it would encourage self-government in Singapore after the war was concluded, and by 1948 had begun to prepare for a fully elected legislature. The first elections, in that same year, were restricted to the island's 22 000 British subjects, disenfranchising most of Singapore's population.

Then in 1951 the colonial government moved towards establishing local government 'so as to popularise self-government at the grass-roots level'. In 1953 a review of the constitutional status of the colony was set up, marking another step towards the joint aim of granting independence and ensuring that Singapore remained non-communist in orientation. The British therefore looked for a suitable anti-communist leader. According to Lee Kuan Yew, that person was a young, independence-minded, British-trained lawyer and former black marketeer: himself[5] (Lee 1998b: 50; Lee 1998a: 72, 89–90). In 1954, with the support of Lim Yew Hock and another union activist, Fong Swee Suan, they formed the People's Action Party (PAP). The PAP was the first non-communist political party to capture the imagination and interest of a large number of Singaporeans. In 1955, as a consequence of the earlier constitutional review, Singapore's first Legislative Assembly was established, consisting of thirty-two members, of whom twenty-five were popularly elected. Ultimate power, however, in the areas of foreign policy, defence and internal security, remained with the colonial government (Shee 1985: 4).

The 1955 election was won by the Labour Front, under the leadership of David Saul Marshall, whose priority was to gain full self-rule. The

PAP won three seats in the Assembly, becoming the opposition. Marshall gained the expansion of the Legislative Assembly to fifty-one seats but, having failed to secure independence through negotiation in 1956, he resigned to lead the opposition Workers' Party. Lim Yew Hock, who was more compliant to Britain's wishes, became Chief Minister in Marshall's place. A more inspiring potential leader was the PAP's Lim Chin Siong who, during a time of strikes and riots against British rule, rallied support among ordinary Singaporeans. However, because of his leftist sympathies, he was repeatedly jailed by the British.

A SPLIT IN THE PAP

A delegation led by Lim Yew Hock and including Lee Kuan Yew succeeded in gaining Britain's agreement, in 1957, for a fully elected and more fully self-governing Legislative Assembly in 1959. The head of state under this system was to be the Yang di-Pertuan Negara, or the equivalent of the governor-general in other Westminster-styled parliamentary democracies. This person, appointed on the recommendation of the prime minister, in turn called upon that person who appeared most likely to command a majority in the Legislative Assembly to form a government and assume the position of prime minister. The prime minister in turn appointed the cabinet, which was responsible to the Legislative Assembly. In all, it was a conventional Westminster parliamentary model. The primary exceptions to complete self-rule under this agreement were that foreign affairs would continue to stay with Britain, while internal security would be maintained by an Internal Security Council, consisting of three representatives each from the Singapore and British governments.

It was at the time of a heated debate with Lee about the ideological future of the PAP that Lim Chin Siong was arrested under the ISA. With Lim in jail, this left the party in Lee's hands. In 1957, the left wing of the PAP rallied against Lee, but a continued British crackdown on alleged communists, including those within the PAP, ensured Lee's long-term control. Lee continued to rely on the support of his jailed party members in the lead-up to the 1959 elections, which would provide the island with its first government under independence. He even promised to have his left-wing factional allies freed from jail before taking office. But, just before the elections were held, Lee asked voters for an absolute majority for his right-wing faction of the PAP. The result was an overwhelming victory, with the Lee-dominated faction of the PAP taking forty-three of the fifty-one seats (Chee 1998: 249–53; Shee 1985: 5–7; Turnbull 1998: 264–70). Lee subsequently left Lim in jail.

There were numerous early debates about Singapore's status and its relationship with Britain. In 1960, as a consequence of these debates and the factionalism that inspired them, the Minister for National Development, Ong Eng Guan, was sacked from the cabinet and the party, precipitating a by-election the following year which he overwhelmingly won. Three months later, the death of a local PAP member of the Assembly led to another by-election, which was won by the leader of the Worker's Party, David Marshall. Among other things, Marshall demanded the abolition of the Internal Security Council, the dismantling of British naval facilities in Singapore, and complete independence. A final blow to the PAP came when, soon after, eight PAP members of the Assembly openly supported demands by six trade unionists for full self-government and resigned from the government.

In 1961, Lee formally split with Lim over their ideological differences, with Lim and the resigned MPs forming the Barisan Socialis (Socialist Front, or BS). The PAP members of the BS believed that they could not achieve power from within the party, but would be able to do so from outside. They also believed that Britain would not hinder their plans so long as British interests were not threatened.

SINGAPORE AND MALAYSIA

In 1961, the PAP strengthened its appeals to the British government to have Singapore included in or otherwise associated with the new Federation of Malaysia. Inclusion within Malaysia was, the PAP believed, the only realistic means of halting the increasingly popular BS from achieving government. Apart from diluting the political presence of the BS within a larger political framework, the PAP knew that federation with Malaya under a right-wing Alliance government would bring with it tighter internal security rules which would hamper the BS. However, within this framework there was a continuing desire by the PAP to maintain self-government in the areas of education and labour. The BS labelled the planned association a 'phoney merger'. Further, being aware that a conventional democratic process might not continue in the PAP's favour, by 1962, Lee was already talking about a specifically 'Asian' form of democracy[6] (Chee 1998: 254–5; Shee 1985: 6–7; Bellows 1970: 41–5).

In 1963, Singapore voted to join the Federation of Malaysia in what Chee has identified as a rigged ballot. Five days after the merger with Malaya went through, on 22 September 1963, the PAP called elections. With just nine days allowed for campaigning thirty-seven seats went to the PAP and thirteen to the less well prepared Barisan Socialis. The year 1963 marked the beginning of the end of a viable political opposition in Singapore.

The incorporation of Singapore into Malaysia had been opposed by both Indonesia and the Philippines, as well as by Singapore's own BS. Lee campaigned, in part, on a platform that said that 'a vote for the Barisan was a vote for Sukarno'[7] (Lee 1998b: 53). However, after the elections there were serious tensions in the relationship between Singapore and the rest of Malaysia. Lee continued to insist on using the title 'Prime Minister', which irked non-Singaporean Malaysians. Lee spearheaded aspirations on the part of the PAP to achieve government in Kuala Lumpur. This was the beginning of what was Malaysia's primary opposition party, the Singapore-linked Democratic Action Party (DAP). The Malaysian Chinese Association, a party in the Malaysian government's Alliance with the United Malay National Organisation (UMNO), had earlier sent organisers to Singapore to oppose Lee which also created tension. There were also ideological differences, with concern over what Lee acknowledged as Singapore's pursuit of perceived socialist-oriented policies (Lee 1998b: 51). And there was real concern over Lee's refusal to allow Singapore to become financially or politically subservient to Kuala Lumpur. Most importantly, there was long-standing concern among ethnic Malays that the inclusion of Singapore into the Federation would help to establish an ethnic Chinese majority in Malaysia. It could not, as only 42 per cent of Malaysians at that time were ethnic Chinese. But with ethnic Indians, the balance would have been enough to tip the ethnic scales away from Malay domination. Conversely, Lee Kuan Yew claimed that rather than aim to establish a multiracial society, UMNO was intent on establishing a society politically dominated by Malays. After the Malaysian general election of 1964 resulted in the defeat of PAP candidates on the Malay Peninsula, the five ministerial members of parliament representing Singapore were moved to the Opposition benches 'to join seven others already there' (Lee 1998b: 54).

In July 1964, events began to come to a head, with Chinese-Malay riots in Singapore. Over the course of three days, at least twenty-three people were killed, with a further 454 injured. Lee later blamed UMNO for being behind the riots to gather Malay support in Singapore and to consolidate support for UMNO on the peninsula. There were further clashes in August. In December, Malaysian Prime Minister Tunku Abdul Rahman told Lee that the constitutional arrangement which included Singapore in the Federation should be changed. Trade was to be independent but defence would remain Kuala Lumpur's responsibility, to which Singapore would contribute. Lee countered with the idea that the Malaysian and Singaporean governments should operate independently within their respective spheres of influence. 'Not surprisingly, we made no progress with the "rearrangements" ... What was suitable for Singapore was not suitable for Malaysia and vice versa. Merger had been a mistake' (Lee 1998b: 56–7). After ordering financial arrangements for its central bank, on 9 August 1965 Lee Kuan Yew announced in an emotional speech that Singapore had separated itself from Malaysia. A similar, and irrevocable, announcement was made in Kuala Lumpur at the same time.

POLITICAL LIMITATIONS IN SINGAPORE

From 1965, the PAP increased its use of the intelligence apparatus to watch the Opposition. The following year, when Chia Thye Poh was elected as a candidate for the Barisan Socialis, he accused the ruling PAP of harassing BS leaders. In response, Chia was arrested and jailed under the Internal Security Act until 1989. Even then, he was held under house arrest on Sentosa Island for a further two years and was thereafter banned from writing or publishing, travelling overseas without government per- mission, or belonging to any organisation (Chee 1998: 241–7). Following the arrest and detention of Chia, the BS withdrew from the parliamentary process, citing the impossibility of participating in the political environment while the PAP exercised regressive measures against duly elected members.

The by-elections of 1967, caused by BS resignations from the Assem- bly, gave the PAP forty-nine of the fifty-one available seats. In 1968 all fifty-one PAP candidates were returned unopposed. Five independents and two Workers Party candidates challenged seven PAP candidates, with the PAP candidates winning all contested seats. Singapore had started with thirteen political parties contesting the 1959 elections, and by 1970 a dozen parties were still registered although only one, the PAP, was viable. From then on the PAP completely dominated the political landscape.

One factor that did tend to aid the consolidation of power by the PAP was the 'siege mentality' engendered by the government in response to Singapore's economic development and, to some extent, to its changed security environment. Despite Britain's catastrophic 'defence' of Singa- pore in 1942, after the war it was rebuilt as a major British naval base. It became increasingly obvious, however, that Britain's time as a world and colonial leader was fast coming to a close. Britain maintained international military links as long as it felt able to do so, but World War II had ended Britain's period as a great power, both in an economic and military sense. As it shed its colonial empire, Britain also moved to reduce its overseas military commitment. By the late 1960s it had decided on a policy of withdrawing all forces 'east of the Suez', including withdrawing its forces from Singapore in 1971. While Britain's material withdrawal was replaced by the Five Power Defence Agreement,[8] Singapore, as a small and physically vulnerable state surrounded by potentially hostile states, had its sense of insecurity aroused by their leaving.

Although economic development during the 1960s was satisfactory, the withdrawal of British forces from Singapore also precipitated a rise in unemployment of approximately double, up to around 100 000 in a workforce of a little over 500 000 (Bellows 1970: 113–14). Singapore's already challenged political pluralism was 'regressing before the exigencies of economic survival'. Bellows pointed out that by the late 1960s Singapore was already choosing to go down an essentially non-democratic path. He noted in 1970 that a 'tightly organised society which demands order, discipline, involvement, and commitment on the part of each individual as the *sine qua non* for basic survival bodes ill for the continuance or renaissance of a competitive party system' (Bellows 1970: 114).

As early as 1960 Lee Kuan Yew had indicated that he did not think that democracy, in the conventional sense of one-person, one-vote, was suitable for developing countries, within which he included Singapore. He said that he believed for a government to at least give the impression it was effective it must be seen as enduring. In this sense, an effective government, according to Lee, could not be subject to the vagaries of the electoral process. 'If I were in authority in Singapore indefinitely without having to ask those who are governed whether they like what is being done, then I have not the slightest doubt that I could govern much more effectively in their interests' (Josey 1970: 8–10). These words, uttered in a radio interview in 1960, turned out to be prophetic.

While it is open to debate whether the PAP under Lee had governed 'in the interests' of all Singaporeans, it is true that Singapore did achieve remarkable economic development under his rule. The primary policy used to achieve this was a high level of government investment in and support for private industry, based on a high level of (enforced) savings (Low & Quan 1992: 15–27).

It is also true that, in practice, Lee and the PAP did not have to ask Singapore's people whether they liked what was being done. When some announced that they did not, in fact, like what was being done, they tended to be persecuted by the state through a variety of non-democratic means. According to Vasil, the PAP's leaders did not believe that a conventional representative democracy was workable in an economically developing society. 'The open and competitive system also had proved to be a source of special problems of political management in multi-racial societies. Furthermore, it was obvious that it acted as a barrier to rapid and substantial social and economic change and progress' (Vasil 1984: 115). And further, '... the PAP leaders were clear in their minds that they could not afford to allow any independent centres of power' (Vasil 1984: 117). Despite Singapore's undoubted economic development, this guiding philosophy has not altered since that time.

Lee went on to develop his views on autocratic government citing what he called 'Asian values'. He later modified this rather vague term to 'Confucian values', which he regarded as more culturally authentic and more closely fitting with Singapore's predominantly ethnic Chinese population. Within this idea, Lee identified loyalty to and the dominance of the group, respect for authority, and a paternalistic decision making process. Lee's understanding of Confucianism reflected the reinterpretation of Confucius under the Sung Dynasty, which wished to re-impose authoritarian rule in China. It was a very particular interpretation of Confucius, and certainly not the only one that was available. Lee adopted his version of Confucianism to suit his political style, employing it as legitimising rhetoric. In so far as Lee was criticised for this position, he defended himself and his political style by denigrating the circumstances and values of Western states, very often to the point of caricature.

Singapore unicameral parliamentary democracy has a maximum life of five years, although elections have generally been more frequent, maintaining the façade of democracy. A chiefly ceremonial president heads the state, while real power resides in the hands of the majority party of parliament. The PAP has always held the majority of seats, but from 1968 to 1981 held all seats, and has since then always held no fewer than seventy-seven of a total of seventy-nine available seats.

In 1990, Lee handed the prime ministership to Goh Chock Tong, but retained the title of Senior Minister Without Portfolio and, as chairman of the PAP, was seen to still control events in Singapore. Goh was regarded as a 'seat warmer' while Lee's son, Lee Hsien Loong, was being groomed for the prime ministership. However, in late 1992, Lee Jnr was diagnosed with cancer, throwing the future leadership of the PAP into some doubt. Goh secured the position of prime minister, even though Lee Jnr later entered into remission from the disease. At the beginning of the twenty-first century, Lee Jnr was again being touted as Singapore's next prime minister.

BEING IN OPPOSITION

Electoral support for the opposition party, the Singapore Democratic Party (SDP), was between 20 and 40 per cent of votes in seats contested and, at the end of the 1990s, appeared to be growing. This was a fairly remarkable achievement given the restrictions placed on the SDP by the government through its control of the media, its use of legal action against SDP members, its control of the grass roots Residents Committees, and its frequent recourse to changing electoral rules prior to elections.

That the SDP survived in such a climate of harassment and official surveillance was in itself remarkable, although party membership was limited to about 200 by the significant personal costs borne by not just membership but by association. 'With control of various organs of government in the hands of the dominant party or family, individuals participating in opposition politics are vulnerable to various methods that undermine their pursuit of public office.' These include public vilification, lack of recourse to action against attacks, defamation suits against critics of government members, contempt of court charges for criticism of the legal process, vigorous tax audits, and police surveillance, among many others (Lingle 1996: 22).

MAINTENANCE OF POWER

Methods of maintaining PAP political control were various, but three key points stood out as gross breaches of conventional democratic parliamentary behaviour. The first was the 'gerrymandering' of electoral boundaries. In this process, electoral boundaries of unsafe or challenged seats were reconfigured to isolate polling booths that returned a strong anti-government vote. The effect of this was to incorporate those anti-government areas into more strongly pro-government electorates, hence diluting the anti-government ratio of the vote, or fragmenting the growth of anti-government sentiment within a particular area. For example, the government altered the boundaries for electoral districts in October 1996, just three months before the 1997 elections.

The second key method for the government to maintain political control through the electoral process was to change the electoral rules just prior to elections, and sometimes after election campaigns had already commenced. For example, Singapore began as a one-person, per-seat parliamentary system, but later introduced Group Representational Constituencies, a multi-person, per-seat system. This system required a particular ethnic mix of candidates for certain seats, the ostensible intention being to guarantee proportional ethnic representation in the parliament. However, the short notice with which this requirement was introduced and the organisational difficulties associated with standing a pre-determined number of ethnically specific people in a particular seat presented major hurdles for opposition candidates to overcome. Under a conventional parliamentary system, if an individual candidate drops out he or she only invalidates their own candidature. Under the Singaporean system, if an individual candidate drops out of a multi-candidate team, the whole team is invalidated.

The third main method of maintaining political control was by instilling a degree of fear into the electorate. Residents Committees were used as a means of surveillance of disgruntled citizens and as a conduit for threats of loss of access to government services. An extension of this was that constituencies that vote away from the government were warned that their vote could earn them *en masse* a loss of government services. The Residents' Committees (RCs) and the more recent, government organised and funded Community Development Councils acted, in effect, like the grass roots or local branches of the PAP.

These RCs were formed in the numerous tower blocks which dominate much of Singapore's architectural landscape, which themselves lend a 'Brave New World' feel to the physical infrastructure of the city. Although not formally founded as a part of the PAP, the chairman of each committee is usually a PAP member or is otherwise linked to the network of patronage within the PAP. RCs are used for various purposes, including fundraising and as a means of 'vote buying' at election time. In this sense, there was a parallel between the RCs and village or neighbourhood committees in communist states or under the New Order government of Indonesia. Participation in RCs was encouraged by inducements, such as enhanced ease of access to municipal services (for example, educational facilities), and through localised public works (for example, footbridges, street beautification, local infrastructure maintenance). A negative inducement for staying away from RC meetings was increased difficulty of access to municipal services or, on a wider scale, a loss or relocation of public works.

As with most states that fail to distinguish between the party and the state, active participation in RCs or membership in the PAP by individuals in the civil service had a tendency to smooth career paths. Alternatively, non-particpation in RCs or the PAP, or, worse, opposition, quickly led to the discovery of a 'glass ceiling' to professional development. Loss of employment was not uncommon for government opponents. An employee so affected could not, in most cases, appeal to their union because there were few independent trade unions. Of the eighty-two unions that exist in Singapore, seventy-two were affiliated with the National Trade Union Congress (NTUC), which was closely linked to the government.

EMPLOYMENT

The relationship between the PAP and the NTUC was so close that it was described by both as 'symbiotic' (Wong 1992: 145). Indeed, the NTUC's general secretary, Lim Boong Heng, was at the end of the twentieth century also a PAP government minister, being Minister Without Portfolio (previously Minister for Trade and Industry). His predecessor, Singapore's President Ong Teng Cheong, was NTUC secretary general and Deputy Prime Minister simultaneously. As a consequence of the nominal nature of the trade union movement, there were no mechanisms for redressing worker grievances. To illustrate this point, if a worker or group of workers were sacked or retrenched, this occurred without notice and was done in such a way that the workers were individually removed from the workplace, meaning they could not share their grievances with other workers. Further, while not all employees were directly subject to the whims of the government, the government was the single largest employer in Singapore, with a majority of all employment made up between it and government-linked corporations or government-friendly multinational corporations.

Very little strike action has been taken by Singapore's workers in support of claims, the last such strike being in 1986. In part this reflected a relatively high degree of worker mobility, almost full employment and overall real wage growth. But in part it also reflected a controlled dispute management system, through the Ministry of Manpower and the Industrial Arbitration Court, and through the unwillingness of most unions to confront the government.

Because of a long-standing labour shortage, Singapore had about 460 000 'guest workers', constituting around a quarter of the total workforce. A great majority of these workers were unskilled labourers and many lived at or near their places of employment, often in substandard conditions. Of this group, there were about 100 000 maids in Singapore, mainly from the Philippines, Indonesia and Sri Lanka. Most maids worked from early in the morning to late at night and were allowed between one day off a week and one day off a month. Not including room and board, maids were paid around S\$250 a month (in 1999), although for the first few months of employment this was paid to a 'placement' agent. The cost of living in Singapore was at the level in which S\$250 would be considered about half of a low weekly income. Most low-paid 'guest workers' were not covered by the Employment Act and did not qualify for the free legal assistance that is available to citizens.

THE PRESIDENCY

While the position of president of the state in Singapore was not a powerful one—that was left to the Special Ministership and the Prime Ministership—the candidacy for becoming president was even more tightly controlled than for ordinary parliamentary constituencies. Strict prerequisites were required to be president, including having held one of several senior public offices which meant being appointed by a government minister, which in turn required at least total loyalty to and usually membership of the PAP. One exception to this requirement was the prospective candidate being the chief executive of a company with a capital value in excess of S\$60 million. All candidates had to be vetted by a three-person committee, of which two members were government appointees. Only around 400 Singaporean citizens could meet the first set of criteria for election as president, while applications by two opposition candidates were rejected by the three-person screening committee (Lingle 1996: 93).

Given these circumstances, while most Singaporeans are happy not to rock the boat, there has been some political disquiet. Criticism of the Singaporean government and the PAP has centred on its authoritarian style and its questionable dealings with political opponents. The government has employed the Internal Security Act to arrest people allegedly involved in subversion conspiracies, and in one case had a successful opposition candidate disqualified, in absentia, for income tax evasion —charges which were poorly supported in law. The ISA continues as a statute and may be employed against any person deemed by a PAP committee to have threatened the interests of the state (the interests of the state and the interests of the PAP usually being conflated).

The Singaporean government exercised relatively strict control over a number of elements of Singaporean life, including the media and, perhaps less importantly, public behaviour. Singapore has been an economic success, in large part due to activist government policies. 'The PAP has maintained its political dominance in part by developing genuine voter support through honest, effective administration and its strong track record in bringing economic prosperity to the country and, in part, by manipulating the electoral framework, intimidating organised political opposition, and circumscribing the bounds of legitimate political discourse and action' (US Department of State 1999b: 11).

But most Singaporeans seemed happy with their government and did not appear to feel a strong need for political change, which is even acknowledged by opposition activists. Indeed, they say, the prime concern of most is material development, with the maintenance of such being the first priority. Hence, if the government can deliver material development and challenging the government can remove it, there is considerable incentive for supporting the government rather than opposing it. Combined with the government's tight control over the flow of information and its own active information campaign, there has developed in Singapore what has been described as a fairly clearly defined sense of hegemony. Where a hegemonic framework can be said to exist in any politically stable society, in Singapore the presentation of its construction is very clear.

FREEDOM OF SPEECH

Perhaps the best known means of controlling dissent in Singapore is the use of law. The most common method of silencing dissent was to sue dissenters for defamation. In Singapore, defamation was equivalent to expressing disapproval of a member of government, the implication being that such disapproval somehow lowers the public standing of the politician. Fines in defamation cases commonly run to the value of between S$200 and S$500 000. In 1995, the *International Herald Tribune* was sued for a record (for a publication) US$678 000 in a highly publicised and, outside Singapore, doubtful defamation case concerning the political rise of Lee Kuan Yew's son, Lee Hsien Loong. The use of defamation damages was often enough to cause bankruptcy, which disqualified one from standing for parliament. The use of defamation was also usually sufficient to otherwise financially ruin the person so sued, and acted as a considerable disincentive to criticism of the government.

Following the 1997 elections, Workers' Party candidate Tang Liang Hong was sued for defamation by Goh Chock Tong, Lee Kuan Yew and nine other current or former members of parliament. Tang was ordered to pay a record S$5.77 million, while tax authorities also charged Tang with tax evasion. Tang subsequently fled to Malaysia. Tang's WP colleague, J. B. Jeyaretnam, was also sued for defamation by telling a political rally that Tang had filed police reports against 'Goh Chock Tong and his people'. In the first suit, Jeyaretnam was required to pay 10 per cent of Goh's damages claim and 60 per cent of his legal costs. Goh appealed and the figure was increased to half of his claimed damages and all of his legal costs.

The most significant element of 'free speech' was reflected in the mass media. In Singapore, however, the mass media was tightly controlled and the government 'intimidates journalists into practicing self-censorship. The Government's authoritarian style has fostered an atmosphere inimical to fully free speech and the press' (US Department of State 1999b: 5). One means of influencing the mass media, in particular the print media, was through the government's close ties to Singapore Press Holdings, which owned all the official language mass circulation newspapers in Singapore. The government also had veto over holders of management shares in the company, who in turn appointed all directors and staff.

While publications from Malaysia were banned, a wide range of other foreign newspapers and magazines were available in Singapore. However, these publications had to post a bond of S$200 000 and have a legal nominee. The government could also ban foreign publications under the ISA and Undesirable Publications Act, and limit the circulation of foreign publications under the Newspaper and Printing Presses Act. The circulation of *The Asian Wall Street Journal*, the *Far Eastern Economic Review*, and *Asiaweek* was limited, although approximated demand. However, this acted as a disincentive for the publications to be critical of the Singaporean government. The government also denied residency to a number of foreign correspondents, although it has become increasingly more lenient in this area.

The Singapore Broadcasting Authority regulated the broadcasting industry, including the Internet, from which it filtered material (almost entirely pornography). The government-linked company Singapore International Media has a near monopoly on broadcasting, operating all four free television stations and ten of the fifteen radio stations. Of the other five radio stations, two were operated by the Armed Forces Reservists' Association, two by the government-controlled National Trade Union Congress, with only the British Broadcasting Corporation World Service being fully independent of the government. A government-controlled cable service was also available and, while Malaysian and Indonesian services can be received, satellite receiving dishes were almost entirely banned (see also Gomez 2000: 41–54 for discussion of censorship in Singapore).

SPEAKING AS A POLITICAL ISSUE

Public speech was also tightly restricted, under legal provisions enacted by the colonial British government as a means of restricting communist dissent during the 1950s. Speaking in public required an 'entertainment permit', yet there was usually insurmountable difficulty in obtaining such a permit. Such difficulties vary from outright refusal to granting a permit at such short notice that it is practically impossible to organise the event to be addressed. In the 'free speech trials' of the Secretary-General of the Singapore Democratic Party, Chee Soon Juan, in January and February 1999, evidence was produced confirming that a refusal to grant 'entertainment permits', or refusal to grant them in a timely manner, for the purpose of political speeches was departmental (and hence government) policy. The ostensible reason for retaining this law was to guarantee 'public order'.

The requirement for an 'entertainment permit' seemed to contradict the Singaporean Constitution, which guaranteed freedom of speech. However, Singapore's courts ruled that there was no conflict between the permit requirement and the constitutional guarantee. It was an intentional irony that Chee Soon Juan's second public speech for which he was tried included that part of the Singaporean Constitution that guaranteed freedom of speech. Not surprisingly, government members were exempted from the requirements of this legislation and may speak in public at their whim, including speaking in what might be considered a defamatory manner against their political opponents.

THE LAW AND POWER

Beyond this, freedom of association was restricted by the government which required regular meetings of groups of more than ten people to be registered under the Societies Act. While this can and has been applied to restrict the forming of illegal associations, such as criminal gangs, it also prohibited organised political activity other than by registered political parties.

The Singapore government retains the Internal Security Act, which allows the indefinite detention without trial of a person charged under it. The ISA was introduced in order to combat the communist insurgency in the 1950s, although it has been used against non-insurgent political opponents. Similarly, under related provisions, the government or its agents can and do undertake a wide range of surveillance procedures, including tapping telephones and otherwise monitoring private conversations, as well as monitoring Internet usage. Numerous claims that the government routinely conducts surveillance of opposition figures was borne out in evidence presented in the second 'free speech' trial of Chee Soon Juan, when the public prosecutor led evidence outlining detailed and precise movements of two SDP party members. One was an alleged 'offender' having assisted Chee Soon Juan in speaking without a permit, while the other was not charged with any offence. Beyond that, Chee Soon Juan was clearly under surveillance by a government agent while he sold books in 1999. The real question about such surveillance, apart from its obvious misuse of a state aparatus to thwart democratic process, was whether it was made obvious in order to alert and therefore intimidate Chee, or whether the agents were simply inept at being discreet about their activities.

SEPARATION OF POWERS

Although Singapore claims to derive its political processes from Britain, its practices were very far from those of a functioning democracy in which all people are regarded as equal before the law and the law is applied in an even-handed manner. The use of the law for political purposes would not be a tool available to the government under the conventions of the Westminster parliamentary system, nor under any system which accepted the necessity of maintaining a separation of the roles and influences of the political executive and the judiciary—the so-called 'separation of powers'. However, under the Singaporean system, there was no effective separation of powers and, as a consequence, judges often handed down decisions based less on law than on political expediency.

Subordinate Court judges and magistrates, as with public prosecutors, had their area of operation determined by the Legal Service Commission. The Commission allocated judicial responsibilities and had the authority to transfer judges from the bench to non-judicial duties as a matter of bureaucratic decision making. The appointment of new Supreme Court judges required the recommendation of the Prime Minister in consultation with the Chief Justice. Subordinate court judges were appointed on the recommendation of the Chief Justice. According to the United States State Department, 'Many judicial officials, especially Supreme Court judges, have close ties to the ruling party and its leaders' (US Department of State 1999b: 4). The Singaporean Constitution also allowed the Prime Minister or the Chief Justice to convene a tribunal for the purpose of removing a judge on the grounds of misbehaviour or inability, although this had not been used.

What this meant in a practical sense was that for a legal worker to be appointed to a judgeship he or she must be accepted as trustworthy by the PAP. Future promotion depended on continuing to satisfy political as well as legal requirements. One judge who handed down a decision contrary to the interests of the government was quickly transferred into a bureaucratic position, which he soon resigned. The lesson to other judges was clear.

Beyond the threat and reward system of having judges hand down politically desirable decisions, and the appointment of 'suitable' candidates in the first place, was a type of legal hegemony. What this meant in practice was that there developed a kind of culture or world-view which regarded the PAP as not only the legitimate government of Singapore but also the 'natural' government of Singapore. That is, there could not really be an alternative. As a consequence, opposition figures and other critics were not legitimate political participants but troublemakers intent on accidentally or intentionally arousing antagonism and ill will. In a society that so highly valued order, critics of the government were implicitly culpable. In this sense, the letter or even the meaning of the law was less important than the 'common sense' of the judge as understood from a peculiarly pro-PAP perspective.

While judicial appointments were usually made on the basis of 'suitable' but otherwise anonymous candidates, it was not always so. In particular, there was the case where a long-time law school friend of Lee Kuan Yew was appointed to the High Court Bench and, within a year, was elevated to the position of Chief Justice, the most important legal position in the country. Lai Kew Chai had not practised law for twenty years (spending much of that time in business in Malaysia), and both his initial appointment and his quick rise to power shocked even Singapore's compromised legal fraternity. Not only was Lai a friend of Lee Kuan Yew, but he had formerly been employed as a lawyer with the Lee family legal firm, Lee and Lee. His appointment was a fairly blatant example of achieving pro-Lee/PAP political outcomes from ostensibly legally unbiased situations. 'The complicity of the courts' has been noted, by the US State Department and human rights organisation Asia Watch. 'Government leaders historically have utilized court proceedings, in particular defamation suits, against political opponents and critics. Both this practice and consistent awards in favour of government plaintiffs have raised questions about the relationship between the government and the judiciary and led to a perception that the judiciary reflects the views of the executive in politically sensitive cases.' (US Department of State 1999: 4). As one critic noted, 'the regime has a near perfect record in winning court cases against its opponents' (Lingle 1996: 92).

Interestingly, to say that the judiciary in Singapore is corrupt or unduly influenced by external powers is to beg being charged with contempt of court. In 1995 Dr Christopher Lingle and the *International Herald Tribune* were sued for contempt of court (as well as through a related defamation case) for suggesting that Singapore's courts were politically influenced.

CRONYISM AND CORRUPTION?

It is a truism in politics that a government too long in power will become corrupt. The temptations associated with the power of office are great, while the lack of needing to genuinely face a test of political popularity in a free and fair election means that corrupt activities will not have to be accounted for. Given the Singaporean government's propensity towards suing any person who suggests such misdeeds, there could be no claim here that the Singaporean government or its members are corrupt or engage in illegal cronyist activities. However, the family of Senior Minister (former Prime Minister) Lee Kuan Yew has done particularly well out of Singapore's economic development. It has been suggested that one of the reasons that the PAP is loath to even begin to allow a genuine opposition to become active in Singapore is because it could uncover activities which might not be regarded as strictly acceptable, most damagingly if the PAP was no longer in power.

One such incident, in which the family of Lee Kuan Yew did particularly well, revolved around the purchase of condominium properties called Nassim Jade in 1995. Shareholders of the public company Hotel Properties Limited were grumbling about what they perceived to be favours done for some people with political clout, such favours costing the company potential profits. Luxury condominiums, valued at millions of dollars per unit before the property value slump in 1998, were sold to the Lee family at a discount, while shareholders were waiting to pay full price for the same condominiums.

After an investigation, the Stock Exchange of Singapore publicly censured the company for not seeking shareholders' approval for the discounted sales. Dr Lee Suan Yew, younger brother of Lee Kuan Yew, was on the board of directors of the company, himself buying one of the properties. Other purchasers of the properties included another Lee brother, Freddy Lee and his wife Eleanor Ngo Puay Chin, as well as Lee Hsien Loong and Ho Ching, Lee's son and daughter-in-law. The Chief Justice of the High Court and close Lee friend, Lai Kew Chai, and his wife Dorothy Yip also purchased one of the condominiums. The cost of the condominiums was between S$3 342 800 and S$4 734 600, representing a discount of between 7 and 12 per cent. Even at 'soft launches' of property sales, a discount of 5 per cent was usually regarded as the maximum allowable. Lee Kuan Yew and Lee Hsien Loong also purchased two properties at another HPL development, Scotts 28, for S$2 791 500 and S$2 776 400 respectively, each securing a discount of 5 per cent. In total, Lee senior received discounts totalling S$416 252, while Lee junior received discounts totalling S$643 185. The total of the purchases amounted to more than S$10 million, yet no mortgages or loans were taken out to secure the purchases.

Other family members who were found to have made purchases in the Nassim Jade complex included Lee's daughter Lee Wei Ling, sister Lee Kim Mon and, as well as Freddy, another brother Lee Kim Yew (Dennis). Kwa Kim Li, a niece of Lee, and Lee's sister-in-law, Gloria Lee, also bought condominiums in the project at a discount.

Confronted with the evidence, Lee Kuan Yew openly admitted that he and his son, Lee Hsien Loong, were given preferential treatment in the purchase of the Nassim Jade properties. 'There is no way,' he said, 'and I say this with some sympathy for the young and aspiring professionals or young executives, for them to have the same value to a seller of a product as a well-known figure or sports star or a TV star' (*Business Times* 1996). Lee's response came after two newspaper editors told Lee that 'the fuss was over equity, not legality. The common grouse was that ministers, senior civil servants and MPs on the "inside track" were invited to soft launches, while ordinary folk had to queue' (*Business Times* 1996). 'It's a fact of life. There is no way of me having to join a queue to buy a house, or my wife,' said Lee. He also said that it was normal for a well-known or elite figure to receive preferential treatment in a variety of circumstances (*Business Times* 1996).

Despite the regional economic downturn, Singapore's major companies granted a number of board members big pay rises at that time. Kim Eng Holdings paid its board S$12.5 million, divided among eight board members. Its chairman, Gloria Lee, would have received at least S$1.5 million for her services. Similarly, Tat Lee Bank was given a banking licence in the mid 1970s, at a time when it was against government policy to grant private commercial banking licences. One of the directors of the bank was Lee Kim Yew. Despite a S$39 million—35 per cent—loss primarily due to unwise investments in Indonesia, directors were paid S$3 million. In December 1998, Tat Lee Bank was merged with the publicly owned bank Keppel. Tat Lee Bank's losses were not revealed until after the merger between the two. Similarly, the brokerage firm of which Freddy Lee was chairman was bailed out by the publicly owned Singapore Technologies in December 1998. Singapore Technologies' head is Lee Hsien Loong's wife, Ho Ching, who is therefore Lee Kuan Yew's daughter-in-law and Freddy's niece by marriage. (A Singapore Technologies subsidiary company is Chartered Industries, which is a major weapons supplier to the government of Burma.)

More notably, Lee's son, Lee Hsien Loong, joined Singapore's peacetime army at the age of twenty-six and, within five years, at the age of thirty-one he was promoted to the rank of Brigadier-General. Six months later he was elected to parliament and quickly rose through the party structure to become Deputy Prime Minister. Lee Kuan Yew sued the respected newspaper, the *International Herald Tribune*, for referring to the existence of dynastic politics in SEA, including in Singapore. Regardless of the competence, or otherwise, of a child of a political leader, their succession to leadership does reflect the creation of a dynasty.

Perhaps the most intriguing aspect of Singaporean politics was the question why, so long after Singapore has become established, its government continued to rule using such authoritarian methods. There are no simple answers to this. Some suggestions, however, have revolved around the personality and continuing political grip of Lee Kuan Yew, while others refer to the established style of the PAP, which remains dominated by Lee. Other responses include that Singapore's style of government genuinely reflected the wishes of the majority of its people. This may well be correct, although it did raise the issue of the extent to which political thinking in Singapore (so far as it exists at all) was shaped by four decades of one-party domination. A more subtle approach would talk of the creation of a hegemonic framework, in which economic reward, political pressure, the legal system, and the provision of information all worked together to create a sense of the status quo being the only way. In late 1998 there were faint signals that Singapore was about to begin experimenting with liberalisation, but they soon disappeared and were quickly buried by the re-emergence (and repression) of Chee Soon Juan and the SDP as a force to openly challenge the PAP.

In the 1960s and perhaps even into the 1970s, the PAP could legitimise some of its action on the twin grounds of the threat of communism, however shallow that had become, and the need to develop in economic terms. At the beginning of the twenty-first century, the political style of the PAP as Singapore's government was beginning to look arthritic.

NOTES

1   *To be free: stories from Asia's struggle against oppression*, by Chee Soon Juan, was published in 1998 by the Monash Asia Institute's publications committee, which was chaired by the author of this text. Chee was, at the time of publication, a Research Associate of the Institute.

2   This ban was later rescinded.

3   Stated in evidence during his second 'freedom of speech' trial, February 1999.

4   'Nanyang' was the term coined to denote the 'southern Chinese' community. It literally means 'Southern Seas'. While Singapore was and remains the outstanding example, other major Nanyang centres included Penang, Kuala Lumpur and Kuching.

5   Lee not only regarded himself as a suitable leader but also he came to identify his views and Singapore's interests as one and the same. Indeed, his failure to distinguish between himself and the state was reflected in the title of his autobiography, *The Singapore Story*.

6   Lee noted in his autobiography that as early as 1955 he had recognised 'the folly of adopting a democratic Constitution' (Lee 1998a: 271)

7   At this time, Sukarno was arguing that the creation of the federation of Malaysia was a product of neo-imperialism and proposed that Malaya be incorporated into a Greater Indonesia. The failure of this proposal led to the 'Confrontation' between Indonesia and Malaysia of 1963–66.

8   The FPDA was a formal alliance of Britain, Australia, New Zealand, Singapore, and Malaysia, intended to provide security for Singapore and Malaysia in the event of external aggression.

9   English, Chinese, Malay, and Tamil.

14

Indonesia: Diversity in Unity

The throng of happy, dancing, yelling people clogged the smoke-filled streets, banging drums and revving engines to a symbolic rhythm, with the procession of trucks, cars, motorcycles, and bicycles moving at less than walking pace. Virtually all were wearing red and particularly red T-shirts with the angry bull logo of Partai Demokrasi Indonesia—Perjuangan (PDI-P, or Indonesian Democratic Party—Struggle), and there were red banners everywhere. The mood was festive, with the atmosphere that of a street carnival. From the roof of a big hotel, the red banners and T-shirts could be seen streaming back from the Hotel Indonesia Circle along the main boulevards and side streets in every direction.

This extraordinary and overwhelming scene was the last rally of the PDI-P before Indonesia's first democratic elections in forty-four years. It was less a political rally than a celebration of the ability of Indonesian people to express their opposition to the government and their hope for the future. The final estimate was that more than one million people took part in the rally, a figure that matched the seemingly endless flow of humanity. It was Indonesia's biggest ever political gathering, and a massive display of political mobilisation. However, both PDI-P's biggest challenge and that facing Indonesia was less how to get people onto the streets, or even into the polling booths, than it was how to translate mobilisation into political participation, and then policy development.

To say that Indonesia is a large and complex place is but to gently scratch the surface of myriad cultures and societies, political and economic agendas and a geography which spreads itself across almost the entire width of southern SEA. Once a colonial empire, the post-colonial

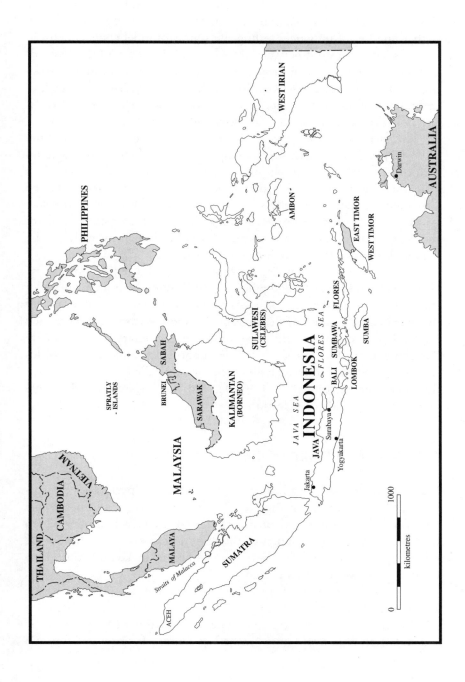

state reflects tensions both recent and old, local and global, and immediately pressing and deeply underlying. Since the collapse of the rule of President Suharto in May 1998, the state has ebbed and flowed along the shores of disintegration. Regionalism in particular has come to the fore, with a number of provinces testing the waters of independence. This in turn has led to tensions between the original inhabitants of these islands and the transmigrants who have come to comprise a significant proportion of their populations. Religious difference, too, has developed, as orthodox Muslims cling more firmly to their faith, while non-Muslims and non-orthodox Muslims seek answers elsewhere.

This chapter on Indonesia will briefly note the development of the idea of a pre-colonial archipelagic empire and its influence and move on to look at some of the implications of Dutch colonialism. It will then note the rise in 'Indonesian nationalism' and the construction of the post-colonial state as, in effect, a Javanese empire. Problems with this concept, reflected in regional rebellions, the rise of the political role of the army, and the suppression of regional political identity, will then be explored, along with competing political visions.

It will move on to look at how Suharto consolidated his power base both militarily, financially and politically (including the dismembering of the party system), the institutionalisation of high-level corruption, and the eventual beginnings of the division between Suharto and the armed forces. This then moves into the more contemporary period, where Suharto courted Islam as an alternative support base and the issue of his succession became increasingly the focus of political life. It will also cover the economic meltdown of 1997–98, and the period after the 1998 assembly and presidential elections.

PRE-COLONIAL HISTORY

Indonesia does not have a history as such before the period of colonialism, as the state known as the Republic of Indonesia is a post-colonial construction. Before the colonial period there were two empires which held sway over some or much of the region now known as Indonesia, but the greatest of these was short-lived and could make no lasting claim to suzerainty over the archipelago.

Human occupation of Java, the most heavily populated of the Indonesian islands, dates back well into pre-historic times, but began to develop most noticeably after the migration of ethnic Malays from the south-eastern region of China in the last century before the Common

Era. These migrants brought with them wet-rice agriculture, which was not only suited to the well-watered and fertile volcanic soils of the island but which also encouraged a relatively high level of population growth. It has also been suggested that this wet-rice agricultural system, which required the investment of labour in preparation and thus did not encourage social movement, either led to or allowed the development of a relatively permanent military–political elite (see Wittfogel 1957; Missen 1972: 51–2, 97–104). This gave rise to powerful and complex political structures which, being both centralised and relatively stable, developed an autocratic political form. Court life became increasingly removed from village life other than through the payment of taxes or tribute and acknowledgment of loyalty.

Along with the development of a centralised and sophisticated court structure came the adoption of a formalised and hierarchical religion, Hinduism, from around the second century CE. This was most fully established by the eighth–tenth centuries, including a brief encounter with Buddhism (which was viewed as a type of Hinduism). However, traders from both the Middle East, India and, increasingly, the Malay Peninsula, brought Islam to Java, which began to take hold from the fourteenth century (Caldwell & Utrecht 1979: 8–10; Grant 1966: 4–8; Geertz 1960: 121–5). The region of Central Java in the Yogyakarta-Surakarta-Kartasura area and to the near east, the most fertile and productive on the island, supported Java's most powerful rulers, the Sailendra, the early Mataram, Majapahit, and the late Mataram. What was most probably the first great sea power of the region, from the seventh to the thirteenth centuries, the Buddhist coastal state of Sri Vijaya on the Palembang river in southern Sumatra, challenged the land-based Javanese states for the greatest regional hegemony. The Sri Vijayan empire joined the Sailendras (Coedes 1968: 144–7, 248), leaving as their legacy the mighty Borobudur monument in central Java. But being a maritime state, Sri Vijaya also had to contend with other sea powers, including the rise of Malacca, and its fortunes declined while those of the succeeding Javanese rulers continued.

The Sri Vijayan empire, at its height, probably claimed suzerainty over most of Sumatra and the Malay Peninsula and perhaps some outlying islands. The greatest empire, however, was that of Majapahit, founded in 1293. At its peak it probably commanded loyalty from the whole of Java and Madura, much or all of Sumatra, northern and western Kalimantan (Borneo), Sulawesi, Maluku, Bali, Lombok, and Sumbawa. It also traded with and politically influenced the state of Champa on the Indo-Chinese peninsula and was politically involved with the precursor states of Cambodia as well as trading with the precursor states of both Thailand and Vietnam, and being acknowledged by China as a regional power. By 1389, however, Majapahit was in serious decline, though it struggled on for a little more than another hundred years (Zainud'din 1980: 48–51). Despite this relatively brief and ancient flourishing of empire, it continues to be portrayed in Indonesian schools as the precursor state to Indonesia.

TRADITIONAL POLITICAL POWER

Throughout this period, a particular political style emerged which continues to be reflected in contemporary Indonesian political development. That style acknowledged that political power, or just power, was both more complex than the European concept and that it was at another level more simple. In Javanese terms, the closest word to the English term 'power' is *kasekten*, which implies power, legitimacy and charisma. However, in contemporary terms, while this idea still has currency it has also been modified both by European political concepts as well as by the internally evolving state of Javanese (and Indonesian) thinking. The other significant aspect of *kasekten* was that it was without moral implications. That is, power was neither legitimate nor illegitimate; if it existed it simply *was* (Anderson 1972: 1–8; see also Moedjanto 1993; Proudfoot 1980; Zainud'din 1980: 97).

A related idea that continues to find reflection in contemporary Indonesian political thinking is that of the *mandala*. The Javanese conception of power dispersed towards the periphery and was 'fluid and unstable, always ready for dispersal and diffusion'. As a consequence, 'interstate aggression necessarily becomes a basic assumption about interstate relations' (Anderson 1972: 31). This 'doctrine emphasised the cult of expansion ... as the dynamic factor calculated to disturb the equilibrium of interstate relations. A state's belligerence is in the first place directed towards its closest neighbour(s) ...' (Moertono 1981: 71). If the *a priori* enemy of the state is its closest neighbour, Java is happier in a dominant rather than equal (or power sharing) role within the wider modern state. Implicit in this conception is the idea that Indonesia is therefore not a state in which all parts are equal, but rather it suggests that Indonesia is a reinterpretation of a Javanese empire.

Related to this mandalic conception of the state is the idea that, personifying the state, the president finds a parallel with former monarchs. The office of the monarch was exemplified by the person of the monarch, thus making the person of the monarch the centre and source of power, authority and legitimacy. Similarly, the office of the president is at the centre of Indonesia's administrative structure, with authority, legitimacy and at least nominal power being held by the person of the president. Sukarno adopted this posture, particularly from the late 1950s until political circumstances began to slide from his grip after October 1965, while Suharto increasingly did so also towards the end of his rule. But like earlier monarchs, both presidents had to balance the competing forces that comprise the *kraton* (palace), or the body politic. Both ultimately failed. Suharto's eventual successor as president, Abdurrahman Wahid, reflects a more benign version of that style of power.

RELIGIOUS DIFFERENCE

The spread of Islam through the Indonesian archipelago varied in intensity and reach. Some regions, such as Aceh in northern Sumatra, were deeply influenced by Islam as were parts of Java and Madura. However, inland Java and a number of other islands remained inured to Islam's reach or appeal. As such, a number of outlying islands or more remote regions retained their earlier religious practices, such as Hinduism in Bali and animism in a number of other areas. Where animism predominated Christianity, following colonialism, tended to take root. Within Java and to a lesser extent Sumatra, Islam fell into two broad camps, being formal (*santri*) Islam and informal or nominal (*abangan*) Islam.

In part the less formal *abangan* interpretation of Islam can be attributed to the mystical Sufi version which made its way from India to the region. But perhaps the traditional resilience and syncretism of pre-existing Javanese animist beliefs are more responsible for the distinction between those who profess a formal Islamic belief and those who are more nominal. In the provinces last to be colonised, animism remains a dominant religious form although it is not formally accepted by the government, which requires people to profess Islam, one of two forms of Christianity (Protestantism or Roman Catholicism), Hinduism, or Buddhism.

The rise of Islam as a political force in Java was at its most developed during the period of the Mataram empire. Mataram can be traced back to the Hindu kingdom of the seventh century, flowing and ebbing over the following centuries and reaching its final peak as an Islamic sultanate in the sixteenth–seventeenth centuries, when it dominated all but the western edge of Java, as well as the nearby northern island of Madura. At this time, the sultanate of Aceh was at its most powerful, dominating the north-western end of the archipelago, while the sultanate of Ternate, a

small island in the Maluku group, dominated the east. The rise of
Mataram might have continued unchecked except that the period of its
ascendancy coincided with the arrival of the Dutch at Banten.

Until well into the period of Dutch colonialism, the basic unit of
social and political life for the vast majority of Javanese (and others of the
archipelago) was the village. Being a small and relatively closed unit, the
village encouraged mutual participation, consensus as a decision making
process, and a disinclination to air grievances publicly. Given that the vast
majority of the population lived in villages and that moving from villages
to cities in substantial numbers is a relatively recent phenomenon, it is
unsurprising that many village customs live on. This aspect of traditional
life finds a particular reflection in the Indonesian political system, which
both officially and unofficially regards conceptions of individualism and
the rights of the individual as having little correspondence with the
'traditions' of the state.

THE COLONIAL PERIOD

The influence of the Dutch on Indonesia's political development was
important in two respects. In the first instance, through the colonial
experience, the Dutch geographically defined what was to become
Indonesia. The Dutch also restructured the ruling elites to serve their
colonial interests, helping to re-invent and re-impose elite privileges
beyond traditional limits, the influence of which remains.

The initial goal of the Dutch in what they termed the 'East Indies'
was to seek spices and other tradeable goods, as well as routes through to
and from China and the Pacific. In 1602 the Dutch East India Company
(Verenigde Oost-Indische Compagnie—VOC) was established, initially
based at Banten on the western edge of Java, although in 1619 the Dutch
seized Yacatra (Jakarta), renaming it Batavia, on the north-west coast of
the island. From here they could trade with the other islands and further
afield, as well as counter the strategic Portuguese stronghold in Malacca,
which the Dutch captured in 1641.

The Dutch quickly recognised Java as a potentially rich colonial
'resource'. Although the Dutch had some technological and military
advantages over the Javanese, the primary method of political and military control by the Dutch was to play off royal Javanese households
against each other or to exploit divisions within them (Ricklefs 1993a:
147, 1993b). Those royalty who sided with the Dutch or agreed to
Dutch terms remained intact and continued to exercise rule over vast

tracts of the island; those who did not were subjugated. Even though the royal houses of Java remained, the Dutch were the real power behind the various thrones.

The economic system employed by the VOC relied on a monopoly of trade and coerced cash-crop (*preanger*) bonded labour on coffee and sugar plantations throughout those parts of the archipelago it controlled. But due to corruption, mismanagement, piracy, and changing patterns of trade, the economic fortunes of the VOC steadily declined. When the company's charter expired on the last day of 1799 it was not renewed (Caldwell & Utrecht 1979: 14–15; see also Geertz 1963: ch. 4). Britain by this time had begun to move into the region and, following Holland's subjugation during the Napoleonic Wars, Britain occupied and administered the East Indies from 1811 to 1816. The consequent Anglo–Dutch Treaty of 1824 reflected the growing Dutch hegemony in Java and Sumatra and the British control over the Malay Peninsula, formalising the situation and requiring the British to vacate the footholds it had gained on Sumatra, while the Dutch abandoned Malacca on the Malay Peninsula. The effect of these changes was to formally partition the Malay world along the Straits of Malacca and (from 1912) through northern Borneo, defining the borders of the post-colonial state.

Following economic and military catastrophes in Holland, and the devastating Java War of 1825–30, in 1830 the Dutch raised the Royal Netherlands Indies Army (Koninklijk Nedlandisch Indisch Leger—KNIL), which was largely manned by outer islanders and was used to quell uprisings in other parts of the archipelago. The KNIL later constituted a significant basis for outer island opposition to the government of what was then the new republic. The Dutch also introduced the *cultuurstelsel* (cultivation system), a more systematic, methodical and widespread form of the *preanger* system (Geertz 1963: ch. 6). Under the *cultuurstelsel* Javanese peasants were obliged to grow commercial crops for the government on one-fifth of their land, although in reality it was often two-fifths or more. Further, though earlier Dutch (and British) administrations had attempted to limit the power of the *priyayi*, or traditional aristocracy, under the *cultuurstelsel* their rights were not only restored but reinforced, rewarding both Dutch and *priyayi* supervision of the system with a percentage of profits. It also introduced government more directly into the affairs of villages, which had previously been left relatively untouched. This detached the *priyayi* from ordinary Javanese society and removed the restraints upon them which had been applied under *adat* (traditional law) (Ricklefs 1993a: 121–2). This exaggerated status of the elites, made all the more tense and brittle by their lack of real power, carried over into modern Indonesian interpretations of the methods and extent to which power could be 'legitimately' employed.

THE LATE COLONIAL PERIOD

Between 1856 and 1865, the *cultuurstelsel* system was abandoned and increasingly replaced by private capital. This thus set the scene for more fulsome colonial economic exploitation in the latter part of the nine-teenth century and the first four decades of the twentieth century (Caldwell & Utrecht 1979: 18–22).

While Dutch political hegemony was well established in Java and much of Sumatra by the nineteenth century, its control over the wider archipelago was not fully achieved until the early twentieth century. Aceh maintained its political integrity when deprived of British protec-tion in 1871, holding out until 1908. Bali was occupied in 1906 and eastern Nusa Tenggara, inland Kalimantan and Sulawesi were effectively ignored until being 'pacified' between 1900 and 1910 (Grant 1964: 14). This completion of Dutch domination over the East Indies had a number of consequences, one of which was to transport indigenous troops from one area to assist in repressing the peoples of another. This had the effect of spreading the old, simple Sumatra–Melayu-based trad-ing language of market Malay. Increased trade between the islands also furthered the development of this language and, already the most common language between ethnic groups, it increasingly became the lingua franca of indigenous Dutch East Indians wishing to communicate with each other, providing the disparate ethnic groups with their first sense of common identity.

In response to humanitarian indignation in Holland and a decline in the well-being of the local population, early in the twentieth century the colonial authorities also introduced what was called the 'Ethical Policy'. This policy had its most important impact in the field of education, which had the benefit of training indigenous peoples to assist in the rapidly growing primary sector of commercial cropping. One main con-sequence of this rise in educational levels of indigenous peoples was the growth and influence of Western educated local people, who began to question and rebel against the caste structure implemented by the Netherlands East Indies authorities. Thus was born the beginnings of Indonesia's independence movement.

TOWARDS INDEPENDENCE

Despite some changes in form, the Dutch pre-WWII administration within the East Indies retained a paternalistic ethos and continued to be both unitary and centralised in its political structure. The Japanese occupation of 1942–45 further entrenched this and, as a consequence, the political characteristics of paternalism, unitarism and centralism deeply influenced the new Republican government not only throughout the 1950s (and especially after the proclamation of 'Guided Democracy' in 1958), but into and throughout the New Order government of Suharto after 1966.

One notable influence of the Japanese was that they founded organisations which would play a key role in the establishment of the republic. For propaganda purposes the Japanese brought together the major Islamic organisations, notably Muhhamadiyah and Nahdlatul Ulama, under the umbrella group Masyumi, which later became a significant political player. They also trained Indonesian youths in Islamic and nationalist military units, both to police the colony and to assist in fending off expected Allied attacks. By 1943, there were over 35 000 men in the Javanese auxiliary army alone (Feith 1969: 198). This organisation, the Volunteer Army of Defenders of the Fatherland (Tentara Sukarela Pembela Tanah Air— Peta) was to become the basis of the revolutionary army and later the foundation of the army (Angkatan Bersenjata Republik Indonesia or ABRI, from 1999 Tentara Nasional Indonesia or TNI). Another impact of the Japanese military influence, which Mangunwijaya described as 'fascist' in character,[1] was to bring to Indonesia's incipient armed forces a notion that society could and should be controlled, and that the armed forces should be allied with government in closely directing and controlling Indonesian society (Mangunwijaya 1992: 6).

Under mounting pressure from nationalist leaders, but probably more as an attempt to forestall Allied military advances in the Pacific, Japan encouraged moves towards Indonesian independence. Two days after Japan surrendered, on 17 August 1945, Sukarno and Hatta proclaimed the Republic of Indonesia, of which Sukarno was to be president and Hatta vice-president, with an advisory Central National Committee of 135. The republic received almost immediate widespread support in the former colony and by the end of September had obtained arms from surrendering Japanese soldiers to battle the Dutch and possibly the Allies in the period after the cessation of hostilities with Japan.

THE REPUBLIC

The Constitution of the Republic, referred to as the 1945 Constitution, which was proclaimed at that time, was a short and in many respects ambiguous document, the intention being that it allowed considerable scope for decision making on the part of the President. The Constitution vested primary authority in the person of the president, who selected a cabinet and directed the affairs of state. The Constitution was changed in 1949 and again in 1950, to vest authority in the cabinet, with the Prime Minister being the senior office holder. This accorded with the 'parliamentary democracy' period of 1949–57. However, following the move towards 'Guided Democracy' from 1957, in 1959 the 1945 Constitution was re-adopted in the final act of abandoning the authority of parliament, the party system and democratic processes. It is the 1945 Constitution, slightly modified, that prevails still.

NATIONALISM

While Indonesia as a state has a clear association with the former colony of the Dutch East Indies, the Dutch considered the colony a group of essentially separate subcolonies linked to the administrative centre of Jakarta. This was the case with Irian Jaya, or West Papua, which remained a separate colony until 1963, with formal incorporation in 1969. In creating the state, one influential school of thought (nominally led by Sukarno) in Indonesia's formative period took a larger view, incorporating not only the whole Dutch colony and Portuguese (East) Timor but also the Malay peninsula, northern Borneo and even the Philippines. As it transpired, the greatest conception of the Indonesian state was not to be, although the state as it now exists is larger than many imagined it would have been, particularly among those regionalists who retained aspirations to local autonomy or independence.

Yet while there remains considerable regional identity throughout Indonesia, there is also a strong identification with the concept of the Indonesian state as it currently exists. This has in large part been brought about by the standardisation of a common, if synthetic, language, Bahasa Indonesia (Anderson 1990: 123–51), and the imposition of a 'national' culture (see Atkinson 1987; Tsing 1987: 196–200). The efforts of both the Sukarno and the Suharto-led governments further assisted in cementing the idea of Indonesia in the minds of ordinary Indonesians. This national culture, however, strongly reflects aspects, often reconstructed, of the political culture of Central and Eastern Java. That aspect of Indonesian culture which relates to a confluence of a Central Javanese understanding of power, received its modification under Dutch colonialism, with borrowings from the Western tradition of the nation state, and the exigencies of the survival of both the nation state and its elites. This political structure was then effectively imposed on the state as a national ideology.[2]

This national ideology is called the Pancasila (the five principles), which exists alongside the 1945 Constitution. The five principles are social justice, a just and civilised humanity, belief in one god, Indonesian unity, and government by deliberation and consent. However, the wording of the five principles has changed since they were first enunciated, for example with government by deliberation and consent originally being interpreted as the people's sovereignty, while unity was interpreted as nationalism. These interpretations are not necessarily contradictory, but they do allow considerable scope for the derivation of meaning.

The 1945 Constitution, which was to have been temporary, was replaced, twice, although its replacements were themselves also short-term documents, looking forward to the creation of a more complete and representative document. However, because the 1945 Constitution places considerable power in the hands of the president and because it is both short and ambiguous, it is highly interpretable and has been claimed to mean many different things since it was reintroduced by Sukarno to help usher in the period of 'Guided Democracy'. Like his predecessor, Suharto also viewed the 1945 Constitution as a suitable vehicle for a strong presidential rule. And as with the Pancasila, strict adherence to the 1945 Constitution is required by all Indonesians. Yet what is required to be adhered to has shown itself to be indistinct and quite politically malleable.

THE REVOLUTIONARY PERIOD: 1945–49

While the Republic of Indonesia was proclaimed on 17 August 1945, it was clear from the outset that such a unilateral declaration would still need to be 'negotiated' with the former colonial power. Given the manner in which WWII had been fought, the Netherlands government and those of the Allies initially regarded the establishment of the Republic as an instrument of Japanese warfare, which, from the Japanese perspective, was correct.

Allied, mostly Australian, troops had been involved in 'mopping up' campaigns in the outer islands in the final months of the war and upon the cessation of hostilities moved to take authority from the defeated

Japanese. Within weeks British troops had begun to land in Java and Dutch troops began to return soon after, assuming the role they had occupied before the war. At the same time, local units loyal to the Republic had begun seizing arms from surrendering Japanese. In this situation, where authority was claimed by two armed groups, fighting inevitably broke out between the Republicans and the British, particularly in Java and Sumatra.

Within the Republic, there were political and administrative changes to make it more effective and, recognising the different sources of nationalist sentiment, there was a call for the establishment of political parties. Of the major groups, one was Masyumi (Consultative Council of Indonesian Muslims) which was led by both wartime Masyumi members as well as newer members. Another was the Indonesian Nationalist Party (PNI) which was led by many of the older leaders established by Sukarno in 1927 and who were active under the Japanese administration, and, finally, there was the Socialist Party (PSI), which had a strong youth wing. The Indonesian Communist Party (PKI) was also re-established and a number of smaller parties, often nationalist–communist in orientation, also sprang up.

The period from 1945 to 1949 was marked by both negotiation and fighting. The Dutch military forces were stronger in the cities and surrounding areas but had little influence in the hinterland. By the middle of 1947, the Dutch had 150 000 soldiers in Indonesia and, with the negotiations failing, launched a full-scale attack on the Republic. The United Nations Security Council pressured the Netherlands to settle, while within the Republic the more radical, anti-negotiation socialist Amir Sjarifuddin headed the cabinet.

In August 1948, the communist leader Musso returned from a twenty-year exile in the Soviet Union and welded together the fledgling republic's left-wing parties into an expanded and significantly more influential Communist Party, which he headed. Sjarifuddin's cabinet was replaced by a moderate Masyumi–PNI coalition. In response, in September a group of second tier leaders in the PKI at Madiun in Central Java announced a revolt against the Sukarno–Hatta government, believing the new government would move to disband local communist-led armed units (Hindley 1964: 21). The Republic's army attacked the rebels and Musso, Sjarifuddin and a number of other senior leaders were killed in the following weeks, all of which constituted a severe blow to the PKI. The Madiun Affair, as it was called, was regarded by the Republic's regular army as treachery during hostilities with the Netherlands. It marked the beginning of a distrust between ABRI and the PKI which culminated in the events of 1965–66.

A second major attack by the Dutch in December 1949 resulted in military successes on the ground but also in increasing pressure from the UN and in particular from the United States, through its post-war Marshall Plan, to resolve the dispute. In November 1949, the Netherlands agreed to a settlement in which fifteen outlying, Dutch created, states would come together with Java and Sumatra in a federated Republic of the United States of Indonesia (RUSI). The creation of the outlying states accurately reflected local conditions and loyalties, as well as the Netherlands' conception of its colony as comprising a number of smaller colonies rather than being a large, unified colony. But it was an unworkable structure if the state was to remain intact. The republic was also required to assume the Netherlands' East Indies debt of 4300 million guilders, of which 1291 million guilders (US$339 million) was external debt repayable in foreign currency (Feith 1964: 203). From the very beginning, Indonesia's economic position was compromised, a situation which was exacerbated in the following decade by questionable economic decision making and management, and which pushed the state to the brink of self-destruction.

INDEPENDENT INDONESIA: 1949–65

On 27 December 1949, Sukarno was sworn in as President of RUSI, while Hatta was chosen as Prime Minister. The cabinet reflected ministers from Masyumi and PNI as well as non-party ministers, and five ministers chosen from the federal states. But federalism was quickly abandoned.

Sukarno's vision for the state as manifested in government policies was not universally accepted, particularly as it focused not only power but also economic resources in Jakarta, and thence Java, at the expense of the wider archipelago. Divisions in Indonesian politics therefore date back to the first years of the struggle for independence. In order to address these divisions, and to develop a state ideology that not only drew on traditional political forms but incorporated modern political concepts, Sukarno included a clearly defined version of nationalism into his conception of politics.

Sukarno's nationalist aspirations for Indonesia were shared by many intellectuals and by the newly emergent armed forces, but among the peoples of the former Dutch colony there was at least as much to separate as to bind. With the abandonment of the 1949 Constitution in 1950, former KNIL troops on the island of Ambon in the Maluku group raised themselves in revolt against the central government until defeated towards the end of the year. More significantly, from 1950 there was a fundamentalist Islamic rebellion, known as the Dar'ul Islam Revolt, in West Java,

South Sulawesi and Aceh. In this case, the rebellion was based on irregular Islamic military units that had been fighting since the Japanese occupation as well as later against the Dutch. These militant Islamic groups had always been outside the control of the central government and were unwilling to bow to central government directives. By December 1948, the Islamic guerrillas, under Kartosuwirjo, proclaimed the Negara Islam Indonesia (Indonesian Islamic State). Kartosuwirjo announced that the republic had ceased to exist and that the NII was the true embodiment of the revolution. After Indonesia gained practical independence in 1949, the so-called Dar'ul Islam (Islamic state) movement continued to defy the central government, at times extending its influence into Central Java and over Aceh and much of South Sulawesi. The Dar'ul Islam rebellion probably had most impact in the period from 1957 until 1961, largely as a reaction to the growing influence of the PKI in government. It also received a significant boost when rebels in South and Central Sulawesi joined the movement in 1952 and 1958 respectively, having been in their own state of rebellion since 1950. With the capture of Kartosuwirjo in 1962 the movement in West Java was militarily wiped out. The Dar'ul Islam revolt was Indonesia's longest sustained rebellion.

While the Dar'ul Islam revolt had never threatened the cohesion of the state of Indonesia in the way that the PRRI-Permesta rebellion of 1957–58 did, even into the late 1990s there were signs that the values which engendered it—primarily a desire for an Islamic state or independent Islamic states and a distrust of the central government in Jakarta—were still strongly held (notably in Aceh). Other inter-ethnic clashes took place throughout Indonesia, particularly after the fall of Suharto in May 1998. Thousands of people were killed in these riots and damage to property was often devastating.

While the commitment to liberal democracy in the years from 1949 until the middle to late 1950s was less than total, there was a practical adherence to democratic forms. In 1952, the Nahdlatul Ulama (NU— Awakening of Religious Scholars) left Masyumi, embarking as a political party in its own right. This division in the Islamic vote reflected deeper tensions between Indonesia's Islamic organisations and how Islam was viewed, particularly in Java. However, despite the Islamic parties' stated desire to create an Islamic state, they remained a part of the democratic political system. One consequence of the Republic's commitment to democratic processes, combined with the Republic's multi-party system, was the regular rise and fall of coalition governments which divided over a series of issues. This constant division, lack of political stability and tendency to compromise created an inability to engage in forward economic planning. Tensions grew between two broad groups within the political system, outlined by Feith and referred to as 'administrators' and 'solidarity makers' (Feith 1962) as the sometimes chaotic events of the 1950s began to unfold.

Even from the earliest days there were major political difficulties. The political consensus which had marked policies until that time began to fall apart, with the party's positions becoming polarised. On one side, there was Masyumi, the Socialists and the two small Christian parties (Protestant and Roman Catholic); on the other side was the PNI, the PKI and several smaller parties. Political differences hardened and, by the time of the elections of December 1955, political bitterness including a marked split between Masyumi-supporting *santri* Muslims and the PNI-supporting *abangan* Muslims had become extreme. Political consensus was effectively dead, government bureaucracy had divided along partisan lines, and increasingly there was a view that an alternative political system had to be found (Feith 1964: 204–7).

In December 1956, matters worsened, highlighting the division between both the centre and the periphery of the republic, between Javanese and non-Javanese Indonesians, between former revolutionary soldiers and former members of KNIL who were incorporated into the Indonesian army, and between the two main political groupings. Blood-less coups were enacted in the three provinces of Sumatra, in which newly established 'revolutionary' councils headed by indigenous (often former KNIL) army officers claimed power, rejecting the central government and accusing it of excessive bureaucracy, over-centralisation, neglect, corruption, and being too tolerant of the PKI. To effect their de-recognition of the new government, the officers channelled exports directly to world markets which, along with extensive smuggling often sponsored by army units, deprived Jakarta of foreign exchange. In March 1957 a similar bloodless coup gave power to an army-led council in East Indonesia (Sulawesi, Maluku and Nusa Tenggara). The outer islands thus came to most strongly represent Masyumi-Socialist interests, while the centre was more strongly PNI–NU–PKI.

Of all the events of the 1950s, perhaps the most important was the effective nationalisation of Dutch property in 1957, which was formalised in 1958. This nationalisation of Dutch interests was ostensibly a response to a failed UN bid to settle the outstanding problem of the incorporation of Dutch New Guinea into the Republic, as well as to end Dutch 'economic imperialism'. The process of nationalisation of Dutch interests had the combined effect of halting foreign investment in the Republic and cutting shipping within the multi-island state by the

Dutch-owned shipping company, KPM (Koninklijke Paketvaart Maatschappij), which had provided about three-quarters of the transportation between the islands. The economy, saddled with debt from the outset, plagued by unstable government and almost no economic policy, slid further and further into ruin.

'GUIDED DEMOCRACY'

When the Ali cabinet resigned in March 1957, the seventeenth cabinet since 1945, parliamentary democracy was finally abandoned and Sukarno's 'Guided Democracy' was adopted in modified form. Along with 'Guided Democracy' came martial law, on 14 March, strengthening the position of the army's central leadership under its chief of staff Major General Abdul Haris Nasution. This provided legal grounds for army intervention in civil affairs and laid the groundwork for the military's 'dual function' (*dwifungsi*) of both protecting and helping to run the state. The Indonesian army had never confined itself to a purely military role and, to that end, ran a parallel administrative structure to that of the state, from cabinet level to local administrative regions, even down to the village level.

Alienated both politically and economically from the central government, the 'revolutionary councils' of Sumatra and Sulawesi raised themselves in revolt, in what was called the PRRI-Permesta Movement. The Sulawesi-based Permesta (Perdjuangan Semesta, or Overall Struggle) revolt was formally proclaimed on 2 March 1957. On 10 February 1958, rebellious officers in Padang, West Sumatra, demanded full autonomy and proclaimed the PRRI (Pemerintah Revolusioner Republik Indonesia, or Revolutionary Government of the Republic of Indonesia). With this proclamation, the leaders of the councils had demanded that the cabinet installed by Sukarno resign and be replaced by a new cabinet under either Hatta or the Sultan of Jogjakarta, with attendant changes to financial arrangements with the outer islands. With no change in Jakarta, on 15 February a revolutionary government was proclaimed at Padang in West Sumatra. The PRRI invited other rebel groups outside Java to join it in opposing the Jakarta government and to accept its authority. The Permesta group complied, but those areas already embroiled in the Dar'ul Islam revolt remained aloof from this further conflict. Within two months, the army had crushed the PRRI rebellion and moved on the rebels in Sulawesi, defeating them three months later.

While the army formally included itself in government, the PKI also increased its standing, both as an independent political party and within the government. Acknowledging the growth of the PKI during this period, Sukarno promoted socialist and later communist ideologies for their economic egalitarianism, their potential to act as an organising principle for revolution, their contribution to social development, and in order to more closely identify with a number of other post-colonial states. Along with his support of nationalism and religious practice, Sukarno coined the term *Nasakom*, incorporating and syncretising the 'ideals' of *nasionalisme, agama* and *komunisme* (nationalism, religion and communism). It was, in practice, a grab-bag of political ideas. In such a confused framework, based on low levels of economic development and little infrastructure within a rapidly declining economy, it is not surprising that Indonesia under Sukarno was politically unstable.

By 1965, the government under Sukarno had effectively lost control of the economy. In that year, the general rate of inflation had reached 500 per cent and the price of rice had risen by 900 per cent. The budget deficit had risen to 300 per cent of government revenues, and if foreign debt repayments for 1966 were to be made on schedule they would have amounted to almost the total of the nation's export income (Crouch 1988: 204) Then Sukarno's health appeared to begin to fail. With the process of succession left unresolved the country's two biggest political players, ABRI and the PKI, viewed each other with increasing suspicion.

At the height of chaos under what was later termed the 'Old Order' government of Sukarno, an incident took place on 30 September 1965 in which six senior generals were abducted and killed. This precipitated a massacre of PKI members and suspected sympathisers and a change in the presidency. The abduction of the generals was organised by mid ranking officers loyal to Sukarno who believed that the six generals were planning a coup against the president for 5 October 1965 (Armed Forces Day). In the abduction, the officers were probably assisted by, or had at least informed by, senior PKI members. After the events, the leader of the affair, Lieutenant Colonel Untung, announced the formation of a new 'revolutionary council' under Sukarno. However, it seems that this was a desperate attempt to make the best of a botched abduction rather than a planned reorganisation of Indonesian politics.

Tensions between a majority faction of the army and the PKI had reached an almost hysterical pitch by 1965, with the PKI gaining more and more influence in Sukarno's government and the armed forces being required to compete with what it had previously considered an untrustworthy organisation. The army and the PKI were at odds over a host of fundamental issues and each viewed the other with great hostility (Hindley 1964: 286–97).

What was later termed an 'attempted coup' by the PKI (not by the Untung-aligned officers) was put down by forces still 'loyal' to the formal military hierarchy under the command of Kostrad (Army Strategic Reserve Command) leader General Suharto. Interestingly, a long-held belief that Suharto was forewarned of the attack on the generals was confirmed when one of the 'coup' officers, Colonel Abdul Latief, was interviewed in prison after Suharto's political fall in May 1998. Latief said he had spoken to Suharto about the plan, 'because he is one of us', and had actually discussed the plan in detail with Suharto some days before (Poulgrain 1999). Over the next several months, being caught both unprepared and unarmed, the PKI was crushed by the Army, with perhaps a half million members, suspected sympathisers, and victims of long-standing local feuds being killed. Some estimates put the figure at up to 1.5 million political deaths over the period 1965–70 (Defence of Democracy Groups 1985: 4).

RISE OF THE NEW ORDER

Sukarno gave almost *carte blanche* to Suharto to 'restore order' in a letter of 11 March 1966. The day after the letter was signed, Suharto formally banned the PKI. Four days later, after Sukarno refused to agree to an army demand to dismiss cabinet ministers distrusted by the army leadership, the army arrested them. The signing of the letter by Sukarno marked the effective transition of power from the president to the general. In formal terms, the struggle for power between Sukarno and Suharto went on for another two years, but from 11 March 1966 (and even since late 1965) power had been increasingly with Suharto. In the political manouevring between late 1965 and March 1967, Suharto and his supporters in the army not only purged the armed forces but also cleared the civil service of pro-Sukarno elements. A part of the process of bringing the bureaucracy to heel was through the Army's political organisation Golkar, originally the 'organisation of functional groups' (Golongon Karya), which rapidly assumed the status of an institutionalised government party. The MPR, similarly purged of its old PKI and leftist members, formally stripped Sukarno of the presidency in March 1967, from which time Sukarno was effectively placed under house arrest until his death in 1970. Riding a wave of at least partly engineered anti-Sukarno sentiment and his own growing authority, Suharto was named as acting president and was formally endorsed by the MPR as president in 1968.

Under the provisions of the letter of 11 March, Suharto used the establishment of the 'Operations Command to Restore Security and Order (Kopkamtib)'[3] as his prime vehicle of control during this period. Kopkamtib not only had authority for tracking down remaining PKI members and sympathisers but also soon took responsibility for quelling other signs of dissent, including the issue and withdrawal of licences to publish. A parallel body was the Special Operations (Operasi Khusus or Opsus), which was built up by General Ali Murtopo and used for covert operations, such as arranging the outcome of the 'act of free choice' in Irian Jaya in 1969, organising key aspects of the first New Order elections in 1971, and the East Timor dispute, among many others (Lowry 1996: 71).

There was also a more clandestine body, the State Intelligence Coordinating Body (Bakin), established in 1967, which was a type of military-dominated secret police with responsibility for intelligence assessments and action aimed at the non-military population, such as political parties, dissidents, the Chinese community and the possibility of a communist revival. After 1974, intelligence agencies were streamlined and concentrated under General L. B. (Benny) Murdani, then its nominal deputy head. From 1983, when Murdani was appointed commander in chief of ABRI, both domestic and military intelligence organisations were further concentrated under Murdani through Bakin. Like Opsus, Bakin was originally constructed as a pro–Suharto organisation and operated in that manner, until Murdani fell out with Suharto and Bakin, still under Murdani's influence, was dismantled and the intelligence organisations brought under tighter control in the early 1990s.

From the outset there were those in the army who were concerned with Suharto's style and in particular his personal domination of the political process. But Suharto quickly moved to marginalise or oust his opponents, both real and perceived, and increasingly consolidated his position as a fulsome and in some senses a more traditional successor to Sukarno's recreation of the role of the Javanese king.

Economic development and official corruption, public pronouncements and secrecy, and favour and repression have been issues which have captured the attention of the country's elites as well as its more broad population in particular since the last years of the 1960s. This was all overlaid by a commitment to 'consensus', in which the whole Indonesian 'family' would work together for mutual benefit and dissenters would be dealt with harshly.

THE PARTY SYSTEM

In 1973, Suharto abolished the plethora of small political parties and created two new parties, the United Development Party (PPP), which comprises former Islamic parties, and the Democratic Party of Indonesia (PDI), which comprises the two small Christian parties, the Partai

Nasional Indonesia (PNI) and other nationalist parties. Golkar, which is in effect the party of government, was not formally considered a party for the purpose of this exercise.

In the 'elections' held between 1971 and 1997, Golkar won between sixty-two and 73 per cent of the vote. The PPP (or its predecessors in 1971) had achieved almost a third of votes, but its political strength was severely diminished when the NU pulled out in 1987 and its vote plummeted to 16 per cent. The PDI (or its predecessors in 1971) achieved a low of 8 per cent in 1982, but a high of 15 per cent in 1992 and looked to be gathering strength before its was split by government intervention in 1996, ahead of the 1997 election.

There were numerous reports of voting irregularities, such as when more votes were cast than there were voters, when in Sulawesi a total vote strongly favouring Golkar was fully counted before counting in Jakarta had barely started and when ballot boxes were interfered with. Also, with some electorates broken down into voting stations of as few as 200, officials were easily able to identify the general voting tendencies of those stations. With some stations located in factories or offices, senior officials were pressured to ensure a strong vote in favour of Golkar.

As Golkar was formally not a party, it could conduct its affairs as it liked. However, as the PPP and PDI were formally political parties, they were restricted in when they could conduct meetings and could not campaign outside the election period. Further, the PPP, and perhaps even more the PDI, were deeply influenced by government and ABRI agents, to the extent that the PDI 'pro-democracy' push of the early to mid 1990s in effect reflected the political aspirations of a significant faction of ABRI. The ousting in 1996 of the PDI's leader, Megawati Sukarnoputri, by a government-supported rebel PDI congress, reflected more her gaining too much popular support and Suharto wishing to see a potential competitor deposed.

NEW ORDER POLITICAL STRUCTURE

In structural terms, Indonesia had a political system in which the executive was independent of what approximates the legislature. Until 1999, the 'legislature' itself also comprised half of the electoral assembly that chose the president and vice-president on a five-yearly basis. Indonesia's legislative assembly, the Dewan Perwakilan Rakyat (DPR) had no effective legislative function until 1999, such a function being decided by presidential decree. The DPR had 500 members and is divided into committees and oversees the work of government. From 1967 until 1999, one fifth was directly appointed by the president with a further thirty-eight (reduced from seventy-five and before that 100) positions being reserved for senior ABRI (later TNI) officers. To balance this, members of ABRI were not allowed to participate in the voting process.

Beyond the DPR, the political structure which formally supported Suharto and the New Order government relied for its legitimacy on the 'will' of the People's Consultative Assembly, the Mejelis Permusya-waratan Rakyat (MPR), which until 1999 had 1000 members and is in theory Indonesia's highest sovereign body. It is the MPR that elects the president and approves broad outlines of state policy. Members of the DPR have representation as members of the MPR. Until 1999, the president also directly appointed 100 members of the MPR (formerly a third), while about half the assembly was comprised of members of the bureaucracy, ABRI and other social organisations. Only 40 per cent of the MPR was freely elected. Even then, given the provisions of the Indonesian electoral system in which Golkar was, until 1999, assured a majority of around two-thirds or more of the total vote, the president commanded a very large and secure majority within the MPR.

Despite Suharto's firm 'electoral' grip on the presidency, until just before his resignation, he did face challenges, most notably over the appointment of the vice-president. In the April 1987 elections, ABRI opposed the election of Sudharmono as Suharto's vice-president. As State Secretary, Sudharmono had helped engineer the decline of ABRI's influence over the bureaucracy income generation. As Golkar chairman between 1983 and 1988, Sudharmono also reduced ABRI's grip on power by cultivating civilian politicians. In 1988, as a consequence of his suggestion that Suharto rein in his children's business interests and because of his pointed opposition to Sudharmono as vice-president, then ABRI commander General Benny Murdani was sacked in 1988, being given the less powerful position of Defence Minister. ABRI vehemently opposed Sudharmono's appointment in the MPR, but lost the battle. Along with the gradual removal of senior ABRI officers from senior ministerial posts,[4] this had the effect of finally splitting Suharto's close links with ABRI. In 1993, ABRI got its own back by having ABRI commander Try Sutrisno elected as vice-president against Suharto's wishes. In turn, Suharto moved to reduce ABRI's influence in Golkar.

This series of events marked the formal rift between Suharto and the 'Red and White' (nationalist-secular) group within ABRI which was headed by General Wiranto. Recognising this rift, Suharto cultivated an

Islamic support base, through an intellectuals organisation (ICMI), through supporting mosque-building funds, making the hajj, and, most importantly, appointing more strongly Muslim officers to senior positions within ABRI.

THE ECONOMY

It is a common view that Indonesia's economy in the 1990s went from being a showcase for economic development to a basket case within the space of a few months. In early 1997, Indonesia's economy was still officially recording a growth rate that corresponded to 7 per cent or more a year. A little over a year later that figure had plunged to an economic contraction of around 20 per cent a year (government estimates suggested 13 per cent), with consequent social and political upheaval. Needless to say, the official picture of Indonesia's economy had long been overly optimistic while structural problems were largely ignored. The economic collapse, then, was not so much unexpected as its looming causes were not paid the attention they clearly deserved. To start with, however, Indonesia's economy under the New Order government looked to be improving quickly.

Suharto's first steps, having attained power, were to placate what would be his military support group and to get Indonesia's economy back on to some sort of viable footing. The economy he inherited from Sukarno was at least as much of a shambles as it was in 1998, with rice production below consumption requirements and the state unable to meet its foreign debts. Economic growth over the period 1960 to 1967 was at less than 2 per cent a year, while inflation was rampant. Based on 100 units in 1957, by 1966 the cost of living had risen to 150 000 units (Winters 1996: 48). The inflation rate for 1966 was just under 1500 per cent.

In his first move, Suharto established an economic environment that was attractive to foreign capital, which in turn helped resuscitate Indonesia's collapsed economy. Allied to this, Suharto ensured that his senior supporters were well looked after. But it was the unplanned and unexpected oil boom, which resulted from the rapid rise in world oil prices in the early 1970s, that cemented Suharto's early years. While there were problems at home, the inflow of wealth from oil ensured that, by the time the boom ended, he would be firmly entrenched in power and the economy would be on a general growth trajectory.

The New Order government instituted a number of policies to attract foreign investors, as well as to get domestic investors to rejoin the market. The first move, in 1966, was to invite the International Monetary Fund, banned by Sukarno, back into the country and to bring in a World Bank mission soon after. In 1967, Suharto turned his attention directly towards private investors, sponsoring meetings and summits for both investors and the media, in which representatives of the Indonesian government outlined new strategies to make Indonesia a more favourable place to invest.

However, official corruption, which had been a significant feature of Indonesia's economic landscape since the first days of the republic, remained institutionalised. This was enhanced by a complicated bureaucracy, through which one could navigate only by the payment of bribes. At about this time, a number of senior army officers began involving themselves in foreign investment programs from which they could personally benefit. Further, Suharto topped up the officers' incomes through his access to revenue from the sale of oil, by the head of the state-owned oil company Pertamina, General Ibnu Sutowo. Both Suharto and Sutowo had, in the late 1950s, been punished by the army for corrupt activities. From 1968, Suharto had received funding from Sutowo. In exchange, Sutowo was given almost entirely free reign over Pertamina, which was easily the country's largest source of foreign income and which operated in a manner effectively independent of official government policy. Sutowo's primary method of raising funds was to borrow against the value of Pertamina, outside the existing government borrowing regime. The effect of this process of unofficial fund raising was that Indonesia ended up running a 'two track' economic system (Winters 1996: 84).

By 1972, the rogue economic policy of Pertamina was of such concern that, in support of IMF attempts to curtail the organisation's borrowings, the United States suspended eligibility for program loans (Winters 1996: 89). With long-term borrowing no longer available, Pertamina's debt became unsustainable. This flowed over into the conventional economy, with built in cross-over provisions meaning that should the Indonesian government not guarantee Pertamina's debts, it would default on its own borrowings and all debts would have to be repaid in full. Sutowo was effectively put out of business and formally sacked from his job by Suharto in 1976. When Pertamina finally collapsed, it had over US$10 billion worth of debts (Mackie & MacIntyre 1994: 14; Hill 1994: 69). The political fallout was significant, but by then the unexpected income from the first surge in world oil prices, soon to quadruple the price of oil, had begun to come in. Indonesia's overall economy became buoyant, providing Suharto with yet another method of ensuring development and increasing his system of patronage.

SUHARTO AND CORRUPTION

With the new revenues from oil many Indonesians, including Suharto, felt they could be less reliant on foreign investment and could afford to run a more nationalistic approach to economic development. Economic policies subsequently became more restrictive for international investors, opening the way for local business people with close links to Suharto to expand their business interests. There was considerable resentment towards this policy, however, which was reflected in riots in Jakarta in 1974, which coincided with a visit by the Japanese prime minister, Kakuei Tanaka. The outward purpose of the riots was against perceived excessive Japanese investment and Chinese ownership. The rioting soon developed an anti–Chinese sentiment, reflecting a long-standing concern by ethnically indigenous Indonesians, referred to as *pribumi*, about what some Indonesians regarded as an excessively firm ethnic Chinese grip on the domestic economy. In particular, one small group of ethnic Chinese financiers and other intermediaries had provided funds and supplies to ABRI in return for political favours, and corruption and profiteering were rampant. One outcome of the riots was to give considerable impetus to what were becoming stricter foreign investment laws. However, the so-called *Malari* riots, in greater part, also reflected growing political tensions within ABRI and a desire on the part of some senior officers, in particular Kopkamtib commander General Sumitro, to see Suharto replaced.

As the government took tighter hold on the economy, Suharto began to build his own slush fund, as well as reap rewards from private deals and allocate lucrative government contracts to his family and friends. By 1978, Indonesia's economy was dominated by a system of patronage and discretion that exceeded the heights of the Sutowo era. But it was not to last, with the first move towards a shake-out coming with criticism from the World Bank in 1980 (*FEER* 1981: 46). It was not until the oil price collapse of 1982–83 and again in 1985–86 that Indonesia's New Order government began to seriously rethink its economic policy direction and, along with it, the relationships that had developed between members of the country's political, military and economic elites.

In some senses, 1986 was a more difficult year than most for Suharto. With the price of oil having dropped to real pre-1973 prices, Indonesia's main source of income had all but dried up, its non-oil economy was a shambles and the funds for 'patronage' through which Suharto continued to derive support were becoming increasingly difficult to come by.

As a consequence of the collapse in oil prices, from 1983 until 1989, Indonesia's 'Berkeley Group' of (pro-free market) economists was able to re-assert its influence over economic policy and the New Order government implemented a number of initiatives aimed at restoring the country's economic health. Perhaps the most significant changes during this period concerned taxation. Income tax in Indonesia was effectively completely divorced from the limited earnings of ordinary people and in particular farmers, which meant the government did not have access to this otherwise conventional source of revenue. This lack of access to tax-based funds was primarily addressed with the introduction of a value added tax on goods.

Despite the after-taste of the Pertamina scandal, high and growing levels of corruption and economic policy that zig-zagged between a type of free-market rationalism and crony-oriented profit-taking, by the late 1980s foreign investors were considering Indonesia very closely. The New Order government looked to be securely in control and such political stability has always been regarded as desirable by foreign investors. Suharto and the New Order government were also considered to be 'friendly' to the West, which further enhanced Indonesia's foreign financial appeal.

THE CRASH OF 1997

Although economic growth in Indonesia has been inconsistent, the country had, until 1997, managed to record an average growth rate approaching 5 per cent, with average rates of around 7 per cent growth from 1990 onward. Inflation also significantly decreased and the broader social indicators showed that standards of living had increased significantly since the late 1960s (though they would have been hard pressed not to rise above what was then such widespread absolute poverty). However, there were still serious questions about income distribution and in particular the increasing gap between rich and poor.

The causes of the economic collapse from 1997 were various, but some key points continue to be repeated and appear to be significant. The first was that there was, as a consequence of economic reforms, a greater potential to move capital in and out of the country. The second was that many leading business people had primarily grown rich as a consequence of their links to Suharto. The third was that corruption was rampant and that non-productive investment was unsustainable. The fourth was that Indonesia had amassed an unsustainably high level of foreign debt, often through unscrupulous or haphazard banking practices. The fifth point was that, with Suharto's grip on power becoming shaky in the face of increasingly loud calls for political change, most of the money which had been made in Indonesia during Suharto's rule began to flow off-shore. The timing of this event coincided with a currency collapse in Thailand, which encouraged money markets to re-examine Indonesia. When they did they panicked, and the rupiah plummeted, losing 80 per cent of its value in less than twelve months.

This collapse in the value of the rupiah wiped out any chance of Indonesian companies being able to repay foreign debts, sending most into technical bankruptcy. The economy officially shrank by 13.6 per cent in 1998, unemployment leapt from around 20 per cent, at the government's own conservative figures, to more than 50 per cent, with under-employment accounting for perhaps another 20 to 30 per cent. Starvation, which had effectively been wiped out, reappeared and malnutrition became widespread. Children were withdrawn from schools in vast numbers because parents were unable to meet educational costs, and health problems escalated. Needless to say, the political tensions this engendered quickly broke to the surface, often exacerbated or exploited by factional interests.

THE PRO-DEMOCRACY MOVEMENT

In December 1993, Megawati Sukarnoputri was elected to the chair of the PDI. This was despite Suharto's best attempts to have her election thwarted, but she was successful because of the support she received from senior members of ABRI's Red and White group. Megawati was popularly seen to represent the relative economic egalitarianism of her father, Sukarno, as opposed to the opulence surrounding Suharto's family and friends.

In part it was simply the name of the PDI which gave it its democratic credentials and in part it was that Megawati was increasingly perceived to provide a genuine political alternative to Suharto. That Megawati was the daughter of Indonesia's first president, Sukarno, gave her a pedigree and some legitimacy.

With the highly symbolic election of Megawati, the PDI appeared to grow in terms of popular support. There was a flowering of political optimism and many observers believed that 'democratisation', to be led by Megawati, was just around the corner. This feeling of optimism led to the development of a new breed of political activist in Indonesia, drawing strongly on an emerging middle class and the growing student movement. Some renegade politicians openly defied Suharto—and were quickly jailed for it—while a left-wing student-based political party and some unionists became active, and the Parti Rakyat Demokrasi (PRD—People's Democratic Party) came into existence.

The media had been heavily censored and otherwise constrained during Suharto's period in office. Suharto took control of government amid a wave of press closures, with a second round of closures occurring in 1974 in response to the Malari riots. Radio and television news had to run official government news broadcasts, and friends and family of Suharto owned or controlled very large sections of the media. Outside this direct control, individual journalists were harassed or not allowed to work and, although there were many brave attempts to work against government restrictions, Indonesia's public had to learn to 'read between the lines' of what was openly reported. However, in the developing climate of the 1990s, some media began to test the limits of government control. In May 1994, in response to articles that reflected tensions between ABRI and the government, the government closed three respected publications, *Tempo*, *Editor* and *De Tik*.

Despite this repression, the growth of democratic hope reflected the creation of a political 'space' between the increasingly divided elite, especially within ABRI. In 1996 this 'space' began to close as a number of senior ABRI figures as well as Suharto decided that Megawati's role of leader of the PDI had attracted too much attention. ABRI stage-managed an alternative PDI meeting at which Megawati was dumped and her predecessor, Suryadi, was elected to the chair. Megawati declared the meeting illegal and refused to resign, her supporters barricading themselves in the PDI's headquarters in Jakarta. By July 1996 the situation had come to a head, and anti-Megawati PDI members liberally supported by soldiers in PDI T-shirts stormed the PDI's headquarters. In the mêlée, several people were killed, dozens injured and several went missing. A riot soon broke out and Jakarta experienced its worst social upheaval since 1966. The PRD, members of which had been protesting against the government in front of the PDI headquarters, was blamed for the rioting and declared an illegal organisation, its leadership hunted down and jailed.

SUHARTO'S DECLINE

While the 'pro-democracy movement' was in tatters, the effect of the raid on the PDI headquarters seemed to signal that a final confrontation over Suharto's leadership was looming. It was from this time that Indonesians with money began thinking about their security, and started moving their money off-shore. When the value of the rupiah began to fall in mid to late 1997 it seemed that the country, indeed the region, was caught unawares. Most unprepared of all was Suharto who, in his January 1998 budget speech, outlined economic prospects that were wildly out of keeping with the reality fast befalling the country. This had the effect of further deepening and entrenching the crisis, with the rupiah reflecting the loss of faith in both Indonesia's economy and its political system. From R3500 to the American dollar in June 1997, by 1998 it had plummeted to R17 000 to the dollar. Suharto's patent inability to deal with the crisis called into radical doubt his continuing suitability as president.

Spurred on by material desperation, protests which had been a scattered but relatively constant feature of Indonesia's landscape since 1996 became more frequent, larger and more violent. Ethnic Chinese were frequently attacked by radical Muslim mobs, while students and others increasingly protested in and around universities. ABRI, unsure of how to control the situation, reacted with its traditional violence. In part, however, this reflected the differing strategic interests of its key members. The Red and White faction had by this time decided that Suharto had to go, but had no mechanism short of a coup by which to force the situation. The coup option was favoured by some but not others who had some lingering sense of loyalty to the president, to the office of the president, or to the Constitution. On the other hand, the so-called 'Green' group, by now headed by Suharto's son-in-law Prabowo Subianto, intended to support Suharto and crush public opposition.

Some of the rioting in the first part of 1998 appeared to reflect a degree of organisation not usually associated with a free-for-all. Some Islamic leaders were implicated, the belief being that they wished to strengthen the position of political Islam ahead of any political change. Similarly, troops from the 'Green' group were believed to be acting as *agents provocateurs*. The students, by this stage, were leading the push for Suharto's resignation, daring to say out loud what only months previously would have been unimaginable (Van Klinken 1999b; Berfield & Loveard 1999). Increasingly these students also found themselves supported by Indonesia's elite.

Emboldened by shadowy support from high places, students as far afield as Yogjakarta and Medan and in Jakarta had pushed the limits of what the New Order had regarded as acceptable dissent. Protests were allowed on university campuses, but when they moved outside the campuses they were met with ABRI opposition. Initially these confrontations were relatively non-violent. But then, in Medan, ABRI reaction became violent, with students being severely beaten, rubber bullets and tear gas being fired, and a number of female students being gang-raped by soldiers. This use of rape as a means of inciting terror was to find replication in the weeks after, as mobs rampaged through Jakarta and elsewhere, systematically raping Chinese women.

Then, in Jakarta, while Suharto was attending a meeting in Egypt, students at the private Trisakti University campus joined the protest movement. However, Jakarta was the direct security concern of Prabowo. With Suharto out of the country, the stakes over political leadership were critical and on 12 May Prabowo's men reacted with uncontrolled violence. As students began to run back to their campus, the troops opened fire. The rubber bullets soon gave way to conventional rounds and fleeing students dropped before the gunfire. The final toll was four dead and many more wounded (Richburg 1999; Bourchier, D. 1999). It was subsequently claimed that Prabowo had hoped to trigger a massive social breakdown, which could in turn be used to declare martial law in order to shore up Suharto's worsening political position.

There were more student protests, but increasingly Jakarta's poor and dispossessed began to join in. What had started with a naïve but politically motivated protest soon turned into an orgy of anti-government rioting and looting. Looters were trapped in burning buildings and the death toll quickly rose to more than 1000, with the mayhem being quelled only by the army bringing its armoured cars and tanks on to the streets. The public outcry for Suharto's resignation reached unprecedented levels, with former generals, academics and ordinary Indonesians calling for him to quit. Major General Yudhoyono personally delivered a message from retired generals addressed to ABRI commander-in-chief General Wiranto requesting that Suharto resign. A similar petition was presented to a special session of the MPR of which, in an act of unprecedented defiance, half of the assembly called on Suharto to resign, its repeated calls headed by former Suharto loyalist, MPR chairman Harmoko (Schwartz 1999: 358).

THE FALL OF SUHARTO

Despite Wiranto saying that the call was unconstitutional and advising against planned protests two days later, it was becoming increasingly apparent that Wiranto had done a deal with Suharto; agree to retire quietly and there will be no more violence. On Tuesday 19 May 1998, in a public speech televised live, President Suharto announced the formation of a 'Reform Committee' and a new 'Reform Cabinet'. But more importantly, Suharto also announced that there would be new presidential elections and that he would not stand as a candidate. No date was given for the election and many believed it could be more than a year away, which did not satisfy the protesters. With Harmoko now threatening to have the MPR impeach Suharto, the MPR building swamped by protesters and all credible candidates refusing to join his 'Reform Committee', on 20 May 1998 Suharto began to waver. When Harmoko again spoke against Suharto and ABRI 'fraction' leader in the MPR, Syarwan Hamid, raised his fist in symbolic support it appeared increasingly obvious that Suharto was alone. A visit to his home by three former vice-presidents, Try Sutrisno, Sudharmono and Umar Wirahadikusumah that evening further encouraged Suharto to resign. A visit later that night by Wiranto sealed the arrangement; Suharto and his family would be protected after his resignation. At around 11 p.m., Suharto summoned Habibie and informed him that he would become Indonesia's third president on the following day (Schwartz 1999: 358–66).

THE HABIBIE PRESIDENCY

Habibie's appointment was supported by Wiranto, while Wiranto was reappointed as commander-in-chief of ABRI and defence. The appointment in March of Habibie to the vice-presidency had always been designed to allow Suharto to quietly step away from Indonesian politics during that five-year term of office. After a brief and somewhat ill-conceived show of power on the following day, 22 May, Prabowo was shuffled out of Kostrad to the staff and command college at Magelang and soon after sacked from ABRI. Meanwhile, Prabowo's military allies were similarly moved from influential positions in what was beginning to look like a purge, to be replaced by Red and White loyalists. In particular, Kopassus commander Major General Muchdi Purwopranjono was replaced by Major General Sjahrir. The Red and White faction had not just moved into the cabinet, it had also won control of ABRI.

Despite Habibie's general unpopularity, with Wiranto's support he retained the presidency through months of public protest, including widespread rioting in Jakarta in November 1998. An agreement was brokered over new elections for the DPR, with the presidency to be decided in October 1999. In the days after Habibie took office, he made a number of moves towards establishing his reform credentials. Labour unions previously banned under Suharto were legalised, there were moves towards liberalising press regulations, there was a start to delinking government and business and resolving other conflicts of interest, and it was announced that all political parties could contest future elections. More than 140 political parties formed during this period of openness, while the media attempted to reconstitute itself as a free entity. Economic constraints, however, tempered the media's enthusiasm, while the ownership of some media organisations showed links to Habibie's government. Having said that, in October 1999, under Information Minister Mohamad Yunus, Indonesia formally lifted all political controls over its media (see Anwar 2000).

As importantly, however, was the political and ethnic violence that had been tearing at the fabric of Indonesian society since early 1998. Much of the violence was orchestrated by members of the political elite running competing agendas ahead of the elections. Such agendas included the assertion of Islamic nationalist identities of various types, scapegoating the Chinese for economic problems, redressing local economic imbalances, the settling of ethnic rivalries, claims to separatism, the relative positions of various political parties, and, not least, the role of, and factionalism within, the armed forces.

ECONOMIC REFORMS

The economic reforms that Indonesia was forced to undertake as a consequence of the collapse of the value of the rupiah and the associated economic decline were various and, in part, only haltingly put in place. Suharto initially agreed to economic reforms in late 1997, but failed to implement those agreements either at all or in any meaningful way. His family and cronies appeared to be protected from the full thrust of the IMF's intentions.

However, after Suharto fell from power Habibie realised that some significant reforms would need to be undertaken. His first moves were to delink some more notorious cronies from their monopolies and to end the monopoly system. Loss-making projects were scrapped, such as Suharto's youngest son, Tommy Suharto's 'national car' project, while investigations began into the collapsed banking industry. Between early 1998 and early 1999, more than fifty insolvent banks were closed by the government. One bank belonging to Suharto's middle son, Bambang Trihajmodo, was closed, re-opened under a different name and closed again, while another belonging to Islamic leader Abdurrahman Wahid was also closed. The total cost of reforming the banking sector was estimated at between US$40 and US$50 billion, or about three quarters of the country's foreign debt, while recapitalisation was expected to cost more than US$33 billion.

In March 1999, Indonesia's international economic rating, in the finance industry known as 'junk', was the lowest of any rated country except Pakistan (Hammond 1999). By mid 2000, the sense of growing stability that had marked both the economy and politics by mid 1999 had begun to evaporate, with political uncertainty fuelling continued selling down of the rupiah.

EAST TIMOR

In January 1999, Habibie announced that East Timor, so long a trouble spot for Indonesia, would be given the choice of autonomy within Indonesia or independence. When Habibie announced the decision to Cabinet, he had failed to first informWiranto. Wiranto said nothing at the Cabinet meeting, but immediately after senior officers in East Timor, including those with links to Wiranto, began creating and arming local militias. Ahead of the referendum, some thirteen pro-integration militias comprising around 6000 members had been created in East Timor, spreading fear and havoc and being responsible for hundreds of deaths of pro-independence activists as well as ordinary East Timorese. Even a growing UN presence in the province was not enough to quell the violence.

THE ELECTORAL REFORMS

On 28 January 1999, the DPR approved the legal foundation for a new political party system and the 1999 elections. Of more than 140 political parties, forty-eight were regarded by the Komisi Pemilihan Umum (KPU—National Electoral Commission) as satisfying electoral criteria, having executive boards in nine of the twenty-seven provinces, and in half the towns and districts in each of those provinces. Candidates would be elected proportionally by province, but a party's winning candidates would be chosen on the basis of district results. New parties would also need at least ten seats in the national assembly to stand at the 2004 elections.

Election committees at various levels managed the campaign and elections. Half their membership was drawn from the political parties. For the first time, independent Indonesian and international observers were also permitted to monitor the elections. The number of unelected TNI seats in the People's Consultative Assembly was reduced from seventy-five to thirty-eight. In provincial and local assemblies they were reduced to 10 per cent of the seats. It was decided that civil servants could vote and, provided they took leave from office, could join political parties. The revised regulation allowed for one year of leave on basic pay. The president would continue to be elected by the MPR, which was revised from 1000 to 700. Of these, 238 seats would be appointed (old MPR 575), including thirty-eight military, 135 regional and sixty-five group representatives. Among the forty-eight represented parties, twenty-six were linked to the government party, Golkar, or Suharto's family. The electoral laws that do exist were also seen as biased in their direction.[5]

DEMOKRASI

On 7 June 1999, the first post–Suharto general elections were held in Indonesia. The elections were remarkable for their transparency, lack of violence and the neutral role of the TNI, apart from East Timor, Irian Jaya and Aceh. There were some minor irregularities and the count was slow, which confused many who were used to the results being known sometimes before the elections had been held. But, in all, it was a remarkably successful poll, while the results reflected a coalescing of political support around five main parties.

Partai Demokrasi Indonesia-Perjuangan, led by Megawati Sukarno-putri, was by far the most successful, with more than a third of the votes, followed a distant second by Golkar, which used money, institutional power, the threat of the unknown, and force of habit to secure a little over 20 per cent of the votes. The Partai Kebangkitan Bangsa (PKB—National Awakening Party), led by Abdurrahman Wahid came third, the PPP fourth and PAN a distant fifth. Along with the other seat holders, Partai Bulan Bintang and Partai Keadilan, Indonesian politics coalesced into two broad camps, or coalitions. Of the forty-eight parties that contested the elections, some twenty-six were seen as 'front' parties for either Suharto or Golkar. None of these parties managed to secure a seat in the new DPR.

One of the main consequences of the elections was that 'nationalist–secular' parties won the overwhelming majority of votes, if PKB and PAN were considered within this camp. There was also strong support for parties promoting the continued unity of the state, while political leaders apart from Amien Rais opposed federalism and supported retention of the 1945 Constitution.

While the June 1999 general elections in Indonesia for a while held out great hope for the country's process of democratisation, it became very clear early on that it was only the first step on a very long and difficult path. It seemed clear throughout 1999 that the TNI generally and

386 South-East Asia: A Political Profile

General Wiranto in particular held real power in the country, although it was not entirely clear to what end they wished to use it (see Kingsbury 1999). Violence in Aceh between the Gerakan Aceh Merdeka (GAM, Free Aceh Movement) and the TNI left hundreds, perhaps thousands, of people dead and identified Aceh as a region that radically challenged Indonesia's continuing ideological claim to 'unity in diversity'. In Maluku, too, violence and carnage continued, most obviously in the main city of Ambon, which over 1999–2000 left more than 3000 dead and brought into doubt the capacity of the president to rule. Here tensions revolved around competition between the earlier Christian inhabitants and more recent Muslim arrivals. But behind it, and to some extent events in Aceh, could be seen the hand of the TNI fomenting trouble, at least in part to prove their own necessity. And then came East Timor.

The TNI's support for East Timor's 'militias' (see following chapter on East Timor) was a very clear part of the military's attempt to impose its will, as well as to show what happened to recalcitrant provinces. In the final analysis, however, the TNI—and Indonesia—lost in East Timor. Not only was Indonesia's continuing presence there overwhelmingly rejected in the face of state-sponsored violence and intimidation, but events there came close to turning Indonesia into one of the world's pariah states. The United States, Britain and Australia all suspended defence links with Indonesia over events in East Timor. Indonesia's economy was also further destabilised as the international financial community both wondered about the unproductive military expenditure and punished Indonesia for its stand. This in turn led to a renewed collapse in the value of the rupiah, to more than R8000 to the US dollar. To deflect attention from these troubles, senior Indonesian authorities began to look for scapegoats for their problems, in particular focusing on near neighbour Australia for 'interfering in its internal affairs'.

In late September 1999, the TNI pushed through the DPR a new 'security' law, which allowed the TNI greater scope for imposing one of three levels of 'emergency control' (which was quickly suspended in the wake of violent public protests). The first was for the TNI, or the government, to be able to declare a 'danger to security', the second to declare 'unusual conditions', and the third to declare a 'state of emergency'. This would have given the president and/or the TNI unprecedented powers over the civilian population at a time when most Indonesians had expressed a desire for less control over the population. It was clearly an anti-democratic step and one against which many students protested, leading to a number of deaths among both protesters and soldiers. Perhaps what the clashes over this legislation indicated was that, at the end of the twentieth century, Indonesia was still a very long way from having resolved many of its fundamental and seemingly intractable problems. Increasingly, its critics argued, the idea of the state of 'Indonesia' was itself under serious challenge.

GUS DUR AS PRESIDENT

The election of Abdurrahman Wahid—Gus Dur—as president on 20 October 1999 came as a shock to most people, not least the thousands of Megawati supporters in the streets outside the MPR building who immediately began rioting. A car bomb exploded, killing three people, while riot police fired tear gas into the angry crowd. The election of Gus Dur was a triumph of clever politicking over what appeared to be nat-ural justice. While Gus Dur was clearly aiming for the top job, he had to work to achieve it.

By contrast, Megawati, who could have secured it, failed to put in the work necessary to build a coalition of support. Instead, she remained aloof and indecisive. Habibie had thought he could stitch together a coalition to retain the presidency, despite factional intrigues against him from within his own party. In particular, Akbar Tanjung and Marzuki Darus-man were equivocal in their support for his bid for the presidency. But what really sank Habibie's chances was when he announced that Wiranto would be his vice-presidential running mate. Wiranto was interested in the vice-presidency, but after a day of deliberation publicly announced that he would not stand with Habibie. Habibie was humiliated and could clearly not muster sufficient support to make his bid tenable. The rejec-tion of Habibie's 'accountability speech' to the MPR, at 2 a.m. on 20 October 1999, was the final humiliation, although it reflected more Habi-bie's lack of personal and political popularity than it did the substance of the text. Even Golkar members voted against accepting Habibie's speech, following an open split within Golkar on 18 October (Tesor & Loveard 1999). The final count was not completely one-sided, at 355 against and 322 for (nine abstentions and four spoiled ballot papers) but, as the equiv-alent of a no-confidence vote, it was humiliating enough. With this final blow, Habibie withdrew his candidacy for the presidency. 'Morally,' he said, 'I cannot continue.'

GUS DUR GAINS THE PRESIDENCY

Between Habibie's announcement that he would not stand as a presiden-tial candidate and the start of the presidential voting process some ten hours later, there was a flurry of political activity as promises were made, deals were done and political dreams were shattered and, in one case, realised. With just 10 per cent of the vote, Gus Dur's PKB did not look like presenting him as a strong contender for the top position. But following Golkar candidate Akbar Tanjung's withdrawal from the ballot, Golkar's votes shifted in behind Gus Dur, rather than Megawati. In exchange, Gus Dur agreed that Golkar could have a number of cabinet posts. With Rais' support already secured, Gus Dur then cemented his alliances with the small Islamic parties (Wagstaff 1999). In a two-horse race, Gus Dur's team had been quicker and more conscious of the need to form coalitions than had PDI-P.

Amien Rais was central to the election of Gus Dur to the presidency, by helping to swing behind him the votes without which he would certainly have not gained the presidency. While this was interpreted as reflecting Rais' increasing political power, it also reflects Gus Dur's support for Rais' gaining of the chair of the DPR. In the final analysis, Gus Dur won by seventy votes, or a little more than his party, PKB, held. In obtaining the presidency, Gus Dur made commitments to share power. This was later reflected in the appointment of cabinet ministers.

AND MEGAWATI GAINS THE VICE-PRESIDENCY

Megawati was humiliated by her defeat for the position she believed was rightly hers. But with only 34 per cent of the vote, two-thirds of the population did not explicitly support her. As her supporters rioted upon the election of Gus Dur, he knew that if she and they were not assuaged there would continue to be trouble, possibly into the longer term. And, in building an inclusive government, Megawati's involvement at the highest possible level would be critical. With Gus Dur's support, Megawati was voted in as Vice-President.

The structure of the government under Gus Dur reflected the new political reality of Indonesia. As expected, it was an inclusive government, drawing in representatives from the five major parties (PDI-P, Golkar, PKB, PPP, PAN) and the TNI. PAN was represented by Amien Rais being voted to the seat of chair of the DPR, while Golkar's Akbar Tanjung was elected as chair of the MPR. Cabinet postings fulfilled the rest of the inclusive requirement.

In the first few months of Gus Dur's presidency, he initiated a number of significant reforms, gradually asserting his authority. His biggest task was to reform the TNI, which he started by sacking Wiranto as Coordinating

Minister for Politics and Security in February 2000. Wiranto's appointment to the ministry by Gus Dur in October 1999 had not weakened his grip on the TNI and he was increasingly seen to be exercising power outside Gus Dur's control. Gus Dur then moved to shake up the TNI, promoting officers he felt were more loyal to him, or in favour of reform.

Gus Dur attempted to resolve the Aceh problem, with little success. His main move in Irian Jaya was to change its name back to West Papua. Problems continued, however, in Ambon and to a lesser extent in many of the other outer islands. Similarly, while the economy had begun to stabilise, fundamental reform was still slow in coming and the country's banks were still technically insolvent. Moves to call Suharto to account for his corruption were slow and hamstrung by legal problems and later a series of bombings, although moves were made to reduce corruption elsewhere, and to make some former cronies accountable.

Perhaps Gus Dur's greatest achievement in his early days as president was that he simply survived, employing a mix of charisma, home-spun charm and wiliness. Indonesia remained beset by problems, not least of which were controlling its many fractious elements bent on causing mischief or breaking away. In this sense, Gus Dur's future was somewhat uncertain. While his legitimacy was secure, as Indonesia's first genuinely elected executive president, the factions that comprised his cabinet were increasingly divided. In early 2000 this in turn led to the formation of two political coalitions, the Poros Tengah (Central Axis) and the Poros Indonesia (Indonesia Axis). The Poros Tengah was established with the intention of asserting political Islam in the DPR and, ultimately, over the presidency. The Poros Indonesia had a more nationalist-secular outlook and was, ostensibly, non-political. However, it was openly admitted by its members that it was a coalition designed to oust Gus Dur as president, the biggest delay to its plan being the lack of a suitable alternative. This political instability again destabilised the rupiah, dropping it to 9500 to the US dollar. But more importantly, it again raised the troubling question of whether it was possible to govern Indonesia under a democratic political system.

NOTES

1   D. Bourchier has also argued that the political forms which took root in Indonesia, especially in the New Order period, derived from Japanese 'organicism', although they were also strongly influenced by European 'organicism' (that is, fascism) (Bourchier 1996)

2   Pemberton discusses Javanese tradition and culture and the construction of the Indonesian state from a particularly critical perspective in his *On the subject of 'Java'* (Cornell University Press, Ithaca and London 1994).

3   Kopkamtib was formally dismantled in September 1988 in response to international criticism and to lower the profile of the army in internal security. It was replaced by the Body for Coordinating National Stability and Security (Badan Koordinasi Bantuan Pemantapan Stabilitas Nasional), known as Bakorstanas. Bakorstanas worked under the same legislative provisions as Kopkamtib.

4   Until 1998, no serving officer had been appointed to a senior ministerial post since 1980.

5   These details are based on notes taken at KPU briefings as an official election monitor.

15

East Timor: The Difficult Birth of a New State[1]

The storm of dust and debris forced the crowd of officials, police and other onlookers to turn their backs as the big United Nations helicopter lifted off from the soccer field in front of the UN compound in Maliana, only a short distance from East Timor's border with West Timor. One UN Assistance Mission to East Timor (UNAMET) military liaison officer, who had been working in the Bobonaro district around Maliana since the UNAMET mission was first established, turned into the storm and, squinting, held up his hands and applauded. He then turned and shook hands with the paramilitary Mobile Brigade police sergeant standing next to him. The helicopter had just lifted off for the East Timorese capital of Dili, carrying the district ballot papers from the territory's referendum on what amounted to self-determination.

It had been a long and hard ten weeks, in which many local people had been killed by members of the district militia in connivance with the Indonesian army and the police. Houses had been burned and the population had been thoroughly terrorised. Yet despite this violence and intimidation, which was expected to make a 50 per cent showing of registered voters a good turn-out, the people of Bobonaro district were lined up in their best Sunday clothes before dawn. More than 90 per cent of the district's people voted, helping bring East Timor's total turnout to the poll of registered voters to 98.6 per cent. Across the territory, again despite the terror, the trucking in of many questionable voters from West Timor, and the fact that many voters did not believe their votes were secret, 78.5 per cent of registered voters opted for independence from Indonesia, setting in train the process of establishing a new state.[2]

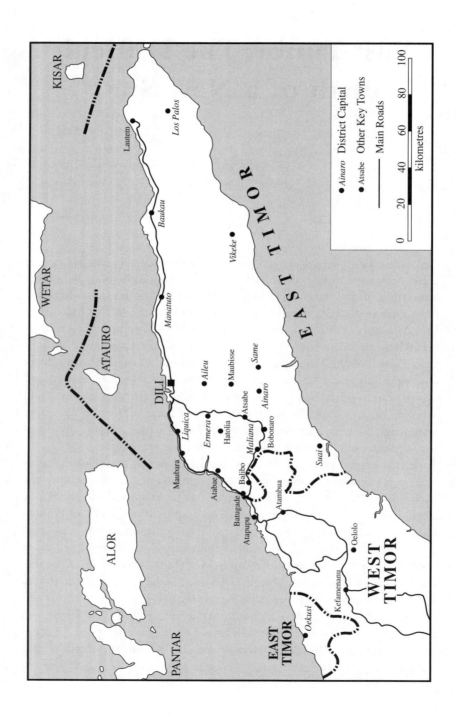

But before moves could be made in this direction—indeed within minutes of the ballot result being known—the sea of violence that had washed over ordinary East Timorese people until that time broke anew in a wave of fury. It left thousands butchered and had displaced most of the population of 850 000, with around 250 000 being forcibly removed to West Timor. This violence, conducted by so-called militias of thugs hired often from West Timor and led by members of TNI, outraged world opinion. As a result, although somewhat belatedly, a number of countries under the banner of the UN organised a peace-enforcement mission to East Timor, which was the forerunner of a UN-organised interim administration, the UN Transitional Authority in East Timor (UNTAET) ahead of full self-government. The task of this interim administration, and the government to follow it, was to build a state from the ground up, bringing into focus the full range of political, economic, and socio-cultural issues that creating a new state implied.

EARLY HISTORY

East Timor's history is more complicated than many, at least for such a small (19 000 square kilometres) and relatively obscure place. Prior to the Portuguese establishing a Dominican religious order and trading ports in the mid sixteenth century,[3] Timor (*Timor Loroe Sa'e* or Land of the Rising Sun) was a collection of small and competing states. The southern part of Timor was predominantly Polynesian in ethnic make-up, the north mostly Melanesian, and the central regions largely aboriginal. Added to this ethnic mix, Chinese traders seeking sandalwood had been visiting the island for centuries before the Portuguese arrived, while traders from other nearby islands were regular visitors. As a result of the ethnic variety and the rugged, difficult terrain, some sixteen separate linguistic groups along with around thirty-five further dialects developed in that last area controlled by the Portuguese, corresponding to contemporary East Timor (see De Matos 1974; Leitao 1952).

During the sixteenth and seventeenth centuries, the small states of Timor were frequently at war with each other, primarily in a bid to control the island's lucrative sandalwood trade. Their reception of the Portuguese was little different. Portugal only gradually extended its control over the island, facing several rebellions. By the time it had managed to subjugate most of the *liuri* (local kings) the Dutch had begun to expand their regional interests into this Portuguese territory. In two wars, in 1859 and 1913, Timor was partitioned along its present lines, leaving the enclave of Oecusse within the Dutch territory (Hiorth 1985: 6–7). This was the state of the island when Japanese forces occupied Dutch Timor in February 1942.

The Japanese left Portuguese Timor, as it was a colony of the fascist but otherwise neutral Portuguese government. However, Australia, concerned about the potential for Timor to be used as a base for the launch of an invasion, violated Portugal's neutrality by sending 200 commandos to operate in the territory on 17 December 1941. In the ensuing conflict, the local people supported Australian commandos in their work against the Japanese. The price for these people was that some 40 000 of them were killed by the Japanese in retribution, with more dying in later Allied bombing (Jardine 1995: 21–2). It was from this time that many Australians began to identify a special relationship with the people of East Timor, which has both assisted and complicated East Timor's bid for independence in the last quarter of the twentieth century.

EXIT PORTUGAL

Portuguese Timor's postwar period was quiet, with the colony being perhaps the least developed of Portugal's overseas possessions. However, the cost of retaining its colonies burdened Portugal and, with the winds of political change sweeping the Iberian Peninsula, on 24 April 1974 the fascist dictatorship of Marcello Caetano was overthrown by a leftist military uprising. The intention was for Portugal to cast off its colonial dependencies quickly and, as a consequence, political parties began forming in the colony. Founded on 20 May 1974, the Timorese Social Democrats, soon renamed the Frente Revolucionaria de Timor L'Este Independente (Fretilin—Revolutionary Front for an Independent East Timor), was the biggest and most popular party. It was trailed by the Uniao Democratica de Timor (Timorese Democratic Union—UDT), founded on 11 May 1974, comprising small businesspeople, property owners and officials, which initially supported continued integration with Portugal then quickly opted for independence, but later for integration with Indonesia. The Associacao Popular Democratica de Timor (Timorese Popular Democratic Association—Apodeti) and Kliban Oan Timor Aswain (Sons of the Mountain Warriors—KOTA) supported integration with Indonesia and were invented or supported by Indonesia's military intelligence, accounting for less than 10 per cent of popular support (Dunn 1996: 65–6; Hiorth 1985: 21–3; Joliffe 1978: chs 2–5).

Fretilin and UDT initially came together in an alliance in May 1975, seeking independence. An election for a popular assembly to oversee decolonisation was planned for October 1976. But with Indonesian intelligence conspiring against the leftist Fretilin, the UDT was led to believe the leftist party would soon launch a coup. To forestall this possibility, on 11 August 1975, UDT supported by local police made a pre-emptive strike against Fretilin in what was called the 'Revolutionary Anti-Communist Movement of 11 August'. However, Fretilin enjoyed the support of some 3000 Timorese (Portuguese army) soldiers and some thousands more of the local militia (Dunn 1996: 38). Fighting was fierce but it was over within days, costing some 2000–3000 lives. The remnants of the Portuguese administration fled to the nearby island of Atauro and then to Portugal. Never a great colonial master, the Portuguese left the colony in abject retreat. Portugal, however, continued its claim to East Timorese sovereignty, which it finally relinquished to the UN. UDT-Apodeti-Kota (pro-integration) remnants fled to West Timor from where, with the fulsome assistance of the Indonesian military, they began cross-border raids. In the post-'civil war' period, Fretilin put back together the machinery of government and, apart from the security problem in the west, life resumed close to usual under an interim administration (Dunn 1996: chs 8, 9).

ENTER INDONESIA

The first Indonesian-pro-integration raids were on the northern coastal border town of Batu Gade, which was abandoned by Falintil[4] troops in the face of superior numbers and tanks. Skirmishes continued in the border area until October, when Indonesian troops and anti-Fretilin irregulars attacked the town of Balibo, about 20 kilometres south-east of Batu Gade. It was in this attack that five Australian journalists were killed by the invading force, which increased Australian interest in the territory (to have implications almost a quarter of a century later). Despite these forays by Indonesian-backed forces across the border, Falintil put up an unexpectedly stiff resistance, prompting Indonesian military planners to reconsider their approach to what was by now a clear desire to occupy the territory of Portuguese Timor. On 24 November 1975, Fretlin asked the UN to push for the withdrawal of Indonesian forces from its territory, and four days later declared East Timor an independent republic. On 30 November UDT and Apodeti announced their support for East Timor's integration into Indonesia. On 7 December 1975, Indonesia launched its formal invasion of East Timor, starting with a parachute landing on Dili ahead of more than 40 000 troops invading the territory. The wholesale slaughter of East Timorese people by Indonesian troops that immediately followed presaged a major campaign of violence and dislocation. It has been variously estimated that 60 000 people were killed in the first two months immediately following the invasion. In May 1976, hand-picked East Timorese delegates voted for East Timor's incorporation into Indonesia,[5] which was formally endorsed by Indonesia's President Suharto on 17 July. This decision was never accepted by the UN, which voted repeatedly for Indonesia to withdraw its forces from the territory.

Despite the overwhelming presence of Indonesian armed forces in East Timor, Falintil kept up an active military campaign throughout the later 1970s. Quickly abandoning conventional warfare, Falintil opted for guerrilla tactics, which were relatively successful in tying down more than 20 000 Indonesian troops. However, in the late 1970s and early 1980s, Indonesian forces instituted a policy of relocating villagers believed to be supporting Falintil to 'secured' sites. Without adequate food, water or sanitation, by the early 1980s these sites had contributed in large measure to the deaths of more than 200 000 people, a third of East Timor's population (ACFOA 1991: 3).

UNDER INDONESIA

Under Indonesia, East Timor underwent a number of profound changes. Apart from the massive violence and social dislocation, which on a per capita basis matched the atrocities of the Khmer Rouge in Cambodia, Indonesia moved to put its stamp on the territory. The first move was for senior military figures to take over or set up businesses that traded directly with Singapore, bypassing Jakarta and hence the need for taxation or other forms of accountability. For example, the military held a monopoly on East Timor's export of coffee, which until the development of gas and oil was by far its most lucrative trade. This military-dominated economy proved to be a profitable source of income for many officers, although it had the effect of further impoverishing this already poor territory. Businesses and property once owned by Portuguese citizens were taken over by Indonesians. The military made considerable profits by selling established businesses to new Indonesian owners, even though they did not legally hold title.

Under Indonesia, education was expanded and the number of secondary schools increased. In part, this policy of educational development was intended to inculcate in the East Timorese a sense of them belonging to the greater Indonesian 'nation'. The medium of education was Bahasa

Indonesia, which did have the effect of standardising this language among virtually all East Timorese who went to school following the period of Indonesia's occupation.

Indonesia also built a number of health clinics, although most East Timorese felt little benefit from them. Who the clinics and, increasingly, the schools did serve was the influx of 'transmigrants' and economic migrants from around Indonesia. By 1998, it was widely estimated that more than 150 000 non-East Timorese lived in East Timor, with up to two-thirds of them centred in the capital of Dili. Administrative jobs were created to run the territory, but these were often given to non-East Timorese. Those who were brought to East Timor on government business received a 'hardship' allowance of 99 per cent of their salary, which boosted local inflation and artificially inflated the average income of people in the territory. The standard of living for some East Timorese did rise under the Indonesians, but for many it did not. Even the roads that Indonesia built in East Timor, of which it was unduly proud, served in large part to transport troops and equipment from district to district, while many of the major bridges and water supply projects were built with foreign aid.

Throughout all of this, East Timorese people were regarded as less than human by their new Indonesian masters. Women were raped as a matter of course, opponents to Indonesian rule murdered, and people continued to disappear, presumably being killed, with monotonous regularity. At no stage did the vast majority of the East Timorese people ever feel that they lived in other than an occupied territory, while the Indonesian armed forces continued to act like an insensitive occupying force, rather than as the guardians of the state and protectors of the peace. Meanwhile, Falintil continued its guerrilla campaign from the mountains, reduced in the 1980s to a small and desperate force of a few hundred, then rebuilt from the late 1980s on as a small but tough and highly disciplined military group consisting of four semi-independent units totalling perhaps 2000.[6]

POLITICAL CONSOLIDATION

In 1981, after the Indonesian army's notorious 'fence of legs' campaign in which East Timorese civilians were pushed in front of Indonesian troops advancing on Falintil positions, the political parties were more closely coordinated under the overall banner of national liberation. This policy rejuvenated the independence movement. Briefly in 1983 the Indonesian government agreed to enter into peace talks. However, General Benny Murdani, who became commander-in-chief of the Indonesian armed forces in that year, cancelled the peace talks and stepped up the military campaign against the resistance movement. As head of military intelligence, Murdani had been one of the two key proponents and architects of Indonesia's invasion of East Timor[7] and was regarded in Indonesian military circles as militarily aggressive. He was not the sort of military leader who opted for discussion. The East Timorese resistance had little choice but to unite if it was not to disappear entirely (Jardine 1995: 54–7; Singh 1995: 145–6).

As the senior ranks of Falintil thinned out as a consequence of Indonesia's continued attacks, in particular the death of Falintil leader Nicolao Lobato in 1978, in 1981 leadership was formally handed to regional guerrilla leader Jose 'Xanana' Gusmao. Gusmao was born on 20 June 1946 in Manatuto. As a young man he trained at the Jesuit seminary near Dare, just south of Dili. As one of the territory's few well-educated young men, he quickly joined the then newly established political party, Fretilin. By August 1975 Gusmao was working for Fretilin's Department of Information and was elected to the party's central committee. However, following the Indonesian invasion in December that year, Gusmao fled to the east of the island, to a stronghold behind Mount Matebean, where he led the armed resistance movement in that area.

Gusmao's first major initiative as leader was, on 26 April 1986, to establish the Council of National Maubere Resistance (CNRM) as a clandestine coalition of all East Timorese groups, including Fretilin, UDT and the student group Restencia National dos Estudantes de Timor L'Este (Renetil). Maubere, which means 'older brother' in Tetun, was used to describe the relationship between the active pro-independence fighters and ordinary East Timorese. In theory, Falintil was to look after the interests of ordinary East Timorese under this arrangement. In practice, what it meant was that Falintil worked more openly with East Timorese people and relied on them more closely to provide a support base for their activities. This paved the way for the independence movement's next step.

The next major move in the political delineation within East Timorese politics was the formal separation of Falintil from Fretilin in 1987. This division did not reflect any ideological division between the political and armed groups, but rather a recognition of the need for the armed resistance movement to represent all anti-Indonesian political groupings. Despite being Falintil's commander, it was also from this time that Gusmao steered the independence movement away from open armed conflict towards a policy of civil disobedience. The cost of the armed conflict, in terms of lives, and the slim chance that Falintil would ever be able to defeat Indonesia's military in the field, pushed Gusmao to look at attracting international attention to their cause, while still keeping up pressure on the Indonesian authorities within East Timor. The recruitment of young, urban East Timorese—in most cases those born in the years since Indonesia's invasion—into the pro-independence ranks breathed new life into the independence campaign. It was from this time that independence started to look like a faint possibility. The adoption of this policy also stamped Gusmao's personal authority on the pro-independence movement, elevating him from the status of guerrilla leader to cult figure within the pro-independence community.

THE SANTA CRUZ MASSACRE

Despite the already long and bloody history of Indonesian atrocities in East Timor, perhaps the issue that most galvanised world opinion on East Timor was the killing of protestors at the Santa Cruz Cemetery in Dili on 12 November 1991. The protesters were, in theory, attending the burial of a student who had been killed two days previously. However, the event was also clearly an opportunity to protest against Indonesia's continued occupation of East Timor and active repression of its people. The attack against the protesters also corresponded to a planned (but abandoned) visit to Dili by a Portuguese delegation. One version of events had it that the massacre was prompted by the former commander-in-chief of Indonesia's armed forces, Benny Murdani, as a means of embarrassing Suharto's son-in-law, (then) Lieutenant Colonel Prabowo Subianto, who was at that time stationed in Dili. It was also a sign that the army would continue to take a tough line against protesters in East Timor. This incident backfired against this suggested plan, arousing even greater antipathy towards Indonesia among the people of East Timor, while Prabowo was not held accountable for the incident and two key Murdani supporters lost their jobs. A more conventional interpretation of events was that the army was solely trying to reassert its authority over dissident East Timorese, although this seems unlikely given the public nature of the attack (see Kingsbury 1998b: 119–20).

The upshot was that, regardless of the motives behind it, almost without warning, soldiers opened fire on the protesters at close range. They later bayoneted wounded protesters and were alleged to have gone to a nearby hospital where they killed the wounded who had been taken there. Parts of the massacre were recorded on videotape and broadcast and rebroadcast throughout the world. It was a public relations disaster for Indonesia and aroused considerable international sympathy for the East Timorese cause. The Indonesian government exacerbated the situation by initially claiming that only nineteen had been killed with ninety-one wounded, later raising that number to fifty dead after a formal inquiry. However, other accounts put the final death toll from this encounter at 273 (Grant 1996: 40).

It was far from the most bloody of Indonesia's massacres of East Timorese, but it did come at a time when the issue of East Timor was widely thought to have been resolved. In fact, what it showed the international community was two things. The first was that Indonesia's army would not hesitate in using brutal force against unarmed civilians. The second was that popular opposition to Indonesian rule in East Timor continued to be widespread and growing. This in turn reflected the new policy on the part of Falintil, to shift the focus of its campaign against Indonesia from direct armed conflict towards bringing it back to the towns of East Timor, through civil disobedience campaigns. It was a high price to pay, but the Santa Cruz massacre refocused world attention on East Timor in a way it had not been focused since, or perhaps even including, 1975.

It was also from around the time of the Santa Cruz massacre that the Roman Catholic church, already converting East Timorese at a quick rate, began to take on some of the traits of the radical version in Latin America: liberation theology. Most ordinary East Timorese claim the church was slow to accept the independence struggle, but as the ranks of its congregations swelled with pro-independence activists it was transformed from the bottom up. Although he had already begun speaking out about the possibility of a referendum on East Timor's future, by 1992 Bishop Carlos Belo was still very cautious about his role and the role of the church in pressing for independence.[8] However, within three years he had become an outspoken advocate of the human rights of East Timorese people and, by extension, an opponent of continued Indonesian occupation. In 1996 he and Fretilin's international spokesman, Jose Ramos Horta, were awarded the Nobel Peace Prize.

THE CAPTURE OF XANANA GUSMAO

As a part of the independence movement's policy to bring the struggle from the countryside to the towns, Gusmao moved to Dili in 1991. It was from there that he personally directed the civil disobedience campaign. However, living in Dili was a high-risk strategy, which came undone on 20 November 1992. Betrayed by an informer, Xanana was arrested. It was initially thought he would be charged with subversion, which potentially carried the death penalty in Indonesia, but the charges were later modified to those of rebellion, illegal possession of weapons, and separatism. He was initially sentenced to life imprisonment but, following international pressure, in 1993 his sentence was commuted to twenty years in prison.

While Fretilin and UDT had worked closely together since the mid 1980s, there had been some reluctance on the part of their members to form a full coalition. This was based on the ideological differences of the two organisations, lingering animosities flowing from the August 1975 'civil war', and UDT's association, however forced, with the Indonesian army for some years thereafter. However, with UDT increasingly firmly in the pro-independence camp, it became clear to both UDT and to Fretilin that, in order to secure international support, they needed to present a cohesive front. This was done through the establishment in 1997 of the Conselho Nacional de Resistencia Timorense (Council for Timorese National Resistance—CNRT). CNRT became the primary vehicle through which aspirations for independence could be channelled. Leaders from both parties joined the CNRT that became, in effect, a peak body. Both Fretilin and UDT continued to exist as separate political parties. Falintil shifted its political association to the CNRT, bringing some UDT members into its ranks in the process. The make-up of the CNRT included both Fretilin and UDT members at its top level, but Xanana Gusmao, the leader of both Falintil and Fretilin while still in jail, was elected to the position of president of the CNRT, while retaining his title of 'supreme commander' of Falintil.

INDONESIA RECONSIDERS

Following the resignation of Suharto as Indonesia's president in May 1998, his successor, Habibie, moved to assuage concerns of the international community over a range of issues, while also instituting some liberalising procedures. Apart from releasing some political prisoners, lifting many media restrictions and making moves towards cleaning up the most obvious cases of corruption and nepotism, Habibie began to look to further placating a restive international community. The cost of maintaining East Timor, in terms of military presence, the infrastructure required to support both the military and the Indonesian bureaucracy, and what the

Indonesian government claimed was its investment in human infrastructure, through education and health, was higher, at US$50 million a year, per head of population than for any other province. However, 'a lot poured out of it, into the pockets of corrupt military and civilian officials' (McBeth 1999c). Some estimates suggest as much as 30 per cent of spending was lost on corruption. In terms of revenues locally raised and expenditures, 7.6 per cent of local government expenditure was raised within East Timor, with 92.4 per cent coming from Jakarta (Tesoro 1999). But this did not account for the redirection of a massive proportion of East Timor's economy, nor for the disparities in income distribution that were usually defined along ethnic lines.[9]

As a consequence, and because of the international concern expressed over Indonesia's continued involvement in East Timor, on 20 June 1998 President Habibie offered to free Xanana Gusmao, withdraw troops and create a state of special autonomy for East Timor if the world recognised it as a part of Indonesia. It was only the first step in a protracted negotiation, and one that was quickly rejected by Gusmao as 'diplomatic blackmail'. Portugal, however, quickly jumped on the opportunity to re-open dialogue on East Timor, saying that 'If Indonesia is aiming for democracy, it is their duty to guarantee the East Timorese people the right to choose how they want to live' (Spencer 1999). Discussion continued and by November it was becoming clear that Habibie was looking for a genuine resolution to the issue. On 27 January 1999, Habibie announced that the people of East Timor could decide on their future. They would be given the chance to vote on whether they wished to remain a part of Indonesia, under what was claimed would be a wide-ranging autonomy, or to opt for independence.

However, while this offer was at one level widely appreciated, most commentators, including the jailed leader of the CNRT, Xanana Gusmao, asked for a longer time-frame in which the process could be undertaken. The UN, which was to supervise the ballot, also asked for a longer time-frame. Habibie refused, locking the UN into conducting the ballot within seven months. In part, Habibie's refusal to allow a longer time-frame acknowledged that at a later time he would probably no longer be president and that his successor might have a very different policy on the status of East Timor. At that time, Habibie's most likely successor was Megawati Sukarnoputri. Megawati had already made clear her opposition to East Timor becoming independent, a position she reiterated in East Timor just days before the ballot took place.

Further, the agreement that formalised the arrangement, signed on 5 May 1999, precluded the UN from having an armed presence in East

Timor (UN 1999a: pt 4). The Indonesian police would, the Indonesian government claimed, guarantee security. Yet before the 5 May agreement had even been signed, the security situation in East Timor had begun to seriously deteriorate. This reflected a deep reluctance on the part of many senior TNI figures, including the commander-in-chief of the TNI, General Wiranto, to accept Habibie's decision on East Timor. It also reflected a deteriorating relationship between Wiranto and Habibie and what amounted to competing visions for Indonesia's future.

So far as Wiranto was concerned, East Timor was primarily a military issue and secondarily a political issue. Wiranto had spent most of his military career as a Kostrad officer, at least once taking part in anti-insurgency operations in East Timor during the bloody crackdown of 1981. Also at stake was the pride of the TNI, the fact that many hundreds of Indonesian soldiers were buried there (and up to 10 000 more else-where) and that the old bugbear of state unity was perceived to be threatened by one of the provinces achieving independence. It was from the time of Habibie's announcement that East Timor's TNI-backed pro-integration militias became active.

Wiranto was criticised for having failed to contain the activities of pro-integration militias in East Timor. The general belief is that Wiranto was well aware of what had been happening in East Timor (see Tavares 1999) and that, by failing to act against it, despite the explicit wishes of Habibie, he endorsed or even ordered the activities. Soon after Habibie's announcement on East Timor, a 'Crisis Team on East Timor' was estab-lished to wage a 'dirty war' against pro-independence groups (Tapol 1999a). This team was headed by Major-General Zacky Anwar Makarim, who stepped down as head of military intelligence (BIA—Baden Intelijen ABRI) to take up the new position. Zacky was head of intelli-gence in East Timor at the time of the Dili massacre in 1991. Extraordi-narily, Zacky was also appointed as liaison officer between the TNI and the UN in East Timor, which was at that time his official public role.

With Zacky in charge, the 'Crisis Team' set up the 'militias',[10] com-prising around 6000 paid and press-ganged East Timorese as well as large numbers of West Timorese and other islanders in thirteen organisations. The militias included the better known Aitarak, Besi Merah Butih, and Lahorus Merah Putih/Halilintar respectively in the districts of Dili, Liquisa and Bobonaro. Naga Merah dan Darah Merah was set up in Ermera, Laksau Merah Putih was established in Kova Lima, Mahidin was based in Ainaro, Abelai in Same, AHI in Aileu, Mahadomi in Manatuto, Saka in Baucau, Sera in Viqueque, Tim Alfa in Lauten, and Darah Merah in Ambeno. The militias were supported and partially armed by the regional Udayana IX Military Command, and occasionally led in the field by (sometimes former) military intelligence officers, associated with the Satuan Tugas Intelijen (Intelligence Duty Unit, STI) and Kopassus (Special Forces) (Tapol 1999b). Through what it called Operasi Sapu Jagad (Operation Global Clean-Sweep), these gangs were responsible for hundreds of deaths in East Timor between January and August 1999 and caused more than 60 000 people to flee their villages, creating a serious refugee problem. Officials from the key independence organisation, the CNRT, were killed, while its offices in the western part of East Timor were closed (Tapol 1999a). At the same time, tens of thousands of non-East Timorese who had been living there began to stream out of the territory. It was clear that their time of relatively easy living in a relatively safe place was coming to an end. A further element of Operation Global Clean-Sweep was to disrupt the UN process in East Timor (Tapol 1999a). Requests by Habibie, the nominal supreme commander of TNI, for it to rein in the militias and to impose order in the province were contemptuously ignored.

Despite the efforts of the TNI-backed militias, it became clear well ahead of the ballot that the pro-independence vote would succeed. This was even noted in a letter from a senior Indonesian bureaucrat in Dili to Indonesia's Coordinating Minister of Politics and Security, dated 3 July 1999. The letter admitted that, 'We have been left behind in the efforts to win the hearts of the people' (Garnadi 1999: 6) and that 'Special Autonomy will be rejected' (Garnadi 1999: 3). Despite the atmosphere of violence and intimidation, UNAMET functioned with great precision, reaching into the most remote villages and registering the most distant residents. Its public education campaign appeared to sink in at even the most basic level[11] and, in the final analysis, its registration of voters, some 460 000 of the territory's 850 000 people as well as those living in other parts of Indonesia and overseas, was an outstanding success.

THE BALLOT

The weeks leading up to the ballot were marked by a high level of violence and intimidation, having escalated after UNAMET began its active presence in East Timor. The thirteen militias set up by Zacky, under the control of the Apodeti military leader Joao Tavares, operated under the banner of the Pasukan Pejuang Integrasi (PPI—Integration Struggle Troops) (Tavares 1999). Despite the legality of the CNRT as a party to contest the ballot, the 'pro-autonomy' (pro-integration) groups kept up a campaign of violence against CNRT members and offices. The pro-autonomy groups divided into the Forum Perdamaian, Demokrasi dan Keadilan (FPDK—Forum for Peace, Democracy and Justice), the Barisan Rakyat Timor Timur (BRTT—People's Front of East Timor), and the militia-based PPI. Road blocks were put up to stop the movement of pro-independence supporters, and to stop humanitarian assistance getting to the refugee camps that had been established in remote areas. These were manned by militia members armed with often crude homemade weapons. Their guns, in particular, were based on the firing mechanism of shotguns housed in home-made bodies. Throughout August, as they began to hand in their home-made weapons, the militias were increasingly armed with the TNI's own weapons, including M-16, G3, SS-1 and AK47 automatic rifles, 9 mm pistols and, in the period just before the ballot, hand grenades. By this stage, however, the distinction between the militias, the TNI and the police had become effectively non-existent.

In Maliana, the provincial capital of the district that was the site of some of the most obvious militia activity in the pre-ballot period, the local Halilintar militia openly operated out of the local TNI headquarters.[12] The police, mostly from the paramilitary Brimob (Mobile Brigade) group, actively assisted militia members with transport and were reported by eyewitnesses to have shot villagers when militia rampaged through the village of Memo, near Maliana, on 28 August. There were many such reports of close association between the TNI, police and militias. Militia openly occupied police posts between Batu Gade, on the West Timor border on the northern coast, and the outskirts of Dili. TNI officers and non-commissioned officers were, in some cases, belatedly removed from their posts as a consequence of official and repeated UNAMET complaints about their involvement with the militias.[13]

'JUST KILL—KILL EVERYBODY'

Despite such superficial acknowledgment of the links between the TNI, police and the militias, the violence continued almost unchecked. The two moments that it seemed to stop were, in early August, around the day of the visit to East Timor by Australia's Foreign Minister, Alexander Downer, and during the day of the ballot itself. Apart from that, it escalated in ferocity from July onwards. The killings and kidnappings became more frequent, more homes were burned and more villages ransacked. When faced with the prospect that the pro-integration camp might not win the ballot, one of the key organisers of the FPDK, Filomeno Orai, was asked if he would guarantee a peaceful outcome. 'Peace?' he said. 'Why would we want peace? If the vote is for independence we'll just kill—kill everybody' (McBeth 1999c: 13). Even on the night of the ballot, the village of Ritabou, near Maliana, was put to the torch. It was from this time that UNAMET staff, in particular the polling staff, began to pull out of the provinces. This also marked the beginning of the killing of East Timorese people employed by UNAMET, as well as pro-independence supporters.

While the violence during the campaign period and in the days following the ballot had escalated, no one seemed prepared for the tidal wave of killing, burning and looting that took place starting within an hour of the announcement of the ballot outcome. Even if the ballot had been cancelled, there was a widespread belief among UNAMET security advisers and the CNRT that there would be an attempt to kill or scatter pro-independence supporters. As it turned out, the overwhelming vote for independence unleashed a wave of fury the scale of which neither the CNRT nor UNAMET seemed to expect. Despite all of the intimidation and the fact that many people did not believe their vote was secret, an amazing 98.6 per cent of registered voters participated in the poll. Of them, 78.5 per cent voted in favour of independence.

WHY?

The killings were wholesale in many parts of East Timor. The official death toll, based on a body count by UN staff, was less than 2000. However, local reports continued to refer to much larger numbers, such as between 2000 and 3000 people being killed in the town of Suai alone, and with tens of thousands of others still unaccounted for. No one was safe from the slaughter, except for more than 200 000 forced at gunpoint to be shipped to a perilous fate in refugee camps in West Timor (UNHCR 1999). Others were herded in hundreds onto boats, ostensibly to be sent to other islands. Yet the boats began to return within hours, with no refugees on board. The belief was that the passengers had been killed and their bodies dumped at sea. The question has been asked, and at the end of 2000 has still not been adequately answered: why did this happen? Despite claims by pro-integration groups, the violence was not in response to what they alleged was electoral fraud. The ballot was probably the most clean and transparent in Indonesia's history, despite the pre-ballot violence perpetrated by those people who later claimed the vote was somehow rigged. Of all the pro-integration group's feeble claims, perhaps one stands up to some scrutiny. They claimed that UNAMET employed mostly pro-independence workers for their local staff. Given the overwhelming support for independence among ordinary East Timorese, it would have been impossible for a representative grouping employed by UNAMET to be otherwise. This is not to mention the active opposition of the pro-integration groups to the whole idea of a ballot, much less to actively work for it. The other claims, however, were spurious.

At least a part of the attacks on civilians were an attempt to intimidate them into accepting continued Indonesian rule. It was a blunt method, but one that had been used with some success elsewhere in the archipelago in earlier times. In East Timor, it only hardened resistance to the idea. A second reason was to try to provoke Falintil into retaliation, thereby being able to claim a state of civil war and cancel the ballot or annul its result. A third reason was to use East Timor as a lesson to the other provinces of Indonesia considering breaking away: 'this is what happens if you try to leave', it seemed to be saying. The TNI also had problems with the idea that so many of their comrades had been killed in East Timor, and now it seemed to be for nothing. The anger and the sense of betrayal, however misguided, was real for some. And then there was the question of the TNI trying to save face in what was a humiliating defeat, not by force of arms, but at the hands of an unarmed population. It was a rejection not just of Indonesia, but of the idea of 'Indonesia'. The unity of the state was challenged, the concept of nationalism slapped in the face, the guardians of the state made to look foolish. The people of East Timor were made to pay for this.

Perhaps finally, there were also some elements of Jakarta's 'palace politics' being played out in East Timor, where a contest of wills between Habibie and Wiranto, or between 'reformists' and 'nationalists', determined policy on the ground. Clearly presidential aspirant Megawati Sukarnoputri had her fingers burned in the tussle, saying in early August that she would respect the outcome of the referendum. Just days later, seemingly at the behest of her ally Wiranto, she made a quick visit to East Timor where, flying by helicopter from town to town, she reversed that call and said she wanted to see East Timor remain a part of Indonesia. It was notable that, during her visit, Megawati failed to visit the head of the UNAMET mission, Ian Martin, or to speak to any UNAMET staff.

AN ARMED INTERVENTION

In most cases the people of East Timor knew that there would be some sort of retribution. The information about a type of post-ballot pro-integration campaign had been too frequent and too varied in its sources not to have some credibility. There was a widespread belief that it would come regardless of whether the vote was held or whatever its outcome. The pro-independence people would have to be dealt with.

Responding belatedly to calls by observers and East Timorese support groups, members of the international community began to coalesce around the idea of sending an armed mission into East Timor. The United States was reluctant but Australia, the population of which was outraged by events there, agreed to head such a mission. By mid September the UN had given approval to a peace-enforcement mission to East Timor, comprising military from Australia as well as New Zealand, Thailand, Portugal, the Philippines, South Korea, Cambodia, Britain, Ireland, the United States, Singapore, and Malaysia (UN 1999b). There were many empty threats made against the force, in particular the Australian contingent as Australia had been seen by many Indonesians as a driving force behind East Timor's push for independence. Ahead of the landing of the first International Forces to East Timor (InterFET) troops, 'high walled intelligence and interrogation centres were emptied and documents hastily dumped onto bonfires … Two decades of evidence went up in flames' (Murphy & McBeth 1999). As the InterFET troops landed, on 20 September 1999, members of the TNI and the militias had already begun to move across the border into West Timor, taking huge quantities of looted goods with them.

THE AFTERMATH

Even before the ballot, Xanana Gusmao had said that the East Timorese needed to look to the future and forget about the past. Rather than blame those East Timorese members of the militias for the violence, Gusmao laid the blame at the feet of the TNI. 'We will do everything to avoid vengeance and hatred between people,' he said. 'Of course we have to focus on reconciliation between East Timorese' (Gusmao 1999). Gusmao also pointed to the enormous development issues that the new, fledgling state would face: '…we also have to eat,' he said. 'And I can say to you that we have been preparing our development policy since the beginning of April this year' (Gusmao 1999). However, the task of developing the half-island state was complicated by the TNI's 'scorched earth' policy as it left East Timor. Infrastructure, including communications and water supply, was almost non-existent, most major buildings were destroyed or damaged, and industry was also non-existent.

In the years of the Indonesian occupation, most of the disparate peoples of East Timor had been bonded together by a common enemy and by what was increasingly a common religion, Roman Catholicism. The language of Tetun Dili had increasingly become the standard non-Indonesian language of communication, in a similar manner to that of Tagalog in the Philippines. However, most people and in particular those under forty also spoke Bahasa Indonesia, while those over forty often also spoke Portuguese. These were, in short, the identifiable characteristics of a nation, quite distinct from West Timor.

In the period after peace was restored to East Timor, the UN installed an interim administration, the UN Transitional Authority in East Timor (UNTAET), with the task of rebuilding the basic infrastructure and institutions of state. Apart from the obvious infrastructure requirements, institutions such as a bureaucracy, education system (including rebuilding the university), health service and legal service (including courts and police) would need to be established. In particular, the almost overwhelming health problem presented by malaria needed to be tackled as a matter of urgency, a fact recognised by CNRT. Similarly, a security or law enforcement and judicial apparatus was in the process of being established, both for internal policing and to secure East Timor's border with West Timor. There remained concerns that militia groups would continue to attempt to conduct cross-border raids against East Timor after the establishment of the independent state.

A NEW STATE

At one level there were grounds for the establishment of the institutions of state among East Timor's diaspora which indicated, in large measure, its desire to return. But it was clear that there would be external administrative support for East Timor while these institutions were rebuilt. In this respect, the administrative role of the UN was vital to East Timor securing a stable future.

East Timor's economy was also a critical issue. As the second poorest province in Indonesia and as an impoverished Portuguese colony, East Timor never had a strong economy. However, it did have some scope for economic development, which perhaps could provide the basis of a viable state. In the first instance, the Timor Gap gas and oil field reverted to East Timorese–Australian control and began to provide a flow of state income. Although not as lucrative as earlier thought, the gas revenues have not been insignificant and could contribute considerably to the fledgling state's coffers. East Timor also has a strong coffee production industry and, while world coffee prices were not high, it was also another source of foreign income, at around US\$40 million a year.

Despite the damage that has been done to it, East Timor is also in many senses a physically beautiful place and could attract tourism. It has been said that in 1974 East Timor enjoyed the same level of tourism development as Bali. While Bali was perhaps not the best example of tourism development, it was certainly a major revenue generator. The market for sandalwood, once the reason for foreign interest, is now very small. But it is still a natural resource that could be cultivated. Mineral deposits, mostly of marble, were also available for development, while East Timor's coastal region abounds with fish, having the potential to generate income both as exports and from licensed fishing (although this could interfere with an important local food source).

THE END OF CONSENSUS

With the removal of the last Indonesian forces in October 1999 and the effective quelling of the threat from pro–Indonesian militias, political organisations within East Timor began to look to the future, and to their various visions for it. Not surprisingly, this led to divisions within the umbrella body, the CNRT, both along Fretilin and UDT lines, between radicals and moderates within Fretilin, and between younger and older members. Even the armed wing of the CNRT, Falintil, began to identify its interests somewhat separately from those of the 'politicians'. Within Fretilin and CNRT, there were also divisions between those sections of the organisation that wanted to maintain a clandestine political organisation, so successfully built up under Indonesian occupation, and those who wanted CNRT and Fretilin to be fully public organisations. In part this reflected a lack of a sense of security about the prospective political environment, but also indicated where respective political power bases lay. The future relationship between Falintil and both Fretilin and the CNRT was being discussed throughout 2000, with it seeming likely that Falintil would have to reinvent itself as an institution of state (as the police or paramilitary) rather than as an armed wing of a political organisation. At the left-wing end of the political spectrum was the small party, the

Timorese Socialist Party (PST), the Council for Popular Defence of the Proclamation of the Democratic Republic (CPD-RDTL) and the Revolutionary Front for the Independence of East Timor. Both the PST and the RDTL were largely based on a younger membership than Fretilin and were more radical in their views. The Revolutionary Front, however, worked more closely with CNRT. Older, more subterranean distinctions also existed between what might be broadly described as the more ethnically 'pure' *kampones* (peasants), also known as *indijenas* or *rai-na'in*, and the more usually *mestisu* (Potuguese–Timorese mixed-blood) elites. Again, much of the older generation of Fretilin/CNRT leaders, who were more educated, tended to be of the traditionally more favoured (by the Portuguese) *mestisu* background. Even language policy had become divisive, with the older members of the CNRT pushing for Portuguese to be the official language of state and of education. Younger CNRT members, however, strongly preferred Bahasa Indonesia and English as more practical alternatives.

Apart from Fretilin and UDT, pro-integrationists revived themselves as a minor political force. The two main pro-integrationist organisations were the National Union Front for Political Affairs and the Popular Timorese Party (PPT). PPT had expressed an interest in registering for the proposed 2001 elections in East Timor, but doing so from Kupang in West (Indonesian) Timor. While there was some concern for the safety of members of a pro-integration party, the move was also seen as a spoiling manouevre, indicating that the pro-integrationists would not quickly fade away and allow the territory to get on with establishing itself as an independent state. These groups also conducted a spoiling campaign, by continuing to challenge the validity of the UNAMET ballot process and denying its democratic credentials. The National Union Front for Political Affairs also took the view that UNAMET had sided with the pro-independence group during the ballot. These pro-integration groups replaced the PPI and its militias (some of which continued to exist in West Timor), the Forum Persatuan, Demokrasi dan Keadilan (Unity, Democracy and Justice Forum—FPDK) and the Barisan Rakyat Timor Timur (East Timor People's Front—BRTT).

In the period before full self-government, scheduled for 2001, East Timor was formally run by UNTAET, in collaboration with CNRT, as the de facto government of East Timor. This coalition of UNTAET and CNRT was called the National Consultative Council. Elections ahead of self-government were planned to be held in the latter part of 2000. The question that confronted the people of East Timor was whether, after the UN and the aid agencies had packed up and gone home, they would be able to work together, with so few resources, to build a cohesive state that was viable within the wider international context.

Apart from the potential for internal political instability, the greatest threat to East Timor came from across the border, in West Timor. Cross-border militia activity had resumed while an international military presence remained, and maintenance of border security became more problematic even before that international presence left. The first problem was that while many militia had given up the fight, about 2000 remained armed and active in West Timor. These 'clandestine' militia continued to operate with the backing of senior officers within the TNI, who supported them through arranging illegal activities, such as working in 'protection' rackets in Jakarta. These militia and the generals who supported them would remain a potential problem as long as the generals retained their positions within the TNI. This in turn was dependent on the territorial structure of the TNI and its involvement in business, both legal and illegal. Resolution of these issues was on the Indonesian political agenda, but were far from being resolved.

Even more disturbingly, many Indonesian people believed that East Timor had been stolen from them and that it remained within the archipelago and so would eventually be returned. This view was likely to strongly influence policy decisions in Indonesian political and economic relations with East Timor. That East Timor's major neighbour should regard the tiny new state with such ambiguity was a sign that its future was far from settled.

NOTES

1   This chapter is accorded relatively more space than the similarly small state of Brunei. The reason for this is the more tumultuous history of East Timor, as well as the greater number and depth of the issues it raises.
2   The author was in East Timor, on this occasion, as the East Timor coordinator of the Australian NGO observer group, the Australia East Timor International Volunteer Project, from late July until early September 1999.
3   Portuguese explorer Duarte Barbosa was one of the first to visit the territory, in 1518.
4   Falintil—Forcas Armada de Liberacao Nacional de Timor L'Este (Armed Forces for the National Liberation of East Timor)—was the armed wing of Fretilin, later under the CNRT.
5   This was a very similar process by which West Papua was formally incorporated into Indonesia in 1969.

6   This estimate is based on discussions held with Falintil members, aid workers in East Timor and, in 1999, with UNAMET political officers.

7   The other had been Murdani's mentor, General Ali Murtopo, who was head of Opsus (Special Operations), a secretive quasi-military organisation.

8   Based on a conversation between the author and Bishop Belo in Melbourne in 1994.

9   Based on observation and discussions during a visit to East Timor in 1995.

10 Cotton says the militias were 'raised by the Interior Ministry but attached to territorial or combat military groups' (Cotton 1999: 15).

11 Based on personal observation during the campaign period, and on reports by AETIVP members.

12 Based on personal observation.

13 For example, in late August the military head of Bobonaro district (around Maliana) and three NCOs were removed from their posts.

Conclusion

It can be taken as read that any work on South–East Asia presupposes the existence of such a region in other than a purely imaginary sense. Given the diversity within the region referred to, perhaps without some imaginative leap such a construction would not exist. Yet South–East Asia is a part of the world that can be in some broad sense defined, and is occasionally self-defining (for example, ASEAN). South–East Asia is, in the contemporary sense, beyond the immediate orbit of both China and India, although it reflects influences from both. The region is also almost entirely within the tropical belt and is for the large part mountainous, apart from river valleys and very occasional plains, lending an element of geographic uniformity. But more importantly, while retaining distinct cultural elements, there has been considerable exchange throughout the region as well.

Coedes noted the 'Indianised' elements of Java and Sumatra, Cambodia, Burma, Thailand and Laos (1968), and further identified the early Javanese influence in both Cambodia and Champa. Champa no longer exists as a state, although small Cham communities continue in Vietnam and more particularly in Cambodia, to where they fled ahead of the invading Vietnamese. The state may now be extinct, but the culture is not, and to watch contemporary Cham dance is to visit the stone relief of the Khmer Angkor Wat, to see the engraved *apsaras* (heavenly nymphs) in human form. Contemporary Cambodian dance, on the other hand, reflects Thai influences, rather than those of Angkor. The ebb and flow of armies, but more importantly peoples, has similarly spread cultural influences and muddied what some irridentist nationalists would like to claim as distinct identities. The neatness of states indicated by borders is not reflected by the untidiness of physical human drift, although the latter more accurately corresponds to the pre-colonial environment than does the former.

Archipelagic South–East Asia has its own shared, and often confused, identity as well, with maritime and Islamic influences among its predominantly Malay community spread as wide as Sumatra in the west to the Philippines in the east. Where else but among a coastal trading community would identifiable ethnic groups find themselves not only scattered across a region, as are the Bugis, for example, but often living side by side with communities that have also come from elsewhere?

The inland peoples of these regions were less influenced by such trade and cultural mobility and, in many places, developed cultures that were linked only to their nearest neighbours. But common communal patterns and forms of authority were and often are still found in the more remote places. The traditional local chief, the *datu*, is still to be found from remote villages in Sumatra to the mountains of Sabah and the valleys of the Philippines.

It is interesting to speculate on what might have been had South-East Asia not been subject to European colonialism. Assuming no internal catastrophe, Thailand would probably be a significantly larger state now than it is, encompassing Laos, half of Cambodia and the northern peninsular Malay states. On the other hand, Lan Na, centred on Chiang Mai, could have reasserted its independence, and perhaps rejoined with Shan state in Burma. Vietnam, too, would probably be further extended at its southern and western reaches, if it maintained its on-again-off-again unity, while Cambodia, like Champa, would probably have ceased to exist, as it once almost did. Burma might exist in something corresponding to contemporary form, although given its expansionist tendencies in the past it could also be greater, at the expense of neighbouring Thailand. Alternatively, given its composite nature, it might also have fallen apart, as it has so many times in the past.

In the archipelago, it is possible that we could have witnessed the establishment of another Javanese-based empire. Indeed, some critics suggest that is precisely what did happen, after the Dutch left the region. The glory of Majapahit could have been revisited upon the numerous peoples of the nearby islands, though it is possible that they might not have seen—or see—such visitation in equally glorious terms. Equally as possible, the state structure of the region could indicate several independent sultanates or Islamic-based states, in Sulu and Mindanao in the southern Philippines, in Brunei and Sarawak, in Riau, Sumatra, Java, on the rump Malay Peninsula, West and East Kalimantan, north and south Sulawesi, Maluku, and throughout the south-eastern islands towards West Papua.

But history is, more or less, what it is, and the impact of European colonialism is difficult to ignore. One can argue over the costs or benefits of the colonial enterprise but there is little doubt that colonialism effectively defined contemporary frontiers and, through borrowed or modified models, left a variety of forms of government. The pre-colonial versions of a state without defined borders, in particular the centralised authority of the mandala model, are largely gone. Authority may be centralised, perhaps more effectively in some cases than in the past, but the traditional porousness of borders is anathema to the contemporary state, while authority within borders is only ever grudgingly or unwillingly incomplete.

Almost regardless of the political model adopted, or invented, in the region, some more traditional forms of authority continue. Most notably, variations on patron–client relations continue to dominate, running afoul of conventional statist notions of propriety and political party. No state in South-East Asia has shown itself immune to the continuation of this deeply entrenched system of social, economic and political relations, and it has often been manifested in forms that have transgressed modern law, as with corrupt or nepotistic practices. Of course, such relationships are not exclusive to the region, but they are certainly well represented throughout it.

In a similar and related manner, notions of strong authority remain well entrenched throughout the region. Rare and usually short-lived is the government that does not shore up its power base by methods other than direct electoral support. This in turn has had widespread implications for notions of political representation and participation, and led to creative uses of the term 'democracy', some of which have ultimately included its rejection. Similarly, conceptions of civil and political rights have usually received short shrift, mostly on the grounds that they do not conform to local patterns of authority and respect. It is accurate to iden-tify numerous similar models which posit respect for authority as an admirable quality, and which favour the collective good over that of the individual. But the reification of these values, usually in a highly stylised and non-reflexive manner, speak more about the achievement and main-tenance of political power than they do about the practical conventions of village-based, pre-modern society. Not surprisingly, for peoples who have been brought rapidly from institutionalised pre-modernism into the modern or indeed post-modern world in a few short decades, it is not surprising that 'naturalised' values do not quickly disappear, or are recast in a bid to meet contemporary exigencies. What is of concern, however, is that the reification of many of those values has led to rigid or even brit-tle responses to situations that might benefit more from flexibility and adaptation. In particular, the passing on of long-standing political leaders who have deeply personalised power poses problems not just for transi-tion processes but for attendant state stability. Who will genuinely run Singapore after Lee Kuan Yew dies, or Cambodia after Hun Sen, Burma after Ne Win, Malaysia after Mahatir, or Indonesia after Abdurrahman Wahid? There may be people to rise to the occasion, but there may also be a fundamental shift in political processes, as seen after both Sukarno and Suharto in Indonesia, and after Marcos in the Philippines.

Despite such questions, at the beginning of the twenty-first century there is a temptation to be hopeful, to see the uncharted future as pregnant with positive possibilities. It would be fair to say this of the states and societies of the future of South-East Asia, noting the achievements of each, often against the odds, in the post-colonial period. Yet the idea of a century, or a millennium, is in a practical sense arbitrary and its end or beginning is but one point on a continuum. Little of contemporary South-East Asia can be understood without at least a passing reference to its history, and very large parts of that history indicate that while change and growth of one type or another is probably inevitable, much of it is unpredictable. There are certainly no guarantees that the future will correspond to most peoples' desires, much less any sort of democratic-capitalist 'end of history' scenario as outlined by, for example, Francis Fukyama. Notions of democracy might have a normative value for most readers of this text, but it would be a mistake to automatically assume that because they regard it as desirable it is not just a passing phase in a very long evolutionary political cycle. Many have, in the past, considered the divine right of kings, or the cult of the *devaraja*, to be normatively desirable too, yet that has not lasted. It might be that, in some future technocratic age (perhaps not so far away), political decisions will be seen to be too important to be left in the hands of the untrained or unskilled. Yet this itself raises questions about hegemony, and the representation of sectional interests.

Similarly, there are no imminent threats on the horizon either, although with the benefit of an historical cast it should be noted that events that correspond to decades or centuries can rarely be seen from the perspective of the present. We might know what is happening now, or think we do, but can we really know how what is happening fits into a bigger picture? Will political models that exist at the beginning of 2001 still be around in a hundred years, or even twenty? Will state borders remain, or change? Indeed, will states that we are so familiar with continue to exist in their present form into the indefinite future? Perhaps, but one need only look at contemporary Indonesia to understand the tensions that compete with the idea of the unity of the state are not to be underestimated. The idea of East Timor, as a late inclusion into Indonesia, was for that state seen as irrevocably included. Yet at the beginning of the twenty-first century that inclusion had been comprehensively revoked. What might this imply for Aceh, or West Papua, or any other part of the troubled archipelago? What of Malaysia? Singapore left the Malaysian Federation inside three years, and perhaps Sarawak will one day find an independent place in the world, next to Brunei. The

Philippines, too, has serious internal tensions, as does Burma. Or perhaps, as the world becomes more 'globalised', the idea of the state as such starts to recede in significance, the local unit of cultural and political expression perhaps becoming closer and more familiar.

At the beginning of this book we visited the fictional character Ni, taking a moment's break from his paddy field, contemplating just some of the manifestations of changing life in South-East Asia. There is much, probably most, of South-East Asia still, at the beginning of 2001, that is actually very close to Ni's experience. Some people of the region still live in societies little or not at all touched by modernisation, while most are caressed so gently by it they are barely distracted from the concerns and aspirations that preoccupied their forefathers and mothers. Millions of others, though, have been caught up in the rising tide of modernisation and industrialisation, swept up and deposited in factories, schools and offices, living in often teeming cities with marginal infrastructure but limitless opportunity. Or so it seems, often, from the perspective of the paddy. How rich the variety and possibility of the occupants of shiny cars driving fast along new motorways, dashing from one interesting, almost unbelievable, site to another, if seen from the perspective of the uneducated worker standing knee-deep in brown water, shifting mud from one point to another. What unimaginable lives must be led. Perhaps the goal of the modernisation project is to take all the field workers from the paddies, and the political leaders of the region are attempting to do that as best and as fast as they can. But perhaps, just perhaps, the logic of the process is self-generating and that for winners there must also be losers. The distribution of material gain is a manifestation of the distribution of political power. The rhetoric of politics often espouses the ideal, but usually settles for the mundanely practical, or self-serving. The key to understanding the political dynamic of the various states and peoples of South-East Asia is therefore less related to political rhetoric, the espousal of worthy goals or claims to common good, than it is to actual outcomes. It is not what people say, in politics, that is important. It is what they do.

Bibliography

Abinales, P. 1996, 'When a Revolution Devours its Children Before Victory: *Operasyon Kampanyang Ahos* and the Tragedy of Mindanao Communism', in P. Abinales (ed.), *The Revolution Falters: The Left in Philippine Politics After 1986*, Southeast Asia Program Publications No. 15, Cornell University, Ithaca, NY.

Adams, N. 1970, 'Patrons, Clients, and Revolutionaries: The Lao Search for Independence, 1945–1954', in N. Adams and A. McCoy, *Laos: War and Revolution*, Harper & Row, New York.

Agence France Presse 1996, 'Burma Admits Drug Problem, Rejects US Criticism', 3 December.

—— 1999a, 'Drug Lords' Presence a Necessary Evil—Expert', *Bangkok Post*, 25 February, p. 4.

—— 1999b, 'Interpol Endorses Junta's Drug Proposals', *Bangkok Post*, 26 February, p. 5.

Agencies 1999, 'Government Denies Hosting Khmer Rouge Pair', *Sunday Nation* (Bangkok), 3 January, p. 1.

Alford, P. 1999, 'Muslim Surge Sours Mahatir's Triumph', *Australian*, 1 December, p. 7.

Amnesty International 1990, *1990 Report*, Amnesty International Publications, London.

Anderson, B. 1964, 'The Idea of Power in Javanese Culture', in C. Holt, B. Anderson and J. Siegal (eds), *Culture and Politics in Indonesia*, Cornell University Press, Ithaca, NY.

—— 1972, 'The Idea of Power in Javanese Culture', in C. Holt, B. Anderson and J. Siegal (eds), *Culture and Politics in Indonesia*, Cornell University Press, Ithaca, NY.

—— 1990, *Language and Power: Exploring Political Cultures in Indonesia*, Cornell University Press, Ithaca, NY.

—— 1991, *Imagined Communities*, 2nd edn, Verso, London.

Anwar, D.F. 2000, 'Indonesia's Transition to Democracy: Challenges and Prospects', in A. Budiman and D. Kingsbury (eds), *Rethinking Indonesia*, Crawford House Publishing, Adelaide (forthcoming).

AP (Associated Press) 1998, 'Pomp and Bon Jovi Herald a Fresh Heir', *Age*, 11 August, p. 7.

ASEAN Declaration on the South China Sea, 22 July 1992, Manila.

ASEAN Regional Forum (ARF) 1994, *Chairman's Statement*, 25 July, ARF, Bangkok.

A Short History of the Malayan Communist Party 1955, Government of the Federation of Malaya.

Asian Development Bank 1999, *Annual Report*, Asian Development Bank, Manila.

Asiaweek 1998a, 'Estrada's bumbling beginning', *Asiaweek*, 7 August, p. 19.

Asiaweek 1998b, 'The Trigger', 26 December, p. 110.

Atkinson, J. 1987, 'Religions in Dialogue: The Construction of an Indonesia Minority Religion', in R. Kipp and S. Rogers (eds), *Indonesian Religions in Transition*, University of Arizona Press, Phoenix, pp. 171–86.

Aung-Thwin, M. 1998, *Myth and History in the Historiography of Early Burma*, Ohio University Centre for International Studies Monograph No. 102, Athens, Ohio.

Australian Council for Overseas Aid 1987, *Life after Debt*, ACFOA, Canberra.

—— 1991, *East Timor: Keeping the Flame of Freedom Alive*, Development Dossier No. 29.

Australian International Development Assistance Bureau 1989, *Debt and the Developing World*, Australian Government Publishing Service, Canberra.

Bachrach, P. & Baratz, M. 1962, 'The Two Faces of Power', *American Political Science Review*, no. 56.

Baker, M. 1998, 'Power without glory', *Age*, News Extra, 26 September, p. 3.

Bakker, J. and Ferrazzi, G. 1997, Weber's Pure Ideal Type Model of Matrimonial Prebendalism: Testing the Applicability of the Model in Indonesia, unpublished paper to the 92nd annual meeting of the American Sociological Association, Toronto, 9–13 August.

Balfour, F. for Agence France Press 1999, 'Vietnam's Communist Party Wants to Walk a Harder Line', *The Cambodia Daily*, 27 January, p. 10.

Ball, D. 1998, *Burma's Military Secrets: Signals Intelligence (SIGINT) from 1941 to Cyber Warfare*, White Lotus Press, Bangkok.

—— 1999, 'Burma and Drugs: The Regime's Complicity in the Global Drug Trade', *Asia-Pacific*, no. 14.

Ball, D. and Acharya, A. 1999, *The Next Stage: Preventative Diplomacy and Security Co-operation in the Asia-Pacific Region*, Strategic and Defence Studies Centre, Research School of Pacific and Asian Studies, Australian National University, Canberra.

Bangkok Post 1999a, 'Motorcycle Thief Shot and Killed', 13 January, p. 2.

——1999b, 'Sabotage on the Waterfront', 13 January, p. 8.

—— 1999c, 'Opposition Attack Wins Favor', 13 January, p. 3.

Bangkok Post reporters 1999, 'Security Tightened in Bangkok', 15 January, p. 1.

Battersby, P. 1990, 'Border Politics and the Broader Politics of Thailand's International Relations in the 1990s: From Communism to Capitalism', *Pacific Affairs*, vol. 71, no. 4, winter, pp. 1998–9.

—— 1999, 'Border Politics and the Broader Politics of Thailand's International relations in the 1990s: From Communism to Capitalism', *Pacific Affairs*, vol. 71, no. 4, Winter 1998–99.

Bedlington, S. 1978, *Malaysia and Singapore: The Building of New States*, Cornell University Press, Ithaca, NY.

Bello, W., Kinley, D. and Elinson, E. 1982, *Development Debacle: The World Bank in the Philippines*, Institute for Food and Development Policy, San Francisco.

Bellows, T. 1970, *The People's Action Party of Singapore: Emergence of a Dominant Party System*, Monograph Series no. 14, Yale University, New Haven, CT.

Benitez, C. 1954, *History of the Philippines*, Ginn & Co., Manila.

Beresford, M. 1988, 'Issues in Economic Unification: Overcoming the Legacy of Separation', in D. Marr and C. White (eds), *Postwar Vietnam: Dilemmas in Socialist Development*, Cornell Southeast Asia Program, Ithaca, NY.

Berfield, S. and Loveard, D. 1999, 'Ten Days that Shook Indonesia', in E. Aspinall, G. van Klinken and H. Feith (eds), *The Last Days of President Suharto*, Monash Asia Institute, Melbourne.

Berman, L. 1998, *Speaking Through the Silence: Narratives, Social Conventions and Power in Java*, Oxford University Press, New York.

Berry, K. 1997, *Cambodia from Red to Blue: Australia's Initiative for Peace*, Australian National University, Canberra, and Allen & Unwin, Sydney.

Borneo Post 1999, 'Manila Talks with Rebels Expected to Fail', 15 February, Kota Kinabalu, p. 9.

Bourchier, B. 1999, 'Why Indonesia Had to Explode', in E. Aspinall, G. van Klinken, and H. Feith (eds), *The Last Days of President Suharto*, Monash Asia Institute, Melbourne.

Bourchier, D. 1996, Lineages of Organicist Political Thought in Indonesia, PhD thesis, Monash University, Melbourne.

—— 1998, 'More Educated, More Ruthless', *Inside Indonesia*, no. 53, January–March, pp. 14–15.

—— 1999, 'Skeletons, Vigilantes and the Armed Forces Fall from Grace', in A. Budiman, B. Hatley and D. Kingsbury (eds), *Reformasi: Crisis and Change in Indonesia*, Monash Asia Institute, Melbourne.

Bowie, A. and Unger, D. 1997, *The Politics of Open Economies*, Cambridge University Press, Cambridge.

Boyce, D. 1998, 'Investment in Cambodia Plunges This Year', *Cambodia Daily* (Phnom Penh), 8 July.

Brandt, W. (ed.) 1983, *Common Crisis*, Pan World Affairs, London.

Brandt, W. 1985, *Global Challenge*, Pan World Affairs, London.

Brewer, A. 1980, *Marxist Theories of Imperialism: A Critical Survey*, Routledge & Keegan Paul, London.

Brohman, J. 1996, *Popular Development*, Blackwell Publishers, Oxford.

Brown, M. 1974, *The Economics of Imperialism*, Penguin Modern Economic Texts, Harmondsworth.

Brunei Darussalam, Government of, 1988, *Brunei Darussalam in Profile*, Shandwick, London.

Budiardjo, C. and Liem. S.L. 1984, *The War against East Timor*, Zed Books, London.

Burger, W. and Bogert, C. 1988, 'Mahatir's Heavy Hand', *Newsweek*, 2 May.

Business Times 1996, 'Be Realistic about Level Playing Field: SM Lee', Singapore, 22 May.

Buttinger, J. 1967a, *Vietnam: A Dragon Embattled*, vol. 1, Praeger Publishers, New York.

—— 1967b, *Vietnam: A Dragon Embattled*, vol. 2, Praeger Publishers, New York.

—— 1968, *Vietnam: A Political History*, Praeger Publishers, New York.

Cady, J. 1958, *A History of Modern Burma*, Cornell University Press, Ithaca, NY.

Caldwell, M., and Tan, L.H. 1973, *Cambodia in the Southeast Asian War*, Monthly Review Press, New York.

Caldwell, M. and Utrecht, E. 1979, *Indonesia: An Alternative History*, Alternative Publishing Co-operative Limited, Sydney.

Camilleri, J. and Falk, J. 1992, *The End of Sovereignty? The Politics of a Shrinking and Fragmenting World*, Edward Elgar, London.

Camilleri, J. 1994, 'Reflections on the State in Transition', *Arena*, Melbourne.

Camnews (Cambodia News Digest) 1999, 'KR Jailer in Protective Custody', no. 389, May.

Campbell, T. 1983, *The Left and Rights*, Routledge & Keegan Paul, London.

Case, W. 1996, *Elites and Regimes in Malaysia*, Monash Asia Institute, Melbourne.

Chalongphob, S. 1998, 'Thailand's Debt Crisis and Economic Outlook', *Trends*, Institute of Southeast Asian Studies/*Business Times*, no. 893, 1 January–1 February.

Chanda, N. 1986, *Brother Enemy: The War After the War*, Collier Books, New York

Chandler, D. 1983, *A History of Cambodia*, 2nd edn, Westview Press, Boulder, Colo.

—— 1992, *Brother Number One: A Political Biography of Pol Pot*, Silkworm Books, Bangkok.

—— 1994, 'The Roots of Conflict in Cambodia', in D. Kingsbury and G. Barton (eds), *Difference and Tolerance: Ethnicity, Religion and Human Rights in South East Asia*, Deakin University Press, Geelong, Vic.

Chandler, D. and Kiernan, B. (eds) 1983, *Revolution and its Aftermath in Kampuchea: Eight Essays*, Yale University Southeast Asia Studies Monograph Series no. 25, Yale Center for International and Area Studies, New Haven, CT.

Chandler, D., Kiernan, B. and Boua, C. 1988. *Pol Pot Plans the Future*, Yale University Southeast Asia Studies Monograph Series no. 33, Yale Center for International and Area Studies, New Haven, CT.

Chanoff, D., and Doan, V.T. 1996, *Vietnam: A Portrait of its People at War*, I.B. Taurus Publishers, London.

Cheah, Yanchong 1996, 'More Thoughts on the Ancient Culture of the Thai People', *Journal of the Siam Society*, vol. 84, part 1.

Chee, S.J. 1998, *To Be Free: Stories from Asia's Struggle against Oppression*, Monash Asia Institute, Melbourne.

Choong Tet Sieu and Arjuna Ranawana 1998, 'A Case of Order and Disorder', *Asiaweek*, 16 October, pp. 33–4.

Clegg, S. 1989, *Frameworks of Power*, Sage Publications, London.

Clements. A and Suu Kyi, A. S. 1997, *The Voice of Hope*, Penguin, London.

Coedes, G. 1966, *Angkor*, Oxford University Press, Hong Kong.

—— 1968, *The Indianised States of Southeast Asia*, East–West Centre Press, Honolulu.

Cohen, W. 1995, *The Cambridge History of American Foreign Relations: America in the Age of Soviet Power, 1945–1991*, Cambridge University Press, Cambridge.

Colmey, J. and Liebhold, D. 1999, 'The Family Firm', *Time*, 24 May, pp. 36–48.

Comber, L., 1995, 'The Weather … has been horrible': Malayan Communist Communications during "The Emergency" (1948–60), *Asian Studies Review*, vol. 19, no. 2, November.

Communist Party of Vietnam (CPV) 1991, *Report of the Central Committee's 6th Term on the Documents of the 7th National Congress.*

Confucius 1995, *The Analects*, trans. W.E. Soothill, Dover Publications, New York.

—— 1997, *The Analects of Confucius*, trans. S.W.W. Leys, Norton, London.

Constantino, R. 1975, *The Philippines: A Past Revisited*, Tala Publishing Services, Quezon City.

Cook, M. 1977, *The Constitutionalist Party of Cochinchina: The Years of Decline, 1930–1942*, Monash Papers on Southeast Asia No. 6, Monash University, Melbourne.

Corfield, J. 1994, *Khmers Stand Up!* Monash Asia Institute, Melbourne.

—— 1998, 'Detested Confidant of Marcos', *Australian*, 25 November, p. 15.

—— (ed.) (no date), Selected Chronicles from the Reign of King Rama II: Thai-Malay Relations during the Early Nineteenth Century, trans. C. Skinner, unpublished manuscript.

Cotton, J. (ed.) 1999, *East Timor and Australia*, Australian Defence Studies Centre, Australian Defence Force Academy, Canberra.

Cowen, M. and Shenton, R. 1996, *Doctrines of Development*, Routledge, London.

Cramb, R. and Dixon, G. 1988, 'Development in Sarawak: An Overview', in R. Cramb and R. Reece (eds), *Development in Sarawak: Historical and Contemporary Perspectives*, Monash Papers on Southeast Asia No. 17, Centre of Southeast Asian Studies, Monash University, Melbourne.

Crispin, S. 2000, 'Tide of Change', *Far Eastern Economic Review*, 13 April, p. 12.

Crispin, S. and Tasker, R. 2000, 'First Steps', *Far Eastern Economic Review*, 16 March, p. 16.

Crone, P. 1986, 'The Tribe and the State', in J. Hall (ed.), *States in History*, Basil Blackwell, Oxford.

Crouch, H. 1988, *The Army and Politics in Indonesia*, Cornell University Press, Ithaca, NY.

—— 1992, 'Authoritarian Trends, the UMNO Split and the Limits to State Power', in J. Khan and F. Loh Kok Wah (eds), *Fragmented Vision: Culture and Politics in Contemporary Malaysia*, Allen & Unwin, Sydney.

—— 1996, *Government and Society in Malaysia*, Allen & Unwin, Sydney.

—— 1999, 'Wiranto and Habibie: Military Civilian Relations since May 1998', in A. Budiman, B. Hatley and D. Kingsbury (eds), *Reformasi: Crisis and Change in Indonesia*, Monash Asia Institute, Melbourne.

Crowell, T. and Lopez, A. 1999, '"My Ratings Are Down"', *Asiaweek*, 5 November, p. 29.

Dahl, R. 1971, *Who Governs?* Yale University Press, New Haven, CT.

Daily Express 1999a, 'Political Conspiracy Ruled Irrelevant', Kota Kinabalu, 10 February, pp. 1, 2.

—— 1999b, 'Kurup Hits Out at the Traitors', Kota Kinabalu, 10 February, p. 3.

—— 1999c, 'Fat Hopes, Amir Kahar Tells Sis', Kota Kinabalu, 14 February, p. 3.

Davis, A. 1998, 'Rebels without a Pause', *Asiaweek*, 3 April, pp. 30–5.

Davis, A., and Hawke, B. 1998, 'Business is Blooming', *Asiaweek*, 23 January, pp. 46–52.

De Comyn, T. 1969, *State of the Philippines in 1810*, Filipiniana Book Guild, Manila.

Defence of Democracy Groups 1985, 'Suharto Challenges the Human Conscience', *Inside Indonesia*, no. 6, December, pp. 3–5.

De Matos, A. 1974, *Timor Portugues 1515–1769*, Universidade de Lisboa, Lisbon.

Deutsche Presse-Agenteur (DPA) 1999, 'Ousting Gives Communist Party Jitters', *The Nation* (Bangkok), 9 January, p. A2.

De Waal, A. 1997, *Famine Crimes*, African Rights and the International African Institute, London.

Deyo, F. (ed.) 1987, *The Political Economy of the New Asian Industrialisation*, Cornell University Press, Ithaca, NY.

Diaz, C. 1993, comment during interview, *Lateline*, ABCTV, 5 April.

Diokno, J. 1981, 'Untitled lecture, International Council of Amnesty International, Cambridge, 21 September 1978', in R. Alston (ed.), *Development, Human Rights and the Rule of Law*, Pergamon Press, London.

Dodd, C. 1972, *Political Development*, The Macmillan Press, London.

Dommen, A. 1965, *Conflict in Laos: The Politics of Neutralization*, Praeger, New York.

Donnelly, S. 1984, 'Human Rights and Development: Complimentary or Competing Concerns?', *World Politics*, vol. 36, no. 2, January.

Dunn, J. 1996, *Timor: A People Betrayed*, ABC, Sydney.

Easton, A. 1998, 'The Election Follies Roadshow Wows the Voters', *Age*, 25 April, p. 24.

Elegant, S. 2000, 'UMNO's Dilemma', *Far Eastern Economic Review*, 2 March, pp. 19–29.

Embassy of the Union of Myanmar 1998a, 'The New Cabinet', Newsletter no. 1/98, 2 January.

—— 1998b, 'Achievements of the Government in Narcotic Drug Control', Newsletter no. 2/98, 20 January.

Engelbert, T. and Goscha, C. 1995, *Falling Out of Touch*, Monash Asia Institute, Melbourne.

Erikson, J. 1998, 'Little Room at the Top', *Asiaweek*, 21 June, pp. 30–1.

Evans, G. and Rowley, K. 1990, *Red Brotherhood at War*, 2nd edn, Verso, London.

Evans, G. 1998, *The Politics of Ritual and Remembrance: Laos since 1975*, Silkworm Books, Bangkok.

Evans, I. 1922, 'Primitive People's of Borneo', *British North Borneo Herald*, reproduced in *Daily Express* (Kota Kinabalu), 14 February 1999, p. 5.

Evans, P. 1995, *Embedded Autonomy: States and Industrial Transformation*, Princeton University Press, Princeton, New Jersey.

Fan Yew Teng 1999, *Anwar Saga: Malaysia On Trial*, Genting Raya Sdn Bhd, Seri Kembangan (Malaysia).

Far Eastern Economic Review 1981, no. 112, 29 May, p. 46.

Far Eastern Economic Review Yearbook 1997, 'Malaysia', pp. 164–8.

Faulder, D. 2000, 'A State of Injustice', *Asiaweek*, 3 March, p. 24.

Feinstein, D. 1998, text of speech to Foreign Operations, Export Financing and Related Agencies Appropriation Act 1999 to US Senate, regarding political and economic reform in Indonesia, 1 September.

Feith, H. 1962, *Decline of Constitutional Democracy in Indonesia*, Cornell University Press, Ithaca, NY.

—— 1969, 'Indonesia', in G. Kahin (ed.), *Governments and Politics in Southeast Asia*, 2nd edn, Cornell University Press, Ithaca, NY.

Feith, H. & Castles, L. 1970, *Indonesian Political Thinking 1945–65*, Cornell University Press, Ithaca, NY.

Fforde, A. 1999, Current Issues in Vietnamese Socioeconomic Development, in the Wake of the Regional Crisis: Given the Pattern of Investment, Does the Standard Development Model Apply? Seminar paper, Centre for Southeast Asian Studies, Monash University, Melbourne.

Fisher, C. 1966, *Southeast Asia: A Social, Economic and Political Geography*, Methuen & Co., London.

Fitzgerald, C.P. 1966, *A Concise History of East Asia*, Heinemann, Melbourne.

Flower, R. 1984, *Raffles: The Story of Singapore*, Croom Helm, London.

Forrester, G. 1998, 'A Jakarta Diary, May 1998', in G. Forrester and R. May (eds), *The Fall of Soeharto*, Crawford House Publishing, Bathurst NSW.

Fowler, M. and Bunck, J. 1995, *Law, Power and the Sovereign State*, University of Pennsylvania Press, University Park, PA.

Frank, G. 1981, *Reflections on the World Economic Crisis*, Hutchinson, London.

Friend, T. 1969, *Between Two Empires: The Ordeal of the Philippines 1929–1946*, Solidaridad Publishing House, Manila.

Friere, P. 1972, *Pedagogy of the Oppressed*, Penguin, London.

—— 1974, *Education: The Practice of Freedom*, Writers and Readers Publishing Cooperative, London.

Fukuyama, F. 1993, *The End of History and the Last Man*, Avon Books, New York.

Gamble, C. 1986, 'Hunter-Gatherers and the Origin of States', in J. Hall (ed.), *States in History*, Basil Blackwell, Oxford.

Garnadi, H. 1999, Memo Number: M53/TM p4-OKTT/7/99 (General Assessment if Option 1 fails), 3 July, Office of the Minister of State for Co-ordinating Politics and Security, Republic of Indonesia, Dili Command Post.

Gearing, J. 2000, 'Thailand's New Enforcer', *Asiaweek*, 24 March, p. 30.

Geertz, C. 1960, *The Religion of Java*, Free Press, New York.

—— 1963, *Agricultural Involution: The Process of Ecological Change in Indonesia*, University of California Press, Berkeley.

Gehan Wijeyewardene 1991, 'The Frontiers of Thailand', in C. Reynolds (ed.), *National Identity and Its defenders: Thailand, 1939–89*, Monash Papers on Southeast Asia No. 25, Monash University, Melbourne.

Giddens, A. 1987, *Social Theory and Modern Sociology*, Polity Press, Cambridge.

Goldsworthy, D. 1988, 'Thinking Politically about Development', *Development and Change*, vol. 19, no. 3, July.

Goldsworthy, D. (ed.) 1991, *Development and Social Change in Asia*, Radio Australia/Monash Development Studies Centre, Melbourne.

Gomez, J. 2000, *Self Censorship: Singapore's Shame*, Think Centre, Singapore.

Goodin, R. 1979, 'The Development–Rights Trade-Off: Some Unwarranted Economic and Political Assumptions', *Universal Human Rights*, vol. 1, no. 2, April–June.

Gramsci, A. 1971, *Selections from Prison Notebooks*, ed. and trans. Q. Hoare and G.N. Smith, Lawrence & Wishart, London.

Grant, B. 1996 (1964), *Indonesia*, 3rd edn, Melbourne University Press, Melbourne.

Groves, H. 1962, 'Notes on the Constitution of the Federation of Malaya', in K. Tregonning (ed.), *Papers on Malayan History*, Department of History, University of Malaya in Singapore.

Gusmao, J. 1999, 'We Will Forget the Past', answers to Tesoro, J., *Asiaweek*, 3 September.

Ha, T. 1999, 'Inflation Hits Vital Foods by 21.3 pc', *Vietnam Investment Review*, 1–7 February, p. 4.

Hammer, E. 1966, *The Struggle for Indochina 1940–1955*, Stanford University Press, Stanford, California.

Hammond, A. 1999, 'Indonesia Closes 38 Banks', *Age*, 15 March, p. B1.

Handelman, H. 1996, *The Challenge of Third World Development*, Prentice Hall, New Jersey.

Harrison, B. 1966, *South-East Asia: A Short History*, St Martin's Press, New York.

Hashim, S. 2000, 'Salamat Hashim Speaks', *Asiaweek*, 31 March, p. 29.

Hawes, G. 1987, *The Philippine State and the Marcos Regime*, Cornell University Press, Ithaca, NY.

Herz, M. 1958, *A Short History of Cambodia: From the Days of Angkor to the Present*, Atlantic Books, London.

Hettne, B. 1990, *Development Theory and the Three Worlds*, Longman Development Studies, New York.

Hewison, K. 1994, 'Minorities and Human Rights in Thailand', in D. Kingsbury and G. Barton (eds), *Difference and Tolerance: Human Rights Issues in Southeast Asia*, Deakin University Press, Geelong, Vic.

Hewison, K. 1997, 'The Monarchy and Democratisation', in K. Hewison (ed.), *Political Change in Thailand: Democracy and Participation*, Routledge, London.

Hiebert, M. 1998, 'Tactical Victory', *Far Eastern Economic Review*, 2 July, pp. 10–17.

Higgott, R. 1986, *Political Development Theory*, Croom Helm, London.

Hill, H. (ed.) 1994, *Indonesia's New Order*, Allen & Unwin, Sydney.

Hills, B. 1994, 'Darkness Enfolds the Little Lord', *Age*, 25 January, p. 7.

Hindley, D. 1964, *The Communist Party of Indonesia*, University of California Press, Berkeley.

Hinsley, F. 1978, *Sovereignty*, 2nd edn, Cambridge University Press, Cambridge.

Hiorth, F. 1985, *Timor: Past and Present*, South-East Asia Monograph no. 17, James Cook University, Townsville, Qld.

Ho Chi Minh 1994, *Selected Writings*, The Gioi Publishers, Hanoi.

Howard, R. 1983, 'The Full Bellies Thesis', *Human Rights Quarterly*, vol. 5, no. 4, November

Htin Aung 1967, *A History of Burma*, Columbia University Press, New York.

Hutchcroft, P. 1998, *Booty Capitalism: The Politics of Banking in the Philippines*, Cornell University Press, Ithaca, NY.

IMF 1999, *Articles of Agreement of the International Monetary Fund*, International Monetary Fund, Washington.

—— 2000, *Enhanced Structural Adjustment Facility*, International Monetary Fund, Washington.

Indochina Chronology 1999, 'Laos Struggles through 1999', vol. XVIII, no. 4, October.

Indonesia, Republic of, Department of Information 1989, *The 1945 Constitution of the Republic of Indonesia*, Department of Information, Jakarta.

Infante, J. 1980, *The Political, Economic and Labor Climate in the Philippines*, Industrial Research Unit, University of Pennsylvania, Philadelphia.

The Irrawaddy 1998a, 'Burma Making Small Arms', vol. 6, no. 4, 31 August.

—— 1998b, Mid-year Chronology.

—— 2000a, 'Bloody Day at Ratchaburi Hospital', January, p. 6.

—— 2000b, 'Thai Security Net Catches Dissidents, Intruders', February, p. 2.

The Jakarta Post.com 1999, 'Who's Who: Gen. Wiranto', *The Jakarta Post.com*

Jardine, M. 1995, *East Timor: Genocide in Paradise*, Odonian, Tucson, Arizona.

Jayasuriya, S. 1987, 'The Politics of Economic Policy in the Philippines during the Marcos Era', in R. Robison, K. Hewison and R. Higgott (eds), *South East Asia in the 1980s*, Allen & Unwin, Sydney.

Joliffe, J. 1978, *East Timor: Nationalism and Colonialism*, University of Queensland Press, St Lucia.

Josey, A. 1970, *Democracy in Singapore: The 1970 By-Elections*, Asia Pacific Press, Singapore.

Jumper, R. and Normand, M. 1969, 'Vietnam', in G. Kahin (ed.), *Governments and Politics of Southeast Asia*, 2nd edn, Cornell University Press, Ithaca, NY.

Kahin, G. (ed.) 1969, *Governments and Politics of Southeast Asia*, 2nd edn, Cornell University Press, Ithaca, NY.

Karnow, S. 1991, *Vietnam: A History*, Penguin, London.

Keenan, F. 1999, 'Comrades in Conflict', *Far Eastern Economic Review*, 15 April, p. 28.

Keynes, J. 1936, *The General Theory of Employment, Interest and Money*, Macmillan, London.

Kiernan, B. 1985, *How Pol Pot Came to Power*, Verso, London.

—— 1996, *The Pol Pot Regime*, Yale University Press, New Haven.

Kiernan, B. (ed.) 1993, *Genocide and Democracy in Cambodia*, Yale Southeast Asia Studies Monograph Series No. 41, Yale Center for International and Area Studies, New Haven, CT.

Kingsbury, D. 1998a, 'Watch these Five!' *Inside Indonesia*, no. 53, January–March, pp. 12–13.

—— 1998b, *The Politics of Indonesia*, Oxford University Press, Melbourne.

—— 1999, 'The Political Resurgence of the Tentara Nasional Indonesia', in S. Blackburn (ed.), *Pemilu: The 1999 Indonesian Elections*, Annual Indonesia Lecture Series no. 22, Monash Asia Institute, Melbourne.

Korten, D. 1990, *Getting to the 21st Century*, Kumarian Press, West Hartford, CT.

Krader, L. 1976, *Dialectic of Civil Society*, Prometheus Books, New York.

Kremmer, C. 1997, *Stalking the Elephant Kings*, Allen & Unwin, Sydney.

Lacouture, J. 1969, *Ho Chi Minh*, Pelican, Harmondsworth.

Lande, C. 1968, 'Party Politics in the Philippines', in G. Guthrie (ed.), *Six Perspectives on the Philippines*, Bookmark, Manila.

Laski, H. 1934, *The State in Theory and Practice*, George Allen & Unwin, London.

Lau, T. 1997, 'ASEAN Regional Forum as a Model for North-East Asian Security?', in T. Inoguchi and G. Stillman (eds), *North-East Asian Regional Security*, United Nations University Press, Tokyo.

Lee, K.Y. 1998a, *The Singapore Story*, Times Editions, Singapore.

—— 1998b, 'A Statesman's Write of Passage' (excerpt from *The Singapore Story*), *Far Eastern Economic Review*, 25 September, pp. 50–9.

Leffler, M. and Foner, E. 1994, *The Spectre of Communism: The United States and the Origins of the Cold War, 1917–1953*, Hill & Wang, New York.

Leifer, M. 1995, *Dictionary of the Modern Politics of South-East Asia*, Routledge, London.

Leitao, H. 1956, *Vinte e oito ano de historia de Timor*, Agencia Geral do Ultramar, Lisbon.

Liddle, W. 1996, *Leadership and Culture in Indonesian Politics*, Allen & Unwin, Sydney.

Lingle, C. 1996, *Singapore's Authoritarian Capitalism: Asian Values, Free Market Illusions and Political Dependency*, Locke Institute, Fairfax, Virginia.

Lintner, B. 1990, *Outrage*, White Lotus, Bangkok.

—— 1998, 'Final Countdown', *Far Eastern Economic Review*, 10 September, p. 4.

—— 2000, 'Frustrated Reforms', *Far Eastern Economic Review*, 24 March, p. 26.

Lopez, A. 1998, 'The Marcos Cronies Come Back', *Asiaweek*, 31 July, pp. 20–3.

—— 2000a, 'Meeting Force with Force', *Asiaweek*, 10 March, p. 23.

—— 2000b, 'The Nun vs. The President', *Asiaweek*, 31 March, p. 28.

Low, L. and Toh, M.H. (eds) 1992, *Public Policies in Singapore*, Times Academic Press, Singapore.

Low, L. and Quan, E. 1992, 'Introduction', in L. Low and M.H. Toh (eds), *Public Policies in Singapore*, Times Academic Press, Singapore.

Lowry, R. 1996, *The Armed Forces of Indonesia*, Allen & Unwin, Sydney.

Lukes, S. 1974, *Power: A Radical View*, Macmillan, London.

Lyons, J. and Wilson, K. 1987, *Marcos and Beyond*, Kangaroo Press, Sydney.

Mabbett, I. 1968, *A Short History of India*, Cassell Australia, Sydney.

MacDonald, M. 1987, *Angkor and the Khmers*, Oxford University Press, Oxford.

Machiavelli, N. 1998, *The Prince*, trans. M. Musa, Oxford University Press, Oxford.

Mackie, J. 1998, 'What will the Post-Soeharto Regime be Like?', in G. Forrester and R. May (eds), *The Fall of Soeharto*, Crawford House Publishing, Bathurst.

Mackie, J. and MacIntyre, A. 1994, 'Politics', in H. Hill (ed.), *Indonesia's New Order*, Allen & Unwin, Sydney.

Maclear, M. 1981, *The Ten Thousand Day War—Vietnam: 1945–75*, St Martin's Press, New York.

Maha Sila Viravong 1964, *History of Laos*, Paragon Book Reprint Corp., New York.

Mangunwijaya, Y. 1992, 'Some Notes about the Indonesia Raya Dream of the Indonesian Nationalists and Its Impact on the Concept of Democracy', in D. Bourchier and J. Legge (eds), *Democracy in Indonesia: 1950s and 1990s*, Monash Papers on Southeast Asia No. 31, Centre for Southeast Asian Studies, Monash University, Melbourne.

—— 1994, 'The Indonesia Raya Dream of the Indonesian Nationalists and its Impact on the Concept of Democracy', in D. Bourchier and J. Legge (eds), *Democracy in Indonesia: 1950s and 1990s*, Monash Papers on Southeast Asia No. 31, Centre for Southeast Asian Studies, Monash University, Melbourne.

Manich Jumsai 1979, *History of Thailand and Cambodia*, Cahlermnit Press, Bangkok.

Mastura, M. 1999, 'A Plot Gone Awry', *The Manila Times*, 9 February, p. 6.

Maung Aung Myoe 1998, *Building the Tatmadaw: The Organisational Development of the Armed Forces in Myanmar, 1948–98*, Working Paper no. 327, Strategic and Defence Studies Centre, Australian National University, Canberra.

—— 1999, *Military Doctrine and Strategy in Myanmar: A Historical Perspective*, Working Paper no. 339, Strategic and Defence Studies Centre, Australian National University, Canberra.

McBeth, J. 1999a, 'Cameo Role', *Far Eastern Economic Review*, 18 March, pp. 27–8.

—— 1999b, 'Military Challenge', *Far Eastern Economic Review*, 2 September, p. 19.

—— 1999c, 'Bitter Memories', *Far Eastern Economic Review*, 16 September, p. 12.

McCloud, D. 1995, *Southeast Asia: Tradition and Modernity in the Contemporary World*, Westview Press, Boulder, Colo.

McCoy, A. 1970, 'French Colonialism in Laos, 1893–1945', in N. Adams and A. McCoy, *Laos: War and Revolution*, Harper & Row, New York.

McGillivray, M. 1991, 'The Human Development Index: Yet Another Redundant Composite Development Indicator?', *World Development*, vol. 9, no. 10, pp. 1461–8.

McKay, J. 1990, 'The Development Model', *Development*, vol. 3, no. 4, pp. 55–60.

—— 1991, 'Economic and Social Change in the Asia-Pacific Region', in D. Goldsworthy (ed.), *Development and Social Change in Asia*, Radio Australia, Melbourne.

McNamara, R. 1995, *In Retrospect*, Time Books, New York, and Random House, Toronto.

Mietzner, M. 1998, 'Between *Pesantren* and Palace: Nahdlatul Ulama and its Role in the Transition', in G. Forrester and R. May (eds), *The Fall of Soeharto*, Crawford House Publishing, Bathurst.

—— 1999a, 'Nationalism and Islamic Politics: Political Islam in the Post-Suharto Era', in A. Budiman, B. Hatley and D. Kingsbury (eds), *Reformasi: Crisis and Change in Indonesia*, Monash Asia Institute, Melbourne.

—— 1999b, 'From Soeharto to Habibie: The Indonesian Armed Forces and Political Islam during the Transition', in G. Forrester (ed.), *Post-Soeharto Indonesia: Renewal or Chaos?* Research School of Pacific and Asian Studies, Australian National University, Canberra, with Crawford House Publishing, Bathurst.

Mill, J. 1961, *Utilitarianism and On Liberty*, Doubleday & Co., New York.

Miller, J. 1967, 'Communist China's Foreign Policy', in J. Wilkes (ed.), *Communism in Asia: A Threat to Australia?* Angus & Robertson, Sydney.

Milne, R. & Mauzy, D. 1999, *Malaysian Politics under Mahatir*, Routledge, London and New York.

Missen, G. 1972, *Viewpoints on Indonesia*, Nelson, Melbourne.

—— 1991, 'Malaysia: A Tiger or a Mouse Deer', in D. Goldsworthy (ed.), *Development and Social Change in Asia*, Radio Australia, Melbourne.

Mitton, R. 1998, 'Troubled Kingdom', *Asiaweek*, 16 October, pp. 26–31.

—— 2000a, 'Everyone was Shocked', *Asiaweek*, 10 March, p. 25.

—— 2000b, 'Inside "Secret" Meetings', *Asiaweek*, 31 March, p. 30.

Moedjanto, G. 1993, *The Concept of Power in Javanese Culture*, Gadjah Mada University Press, Jogjakarta.

Moertono, S. 1981, *State and Statecraft in Old Java*, Modern Indonesia Project Monograph Series no. 43, Cornell University, Ithaca, NY.

Monk, P. 1990, *Truth and Power: Robert S. Hardie and Land Reform Debates in the Philippines, 1950–87*, Monash Papers on Southeast Asia No. 20, Monash University, Melbourne.

Morris, C. 1998, *An Essay on the Modern State*, Cambridge University Press, Cambridge.

Murphy, D. and McBeth, J. 1999, 'Scorched Earth', *Far Eastern Economic Review*, 16 September, p. 10.

Nasution, B. 1993, 'Human Rights have an Indonesian History', *Inside Indonesia*, no. 34. p. 1.

The Nation 1998, 'Thai–M'sia Bid to Suppress Rebels', Bangkok, 20 September, p. A2.

—— 1999a, 'Foreign Press Curbs Likely', Bangkok, 15 January, p. 1.

—— 1999b, 'PM Reacts over Series of Bombings, Threats', Bangkok, 15 January, p. 3.

Nelson, R. 1968, *The Philippines*, Thames & Hudson, London.

New Straits Times 1999, 'Trial to Proceed Despite Anwar's Absence', Kuala Lumpur, 25 February, p. 4.

Ngaosyvathn, M. and Ngaosyvathn, P. 1998, *Paths to Conflagration: Fifty Years of Diplomacy and Warfare in Laos, Thailand and Vietnam, 1778–1828*, Cornell University Press, Ithaca, NY.

Nguyen, K.V. 1993, *Vietnam: A Long History*, revised edn, The Gioi Publishers, Hanoi.

Nguyen, N. P. 1994, 'Religious Freedom in Vietnam', in D. Kingsbury and G. Barton (eds), *Difference and Tolerance: Human Rights Issues in Southeast Asia*, Deakin University Press, Melbourne.

Norodom Sihanouk 1973, *My War with the CIA*, Penguin Books, London.

Nurdin, A. 1999, 'Military Faces Dilemma at MPR General Session', *The Jakarta Post.com*, 30 June.

Nussara Sawatsawang 1997, 'Minorities Determined to Pursue Autonomy', Democratic Alliance of Burma Statement, 12 February.

O'Donnell, G. 1973, 'Modernization and Bureaucratic Authoritarianism', *Studies in South American Politics*, Berkeley Institute of International Studies, University of California, Berkeley.

—— 1978, 'Reflections on Patterns of Change in the Bureaucratic Authoritarian State', *Latin American Research Review*, no. 13, pp. 3–38.

Olsen, E. and Winterford, D. 1996, 'The Military Role of Asian Countries in the New Pacific Community in the 1990s', in K. Young (ed.), *The New Pacific Community in the 1990s*, East Gate Books, London.

Osborne, M. 1973, *Politics and Power in Cambodia*, Longman, Melbourne.

—— 1997, *Southeast Asia: An Introductory History*, 7th edn, Silkworm Books, Chiang Mai.

Osborne, R. 1985, *Indonesia's Secret War: The Guerilla Struggle in Irian Jaya*, Allen & Unwin, Sydney.

Parmer, J. 1969, 'Malaysia', in G. Kahin (ed.), *Governments and Politics of Southeast Asia*, 2nd edn, Cornell University Press, Ithaca, NY, 1969.

Pedersen, M., Rudland, E. and May, R. (eds) 2000, *Burma Myanmar: Strong Regime Weak State*, Crawford House Publishing, Adelaide.

Pemberton, J. 1994, *On the Subject of Java*, Cornell University Press, Ithaca, NY.

Pereira, B. 1999, 'Malaysian Opposition's Unholy Alliance', *Straits Times*, 24 February, p. 41.

Pettman, R. 1979, *State and Class: A Sociology of International Affairs*, Croom Helm, London.

Philippines Star 1999, 'MLF Reveals Bin Laden Connection', Manila, 2 February, pp. 1, 5.

Pike, D. (ed.) 1999, 'Laos: How to Move the Economy', *Indochina Chronology*, Texas Technical University, Lubbock.

Ping-chia Kuo 1965, *China*, Oxford University Press, London.

Pirenne, H. 1939, *A History of Europe*, George Allen & Unwin, London, 1939.

Plamenatz, J. 1968, *Consent, Freedom and Political Obligation*, 2nd edn, Oxford University Press, London.

Poulgrain, G. 1999, 'Who Plotted the 1965 Coup?', *Inside Indonesia*, no. 57, January–March, p. 24.

Prakobpong, P. 1998. 'PM urged not to amend military's "privilege" rule', *The Nation*, (Bangkok), 21 September, p. A3.

Proudfoot, I. 1980, 'The Early Indianized States: Religion and Social Control', in J. Fox et al. (eds), *Indonesia: Australian Perspectives*, Research School of Pacific Studies, Australian National University, Canberra.

Prudhisan, J. and Maneerat, M. 1997, 'Non-government Development Organisations', in K. Hewison (ed.), *Political Change in Thailand: Democracy and Participation*, Routledge, London.

Puy Kea 1998, 'Former Khmer Rouge Stronghold Enjoys Business Boom', *Cambodia Daily* (Phnom Penh), 6 July.

Pye, L. 1985, *Asian Power and Politics*, Belknap Press, Cambridge, Mass.

Rapley, J. 1997, *Understanding Development*, UCL Press, London.

Ratanaporn Sethakul 1988, 'Political Relations between Chiang Mai and Kentung in the Nineteenth Century', in Prakai Nontawasee (ed.), *Changes in Northern Thailand and the Shan States 1886–1940*, Southeast Asian Studies Program, Institute of Southeast Asian Studies, Singapore.

Rawana, A. 1999, 'The Maps to Power', *Asiaweek*, 5 November, p. 30.

Rawls, J. 1991, *A Theory of Justice*, Oxford University Press, Oxford.

Reece, R. 1988, 'Economic Development under the Brookes', in R. Cramb and R. Reece (eds), *Development in Sarawak: Historical and Contemporary Perspectives*, Monash Paper on Southeast Asia no. 17, Centre of Southeast Asian Studies, Monash University.

Reuters 1999a, 'Deal on Marcos Funds Soon, says Estrada', *The Nation* (Bangkok), 15 January, p. 3.

—— 1999b, 'Vietnam's Communist Party to Clamp Down on Dissent', *The Nation* (Bangkok), 26 February, p. 6.

—— 1999c, 'TNI Stance Raises Megawati Hopes', *Jakarta Post*, 17 June, p. 1.

Rhodes, R. 1970, *Imperialism and Underdevelopment: A Reader*, Monthly Review Press, New York.

Richburg, K. 1999, 'Indonesia's Unintentional Martyrs: Slaying of Four Students Transformed a Nation', in E. Aspinall, G. van Klinken and H. Feith (eds), *The Last Days of President Suharto*, Monash Asia Institute, Melbourne.

Ricklefs, M. 1993a, *History of Modern Indonesia since c. 1300*, 2nd edn, Macmillan, London.

—— 1993b, *War, Culture and Economy in Java 1677–1726*, Asian Studies Association of Australia, no. 24, Allen & Unwin, Sydney.

Rinn-Sup Shinn 1984, 'Government and Politics', in F. Bunge (ed.), *Malaysia: A Country Study*, Foreign Area Studies, American University, Washington DC.

Robison, R. 1985, *Class, Capital and the State in New Order Indonesia*, in R. Higgott, and R. Robison, *The Political Economy of South-East Asia*, Oxford University Press, Melbourne.

Rooney, D. 1994, *Angkor: An Introduction to the Temples*, Asia Books, Bangkok.

Rostow, W. 1991, *The Stages of Economic Growth: A Non-Communist Manifesto*, 3rd edn, Cambridge University Press, Cambridge.

Rowley, K. 1999, Boom, Bust, and Beyond: The Asian Crisis in Global Perspective, unpublished paper, Swinburne University of Technology, Melbourne.

Roy, D. 1998, *China's Foreign Relations*, Macmillan, London.

Roy, R. 1999, 'Old Rivals Become Pen Pals', *Bangkok Post*, 26 February, p. 10.

Runciman, S. 1960, *The White Rajahs: A History of Sarawak from 1841 to 1946*, Cambridge University Press, London.

Sagar, D. 1991, *Indo-China 1945–90*, Facts on File, Oxford.

Said, E. *Orientalism: Western Conceptions of the Orient*, Penguin Books, London, 1991.

Sario, R. 1999, 'Vital Votes of Sabah Muslims', *The Star* (Kuala Lumpur), 26 February, p. 21.

Saritdet, M. and Nussara, S. 1998, 'Bridging the Gap a Second Time', *Bangkok Post*, 17 September, p. 10.

—— 1968, *Viet-Nam and the West*, Heinemann, London.

Smith, S. 1999, 'Hun Sen's Ultimatum', *The Nation* (Bangkok), 18 January, p. 1.

Spencer, G. 1999, 'Indonesia's Leader's Deal on East Timor Rejected', *Seattle Times*, 21 June, p. 1.

Spillius, A. 1998, 'An Era of Extravagance Ends for a Rich Kingdom', *Age*, 8 August, p. 11.

Spybey, T. 1996, *Social Change, Development and Dependency*, Polity Press, London.

Stanley, P. 1974, *A Nation in the Making: The Philippines and the United States 1899–1921*, Harvard University Press, Cambridge, Massachusetts.

Steadman, J. 1969, *The Myth of Asia*, Macmillan, London.

Steinberg, D. 1982, *The Philippines: A Singular and A Plural Place*, Westview Press, Boulder, Colorado.

—— (ed.) 1971, *In Search of Southeast Asia*, Praeger, New York.

Stewart, I. and Alford, P. 1998, 'Mahatir Finds Anwar Guilty', *Australian*, 23 September, p. 1.

Stuart-Fox, M. 1996, *Buddhist Kingdom, Marxist State: The Making of Modern Laos*, White Lotus Press, Bangkok.

—— 1997, *A History of Laos*, Cambridge University Press, Cambridge.

—— 1998a, *The Lao Kingdom of Lan Xang: Rise and Decline*, White Lotus, Bangkok.

—— 1998b, China and Mainland Southeast Asia: Implications of Strategic Culture, paper presented to Asian Studies Association of Australian biennial conference, University of New South Wales, Sydney.

Sturtevant, 1969, *Agrarian Unrest in the Philippines: Guardia de Honor—Revitalization within the Revolution, and Rizalistas—Contemporary Revitalization Movements in the Philippines*, Ohio University, Center for International Studies, Athens, Ohio.

—— 1976, *Popular Uprisings in the Philippines: 1840–1940*, Cornell University Press, Ithaca, NY.

Sulak, S. 1991, 'The Crisis of Siamese Identity', in C. Reynolds (ed.), *National Identity and Its Defenders: Thailand, 1939–89*, Monash Papers on Southeast Asia No. 25, Monash University, Melbourne.

Sunar, T. 1999, 'Don't Play with Fire, PBS Told', *Daily Express* (Kota Kinabalu), 10 February, p. 1.

Suu Kyi, A.S. 1991, *Freedom from Fear*, Viking, London.

Tambiah, S. 1976, *World Conqueror and World Renouncer*, Cambridge University Press, Cambridge.

Tapol 1999a, *The TNI's 'Dirty War' in East Timor*, Tapol, London.

—— 1999b, *The Dismissal and Indictment of TNI Officers for Human Rights Violations in East Timor*, Tapol, London.

Tarling, N. 1998, *Nations and States in Southeast Asia*, Cambridge University Press, Melbourne.

Tasker, R. 1998, 'Safety in Numbers', *Far Eastern Economic Review*, 15 October, p. 21.

Tavares, J. 1999, *Kesiapan dan Kesiagan Pasukan Pejuang Integrasi (Milisi) Dalam Menyikapi Perkembangan Situasi Dan Konisi Di Timor-Timur*, 17 July, PPI, Balibo, East Timor.

Taylor, J. 1991, *Indonesia's Forgotten War*, Zed Books, London.

Tesoro, J. 1999, 'Voting for the Future', *Asiaweek*, 10 September, pp. 24–5.

Tesor, J. and Loveard, D. 1999, 'The Road to Rejection', *Asiaweek*, 29 October.

Thailand Times 1997, 'Burma's Military Rulers Live off Opium', 2 May.

Thayer, N. 1998a, 'The Resurrected', *Far Eastern Economic Review*, 16 April, pp. 23–4.

—— 1998b, 'Dying Breath', *Far Eastern Economic Review*, 30 April, pp. 18–21.

Thitinam Pongsudhirak 1997, 'Thailand's Media: Whose Watchdog?', in K. Hewison (ed.), *Political Change in Thailand: Democracy and Participation*, Routledge, London.

Tiglao, R. 1998a, 'Teflon Friends', *Far Eastern Economic Review*, 16 July, p. 28.

—— 1998b, 'Her Father's Daughter', *Far Eastern Economic Review*, 27 August, p. 24.

—— 1999, 'A Storm at Sea', *Far Eastern Economic Review*, 9 December, pp. 24–5.

Tiglao, R. and Vatikiotis, M. 1999, 'Estrada in Trouble', *Far Eastern Economic Review*, 23 December, p. 22.

Trager, F. 1966, *Burma: From Kingdom to Republic*, Pall Mall Press, London.

Treaty of Amity and Cooperation in Southeast Asia, 24 February 1976, Jakarta.

Tsing, A. 1987, 'A Rhetoric of Centres in a Religion of the Periphery', in R. Kipp and S. Rogers (eds), *Indonesian Religions in Transition*, University of Arizona Press, Phoenix.

Tu, G. 1999, 'Doi Moi Beating Poverty', *Vietnam Investment Review*, 1–7 January, p. 8.

Tully, J. 1996, *Cambodia under the Tricolor*, Monash Asia Institute, Melbourne.

Turley, W. 1988, 'The Military Construction of Socialism', in D. Marr and C. White (eds), *Postwar Vietnam: Dilemmas in Socialist Development*, Cornell Southeast Asia Program, Ithaca, NY.

Turnbull, C. 1977, *A History of Singapore 1819–1975*, Oxford University Press, Oxford.

—— 1989, *A History of Malaysia, Singapore and Brunei*, Allen & Unwin, Sydney.

United Nations, 1999a, Agreement between Indonesia, Portugal and the Secretary General of the United Nations, 5 May, United Nations.

—— 1999b, Resolution 1264 (1999), 15 September, United Nations.

United Nations High Commissioner for Refugees 1999, *Report of the High Commissioner for Human Rights on the Human Rights Situation in East Timor*, United Nations High Commissioner for Refugees.

UNHCHR (United Nations High Commission for Human Rights) 1999, 'Economic Rights', in *Papers of the High Commission for Human Rights*, no. 1, Office of the High Commission for Human Rights, New York.

US Department of State 1996, *International Narcotics Control Strategy Report*, US Department of State, Washington DC.

—— 1999a, *Cambodia Country Report*, February.

—— 1999b, *Human Rights Practices for 1998 Report: Singapore Country Report*, US Department of State, Washington DC.

Van Klinken G. 1999a, 'How a Democratic Deal Might be Struck', in A. Budiman, B. Hatley and D. Kingsbury (eds), *Reformasi: Crisis and Change in Indonesia*, Monash Asia Institute, Melbourne.

—— 1999b, 'The May Riots', in E. Aspinall, G. van Klinken and H. Feith (eds), *The Last Days of President Suharto*, Monash Asia Institute, Melbourne.

Vasil, R.K. 1984, *Governing Singapore*, Eastern Universities Press, Sdn Bhd, Singapore.

Vatikiotis, M. 1993, *Indonesian Politics under Suharto*, Routledge, London.

—— 1998, 'Romancing the Dual Function', in G. Forrester and R. May (eds), *The Fall of Soeharto*, Crawford House Publishing, Bathurst.

Vervoorn, A. 1998, *Re Orient: Change in Asian Societies*, Oxford University Press, Melbourne.

Viravong, S. 1964, *History of Laos*, Paragon Books, New York.

Voltaire 1979, *Philosophical Dictionary*, trans. T. Besterman, Penguin Books, Harmondsworth.

Vu Tuan Anh 1995, 'Economic Policy Reforms', in I. Norlund, C.D. Vu and C. Gates (eds), *Vietnam in a Changing World*, Nordic Institute of Asian Studies, Curzon Press.

Thitinan Pongsudhirak 1997, 'Thailand's Media: Whose Watchdog?', in K. Hewison (ed.), Political Change in Thailand: Democracy and Participation, Routledge, London.

Tiglao, R. 1998a, 'Teflon Friends', Far Eastern Economic Review, 16 July, p. 28.

—— 1998b, 'Her Father's Daughter', Far Eastern Economic Review, 27 August, p. 24.

—— 1999, 'A Storm at Sea', Far Eastern Economic Review, 9 December, pp. 24–5.

Tiglao, R. and Vatikiotis, M. 1999, 'Escuela in Trouble', Far Eastern Economic Review, 23 December, p. 22.

Trager, F. 1966, Burma: From Kingdom to Republic, Pall Mall Press, London.

Treaty of Amity and Cooperation in Southeast Asia, 24 February 1976, Jakarta.

Tsing, A. 1987, 'A Rhetoric of Centers in a Religion of the Periphery', in K. Kipp and S. Rogers (eds), Indonesian Religions in Transition, University of Arizona Press, Phoenix.

Tu, G. 1990, 'Doi Moi Bearing Poverty', Vietnam Investment Review, 1–7 January, p. 8.

Tully, J. 1996, Cambodia under the Tricolor, Monash Asia Institute, Melbourne.

Turley, W. 1988, 'The Military Construction of Socialism', in D. Marr and C.White (eds), Postwar Vietnam: Dilemmas in Socialist Development, Cornell Southeast Asia Program, Ithaca, NY.

Turnbull, C. 1977, A History of Singapore 1819–1975, Oxford University Press, Oxford.

—— 1989, A History of Malaysia, Singapore and Brunei, Allen & Unwin, Sydney.

United Nations, 1999a, Agreement between Indonesia, Portugal and the Secretary-General of the United Nations, 5 May, United Nations.

—— 1999b, Resolution 1264 (1999), 15 September, United Nations.

United Nations High Commissioner for Refugees 1999, Report of the High Commissioner for Human Rights on the Human Rights Situation in East Timor, United Nations High Commissioner for Refugees.

UNHCHR (United Nations High Commission for Human Rights) 1999, 'Economic Rights', in Report of the High Commission for Human Rights, no. 1, Office of the High Commission for Human Rights, New York.

US Department of State 1996, International Narcotics Control Strategy Report, US Department of State, Washington DC.

—— 1999a, Cambodia Country Report, February.

—— 1999b, Human Rights Practices for 1998 Report, Singapore Country Report, US Department of State, Washington DC.

Van Klinken G. 1999a, 'How a Democratic Deal Might be Struck', in A. Budiman, B. Hatley and D. Kingsbury (eds), Reformasi: Crisis and Change in Indonesia, Monash Asia Institute, Melbourne.

—— 1999b, 'The May Riots', in E. Aspinall, G. van Klinken and H. Feith (eds), The Last Days of President Suharto, Monash Asia Institute, Melbourne.

Vasil, R.K. 1984, Governing Singapore, Eastern Universities Press, Sdn Bhd, Singapore.

Vatikiotis, M. 1993, Indonesian Politics under Suharto, Routledge, London.

—— 1998, 'Romancing the Dual Function', in C. Forrester and R. May (eds), The Fall of Soeharto, Crawford House Publishing, Bathurst.

Vervoorn, A. 1998, Re Orient: Change in Asian Societies, Oxford University Press, Melbourne.

Viravong, S. 1964, History of Laos, Paragon Books, New York.

Voltaire 1979, Philosophical Dictionary, trans. T. Besterman, Penguin Books, Harmondsworth.

Vo Tam Anh 1995, 'Economic Policy Reforms', in I. Norlund, C.D. Vu and C. Gates (eds), Vietnam in a Changing World, Nordic Institute of Asian Studies, Curzon Press.